THE REALITY
OF THE MIND

Studies in Phenomenological and Classical Realism

Edited by Josef Seifert and Giovanni Reale
in collaboration with Agustin Basave (Mexico), John Crosby (USA), Michael Healy (USA), Tarcisio Padilha (Brazil), Juan Miguel Palacios (Spain), Tadeusz Styczen (Poland) and Fritz Wenisch (USA)
The International Academy of Philosophy

Ludger Hölscher

THE REALITY
OF THE MIND

AUGUSTINE'S PHILOSOPHICAL
ARGUMENTS FOR THE HUMAN SOUL
AS A SPIRITUAL SUBSTANCE

Ludger Hölscher

ROUTLEDGE & KEGAN PAUL
London and New York

First published in 1986
by Routledge & Kegan Paul plc

11 New Fetter Lane, London EC4P 4EE

Published in the USA by
Routledge & Kegan Paul Inc.
in association with Methuen Inc.
29 West 35th Street, New York, NY 10001

Phototypeset in Linotron Ehrhardt
by Input Typesetting Ltd, London
and printed in Great Britain
by St Edmundsbury Press Ltd
Bury St Edmunds, Suffolk

Library of Congress Cataloging in Publication Data
Hölscher, Ludger.
The reality of the mind.
(Studies in classical and phenomenological realism)
Bibliography: p.
Includes index.
1. Augustine, Saint, Bishop of Hippo—Contributions
in the concept of the soul.   2. Soul—History of
doctrines—Early church, ca. 30–600.   I. Title.
II. Series.
BT741.2.H65   1986   233'.5   85–25572

British Library CIP data also available

ISBN 0–7102–0777–8

'Quid ego sum, deus meus? Quae natura sum?'
Conf. X, 17.

TO MY PARENTS

Contents

Acknowledgments

For the conception and completion of this work I am particularly indebted to Prof. Josef Seifert who through his own studies on the body-mind problem in general and his personal love for Augustine inspired me to choose and write on this topic, which work he then accompanied and furthered with many valuable hints and suggestions.

My sincere thanks I want to express also to my Second Reader Prof. Fernando Inciarte for his kind and spontaneous acceptance of this task.

In a special way, I am committed to Dr John Crosby who not only improved my work stylistically, but who stimulated me philosophically by many critical, yet thought-provoking remarks.

I am also grateful to Fr Tadeusz Styczen and Dr Robert Wood for their critical reading and commenting on this work, and to Fr Placid Csizmazia O. Cist. for his co-operative help with the translating of Augustine into English.

Also I do not want to forget the technical help and moral support that I received from my friends in the German College in Rome during the final stages of completing this work.

At last, I want to thank the entire philosophical community of professors, students and friends, formerly at the University of Dallas and now at the International Academy of Philosophy, for their stimulating interest in the pursuit of philosophy and for the many inspiring discussions in which I could participate, expressing my sincere hope that this 'tradition' may continue and may yield fruit in the service of the *philosophia perennis*.

Introduction

St Augustine (November 13, 354–August 28, 430) is a figure
whose influence on the development of ideas is undisputed. Only
a few thinkers have achieved an equally lasting effect on the history
of thought. This is one main reason for the vastness of the literature
that has been devoted to him. Numerous monographs have been,
and are still being, written on various aspects of his thought and
on him personally as a man who lived a most unusual and extraordinary life. He was, and is, of interest not only for theologians, but
also for philosophers from various backgrounds, for historians,
psychologists, linguists, and for anyone who wants to be spiritually
nourished by his ideas.[1]

In the light of this great number of studies of St Augustine's life
and thought the question could be raised why one should add a
further work to this list. What fruit could it yield to study him anew
after so much work has been done on him? Is such an endeavour
not doomed, from the very outset, to result in a mere repetition of
what has already been found and explicated?

For various reasons, I think that such an enterprise is nevertheless worth pursuing, particularly with respect to St Augustine's
philosophy of mind.

Augustine, to my mind, was a thinker who possessed an amazing
capability of penetrating into and grasping the structures and
reasons of reality in a way that in its originality and depth has
rarely been surpassed. He was one of those minds that in their
'restlessness of heart' are existentially driven to finding truth, trou-
bled by the idea of possibly being in illusion and error.[2] He can

rightly be called one of the greatest 'searchers for the truth' in the history of thought.[3]

From this personal zeal for truth sprang his desire to communicate to others what he discovered as true, encouraging his friends and students to open up their mental eyes and to see 'on their own' what is given in reality. He stimulated them to ask questions and to discuss disputed issues in order to approach reality originally and to grasp ever more deeply its inexhaustible richness.[4]

Any study, therefore, that seeks to follow the countless analyses and hints of reality in Augustine's work can and should constitute a philosophic grasp of things which alone does far more than repeat already existing secondary literature. For to rediscover and perhaps to unfold what a great mind saw is as such a *new* original insight into reality, especially when it brings to light ever deeper dimensions of being.

Surveying the available literature on our topic, one finds a surprising lack of such a philosophical method of studying Augustine, which will more concretely be outlined below. And above all, the wealth of insight that is found particularly in Augustine's argumentation for the spiritual incorporeality and substantiality of the human mind has hardly been studied and developed in one single systematic treatment.[5] Yet it is precisely this topic that not only played a prominent role in Augustine's own thought,[6] but that is also of vital interest for the contemporary state of mind, in which various materialistic positions are predominant. Therefore, in view of the literature, or lack of it, on this question in Augustine, and in view of the present-day discussion of the body-mind problem in general, to 'dig out' his analyses and arguments, even by complementing and unfolding them in the light of subsequent developments of Augustinian thought and by securing them against critical objections not explicitly posed to Augustine, seems to be a particularly needed endeavour. It is in this that I see the main contribution the present study is to make.

1   Starting point and method

In an early work, Augustine writes that he wants to know nothing more than God and the soul.[7] This desire can truly be said to permeate his whole life and thought both before and after his conversion. As he later recounts in his *Confessiones*, his reading of Cicero's *Hortensius* in his youth already awoke in him the striving for timeless wisdom and for God.[8] It led him to join the Manicheans from whom he hoped to find this wisdom. But their dualistic answer of the two equal powers of good and evil, and of the soul being imprisoned in an essentially evil body, left him disappointed.[9] Particularly their solution to the problem of the *origin* of evil was for him extremely dissatisfying. He left the Manicheans.[10] After having gone through a period of sceptical doubt, he heard some sermons of Ambrose in Milan and encountered through him the books of the Platonists.[11] These helped him to overcome his earlier view of God whom he had conceived solely in terms of corporeal images, and to get accustomed to the idea of a purely spiritual being.

Through the Manichean influence Augustine, as he later writes, went through a period in which he was unable to think of anything spiritual. 'Being' was for him what man perceives through the eyes – that is, something corporeal;[12] whatever could not be thought except in terms of bodily extension he held to be nothing at all (*nihil prorsus esse arbitrabar*).[13] Therefore, his image of God was that of some corporeal being that is either infused into the world (*infusum mundo*) or diffused outside the world throughout infinite space (*per infinita diffusum*).[14] Similarly, he imagined the human soul to be like a subtle body diffused through the realms of space.[15] He shared this materialistic belief with most of the intellectuals of his time.[16]

The encounter with Ambrose and the study of the Platonic writers, however, helped Augustine to gain an idea of what it means to be spiritual, and he was inspired to refute the Manicheans with convincing and cogent arguments.[17] He felt interiorly compelled to find reasons that would show the falsity of a purely materialistic view of the world. This intellectual struggle, accompanied and intensified by his final conversion to Christianity, led him eventually to a grasp of the nature of a spiritual being that has since become directive for the development of this notion in the history of thought.[18]

The starting point of the present study is to take up and develop these Augustinian arguments for the spiritual substantiality of man's soul. I want to use Augustine as a source of insight into the nature of the soul, reviving his reasoning and making it fruitful for the contemporary state of discussion. I am convinced that Augustine implicitly sheds light on many 'modern' problems concerning the soul and that his teaching can be vital in dealing with them.[19]

The method to be adopted will be historical as well as systematic/philosophical: historical, however, not primarily in the sense of presenting Augustine's views and ideas as such and in the light of their (Greek, Neoplatonic, Biblical) roots,[20] nor in the sense of studying the growth and development of his views and his personal existential motives for holding them;[21] rather, Augustine is to be studied as a thinker of his time who can also teach the modern mind. His writings on our topic are to be analysed as exactly as possible in order that, as historical sources, they may serve as vehicles for a grasp of what they are trying to communicate, namely the truth of the things in question. This philological/historical enterprise, called for by Augustine himself for the study of Scripture,[22] provides the basis for the philosophical penetration and evaluation of what is pointed out. It means to pose the question of whether the views expounded correspond to reality or not, that is, whether they are true or false. Such a method seems to have been employed explicitly only by a few scholars, such as Anton Maxsein on Augustine's philosophy of heart[23] and Alfred Schöpf with respect to his epistemology.[24] Yet, as the latter rightly points out, this is precisely the old and always new manner of philosophical investigation, which Augustine himself demands – a fact that has surprisingly been little noticed by Augustinian scholars:[25]

> Books are written about things which the reader, under the guidance of reason, has found to be true; not those which he believes to be true on the testimony of him who wrote them, as when history is read, but those which he himself has also found to be true either in himself, or in the truth itself, the light of the mind.[26]

The reader is to find the truth contained in a philosophical work by himself penetrating into the reality referred to, and is to judge the author accordingly. In fact, it is only by truly grasping the things meant that the words and sentences of the book are understood properly;[27] only in the light of what the book is about can one hope to 'decode' the true meaning of an author's terminology, especially in the area of philosophy.

This is particularly true of Augustine's own terminology that, as has often been observed, is generally not highly precise.[28] He himself admits that it may be that perhaps his thought could have been expressed more clearly so that everyone may understand him; but, he adds, nobody has spoken in such a way as to be understood by everyone in everything.[29] There might be two main reasons why Augustine was not a very systematic thinker and writer: his training as a rhetorician which rendered his style close to poetic language, and his ingenious capacity of constantly discovering new and surprising phenomena which he tried to describe in all their aspects by a variety of terms: non-systematicity was 'the heavy price for being so prodigal and flexible a writer.'[30] For this reason, Augustine strongly emphasizes that we should look at the meaning of the things themselves (*rerum ipsarum intellectus*) when discussing an issue, without being concerned too much with how it can or cannot be expressed linguistically.[31] And therefore, he tries to make plain the sense of a term by giving examples.[32] Whoever studies his works is to be led to the reality itself which is meant and not to remain on the level of words.

This task of personally grasping the reality itself, which Augustine considers the proper way for students to *learn*,[33] he also admonishes his readers to take as their highest authority. He does not want to be accepted in his arguments solely on his own authority.[34] Rather, he strongly advises his readers to use their own reason, and to follow a reliable authority only in the case of lack of time and slowness of comprehension; for to believe in an authority, he says, is a great saving and means no labor (*auctoritati credere magnum compendium est, et nullus labor*).[35] It is a lot of work to find the truth, and it is most difficult to avoid errors.[36] But if one does so, there is no human authority that is superior to the reason of a 'purified soul' having come to the perception of truth.[37]

Such a historic-systematic/philosophical approach also implies an attitude that is critical, both in the sense of being corrective as well as ready to learn. Augustine often asks his readers to be critical of what he writes, as much more he prefers to be criticized than to be praised by someone erring or flattering.[38] He challenges them to refute his opinions, but in an attitude of charity and in the interest of truth (*cum caritate et veritate*).[39] For he shall not be ashamed to learn if he is anywhere in error.[40]

Being fully centered on the truth of the issue in question, Augustine invites anyone to a dialogue with him so that they can help each other to penetrate ever more deeply into the subject at stake. It should be a dialogue of mutual respect for the other in which he is truly understood first in what he is trying to say, and in which one waits for the other in case of slower comprehension:

> I ask the readers of this book to forgive me, where they may notice that I wanted to say more than I could, either because they themselves have a better grasp of the subject, or else fail to understand it on account of the obscurity of my language; just as I, on my part, forgive them where they do not understand on account of their own slowness.[41]

In this sense, I want to accept Augustine's invitation and discuss with him the question of the spirituality of the soul. However, as he did not write a single systematic treatise on this subject which would contain all his arguments against a materialistic conception of the soul, my procedure will consist in gathering relevant texts and trying to extract from them a systematic series of his arguments. This will imply both the presentation and unfolding of arguments explicitly worked out by Augustine for the spirituality of the soul, as well as the philosophical elaboration of observations which may be contained in many occasional remarks and which can serve as premises for the same conclusion. In this latter case, I would try to explicate what is virtually present in him in the light of my own understanding of the issue in question and in the light of subsequent developments of Augustinian thought. Besides Bonaventure, Pascal and Descartes, I will mainly introduce some modern 'realist phenomenologists' who, themselves under the influence of Augustine, have to my mind decisively elaborated on and clarified particular aspects of his thought, both explicitly and implicitly. Foremost among them will be E. Husserl, D. v. Hildebrand, K. Wojtyla, and J. Seifert.

This choice of authors as well as the choice of the works and passages of Augustine referred to are made according as to what they make manifest of the particular subject in question. The criterion of choice, therefore, is not determined by a historical interest (unless stated otherwise), but primarily by the degree of insight they contain in my judgment. Regarding Augustine's works, this also means that I will try to unfold those points in them that seem particularly revealing to me, and to pose critical questions with respect to what seems problematic or one-sided in him, in order to clarify the issue by avoiding misunderstandings and perhaps even by suggesting certain corrections of his view.

However, the scope of my study does not allow for a systematic discussion of all possible objections that could and have been raised regarding Augustine's manner of treating the problem of the soul. I will for instance completely prescind from a critical comparison and evaluation of other attempts at explaining the essential difference and relation between body and soul, such as is given in the Thomistic doctrine of *anima forma corporis*.[42] For to discuss and to do justice to the strengths and shortcomings of other positions would require extensive research that can understandably not be offered in this context. Similarly, it would go far beyond the intention and scope of my study to give a detailed defense of fundamental Augustinian presuppositions that I tacitly adopt, for instance, Augustine's basic epistemological realism, his theory of the *rationes aeternae* and of the hierarchy of being, or his acceptance of the classic Euclidian conception of space. These and similar presuppositions cannot be supported and established in this work, for such arguments would themselves require whole treatises.

Thus, except with respect to this self-imposed limitation, I may, like Augustine, also ask my reader to proceed further with me, where he is as certain as I am; to make inquiries with me, where he is as hesitant as I am; to come back to me, where he recognizes that he has committed an error; and to call me back wherever the error is mine.[43] For in this way to strive and struggle for a fuller understanding of the truth of the issue in question would mean also for me to have reaped a most abundant harvest from my labor (*uberrimum fructum laboris huius mei cepero*).[44]

2 Topic and structure

The aim and purpose of the present study is to show man's soul to be essentially distinct from, yet united to, his body by philosophically arguing in various ways, taken from Augustine, for its incor-

poreal and spiritual substantiality.[45] The topic can broadly be desig-
nated to be 'the nature of the human soul approached by means of
Augustinian insights and observations.' However, certain questions
immediately come to mind with respect to such a topic, questions
that shall briefly be answered.

First of all, as in any philosophical enterprise, one who under-
takes a study of the soul must particularly be conscious of the fact
that reality will always be greater than what we see of it, and that
there will never be an end to our labor of penetrating it. Man,
Augustine says, is a great mystery;[46] what can be more profound
than the abyss that is given in his heart?[47] We may work hard, but
we feel our insufficiency when we strive to comprehend exactly
what we are in the inner man.[48] It would therefore be presumptuous
to intend to offer an exhaustive answer to the many problems and
questions related to the soul. Rather, following Augustine's spirit,
I accept the fact that there are dimensions to its nature that will
ultimately remain inaccessible to our comprehending grasp. In this
sense, I understand this work as providing an Augustinian basis
for further studies in this area.

Secondly, the topic will also be limited quantitatively in that its
focus is exclusively centered on the *human* soul (except for brief
references to related subjects made in side-remarks and notes).
This means, for instance, that neither the problem of the nature
of animal-'consciousness' or of plant-'soul,' nor the question of
how man's soul is both similar and superior to that of an animal
will be touched on. As these questions would presuppose extensive
empirical research, and as Augustine seems less interested in them,
they shall be excluded.[49]

Thirdly, within the realm of what is meant by the human soul,
attention is paid exclusively to that 'aspect' of it that is given in
man's inner self-experience. Soul (mind, spirit) is understood to
refer to that reality 'in me' that I am in contact with when I say 'I'
to myself, that is, the conscious personal subject. In this, I again
follow Augustine whose central approach to man is from inner
experience: *ad te redi, te vide, te inspice, te discute*.[50] Hence, questions
concerning the soul as vivifying principle of the body or concerning
the various kinds of unconsciousness (as well as concerning the
origin and the immortality of the soul) are not dealt with as such,
except for treatises that may throw its conscious spirituality into

greater relief (as a discussion of Augustine's notion of *memoria sui*). The aim is to understand more clearly the reality and nature of this self-experienced 'I.'

Fourthly, a special difficulty arises from Augustine's terminology of the soul. As pointed out above, he himself was little interested in developing a strict terminology which he would always observe. His views were to be understood by a personal grasp of the reality referred to. He even confesses that he felt unable to find a single proper term for this nature that the soul is.[51] Therefore, the exact meaning of terms, such as *anima*, *mens*, *spiritus*, is to be gathered from each respective context and from the analyses and descriptions of the datum referred to. A 'definition' of what Augustine means by 'soul' can consequently be given only at the end of our study.[52]

This gradual penetration and understanding of the reality in question is also reflected by the way in which we want to achieve our goal of showing the human soul to be an incorporeal and spiritual substance. The investigation will have the following structure.

In the first chapter, the meaning of the term *corpus* shall be explicated as referring to both any corporeal entity as well as to the human lived body. Each of these two discussions will be followed by an argument trying to demonstrate that there are (psychic) experiences in us that do not have those properties found in bodies. In the form of a negative proof, thus, the *incorporeality* of the soul shall be approached.

The second chapter will delve more deeply into this incorporeality thereby also revealing positive characteristics of the soul, particularly its '*rational spirituality*.' The starting point will be taken from acts of man that could not only not be performed by a bodily being, but that show their underlying subject to possess specifically 'rational' abilities. These acts will be those of imagination, recollection and *distentio animi*, of knowledge in the sense of both sense-perception and intellectual cognition, and of free will.

The third chapter, constituting in a sense the core of the whole, tries to approach the human soul directly through its immediate self-knowledge. Here Augustine's well known *cogitare-seipsum* argument for the spirituality of the soul shall be treated and unfolded in its various aspects. In this way, we shall attempt to grasp as positively as possible what the soul is: a *self-conscious* spiritual being.

The fourth chapter will show the substantiality of this soul as a being that is a subsisting bearer (subject) of accidents (acts), that is one and individual, and that is most real – and that possesses all three of these characteristics of substantiality to a degree of perfection not found in any body.

Finally, in the last chapter the argument shall be presented that this substantial distinctness of soul and body does not jeopardize, but rather enables us to account for, the oneness of man. This discussion can be seen as containing the summarizing thesis of my work.

Thus, the question of what the soul is shall be approached by analyzing what is given in inner experience. This is how Augustine searched for himself, and this is how he advises anyone else to do likewise:

> What does your soul have? Recall, recollect yourself interiorly.
> I do not ask that one puts faith in what I am going to say:
> do not accept anything, if you have not found it in yourself.[53]

CHAPTER 1

The lack of bodily properties in the soul

1 Materialistic theories and their origin

Augustine starts his discussion of the incorporeality of the human soul by presenting various materialistic views of man that have been and are still being held by different people.

Some people think the soul to be the blood, others the brain, others the heart in the sense of that physical organ we see when we open the body.[1] There are others who believe it to consist of very minute and indivisible bodies that they call atoms (which was the opinion of Epicurus);[2] again others think air (Anaximenes)[3] or fire (Stoics)[4] to be the substance of the soul. And those people who somehow realize that the soul cannot be a body, say that it is no substance, but the harmony of our body, or that it is the combining link that joins primary substances together. In these latter senses, the soul would indeed not be a body; yet it would not be any real entity (substance) at all, but merely some incorporeal harmony (*temperatio*) or epiphenomenon of the body, as Simmias puts it using the analogy of the attunement of the lyre.[5] There are still others, Augustine continues, who hold the soul to be a sort of life different from the life of the body, but not a substance. And some add a certain fifth body, of which he does not know what it is, to the four well-known elements of the world and say that it is from this unknown body that the soul stems.[6]

Whatever the particular explanation, all of these views suppose the cause and principle of things to be corporeal;[7] whatever is, is thought to be a material entity, or at least to have a body as its underlying substance. One tries to measure and to account for incorporeal and spiritual realities with the help of corporeal images.[8]

Why do so many people think this way? Why is it that the idea of matter is enforcing itself so strongly on man that he regards even himself to be a material being?

The answer Augustine gives is characteristic of his way of thinking:

> But because the mind is in those things of which it thinks
> with love, and it has grown accustomed to thinking of
> sensible things, that is, of bodies with love, it is incapable of
> being in itself without the images of those things. From this
> arises its shameful error, that it can no longer distinguish the
> images of sensible things from itself, so as to see itself alone.
> For they have marvelously cohered to it with the glue of love,
> and this is its uncleanness that, while it endeavors to think
> of itself alone, it regards itself as being without which it cannot
> think of itself.[9]

Having lost what has been called the *habitare secum*, the dwelling with oneself, and having thrown himself into the sensible corporeal world, man is so taken up by it that he is unable to think of anything except in terms of material images. He is incapable of freeing his thinking from the idea of matter and of grasping himself as such and not in the light of other things.[10]

Such reductionistic tendencies can often be observed as underlying various theories of man, and, as Grabmann rightly points out, it is a great danger particularly for the modern mind, for which Augustine's point contains a serious exhortation.[11] In fact, most 'modern' anthropologies can be traced back to ancient ideas, often being nothing but more refined 'scientific' versions of traditional views.[12]

For this reason, Augustine's exhortation to remove from our thought all corporeal images and to conceive of the soul entirely in its own terms,[13] needs to be emphasized today as much as, if not even more than, 1600 years ago. For the enormous development of natural science has furthered the grave temptation of viewing man almost exclusively in the light of bodily (chemical-electrical) patterns.[14] However, if we want to understand the soul as it is, Augustine admonishes us, we have to free ourselves from thinking in terms of laws and structures taken from the material world, and thus to grasp and describe it *itself* as object of inner experience in its own proper terms.

2   The soul as distinct from bodies in general

(A)   The broader meaning of 'corpus' as referring to any corporeal entity

In order to develop arguments against the claim that the soul is a corporeal being, Augustine must first outline the meaning of the term *corpus* (body). For, as he says, he does not want to argue with his materialistic adversaries about a question of words.[15] Any philosophical enterprise takes its starting point in a clear delimitation of the basic terms being employed. To these terms a specific meaning is to be given, which is gained by a grasp of the particular fact or nature in reality that it is understood to refer to.

What does Augustine aim at when using the term *corpus*? What are the essential properties that he finds in a bodily being?

> Well, I should, to begin with, like to know how you define
> *body*. For if that is not 'body' which does not consist of limbs
> of flesh, then the earth cannot be a body, nor the sky, nor a
> stone, nor water, nor the stars, nor anything of that kind. If,
> however, 'body' is whatever consists of parts, whether greater
> or less, which occupy greater or smaller local spaces, then
> all the things which I have just mentioned are bodies; the air
> is a body, the visible light is a body.[16]

Augustine does not want to restrict the term body to what consists of fleshly members; for in this sense only man, and the animals,[17] would have a body while beings, such as the earth, heaven, stones, etc., could not be called bodies. Instead, he wants to give a broader meaning to the term *corpus*, a meaning that is applicable to all corporeal entities. And thus, he arrives at the following well-known formula (freely stated): *corpus* is what consists of greater and smaller parts of which the greater part is more, the smaller part less extended in space.[18] In this sense of *corpus*, all beings of a corporeal nature can be called bodies.

But let us analyze more carefully the reality meant by this Augustinian formula.

Augustine, first of all, states that each body consists of parts, that is, each body can be divided into parts which, put together, constitute the whole body. (Body and the material mass of a body [*moles*] are understood here to refer to the same reality.)[19] Of these parts, some are greater, others are smaller, depending on how the body is to be cut.[20] The whole body as such, however, is always greater than any single part of it, no matter which part it is and how great it is (*pars quaelibet aut quantalibet*). For instance, heaven and earth are parts of the mass of the whole world, while each itself consists of innumerable parts into which it could be divided. Yet, as great as each of these parts may be, still greater will always be the whole body of the world which is constituted by heaven and earth.[21]

From this law it follows that bodily entities, when united to themselves, increase with regard to their quantitative greatness. For a greater whole will always be constituted by them.[22] Likewise, it necessarily follows from this law that a body suffers the defect of getting reduced in its mass, when something is taken away from it by being cut off. But no amount of cutting could reduce the body to nothing, Augustine points out; for there will always remain a part which itself is a body.[23]

One could ask the question here why it is that whenever a body is divided into parts, these parts are again bodies which could be divided into smaller bodies, and so on. What is it that accounts for the fact that the parts of bodies share the same essential structure as the whole, viz. being bodies? For it is not at all self-evident that parts retain the same constitutive structure as their whole. A word, for instance, can be split up into letters; but since these letters have a different structure than the word, they could no longer be divided into smaller letters. Or a number, such as 1000, could be divided into its single numbers; however, these single numbers are not constituted by smaller numbers into which they could be further divided.

Though Augustine does not directly address this question, the answer to it seems to be implied in what he is saying. For besides the fact that a body can be cut into parts, Augustine points to another, even more fundamental characteristic of bodies, which provides the basis for solving this difficulty, namely that bodies occupy a specific extension of place (*occupare loci spatium*).[24]

With this frequently recurring expression[25] Augustine refers to basically two features about bodies. Each body, first of all, is located at a specific place in space. It occupies a concrete spot in the infinity of space. This necessarily implies that each place in space can only be occupied by one concrete body at the same time. It is essentially impossible for the same place in space to be taken by more than one corporeal entity. Augustine points out this law with respect to the parts of a body. It is impossible, he says, for a body to have one of its parts at the same place as another one at the same time.[26] Therefore, if a specific part is at one place, another part has to be at another place (*quare alia pars eius alibi est, et alibi alia*).[27] One could with Augustine state the general law that each part of a corporeal being occupies its own proper place (*suum locum quaeque obtinet*).[28]

From this spatial standing outside of and next to each other it also follows, as Augustine shows, that there must be intervals of places (*intervalla locorum*) (i.e. of space containing these places) in between what is occupied by bodies and by their parts, however small they may be.[29] These intervals of space can however be crossed by a body. It can move from one place to another (*de loco in locum*),[30] so that this movement necessarily has to be a local movement implying the traversing of places in space.[31] Consequently, the proper way for bodies to move is locomotion (*localiter enim moveri corporis proprium est*).[32] But since everything that is moved in space can be moved only if it is also moved in time,[33] a body can be characterized to be a nature that is spatially and temporally mutable.[34] For its movements must be in space and time.[35]

There is a second meaning of the above mentioned formula of Augustine's that each body occupies an extension of place. In this (second) sense the expression refers to the fact that each body is also spatially extended, filling out a volume of space. Indeed, both meanings of this formula are closely related. For to be located at a place in space implies for a corporeal entity[36] also to be contained in space (*quod enim alicubi est, continetur loco*).[37] If it is placed in space, it also fills out space in that it is extended in the dimensions of length, breadth and height;[38] and vice versa, if something is extended in space, it as a whole cannot be everywhere in space, but only at its own single place.[39] And since, as we saw above, all parts of a body, being likewise extended in space, stand outside of and next to each other, it follows that the body as a whole cannot be in its single parts, but only in all of them taken together.[40] A body as this one whole entity *is* what consists of parts so that it as a whole cannot be fully present in one or more of its parts; rather, it is constituted by the union of all of its parts.[41]

At another passage (in *De Quantitate Animae*), Augustine further develops the insight that a body must necessarily be extended in space in the three dimensions of length, breadth and height. Asking Evodius (his interlocutor) whether he could think of any body that does not have these dimensions, Evodius answers by expressing his uncertainty as to what the term height means. Augustine explains that height is that in a body due to which its interior can be thought of or be perceived by the senses if the body is transparent, as in the case of glass (*illam [i.e., altitudinem] dico qua efficitur ut interiora corporis cogitentur, aut etiam sentiantur, si perlucet ut vitrum*).[42]

This passage should not be misunderstood as meaning that a body, due to height, becomes an (intelligible, ideal) object of thought thereby surpassing the realm of what is perceivable by the senses (as McMahon's translation of this passage might suggest).[43] Rather, Augustine wants to say that it is only because of its height as the third dimension that a body can be understood to have an interior at all, that is, to be a body in the strict sense and that this interior can even be seen by the eyes if it is transparent.

This interpretation is not only supported by what immediately follows in the text: *quanquam si hoc demas corporibus . . . neque sentiri possunt, neque omnino corpora esse recte existimari*,[44] but it also reveals an important insight on Augustine's part into the nature of bodies. For in order to be a body at all, something cannot merely have length, such as a line; indeed, even to have length and breadth, as a plane has, is not enough to be a body, since a plane as such cannot be cut into pieces. ('Plane as such' here does not mean the planelike surface that a body might have which can certainly be cut into pieces because the body is cut; rather, it means the mathematical figure 'plane' which can be outlined or circumscribed into different sections, but never be cut like a body.) Therefore, something is a body only because of this third dimension (of height) which gives it an interior that is extended in space.

There is still another feature of bodies, mentioned by Augustine, which is due to their three-dimensionality, namely the fact that bodies are perceived by the senses.[45] The third dimension, because of which something is a body at all, accounts for the 'sense-perceptibility' of bodies. Only bodies can be perceived by the senses.[46] Length alone, i.e. the mathematical 'line,' as well as the 'plane' are not perceived sensibly, since they are not bodies.[47] If the third dimension (height) is taken from a body, it is no longer perceivable through the senses, because it is no longer a body.[48]

Consequently, these three dimensions of length, breadth and height necessarily belong to a body (*corpora omnia his carere non posse*), as Evodius grants to Augustine.[49] For it is because of them that a body is extended in space.[50]

Spatial extendedness also accounts for the fact that bodies can be measured.[51] Their quantitative volume in space can exactly be determined and be compared to that of other bodies, or to that of their own parts. The extent to which a body fills out space is the (metaphysical) ground of the possibility of measuring it.

Coming back to the question posed above, namely as to why it is that the parts of bodies are again bodies that could be further divided into still smaller bodies, we can now see that this law is grounded in a body's extendedness in space. For precisely because a body fills out a certain volume of space, each part of it does the same according to its size. As much as I might cut a body into pieces, it will still remain a body occupying a place in space, however little it is extended.[52] Hence, the spatial extendedness of bodies is the ontological condition for their divisibility into parts.

Besides these features of bodies, Augustine refers to still other characteristically bodily predicates. He observes that every body has a certain greatness (*magnitudo*), color and shape.[53] At another place, Augustine mentions form, color, and a certain harmony of the body (*temperatio corporis*) (by which he seems to mean the proportionality of the various elements a body consists of) to be inseparably present in a body as their underlying subject.[54] There is a necessary relation between a body and these properties which cannot be broken up. They belong to the very nature of corporeality.

Yet, these properties, though being essential features of bodies, are not dependent on each other: the color and the shape can remain the same though the body has gotten smaller; likewise, the shape and the greatness can remain unchanged though the color has changed; and even if the shape changes, the body can still be as great as before with the same coloring.[55] The same can be said about all the other qualities that might be in a body: a change in one of them does not necessarily imply a change in the others.[56]

A similar independence from each other is given in the parts of a body. Precisely since they are parts of a whole, they in a peculiar way stand next to each other. They do not interpenetrate, so as to depend on or to imply each other. Rather, though together constituting a whole, each part, so to speak, stands on its own feet. Therefore, Augustine draws the conclusion, each body by nature is manifold, and not at all simple (*ac per hoc multiplex esse convincitur natura corporis, simplex autem nullo modo*).[57]

A still more illuminating discussion of this essential multiplicity of bodies is given by Augustine in *De Libero Arbitrio* in the course of arguing that numbers, in particular the number one, cannot be seen by our bodily senses. For, as we discussed above, such a sense perceives only corporeal beings, each of which is not one whole but an intrinsic multiplicity consisting of innumerable parts.[58] In other words, whatever we perceive through the senses is a body; and because it is a body, it cannot be perceived as one simple whole since any body is constituted by a multitude of parts. Consequently, the number one cannot be seen by the bodily eyes.

Indeed, as Augustine goes on explaining, not even the smallest particles of a body can be called a 'one.' For as small as they might be, they nevertheless remain corporeal entities; and therefore, they certainly have a right and a left, an upper and a lower part, a front and a back, ends and a middle. All these properties must be given in any body, even in the very smallest ones. Hence, a body cannot really be one. It always has two halves, each of which, in turn, consists of two halves, and so on.[59]

The question, then, of how we have an understanding of the number one if it is not gained by the bodily senses, Augustine answers by pointing at an inner light of the mind (*luce interiore mentis*), which is unknown to the senses, and in which we grasp the certain truth of number (*certa veritas numeri*).[60] It is only in the light of this mental knowledge of the number one that we are able to count the multiple parts of a body (*non possent tam multa numerari nisi illius unius cognitione discreta*).[61]

At this point, however, one might object to Augustine that these properties he lists as essentially belonging to each body, even to the very smallest ones, such as having a right and a left side, a back and a front, a middle, and various endpoints, are not really *parts* of a body. They do not make up a body in being its indispensable *constitutive* elements. For they themselves are not corporeal parts of a body that could be further divided into smaller parts. Consequently, to refer to them is not to prove a body's essential multiplicity. For could one not in principle think of an infinitely small body that is one simple whole in the sense of no longer being divisible, but that would at the same time have a right and a left side and these other features, if it could be perceived?

To this objection one could respond according to Augustine's mind that it is certainly true that the properties mentioned are not real constitutive parts of a body. They do not add to its mass extending it in space; they could rather be called aspects of a body, when and insofar as it is perceived under a certain perspective. (For whether a side of a body is right or left obviously depends on the point of view from which it is perceived.) They do not constitute the body, but instead, they are themselves constituted by the body and a mind perceiving it.[62]

However, since these properties are by nature aspects of a body, they necessarily presuppose for their existence the body whose aspects they are. And this body, according to its nature, is to be extended in space. Indeed, it is precisely the fact that the body fills out a certain volume of space that enables it to have these aspects. Without being extended (in three dimensions), a body could not be perceived at all, and thus, it could not be viewed under these various aspects.

So as we argued above, a body's extendedness accounts for its being divisible into parts. Since space is by nature infinitely divisible, everything that occupies space is, because of this, equally divisible. And what is divisible, that is, what is in potency of being split into parts, is not a simple, but a manifold being.[63] Thus, Augustine's reference to the multiplicity of a body's exterior aspects also proves a body's constitutive (interior) manifoldness, in that the former necessarily presupposes and implies the latter.

Yet, the objection could still be taken up by asking whether a body, though extended in space, could not be essentially simple and still have these various aspects. Indeed, is one not to assume ultimately simple bodies that can no longer be divided into parts (such as an 'atom' in the Greek sense of something indivisible) as necessary elements of any corporeal being? For without such simple particles a body would ultimately be nothing, which is impossible.[64] If this is so, however, Augustine's definition of body as being essentially manifold does not hold for all bodies, since these ultimate particles must be simple.

It seems to be in full accord with Augustine's thought to make the following distinction between two kinds of divisibility in answer to the objection.[65] It is one thing for a being to be divisible really and actually, without being completely destroyed. Yet, it is another thing to be divisible mathematically speaking, that is, to allow for divisions that are not actually carried out, but that are mathematically possible. (One could perhaps speak here of a *divisio realis* as opposed to a *divisio rationis cum fundamento in re*.)[66] Obviously, actual or real divisibility presupposes mathematical divisibility. But the former is limited in its scope. For whereas a body can be divided infinitely in the second sense (since space is infinitely divisible in mathematical terms),[67] there must be a finite limit to a body's actual divisibility (as was argued above). This limit, however, is not grounded in the fact that a body is extended in space, but it is due to the fact that a corporeal entity (its material mass) must consist of ultimate particles (atoms) that can no longer be actually divided, except by being annihilated altogether.

Distinguishing these two meanings of divisibility, the objection can be answered thus: Augustine's characterization of body as being essentially manifold (and not at all simple) is valid only when it is taken in the sense of mathematical manifoldness (divisibility) which, as a consequence of its spatial extendedness, is the more fundamental one. The definition, thus, does not imply that each body can *actually* be divided; for this, a certain material, not only spatial, extension is presupposed.[68]

We might briefly summarize the results of our analysis of Augustine's notion of *corpus* as that of which a part is less than the whole in the extension of place. We saw that it entails the following implications: (1) a body (*corpus*) is divisible into greater and smaller parts; (2) the whole body must be greater than any of its parts; (3) the body as well as its parts are located at a place in space; (4)

each body has its own proper place that cannot be taken up by another body at the same time; (5) bodies and their parts stand outside of and next to each other in space; (6) the proper movement of bodies is local and temporal motion; (7) as a whole, a body is not present in each of its single parts, but in all of them taken together; (8) each body is extended in space in the dimensions of length, breadth and height; (9) the third of these dimensions is the most important one, because a. it makes up the body by giving it an 'interior,' and b. it renders the body sensible, that is, perceivable by the senses; (10) spatial extendedness is the metaphysical ground of a body's measurability and divisibility; (11) necessary properties of a body that Augustine enumerates are greatness (*magnitudo*), color, shape, form and a certain harmony (*temperatio*) of the body; (12) these properties, though necessarily belonging to a body, are independent from each other; (13) a body must always have a right/left and an upper/lower part, a front and a back, ends and a middle; (14) these properties reveal the essential manifoldness (multiplicity) of bodies which is grounded in their *finite actual* divisibility and, ultimately, in their *infinite mathematical* divisibility.

All these features are necessarily to be found in what Augustine means by *corpus*.[69] They belong to the nature of corporeality as such. Indeed, Augustine says that even if we merely believed in a corporeal thing of which we have only heard or read, but which we have never seen, we would still have to represent it to ourselves as something in the shape and form of bodies.[70] This fact we know with certainty about something corporeal, even though we might not actually see or have seen it, that it must have those essential properties, if it is to be a body at all.

(B) Certain data of inner experience do not have the features of 'corpus'

In the light of the preceding discussion of the essential properties of that nature that Augustine means by the term body (*corpus*) we are in a position to pose with Augustine the question whether also the soul (or certain data of inner experience to be identified later as belonging to the soul) reveals such bodily predicates. If this should prove to be the case, it follows that the materialists are right; if not, the conclusion can be drawn that there is something in man that is not corporeal. Thus, this first way of arguing will be a negative proof that is not meant to bring to light what, positively speaking, is the soul.

Before Augustine can directly address this question as to whether these corporeal properties are also found in the soul, he must invalidate a widespread, commonly held opinion, namely the claim that whatever is must be a body. Many people, he observes, when asked to think of something without bodily images, simply judge this to be absolutely nothing.[71] Whatever does not show bodily properties is thought to be not existing at all. Consequently, each nature and each substance that is acknowledged to *be* can, according to this opinion, only be a corporeal entity. But this manner of viewing and defining things is for Augustine unacceptable (*non admittenda est ista locutio*).[72]

We have already seen that Augustine himself had for a time held this view;[73] and he relates that Tertullian also opined that only bodies are really existing things.[74] For this reason, he (Tertullian) feared that God or the soul would be nothing, if they were not bodies. And since he was convinced of the existence of God and of a soul in man, he thought them to be corporeal, which, Augustine concludes, was an error he made on the basis of a false general assumption.[75]

In his refutation of this general assumption about being, Augustine proceeds by simply referring to an example from outside the realm of the soul. This example deals with entities that *are*, without being bodies. From this it follows that the claim that whatever is must be corporeal, cannot be a universally valid principle. Hence, the attempt to show that the soul also does not have bodily predicates is not as such to imply that it is nothing.

In *De Quantitate Animae*, Augustine develops this argument against Evodius' (his interlocutor's) misgivings that to admit a lack of corporeal features in the soul is to deny its existence.[76] He does so by pointing at the example of justice asking Evodius whether justice exists, and whether it has length or any other bodily predicate. Evodius answers that justice certainly exists; but it cannot be said to be long, or wide, or anything like that. So, Augustine says, if justice does not have bodily predicates, and yet, if it is not nothing, why is it to be assumed that the soul is nothing if it has no length?[77]

Similarly, in *De Immortalitate Animae*, Augustine emphatically states that the objects of our intellect (*intelligentia*), though incorporeal (since only sense-objects are corporeal),[78] nevertheless *are*, indeed, that they are in the highest degree (*maxime sunt*) since they always remain the same (*semper sese habent*).[79] What he means here is that these intelligible objects, which he will later term *rationes aeternae*,[80] *are* as essentially unchangeable and without beginning or end, thereby surpassing all contingent entities not in being more substantial, but in remaining the self-same beings.

Thus, the existence of such immutable realities that evidently do not possess bodily features disproves the assumption that *all* beings, insofar as they exist, must be corporeal. Also the soul, then, is not to be thought as not existing if it lacks corporeal qualities. On the contrary, Augustine says, instead of considering the soul to be nothing, we should rather deem it all the more precious precisely because it does not have bodily features (*sed eo pretiosior et pluris aestimanda sit, quo nihil horum habet*).[81] (As will be shown later, bodies for Augustine have a rank of being and value that by nature is quite inferior to that of spiritual entities, such as the soul.)[82]

Having rejected this widespread empiricistic and positivistic premise (as it could be called in modern terminology), Augustine is free to show that none of the predicates that he found in bodies can be seen to be present in the soul. This conclusively shows the soul not to be a body.[83]

In a very revealing passage of the *Liber de Videndo Deo*, Augustine argues that the soul, or rather some of its acts which he after Paul (Gal. 5, 22–23) also calls 'fruits of the spirit,'[84] are given without any bodily feature. After explaining that even the images of bodies that we have in our mind are not corporeal, though they are strikingly similar to bodies, he continues:

> How much less are those things that bear no similarity to
> bodies, such as charity, joy, longanimity, peace, benignity,
> goodness, faith, mildness, continence, contained in places of
> space and separated by intervening areas, even though the
> eyes of the heart seek out some distinctions (*intervalla*) in them
> by sending out their rays to them and thus see them! Are
> not all these in one without being crowded; and are they not
> known by their own defined terms without spatial
> boundaries? Or tell me in what place you see charity, which

nevertheless is known to you since you can become aware
of it through the gaze of the mind; you know it as being great,
not because you perceive it by seeing a huge mass; nor does
it shout with a loud voice when it speaks to you interiorly that
you should live by it; nor do you direct the light of your
bodily eyes toward it in order to see it; nor do you strain the
strength of your bodily muscles in order to keep it firmly;
nor do you sense its approach when it comes to your mind.[85]

These inner realities, first of all, are not contained in space; they
are not separated by spatial intervals standing outside and next to
each other. Rather, they are all present in one (*in uno*) without
being cramped and crowded, as would be the case with bodies.
Furthermore, though being known by way of 'conceptual limits'
(*terminis*), they nevertheless do not have spatial boundaries by which
they were circumscribed. For this reason, an experience, such as
love, is not located in a specific place; it would be ridiculous to
say, for instance, that I have love in my arm and joy in my foot.
Again, I know love to be great not in the sense of bodily extension.
It, like the soul as such, is not long, or wide, or solid (*neque
illam longam esse, nec latam, nec robustam*) and can therefore not be
measured like bodies; it does not have a bodily quantity.[86] Because
it is not extended in space, it can also not be divided into parts
and be circumscribed by lines.[87] To use an example, I cannot cut
my love into greater and smaller pieces, clearly delineating them
from each other. It simply does not have the contours of bodies
(*lineamenta corporum*); for what should it mean to speak of the
shape, the limbs, or the color of love?[88]

Furthermore, love, or any other inner experience, is not
perceived through the bodily senses as are corporeal bodies.[89] We
do not hear it, since it does not cry out when it interiorly 'speaks'
to us to live by it (as in the experience of conscience); we do not
see it with the light of our eyes; we do not touch and keep it by
the power of our muscles; we do not sensibly feel it when we
become aware of it.[90] Precisely because the soul and its acts are
not corporeal, they do not have a 'sensible' nature that is perceivable
by the bodily senses.[91]

Augustine also shows in greater detail that the movement of the
soul is essentially different from that of a body. For while a body

moves spatially and temporally, the soul is mutable only in time.[92] For example, he argues, the soul moves temporally when it remembers what it had forgotten, when it learns what it did not know, or when it wills what it did not want before. In these instances, the soul 'moves' from one state of its being to another changing or perfecting its nature. None of these movements, however, is spatial; for in remembering, learning, or changing my mind in my intentions, I do not proceed from one place to another traversing intervals of space. These acts are performed only in time.[93] So Augustine states the general law that whatever moves spatially must also move temporally; but not everything that moves in time moves also in space.[94] One could also say that all *contingent* beings (since God moves neither spatially nor temporally)[95] are primarily subject to time, and are subject to space only insofar as they are of a corporeal nature.

Thus, Augustine can draw the conclusion that the nature of the soul is by far different from that of a body (*longe aliud est animae natura quam corporis*).[96] Since it does not have any corporeal predicate, it cannot be understood in terms of bodily images. To do so were to think about it in a deformed and shameful manner (*deformiter de illa et turpiter creditur*).[97]

3   The soul as distinct from the human body

So far the term *corpus* has been used in that wider sense in which it refers to any being that consists of parts which are more or less extended in space. We saw that none of the properties implied in this Augustinian definition of body is found in what is given in our inner experience. In this way, we got a first glimpse of the incorporeality of the human soul.

This understanding can be deepened when we approach our inner being in the light of the narrower sense of *corpus* mentioned by Augustine, that is, in the light of what consists of 'carnal members' (*membris carnalibus constat*): the human body.[98]

Augustine does not explicitly develop a clear distinction between these two meanings of *corpus*.[99] Yet, as will become evident, he is keenly aware of the unique metaphysical status of the *human* body being closely united to man's soul.

For various reasons, a sketch of Augustine's philosophy of the human body in its union with the soul is illuminating for our purposes. For such a treatise would show (1) that Augustine explicitly stresses the unity of the one human being as consisting of body and soul; (2) that he does not consider the human body a mere (Cartesian) '*res extensa*'; (3) that he actually has a much higher opinion of the body than is occasionally attributed to him; and (4) that the soul does not only not possess those corporeal features that are found in any body, but that also its union with the human body gives evidence of its incorporeality, that is, of its distinctness from the latter.

(A) Augustine's view of the human 'lived' body as part of the one nature of man

'*Homo est substantia rationalis constans ex anima et corpore.*'[100] This or similar definitions of man occur again and again in Augustine's writings:[101] man is a rational substance (or, as he says in *De Civitate Dei* V, 11, man is a rational animal) consisting of soul and body. We as men are a composite of soul and body (*ex anima et corpore nos esse compositos, quid est ipse homo*),[102] so that we would not be fully human beings if either one of them were lacking. For neither the body nor the soul could by themselves be called man, since neither would the body be a man if the soul were not there, nor would the soul be a man if a body were not animated by it.[103] To be a man presupposes being constituted by these two distinct realities which are irreducible to each other.[104] Both of them build up the substance and nature of man,[105] because of which man is a man in the full sense (*totus et plenus*).[106] As parts of man they both can, however, be used to *signify* the whole man.[107]

Thus, Augustine says, you are a man, and you have both a spirit and a body (*homo es, et spiritum habes, et corpus habes*); as man you consist of soul and body,[108] more precisely, of rational soul and mortal body.[109] Whoever wishes to separate the body from human nature is a fool, he says, putting the matter very forcefully.[110]

This dualistic view of man, which is deeply characteristic of Augustine's thought, does however not lead him to neglecting or even denying the unity of man as consisting of soul and body: *Tu unus homo, anima es et caro*.[111] Each man is a single unique person: he is one individual being (*una persona, id est singulus quisque homo*).[112] Though his soul has a body, they do not make up two persons but one man.[113]

When we will in our final chapter come back to the problem of the oneness of man we will see that Augustine does not simply maintain it without deeper reasoning. He is aware of the unique interpenetration of body and soul in man. Indeed, he calls the soul the very life of the body (*tota vita corporis anima est*).[114] It is through the soul that the highest Essence (God) has given a form (*species*) to the body by which it exists to the extent to which it exists. The body as animated by the soul does not exist on its own, but subsists through the soul (*per animam ergo corpus subsistit*).[115] My body lives through my soul (*corpus utique meum vivit de spiritu meo*),[116] and it is only as long as the members are parts of this body that they are vivified by the soul.[117]

What Augustine is describing here is precisely the unique reality of a 'lived' body which has recently been paid great attention to by a number of modern phenomenologists.[118] Like Augustine, they point to the fact that man's body cannot merely be viewed as a lifeless corporeal being, but that it is 'lived' from within. It is not a *Körper*, but a *Leib* (to use a linguistic distinction in German) due to its union and interrelation with the soul.

For Augustine, the most certain proof for this animated and vivified reality of the human body (*animatae viventisque carnis certissimum indicium*) is the fact that man can 'feel his body' (*sentire in corpore*), that is, that he is able to sense his body from within (as distinct from feeling his body, e.g. his skin, from without, or from feeling things through 'exterior' sensation). Man's body is not only animated, like plants, by a certain inner motion (*interno motu*), which, for instance, affects his growth or the production of nails and hair.[119] Though this principle of life has an important function for the arrangement and generation of the body,[120] it is distinct from man's ability of feeling his body from within. For this inner sense is not an unconscious, almost automatic dynamism like the animating life-principle. Rather, this sense is connected with the spontaneous (free) movement of the body in order to direct it (*motus spontaneus . . . sensui copulatur ad corporis administrationem*).[121]

Augustine distinguishes here three ways in which the soul is actively related to the body. It is, first of all, the animating source, or the *vitalis intentio*,[122] of the life of the body. In this sense, the soul affects the proper regulation and growth of the whole body as well as of all its organic members. However, this life-principle is not in our spontaneous free power since it is also given in plants. There is, secondly, the soul's faculty of freely moving the body, which, thirdly, is joined to this inner sense by which it is able to feel its body from within. For in order to move and direct the body by a spontaneous act of the will, it is presupposed that the soul has a sensitive inner awareness of it. If it were not also feeling the body from within, it would not be able to exercise its moving power over it (which certainly does not exclude the possibility that it can move *exterior* objects without feeling them from within).[123]

Though we will come back to these last two faculties of the soul when (in different contexts) arguments for the soul's incorporeality will be developed from them, it is still worth noting here how deeply Augustine penetrates into the relation between body and soul in man. He sees that the soul's faculty of moving the body cannot simply be accounted for by its life-giving impetus, but that it presupposes the conscious presence of the soul in the body, the *sentire in corpore*: I can only move spontaneously what I also feel from within; this inner awareness is essentially implied in the act of moving the body.

It is evident that in sensing and moving the body from within, the soul is much more deeply, much more 'really' present in the body than through its animating dynamism. One could say that the soul not only gives life to the body, but that in a sense it *lives* in it consciously. Man, Augustine says, lives in the union of body and soul (*in coniunctione corporis atque animae vivere*),[124] as if there were no essential difference in nature between the two. Indeed, he stresses that both are parts of the nature of man, sometimes calling the body *homo exterior* and the soul *homo interior*, together constituting the one human being.[125]

These two realities of which man consists, body and soul, do not have for Augustine an equal importance and value. The human person is for Augustine much more 'situated' in the soul than in the body, which, among deeper reasons to be discussed in a later chapter, can be gathered from the following. (1) According to Augustine, as we saw, the human body does not subsist through itself, but through the soul; it is through the soul that the highest Essence gives existence and life to the body. Also, though Augu-

stine does call the *human body* a substance,[126] he primarily stresses
the substantiality of both man and the soul; indeed, as we will see
in Chapter 4, the soul has for him a much higher degree of reality
and value than any body. (2) For Augustine man's highest good is
not what is good for his body, but what is the highest good either
for both body and soul together, or for the soul alone.[127] A good
for the soul is also a good for man, which is not equally true of a
good for the body. (3) The personal pronoun 'I' or 'You' is used
by Augustine both in reference to the human being as such, as
well as to the soul (*unus ego animus*),[128] suggesting that the soul is
the center of man's individual personality. (4) According to Augustine, man is made in the image of God not in the body, but in
the soul;[129] it is primarily his soul, as he shows throughout *De
Trinitate*, that is an image of the Blessed Trinity, even though man's
body can, compared to those of animals, be viewed to be created
much more in the image and likeness of God.[130]

From these facts it becomes clear that Augustine considers the
soul to be by far the more important and central constituent of
man's being. And yet, it would be a grave misunderstanding to
think that he simply downgrades the body, seeing no value in it,
beyond that of being a useful tool for the soul.

To substantiate this claim one should, however, point out first
that there is a development in Augustine's view of the human body
from his early works, written under the influence of the Platonic
and Neo-Platonic conception of the body[131] as well as of his own
personal experiences, to his later more mature writings which reveal
most properly the originality and greatness of his own thought. For
the early Augustine does use the Platonic image of the body as a
cave within which we are imprisoned (*in hac cavea inclusis*),[132] but
by the time of writing *De Civitate Dei* he has overcome this view,
speaking now of the excellence of the body's nature which merits
its being raised to heaven at the end,[133] and of the unnatural power
that in death *tears asunder* (*divellitur*) body and soul[134] which are
joined together in this life by a certain natural appetite in the
soul for animating and governing the body.[135] And even though
Augustine often exhorts us to lift ourselves out of the body and to
rise above those sensible things that appeal to our bodily nature,[136]
he does not thereby devaluate the body as such. Rather, he wants
to make us aware of the dangers for our spiritual well-being

resulting from a life according to bodily desires and pleasures in which the highest good for man, the perfection of his soul, is lost sight of.[137] The body as such is not evil. On the contrary, God made the body good.[138] It is, thus, not the body as such that Augustine rejects; but it is its corruption as source of our evil desires against which he warns us and which he admonishes man to hate.[139] Therefore, if the body is to be considered a cave for man's soul, this does not refer to the body *qua* body, but to the body insofar as it is corrupted.[140]

The full value that Augustine sees in the human body is twofold: its intrinsic beauty and its 'borrowed' preciousness as vessel and instrument of the soul. Both together constitute the real value of the body. Let me try to work out these two beautiful lines of thought in Augustine.

'*Inspice pulchritudinem formati corporis*,' Augustine exhorts us.[141] In his great ability to be amazed at the mysteries and beauties of reality, Augustine could not but be struck by the marvellous inner harmony and proportion of the human body. It is held together, he says, by some *species*, that is, by some beautiful form, because of which it is also good.[142]

But Augustine does not merely state his opinion of the inner harmony and beauty of the human body. In a lengthy passage, he describes what it is that makes him marvel at the nature of the body:

> Moreover, even in the body, though it dies like that of the beasts, and is in many ways weaker than theirs, what goodness of God, what providence of the great Creator, is apparent! The organs of sense and the rest of the members, are not they so placed, the appearance, and form, and stature of the body as a whole, is it not so fashioned, as to indicate that it was made for the service of a reasonable soul? Man has not been created stooping towards the earth, like the irrational animals; but his bodily form, erect and looking heavenwards, admonishes him to mind the things that are above. Then the marvellous nimbleness which has been given to the tongue and the hands, fitting them to speak, and write, and execute so many duties, and practise so many arts, does it not prove the excellence of the soul for which such

an assistant was provided? And even apart from its adaptation
to the work required of it, there is such a symmetry in its
various parts, and so beautiful a proportion maintained, that
one is at a loss to decide whether, in creating the body,
greater regard was paid to utility or to beauty. Assuredly no
part of the body has been created for the sake of utility
which does not also contribute something to its beauty. And
this would be all the more apparent, if we knew more
precisely how all its parts are connected and adapted to one
another, and were not limited in our observations to what
appears on the surface; for as to what is covered up and
hidden from our view, the intricate web of veins and nerves,
the vital parts of all that lies under the skin, no one can
discover it. . . . But if these could be known, then even the
inward parts, which seem to have no beauty, would so delight
us with their exquisite fitness, as to afford a profounder
satisfaction to the mind – and the eyes are but its ministers –
than the obvious beauty which gratifies the eye. There are
some things, too, which have such a place in the body, that
they obviously serve no useful purpose, but are solely for
beauty, as e.g. the teats on a man's breast, or the beard on
his face; for that this is for ornament, and not for protection,
is proved by the bare faces of women, who ought rather, as
the weaker sex, to enjoy such a defence. If, therefore, of all
those members which are exposed to our view, there is
certainly not one in which beauty is sacrificed to utility,
while there are some which serve no purpose but only beauty,
I think it can readily be concluded that in the creation of
the human body comeliness was more regarded than necessity
(*in conditione corporis dignitatem necessitati fuisse praelatam*). In
truth, necessity is a transitory thing; and the time is coming
when we shall enjoy one another's beauty without any lust.[143]

Man's body was created in such a way that it could serve a soul
endowed with reason. Its form perfectly fits to the functions the
soul has to perform in and through the body. But apart from its
role as assistant of the soul, there is a symmetry (*congruentia*) and
a proportion (*parilitas*) in the body that is beautiful and simply
amazing. If one thinks of how the organs are connected and adapted

(*coaptatio*, a term especially coined by Augustine to express this
fact) to each other, one is at a loss to decide, he comes to the
conclusion, whether the body was created more for the sake of
utility or of beauty.[144] Indeed, I think Augustine would have been
even more struck by amazement, had he had a chance of taking a
glimpse also at the inside of the body; he would have felt the same
awe and wonderment as many scientists after him.[145]

So Augustine arrives at the conviction that in creating the body
more attention was paid to beauty and dignity than to utility and
necessity;[146] for there is no part of it that does not contribute to
its beauty, though some parts do not have any useful purpose.[147]

Yet, there is another dignity bestowed on the human body. We
just heard how Augustine considers the body an assistant of the
soul. It stands in the soul's service, so to speak. The soul operates
in the members of the body as if they were instruments (*anima in
partibus corporis tanquam in organis agit*).[148] It needs the body to
carry out activities such as writing, speaking, sense-perceiving and
others.[149] In this sense, the body serves the soul; for without it,
these activities could not be performed.

But this usefulness may not be interpreted as downgrading the
body's own value. It is not merely that the body has a value as long
as it is useful for the soul. On the contrary, precisely because the
body is used by the soul it gains a lasting dignity resulting from its
participation in the excellence of the soul it serves.

Let me develop this thought of Augustine's in more detail, as it
is found in *De Civitate Dei* (in a passage which was literally taken
over by Augustine in *De Cura pro Mortuis Gerenda* III, 5):

> Nevertheless the bodies of the dead are not on this account
> to be despised and left unburied; least of all the bodies of
> the righteous and faithful, which have been used by the Spirit
> as his organs and instruments for all good works. For if the
> dress of a father, or his ring, or anything he wore, be precious
> to his children, in proportion to the love they bore him, with
> how much more reason ought we to care for the bodies of
> those we love, which they wore far more closely and
> intimately than any clothing? For the body is not an extraneous
> ornament or aid, but a part of man's nature.[150]

We find here, *in nuce*, Augustine's view of the human body. It

is based on an important insight into what could be called 'preciousness by participation.' In arguing for the fact that corpses should
not be despised and cast away, Augustine points out how these
dead bodies have acquired a special dignity from their union with
the soul.

The body is, as it were, the instrument and the vessel (*organum
et vas*) of the soul – a recurring notion in Augustine. As instrument,
it is used by the soul (*spiritus*) for certain outside activities. And it
is used in a holy manner when the soul performs good works
through it. Though it is primarily the soul that becomes good as
the agent of these good works, the body, too, participates in this
goodness insofar as it stands in the soul's service. As secondary
agent of these works, the body has its own share in their value.
It becomes good *secundum quid*, as one might say in Scholastic
terminology.

But this acquired goodness is not only due to the body's assist-
ance of the soul in the performance of good exterior acts. Augustine
also shows that the body receives a special value simply by being
a part of man's nature. To bring out this value more clearly,
Augustine uses the analogy of the dress or the ring of a deceased
father. Such a ring does not only have a (material) value as does
any other ring, but it has gained a special preciousness because it
was the ring of a beloved person. This preciousness is not intrinsic
to the ring, it is not essential to its nature as such. One might
rather say that it is superadded on it by the fact that it was worn
by someone special to me, by my father. And the dearer he was to
me, the greater is the ring's value for me. Thus, it is only *for me*
that the ring is precious in this special way. Since I chose this ring
to be my particular memento of my father, and since I dearly loved
him when he was alive, this ring has gained a value *for me alone*, a
value that is nevertheless intrinsic to the ring *insofar as* it represents
my father. If it were stolen, I would be sad not only because I lost
something of material value, but above all, because I lost *this*
memento particularly valuable to me.

Applying this example to the human body, Augustine points out
that the bodies of deceased men should for an analogous reason
not be despised, because they have been worn even more intimately
and closely than any dress. Because these bodies were the vessels
of souls which by nature have an intrinsic excellence and which,

in the case of righteous and faithful persons, have become even more precious, they participate in this preciousness of the soul, acquiring a 'borrowed' dignity that renders them worthy of due respect. In fact, Augustine calls the soul itself the ornament of the body.[151]

Furthermore, as Augustine explains, the relation between soul and body is even more intimate than that between a person and the dress or the ring he wears. For the body is not merely an ornament or a subsidiary attached to us *externally*, but it is an essential part of our nature as human beings.[152] It is intimately united to our soul. For this reason, the body shares even more directly in the dignity and goodness of the soul thereby acquiring this peculiar 'preciousness by participation.'

One could develop Augustine's thought by showing that it is precisely the closer intimacy between body and soul that renders the bestowed preciousness much more intrinsic to the nature of the body than is the case with the adopted value of the ring. For whereas the ring possesses its superadded value for me alone, and not for anyone else, and only because I chose it to be a special memento of my father, the received dignity of the body as vessel of the soul is a part of its nature, in the sense that the body is not only precious *for* someone, such as for the family of the deceased, but that it is precious by nature, not as mere body, but *as* united to the soul. In this, it is more objective than the memento-value of the ring which for its constitution as value presupposes the relation to the person to whom it is precious. Again, the body is not to be chosen as one among other items to be the 'representative' of the deceased man as is his ring; rather, it is *the* memento, because it formed part of his nature. Thus, the much closer intimacy between body and soul effects that the kind of relational character, which is still present in the superadded value of the ring, is lacking in the constitution of the body's dignity. Though resulting from a participation in the preciousness of the soul, this dignity is nevertheless intrinsic to the body.

As an outward expression of this acquired dignity, the human body, unlike the body of an animal, has a form that is erect and looking heavenwards.[153] This should be an admonishing reminder, Augustine says, to pursue the things that are above, as the soul that is fitted (*congruit*) to the body should go beyond the corporeal to the higher spiritual world.[154]

Another indication which shows how the excellence of the soul is expressed in the body is through this amazing suitability of bodily organs for acts of the soul. Augustine marvels at this wonderful mobility which is given to the tongue and the hands, fitting them to speak, to write and to perform many acts and duties. (One need only imagine a man writing with the paw of a dog or speaking with the beak of an eagle to see Augustine's point.) Now that such a body is put in the service of the soul, is that not enough evidence, Augustine wonders, for the greatness of this soul which is reflected in the body? Precisely because the body is made so properly fitting to the soul, it expresses, and thereby participates in, its dignity.[155]

It should be clear now that Augustine does not in fact hold the negative view of the human body that is occasionally attributed to him. Though clearly warning and admonishing us to see the body in a 'holy manner' and to reject the temptations to a life of mere bodily pleasure that will prove fatal for the soul, Augustine convincingly shows the value of the body as part of man's nature in being united to the soul. The one individual man is constituted by both soul and body of which the soul is the source of life and value participated in by the body.[156]

(B) The soul's presence in the human body as proof that it itself cannot be a body

We have seen in the previous section how Augustine shows that the human body is not merely a lifeless *res extensa*, but that it is animated and formed by its union with the soul. In a sense, the soul lives in the body and is able to feel and experience it from within (*sentire in corpore*). Though the human body, like any other body, is extended in space, consists of innumerable parts, can be measured and weighed, etc., it is a very unique kind of corporeal entity: it is a lived body vivified by the soul.

From this peculiar phenomenon of an animated body that can be felt from within Augustine develops an argument for the incorporeality of the soul which shall be sketched out in the following in somewhat greater detail.

In our discussion of the characteristics of corporeal entities we have already pointed out that it is essential to bodies to be located only at one specific place at the same time. Each part of a body occupies its own place in space that cannot be taken by another part or even by the whole body as such, at the same moment in time. Therefore, the body as a whole cannot be at the place of one of its parts, since it consists of all of them taken together.[157]

But is this also the way in which the soul is in man's body? Is the soul also extended in the body so that its parts are present at the respective parts of the body? If this is so, the soul would be nothing but another body, that, due to its fine subtility, is able to diffuse itself into all parts of the human body.[158]

Augustine's answer to this question again reveals his genius of penetrating into and describing reality. Taking the phenomenon of the soul's presence in the body as it is given in experience, he argues that this cannot be explained in terms of the intermingling of two bodies, but that it must be the result of the union of a corporeal body with an incorporeal soul. Let me develop Augustine's argument as it is presented at different places in his writing.[159]

First of all, he states that for this argument he does not want to analyze the soul insofar as it is that power in us through which we know truth; rather, he wants to pay close attention to its 'lower' faculty by which it keeps the body together and feels in it (*illa inferior qua continet corpus et sentit in corpore*).[160] Thus, it is precisely this unique phenomenon of *Leibgefühl*, of feeling the body from within, that Augustine is interested in.

The most comprehensive and revealing text stating this argument is found in *Epistola CLXVI*. By complementing this text with references to other passages, we might be able to become more aware of the mysteriousness of the phenomenon in question which conclusively shows the presence of an *incorporeal* soul in man:

> If body be used to designate nothing but that which, whether
> at rest or in motion, has some length, breadth, and height,
> so that with a greater part of itself it occupies a greater part
> of space, and with a smaller part a smaller space, and is in
> every part of it less than the whole, then the soul is not
> corporeal. For it pervades the whole body which it animates,
> not by a local distribution of parts, but by a certain life-giving
> impetus, being at the same moment present in its entirety

in all parts of the body, and not less in smaller parts and greater in larger parts, but here more attentively and there more remotely, it is in its entirety present both in the whole body and in every part of it. For even that which the mind perceives in only a part of the body is nevertheless not otherwise perceived than by the whole mind; for when any part of the living flesh is touched by a fine-pointed instrument, although the place affected is not only not the whole body, but scarcely discernible in its surface, the contact does not escape the entire mind, and yet the contact is felt not over the whole body, but only at the one point where it takes place. How comes it, then, that what takes place in only a part of the body is immediately known to the whole mind, unless the whole mind is present at that part, and at the same time not deserting all the other parts of the body in order to be present in its entirety at this one? For all the other parts of the body in which no such contact takes place are still living by the soul being present with them. And if a similar contact takes place in the other parts, and the contact occurs in both parts simultaneously, it would in both cases alike be known at the same moment, to the whole mind.

Now this presence of the mind in all parts of the body at the same moment, which implies that the whole mind is present in every part of the body at the same moment, would be impossible if it were distributed over these parts in the same way as we see bodies distributed in space, occupying less space with a smaller portion of itself, and greater space with a greater portion. If, therefore, mind is to be called corporeal, it is not corporeal in the same sense as earth, water, air, and ether are corporeal. For all things composed of these elements are larger in larger places, or smaller in smaller places, and none of them is in its entirety present at any part of itself, but the extension of the bodies is according to the extension of the space occupied. Whence it is perceived that the soul, whether it be termed corporeal or incorporeal, has a certain nature of its own, created from a substance superior to the elements of this world, – a substance which cannot be truly conceived of by any representation of the corporeal images perceived by the bodily senses, but which is apprehended by the mind and felt by its life.[161]

After restating his definition analyzed above of what a body is, Augustine argues that this definition cannot be applied to the soul. For the soul animates the body not by being spatially diffused in it (*locali diffusione*), but by a certain vivifying intention (*quadam vitali intentione*) that is not larger in larger parts of the body and smaller in smaller ones. Rather, the soul is present as a whole (*tota*) in all parts of the body at the same time (*simul*). Augustine investigates this amazing fact which reveals the distinctness of the soul from any corporeal being in still more detail.

The soul feels the parts of the body not by a part of itself, but as a whole. It is present in its oneness (*tota*) everywhere in the body and, thus, it is present in its full being (*tanta*).[162] This is why even the smallest touch of a part of the body, for instance when a needle pricks a tiny spot on the skin, is sensed by the *whole* soul.[163] The (spatially) small sensation is not felt by a small part of the soul (which would have to be the case if the soul were another body whose parts would be in physical contact with the parts of the body). Instead, it is a fully experienced sensation (and not a 'half-sensation' or 'quarter-sensation') involving the soul as a whole.

But though the soul is present in the whole body, it need not feel the body as a whole when it experiences a particular sensation in a part of it. This sensation is felt by the soul not through the whole body, as if it had to run through many of its parts (*neque id quod sentitur, per corporis cuncta discurrit*); rather, the sensation is experienced *only* at that spot on the body where it occurs (*ibi tantum sentitur ubi fit*).[164] The soul, thus, has a full awareness of this sensation as being located at a particular part of its body. Does this mean, then, that the soul being wholly present at this one place is no longer present in the whole body? Is it the same situation as with bodies that when placed in one spot, leave behind them the place where they were located before?

Precisely here Augustine touches upon the mysteriousness of this body-soul relation. For when the soul, experiencing a sensation in a part of the body, is wholly present in this particular sensation, it does not abandon the other parts of the body. It does not accumulate itself at this one felt spot. Instead, as this whole soul, it at the same time remains present not only in the body as a whole, but in its single parts as well (*et in omnibus tota, et in singulis tota est*).[165] For when we experience a particular sensation, let us say in the finger, we could at the same time experience another sensation in the foot; both sensations would be felt by the whole soul.[166] It does not cease being present at and feeling other parts of the body when it experiences a sensation in one of its parts. This is why it is possible that, in the case of a pain in the foot, the eyes can look at it, the mouth can speak of it, the hand can reach for it, all at the same time.[167] For a corporeal being, which is present only at one place at a time, this would by nature be excluded. It can only be an incorporeal soul that is present at these various single places of the body which are spatially distant from each other (*in singulis distantibus locis*).[168]

For this reason, the inner presence of the soul in the body is different, for instance, also from the manner in which whiteness or any other such quality is present in the body. As each part of the body has a particular 'whole' color, one could imagine that the soul might be attached to the body like such a quality. But this is not the case, Augustine argues. For a change in the color of one part of the body does not have an effect on the color of another part of it, whereas, as the example of the footache proves, the soul's feeling in one part of the body can and mostly does affect the soul feeling and acting in other parts.[169]

Thus, while a quality, such as a color, is present *as* this whole color only at a specific spot on the body, the soul is fully present in the single parts of the body at the same time. It, so to speak, has a simultaneous overall awareness of the body from within. It is clear, therefore, that it must be one and the same soul (and not a variety of souls in me) that wholly (*tota*) feels in these numerous parts of the body; otherwise, such simultaneous awareness of sensations occurring at different places throughout the whole body could not be given to it.[170]

This overall presence of the soul in the body, however, does not exclude that the soul can be more or less attentive (*intentius*) at the different parts of the body. I can, for instance, 'intentionally' feel a particular part of my body from within by fixing my special attention on it. There is an *intentio animi*[171] that can be directed toward one particular spot of the body which implies that lesser attention (*remissius*) is being paid to other parts.[172] In this sense of attentiveness, the soul can be more present in one part than in another one. Yet, as this one soul, it fully remains in the single parts of the body.[173] To express this mysterious phenomenon more clearly, one could say that the soul as one constituent of man is present within and throughout the whole body, so that it could feel its parts (that is, obviously only those parts accessible to being felt) from within at any time; but beyond that, it can pay a special conscious attention to a particular part of the body, which does not affect its overall feeling presence in the body at all.

So Augustine can draw the following conclusion. Since each body is by nature extended in space (a greater part of it occupying more space than a smaller part) and since it is present only at one place at the same time, the soul cannot be a body. For no body could be present in the human body in the manner that the soul is. Since it does not fill out space in the body as does water in a skin or a sponge, it is 'mingled' with it in wonderful incorporeal manners (*miris modis ipso incorporeo nutu commixta*).[174]

This presence of the whole soul in the single parts of the body is also a strong indication of the greater simplicity of the soul in comparison to that of the body, about which more will be said later.[175] For only an essentially simple being that does not consist of parts can be present in the body in this unique manner.[176] Thus, if the soul is to be called corporeal, Augustine says, it is so not in the sense in which the four material elements are corporeal; it must have a nature essentially different from any body, a nature that is particularly its own.[177]

And yet, one could still be hesitant to agree with this conclusion by pointing out that the soul precisely by being 'in' the body appears to share in the spatial extension of the body. Evodius seems to struggle with the same difficulty when asking Augustine why it is that the soul can feel wherever the body is touched, if it does not have the same magnitude as it.[178] For the soul must somehow be as great as the body since it is sensitively present in its parts that are distributed at various places in space. In spite of the argument just developed, is one, after all, not to assume, then, a kind of physical extension of the soul, due to which it could be considered a body?

Instead of restating Augustine's answer to this question of

Evodius', which answer is complicated and unclear rather than helpful – he tries to argue that in a sensation the soul does not feel a part of the body, but that it feels something outside of it, so that it is not really present '*in*' the body at all.[179] Let me attempt to solve this difficulty by distinguishing between three kinds of relations to space which seem to be implied in Augustine without being explicitly discriminated.[180]

The first of these kinds is the filling out of space which, as Augustine points out, is an essential characteristic of bodies. A second way of relating to space is the localization in the body of certain sensations, for instance the pain in the foot that Augustine mentions, which are felt only in one particular spot on the body. Thirdly, man's whole soul is in a sense contained in space *insofar as* it constitutes with the body the one man. For since the body fills out space and is always located at a particular place in space, the soul, in virtue of its being united to the body, is present at the same place. The body keeps the soul at a given place in space, not *qua* soul, but *qua* being united to it.[181]

These three ways of relating to space are fundamentally distinct and independent of each other. For neither does the pain, which is located in the body (second way), *as* this one conscious experience also fill out space (first way); nor is the soul as such extended in space (first way) only because it is located at a particular place in space *insofar as* it is a part of man consisting of body and soul (third way). This precisely is the 'mystery of man' that he consists in a union of a corporeal element filling out space and an incorporeal soul that, though itself being unextended in space, is yet present in space in a peculiar way (through the body).[182]

On the basis of these distinctions it becomes clear that the soul's presence in the whole (extended) body does not imply its own extendedness in space. On the contrary, as we saw, precisely because the soul is unlike any body, it can be present in the body in a manner that is extraordinary and unique.

The main conclusion that can be drawn from the arguments discussed in this chapter is that the soul can *not* be a corporeal entity, that is, a body. The soul does not have those features that we found in what is meant by the term *corpus*. However, what the soul actually is, has not been shown so far. We will begin to understand that, particularly with respect to its rationality, when in the following chapter we will be discussing after Augustine specific faculties or acts given in inner experience that can essentially be performed only by an incorporeal subject possessing rational abilities, and not by the body or a part of it.

CHAPTER 2

The 'rational' incorporeality of the human soul shown by basic faculties

The next step in our investigation of the nature of the human soul as it is analyzed by Augustine, consists in discussing certain characteristic faculties of man which, when fully understood, can evidently not be attributed to a corporeal entity. Their very essence and structure requires a subject that possesses completely different marks than are found in bodies. By analyzing these faculties, a further basis of arguments for the incorporeality of the soul will be provided.

Though the form of these arguments is, strictly speaking, that of a negative proof (these faculties presuppose a subject that can *not* be a body), these arguments are much more positive than those treated in the previous chapter. For by investigating and penetrating into the basic faculties of man, we will get some understanding of the positive determinations of their underlying subject. Particularly, we will get a glimpse of what it means to speak of man as a 'rational' being.

Before entering into this discussion, however, the subject needs to be restricted. As the nature of man is an overwhelmingly rich field of philosophical inquiry, and as Augustine, perhaps more than anyone, was able to delve into and to describe man's faculties, we find in him an extremely rich philosophy of man, valuable for both philosophers and psychologists. Yet, from this wealth of insight only those aspects shall be treated that are either used for arguments against a materialistic view of man by Augustine himself, or that play a prominent role for Augustine in throwing the nature of man into relief, even if he does not explicitly conclude from them to the incorporeality of the soul. Thus, we want to restrict the discussion in this chapter to three 'groups' of faculties in man: his imaginative and memorial faculties, his cognitive faculties, and his free will. Needless to say, we can only concentrate on some essential aspects of these faculties without going into many details, as Augustine occasionally does. For since our primary concern is to prove the incorporeality (and also 'rationality') of the soul through them, it suffices to point out their characteristic features without rendering them the prime subject-matter of the investigation.

We will, therefore, exclude from the discussion acts of the human being that are mentioned by Augustine (above all in the *Confessiones*) and that would as well prove the incorporeality of the soul, such as acts of joy, of sadness, of hope, the experience of conscience, of friendship or of religious feelings like repentance, restlessness of heart, the awareness of being guided and loved by God, and many other acts. Though we find in Augustine a great richness of observations and insights into these acts and experiences, and though each of them, when closely analyzed, would reveal an incorporeal nature as its performing subject, we have to limit this chapter to an inquiry into the most fundamental faculties of man.[1]

1   Man's imaginative and memorial faculties

In this section, those arguments for the incorporeality of the human soul shall be presented that Augustine develops from certain acts of imagination and recollection given in man's inner experience. Though these acts are not specifically 'rational,' their analysis will nevertheless reveal them not only to presuppose a performing subject that cannot be corporeal, but that must also possess some 'rational' (spiritual) features.[2]

Augustine refers to these faculties quite often in his writings. He was simply amazed at the fact that man is able, so to speak, to have the whole world contained in himself in the form of mental images and memories. How could it be that so huge a reality is 'present' in a single man? Trying to come to grips with this question, Augustine in a very original manner penetrated into and attempted to grasp what is given in these acts. Though we will propose some corrections of his analyses and point out certain insufficiencies of the arguments for the soul's incorporeality that he bases on these investigations, it remains true to say that we find in Augustine a phenomenology of this aspect of man's being that is highly inspiring and illuminating even today.

(A) Imagination

In a chapter of *De Genesi ad Litteram* (XII, XXIII, 49), Augustine gives a very fine summary of various acts that fall under the broad term imagination. Though his terminology for the act of imagining is characteristically manifold and flexible (*cogitare, intueri, similitudines sive imagines formare*, etc.), his description of these acts makes it clear that what he has in mind here are specific kinds of imagination in the sense of the inner representation of images thought. For all these acts share one basic feature: they are directed toward an object that is not a particular real thing standing over against me, independent of my perceiving it, but that in some way is shaped and constituted by my acts of imagination. Let me quote an excerpt from the chapter just referred to so that by a more detailed enumeration of these various acts of imagination clearer evidence may be gained of the fact that these acts could not be performed by a bodily entity, but presuppose an incorporeal soul:[3]

I think I am emphasizing clearly enough: it is sure that there is a certain spiritual nature in us in which the images (*similitudines*) of corporeal things are formed. This happens when we touch a particular body with a bodily sense, and its image is immediately formed in the mind and stored in memory; or when we think of absent bodies that are already known to us, so that a certain spiritual appearance (*aspectus*) is formed out of them, which were already in the mind even before we thought of them; or when we mentally regard the images of bodies that we do not know, but of whose existence we nevertheless do not doubt, images which are not exactly as the objects really are, but as they appear to our mind; or when we think according to our own whim and conjecture of other bodies that do not exist at all or whose existence is unknown; or when various forms of corporeal images come up in our mind from wherever without us affecting or willing it; or when we are about to do something in a bodily manner and arrange and pre-consider in thought (*cogitatione*) all that will be implied in that action; or when in

the very action, either in our speaking or our acting, all
corporeal movements are anticipated in their images within
the mind so that they can be performed: for not even the
briefest syllable would sound in its proper order unless
foreseen; or when one sees dreams in sleep, whether or not
they have a meaning.[4]

In this passage, Augustine distinguishes eight ways of forming
images which are more or less closely related to each other. The
first is the act of forming memory images which, for Augustine,
are derived from the things perceived by the senses and are then
stored in memory. We will have to come back to this act when
speaking about memory in the following section.

The second act he mentions is closely related to the first one.
He seems to mean an act of remembering in which we form a
spiritual intuition of objects that are no longer present to us as real
objects but as objects known. Precisely *as* known objects present
in memory (*in spiritu*), we put them in our mental gaze and gain a
peculiar vision of them. We see them as (being in reality) absent
objects; and yet, we form an image of them as we think of them
from memory. One might add that in this perceptual remembrance
of such objects, we could very well attain new knowledge about
them, even though they are no longer really present, and even
though this knowledge was not gained in the original act of getting
to know the real objects. For instance, we could find in these
remembered objects values or an existential significance that we
did not see in them when actually perceiving them, but that they
really bear, as we realize in retrospect.

The third act that Augustine describes is not built on acts of
memory, but is a mental projection of new images. It is an act in
which we make up images of bodies that we do not know, but
whose existence is not doubtful to us.[5] In contradistinction to the
second kind of imagining just mentioned, this act is directed toward
the image of an object that, as this particular object, was not known
before, so that the image does not fully correspond, but could be
somewhat similar, to a real object. In another context, Augustine
gives an example that might be illuminating.

When we read the writings of the apostle Paul, Augustine says,
we most likely form a mental picture of him and of all the people

that are mentioned in these writings. Even though none of us has actually seen Paul himself, we somehow imagine how he must have looked. Yet, it is obvious that we can never know whether his exterior was really such as we imagine it to be (unless, as should be added, we happen to discover a portrait that has been proven to represent him faithfully). Above all, each of us will have his own particular image of Paul; we all represent him to ourselves in our own way. (This becomes particularly evident if one compares various paintings of one and the same historical person or event, each of which portrays this person in its own way expressing the imagination of its painter. In fact, each painter himself might have imagined the person in a variety of ways, so that his painting need not necessarily correspond to one particular imagination.) Consequently, even though the writings of Paul are the same for all of us, the images we form of him are as manifold, indeed even more so, as there are people who try to imagine him to themselves. However, whether any of these images is exactly corresponding to the real Paul will remain uncertain.[6]

Closely related to this act of imagining is the fourth act on Augustine's list. The only difference between these two acts seems to lie in the fact that the images made up by this latter act are the product of a more random and conjectural imagination. In this case, we would think of objects that might not exist at all, or of whose existence we are unaware. A good example is the image of a four-footed bird that Augustine had never seen or heard of, but that he could easily make up in his mind when he was writing *De Trinitate*.[7] However, when reviewing this passage (in the *Retractationes* II, XV, 2) he points out that when he wrote this passage he had forgotten certain four-footed winged insects that are mentioned in the Old Testament. This incident shows that the images produced by this fourth act of imagining need not, but can have, a correspondence to reality.

Fifthly, Augustine refers to images that are simply present in our mind without us making them up or willing them. These images can come from anywhere. They are not the product of a particular mental activity of ours, though they are somehow in us so that we can 'see' them. Here Augustine seems to refer to what modern psychology calls associations, that is, images that without our free engendering can simply come to mind at times when we are consciously thinking of something else. They can be images that do not have anything to do with what we are presently reflecting on.

At another place, Augustine refers to a somewhat similar form of imagination that might be worth mentioning in this context.[8] Man has the faculty of silently thinking of words without uttering them in the sound of a particular language, or of hearing hymns and melodies inwardly while the mouth of the body is silent, as he puts it. We all know this experience of having a tune in our mind, which might simply 'be there' without us deliberately producing it, even when we do not actually sing or whistle it. Augustine says that these melodies are present in the mind through their own proper kind of incorporeal images (*per incorporeas quasdam imagines suas*); they are not the real melodies sung and heard by the bodily ears, but they are given inwardly without the mediation of the exterior organs of voice and of hearing. (This is why such melodies can only be 'heard' by *myself*, whereas what is sung aloud can in principle be heard by anyone.) This form of imagining also shows that imagination need not always be a visual act, analogous to the act of seeing through the eyes, but that there could as well be an 'imaginative listening,' nay even an 'imaginative smelling, tasting, or touching.'

The sixth act of imagining mentioned in the passage quoted above refers to the pre-conceiving of our own future actions. When we are planning to perform a certain action we can pre-imagine when and how we want to do it. We can form an image of how we want the action to be performed (which does not at all mean that the action will be done this way); and thus, we pre-conceive the action, or rather the image of a possible action. However, I do not think that such a pre-conception can be done only with respect to the images of those future actions that presuppose our body, as Augustine seems to suggest. One can as well conceive of purely spiritual acts of joy or sadness that one might be experiencing in the future. One may not have this pre-awareness by perceiving a 'visually' given mental image of this future act (precisely because it is not a bodily act); however, imagination in the sense of such pre-awareness in thought (*cogitatione*) seems to be possible, in whatever form it may occur, with regard to both corporeal and purely mental future acts.

Seventhly, Augustine applies this pre-conceiving of future acts to the time of the immediate future. While the former kind of imagining refers to a whole future act as it might be performed once, this other (seventh) act of pre-conception takes place in the very performance of that act (which was pre-conceived) with respect to what will or should immediately follow in its performance. In doing something or in speaking (which are Augustine's examples), we anticipate what we will do or say in the very next moment. If we would not do so, we could not even utter a well arranged sentence since, as Augustine says, even the briefest syllable can only sound correctly if it stands in the proper order of the sentence, which, in turn, must somehow be pre-conceived if the syllables are to have their right place. However, it seems questionable to me whether this anticipation of the immediate future occurs always in the form of a visual grasping of a mental image. When it does not, it would not fall under the general heading of imagination in the sense to be discussed here.[9]

Finally, Augustine mentions the phenomenon of dreams that we experience in sleeping. Here it is obvious that our attention is directed to some images fabricated by a more or less consciously awakened activity. Yet, it is hard to say what these images in dreams really are. Augustine suggests that in dreams we ourselves appear to ourselves, as it were, corporeally. However, as he continues explaining, this corporeal appearance is neither of our body nor is it a body at all, but it is the appearance of our soul in the form of an image of our body.[10] According to Augustine, then, what we see in dreams are the actions of our soul (since the body lies motionless in bed) endued with the semblance of a body. Whether or not this is an adequate account of the phenomenon, the essential point in question is that dreaming is another kind of imagination in the sense of the constitution and conception of mental images.

Though this discussion of various forms of imagination in *De Genesi ad Litteram* is a very revealing one, it is certainly not a complete listing of all the imaginative acts of which man is capable.[11] Nevertheless, what is meant by imagination, in the sense being employed here, should have become clearer. It is a faculty by which man is able to perceive mental images which themselves are produced and formed with a certain freedom by his very act of imagining them.

This freedom implied in imagination must still be understood in two senses closely related to each other. On the one hand, there is the more creative freedom of invention that enables us, as Augustine points out, to imagine anything we want in any way we want. We can form images of heaven and earth, add to them or diminish them, contract or expand them, as when we imagine something very great which in reality is rather little or vice versa; we can put them in a proper order or disarrange them, as when we form artistic ideas in literature or speech; we can multiply them or reduce them to a few images or to one single image.[12] In a word, in imagination we can invent whatever we want whether or not that would be possible in reality at all. However, it must be added that this creative freedom is not characteristic of all the kinds of imagination mentioned above, such as associations and dreams. It is, therefore, not *essential* to its nature as such.

On the other hand, imagination implies a kind of freedom by which it is independent of any determination by a real object. Unlike for instance sense-perception, where the 'content' of the perception is determined precisely by the object perceived, imagination is free from such a bond to reality. The object imagined is not a real thing 'giving information' about itself thereby shaping the act of knowing it; on the contrary, the object of imagination is itself precisely formed and determined by the act of being imagined. In fact, this lack of being determined by a real object is the condition for the possibility of the creative freedom just referred to. Only because the image thought is not a really existing thing being determined in and of itself, is it free to receive any kind of formation (which can certainly be inspired by the perception of real things).

It is the freedom primarily in this latter sense that leads Augustine to call these mental images false (*falsa sunt haec figmenta cogitationis*). As he points out, the Rome that I fictitiously imagine is a false Rome; otherwise I would know what is taking place in it right now on the basis of actual perception. Or the sun that I have in my imagination is a false sun, since I can freely place it in my thought where and when I will, while the real sun passes through its own determined spaces and times. Likewise, the friend that I imagine is false, since I can think him to be wherever I want, whereas I do not know where my real friend is right now.[13] I have and perceive a 'false' image insofar as it is free from a strict determination by the (true) reality, which in these cases is not given to me.[14]

Thus, mental images are essentially distinct from real things. Though they might be taken from reality, their mode of being is very different. In imagining we are aware of them as of our own (free) inventions that cease to exist as soon as we think of them no longer. This is why Augustine can say that when we regard the images of those bodies that are not given to the senses, we can clearly distinguish between these images and presently given real bodies.[15] For such images by nature claim to be precisely images that are made up and shaped, and not to be really existing things.

Now the important question for our purpose is: What is this power in us that can produce and form these various images in so many ways? Could this possibly be done by a part of my body, or is it necessary to assume an essentially different, incorporeal faculty to perform these acts?[16]

There are different ways in which Augustine tries to show that imagination is an act that cannot be performed by a body, but only by an incorporeal soul.[17] Indeed, Augustine thinks that it is mainly by these images of our imagination that the incorporeality of the soul is proven. For these images themselves are certainly not bodies; otherwise, the sky, the earth, the sea, etc., of which we think, must really be in us, which to assume is insane (*desipit*). These images are merely the incorporeal similitudes of bodies. Consequently, the fact that they *are* in us shows that they must be contained in an incorporeal subject (soul). For if the soul were a body, it could not take into itself, through thinking or remembering, the images of outside bodies, not to mention these bodies themselves which would by far exceed its own magnitude.[18]

However, one may ask Augustine, are not there instances also in the material world where an incorporeal image is contained in a corporeal body? For example, mirrors, paintings, or photographs, themselves being bodies, contain *in*corporeal representations of spatially extended, corporeal objects. It seems questionable, therefore, whether the mere reference to the existence of similitudes of real bodies in us, different from these bodies themselves, really justifies the conclusion to be drawn.

Yet, precisely in trying to cope with this question it may become manifest that Augustine might have deeply seen something in his discussion that should be brought out in order to clarify and to strengthen his argument.

The nature of these images of bodies given in imagination is quite distinct from that of those images that are contained in mirrors or other corporeal entities. While both kinds share the feature of not being real bodies (precisely because they are their images), as images they reveal important essential differences. For a mirror-image is extended in space, though not in three dimensions as the body which it represents, but in length and breadth; it can be divided into various sections being outside of and clearly delimited from each other; it can be colorful and is perceived by the bodily eyes. But none of these properties is found in the object of our imagination. The 'mountain' I imagine is *not* extended, as is the real mountain, and its representation in a photograph. It is not a two-dimensional likeness of an outside reality which has its various elements located at different sections of the whole; rather, the object imagined is in a peculiar sense one unified image. When I imagine I 'see' one image as a whole that does not allow for being structured according to various sections standing outside and next to each other. In fact, if I took a special element of what I imagine in order to 'see' it more concretely, I would perform an additional act of imagination that is directed at its own *new* object. It would not be a section of the original image, as when I take a part of a painting; instead, it would be another image being one distinct whole. Similarly, these objects of imagination are not colorful. The 'sun' I imagine is not yellow in the same sense as the real sun or as that being depicted in a painting. Though I could also imagine a yellow sun, this imagined color is of a quite different essential nature. Among others, this can be seen from the facts that color in our common sense essentially presupposes a bearer extended in space, and that it can only be perceived through the bodily eyes. Both conditions are not found in imagination: its object is precisely not spatially extended, and our eyes are evidently not involved in the act proper of its being imagined.[19]

From these considerations it becomes obvious that the sense in which an object of imagination is incorporeal is very different from the sense in which an image in a painting or in other material beings is incorporeal. Only if this peculiar kind of incorporeal nature of such imagined objects is understood, can Augustine's argument for the incorporeality of the soul based on the act of imagination be convincing. For to have images of such a kind is impossible for any body.

This impossibility becomes even more evident when one thinks of the act of imagining itself and its relation to its object. The vision through which the image of exterior objects is perceived (*obtutus quo cernitur . . . imago absentis corporis*)[20] is in a sense co-constitutive of this image itself. We have already seen how Augustine mentions various ways in which we form and shape our images. In a wonderful manner, he says, the incorporeal image of a body is formed in thought;[21] that is, the image exists and is what it is only in our thought; without us thinking it, and thinking it this way, it would not be at all. Thus, the act of imagination, together with all the other acts that might be implied in it, such as acts of deliberate planning and pre-conceiving, of imaginary perception to various degrees of awakenedness or of intentional clarity, or of the rational deliberation of whether or not this image could really exist, – such acts are essentially constitutive of the image itself. By nature it exists only *as* being imagined or thought in these various ways.[22]

But if this is so, the question arises whether the power itself of constituting images of such kind can be predicated of a body. Would it be possible that images with this mode of existence, a mode which is clearly different from that of images found in the material world, can be borne by a body? Posing the same question Augustine answers thus:

> What then is this power which discerns these phantasms?
> Clearly whatever it is, it is greater than all these things, and
> it is conceived of without such material images. Find, if you
> can, spaces for this power; extend it throughout places;
> render it a body of huge size. Assuredly if you think well, you
> cannot. For of everything of this corporeal nature your mind
> forms an opinion as to its divisibility into parts, and you make
> of such things one part greater and another less, as much
> as you like; while that, by which you form the opinion of these
> things, you perceive to be above them, not in the local
> loftiness of place, but in dignity of power.[23]

Were this power of imagination a body, Augustine points out, one would find in it spaces; it would occupy places in space; it could be extended to a body of greater size and be divided into more or less smaller parts. But none of these corporeal properties is found in our power of imagining, if we look at it carefully. On the contrary, Augustine concludes, precisely in viewing this power as a body (which it is not), we perceive it to have an ability of imagining that is superior to anything which can be attributed to a body.

Indeed, as Augustine develops this thought in another place, the very fact of man being able to imagine and to think his soul and its faculties in materialistic terms proves its incorporeality. For referring to the views of the soul of some Greek and Roman philosophers, Augustine argues:

> These (the philosophers who supposed the principles of all things to be material) and others like them have only been able to think that which their hearts enslaved to sense have vainly suggested to them. And yet they have within themselves something which they could not see: they imagined to themselves inwardly things which they had seen without, even when they were not seeing them, but only thinking of them. But that which is in the vision of such imagination is no longer a body, but only the similitude of a body; and that faculty of the mind by which this similitude of a body is seen is neither a body nor the similitude of a body; and the faculty which judges it to be beautiful or ugly is without doubt superior to the object judged of. This faculty is man's mind and the rational nature of the soul; and it is certainly not a body, if not even that similitude of a body which it beholds and judges of is itself a body.[24]

Precisely by denying the incorporeality of the soul, these philosophers implicitly prove it, for they could not hold the view that all things, including the soul, are material if they did not have an incorporeal and rational faculty. The very acts of deliberately forming mental similitudes (images) of bodies, of perceiving and thinking about them rationally, of judging them to be beautiful or ugly, that is, deciding on whether or not they correspond to the reality in question – these acts cannot be performed by a body. For, as we argued above, this specific kind of unextended whole which is the object of imagination, and which, unlike any corporeal image, presupposes for its existence the acts of being imagined, is neither experienced as being rooted in and produced by a spatially extended, divisible body, nor is it ever brought about in this way. For it essentially presupposes a being (soul) that is itself unextended and simple in a very special (spiritual) sense.[25]

Though the present argument presupposes results that will only later be argued for in greater detail, we do get some understanding as to why Augustine states that there must be some kind of spiritual nature in us (*spiritualem quamdam naturam in nobis*) where these images of corporeal things are formed.[26] A body does not have the power to form something spiritual (*neque enim [corpus] habet eam vim, ut formet aliquid spirituale*).[27] It might be the cause of such an image in that the latter is taken from it becoming an image of this particular body; yet, the actual act itself of forming and shaping the image is not done by a body.[28]

Thus, Augustine concludes, neither the image of an absent body, nor the vision itself through which it is perceived, is a body.[29] It must be an act of the (incorporeal) soul.

Furthermore, in another line of thought, Augustine argues that these images are not made in us by the body, but by the soul, because they are made in a marvellous quickness that is much different from the tardiness of our body.[30] Or, as he states elsewhere, the movement of the sun is much slower than our thinking; for it takes the sun much longer to move from East to West, than it takes us to imagine its movement in our thought.[31] So Augustine infers that the soul is a spirit and not a body (*animus ergo iste spiritus est, non corpus*), since it is faster than a body.[32]

However, as it stands, this argument seems inconclusive. For there are incredibly fast processes that occur in matter (including our own body) or in cameras taking pictures, which in their quickness cannot even be imagined. How could one, therefore, hold the act of imagination to be faster than the events in the corporeal world?

There might be three considerations that may underlie Augustine's statement of this view and that would throw the incorporeality of imagination into greater relief.

First, if one compares the actual speed of a corporeal movement with the quickness with which the same movement may be imagined, it is obvious that the latter can be immensely faster, as Augustine's example of the sun shows. Because of its 'freedom' from being determined by actual reality, the imagined sun 'runs its course' in an incomparably shorter time. However, it seems that this greater quickness of imagination can only be achieved with respect to those movements that *can* be perceived in their actual speed, and thus be imagined. For otherwise, as in the case of unimaginably fast material (chemical) processes, there would be no basis for comparing the two modes of fastness.

Secondly, there is another sense in which *all* material processes are slower than imaginations, namely with respect to the latter's formation. If it is understood, as was argued above, that the imagined object is co-constituted by the act of its being imagined, it follows that this image is not only formed in a marvellous quickness, but that it comes into being simultaneously with the act itself. Since it cannot exist without this act, there can be no temporal difference between the act and the object of imagination. Both come into being at the same time. Yet, however fast a material process may be, it must have some temporal extension to be a process at all. Between the beginning and the end of taking a picture with a camera, for instance, there must be some interval of time; otherwise the picture could not come to be. In this sense, such a process always requires more time, i.e. is slower, than the formation of images which come into being simultaneously with the act of imagining them. The image is brought about in the very moment in which the act of imagination begins, which act itself, then, implying acts of perceiving the image and of further shaping it, is of course a temporally extended act.

Thirdly, the *kind* of quickness with which we make up images is completely different from that implied in material processes. For the former is a consciously lived quickness that is experienced only by the person himself, and that cannot be measured by instruments from the outside. Such quickness is not found in bodies, but only in man's soul. However, this last interpretation of Augustine's argument is based not so much on quickness as such, but on its givenness through (self-)consciousness, which will more properly be discussed in a later chapter.

These considerations might have motivated Augustine to thinking that there is a much greater quickness involved in imagination than in a body. Not in general but in the senses discussed, this assertion renders the unique incorporeal nature of imagination even more manifest.

All the arguments treated in this section took their starting point in the existence of mental images that can be produced in us through acts of imagination. Similar images are given to us, according to Augustine, when we recollect something. And it is on this faculty of recollection, distinct from, but related to imagination, that Augustine bases further arguments for an incorporeal nature (soul) in man.

(B) Recollection (recordari)

Memory is one of those phenomena at which Augustine was simply amazed, and to which he frequently refers in his writings. He was always astonished anew at the fact that, similar to imagination, we can recollect a variety of the greatest objects that we have once perceived, though we are confined to the smallness of our body. He considered memory something ultimately mysterious and incomprehensible. And he was surprised to see that people do not wonder about it (*nec mirantur*), but instead of being amazed at themselves, go out of themselves to the greatness of nature.[33]

But memory bore for Augustine also a very existential significance: it was through memory that he became aware of how God had guided him, silently without his knowing it, throughout his many struggles and gradual conversions, until he finally could wholeheartedly embrace the Catholic faith. Going back into his past life in memory, Augustine writes the *Confessiones* constantly interrupting the narrative of his life story by expressing his praise and thanks to God, of whose perpetual guidance and care in all his past aberrations he now becomes aware. This is probably the reason why he included the marvellous reflection on memory in the tenth chapter of his personal biography.[34]

For our purpose of showing the incorporeality of the human soul, the act of recollection, as it is analysed by Augustine, becomes important insofar as it provides an additional basis for reaching this goal. Augustine himself often has recourse to memory in order to demonstrate the soul's incorporeality. However, in doing so he mostly argues along the same lines discussed in the preceding section on imagination, as he often mentions these two faculties in the same context.[35]

Leaving aside those aspects of recollection that are similar to imagination, in this section our focus is aimed at the act of recollection proper, that is, of going back into our own past, taking it as a starting point for further arguments for the incorporeality of man's soul. Thereby it will be our first task to try to understand the 'structure' of recollection in light of Augustine's analyses. Particularly, the question shall be asked how the objects of recollection are 'contained' in memory, and above all, what these objects are.

Let us, therefore, see in the following how Augustine deals with this question and let us ask whether his account of memory does full justice to reality. Our contention will be to show that Augustine's theoretical explanation of the act of recollection is not fully adequate to the phenomenon in question, but that this explanation does not truly express his real intention. Such a critical dialogue with Augustine will also provide the basis for a more spiritual conception of memory than is explicitly laid out by him. In this sense, a more detailed discussion of memory is justified, if not required, in the context of showing the soul's incorporeality. Needless to say, however, such a discussion must be restricted to the most essential aspects of recollection which is itself only one among various kinds of memory.[36]

Augustine generally conceives of memory as a sort of storehouse containing the images of things seen in the past. He speaks of the fields and spacious palaces of memory (*campos et lata praetoria memoriae*),[37] which have an immense capacity (*immensa capacitas memoriae*)[38] of storing up the images in, as it were, most wonderful cabinets (*miris tamquam cellis reponuntur*).[39] And they are called for again from its many secret and inexpressible windings (*secreti atque ineffabiles sinus eius*) when we recollect.[40]

Though this is certainly a figurative way of speaking,[41] it nevertheless gives the impression that memory is something like a huge container in which the images of whatever we have perceived are stored waiting to be recalled whenever we want them.[42]

The way these images of things come into memory Augustine explains thus:[43] When I perceive things through the bodily senses, my mind receives certain messages from them. Leaving them outside, it commits their incorporeal images to memory in an incor-

poreal manner. Thus, it is not the perceived corporeal things themselves that enter into memory, but their images, which then become
present in recollection. Augustine wonders, however, in what way
these images are formed; who could say, he asks, how this happens?
What alone can be known is from which sense of the body a
particular image is taken in order to be interiorly stored (such as
the image of a color is taken from the eye, that of a sound from
the ear, etc.).[44]

So Augustine assumes a power that in the act of sense-perception
produces an image of the object perceived which is stored in
memory. And it is this image which is re-perceived when I recollect
the object from memory.[45]

The important question which arises is whether this theory does
full justice to the act of recollection given in experience. There is
one decisive problem implied in this conception of memory. Augustine puts his finger on it explicitly when, drawing out the logical
consequences of his theory, he says in *De Magistro* that in answering
questions about things sensed in the past, we do not speak of these
things themselves, but of images that are impressed on us by them
and committed to memory (*non iam res ipsas, sed imagines ab iis
impressas memoriaeque mandatas loquimur*).[46]

Yet, is it really true that, when I tell someone, for instance, about
a vacation trip I took some while ago, I mean to tell him merely
about an image I have in my memory and not about what I really
saw? As Gareth Matthews rightly points out, this is nothing but
changing the subject; it is not a talk about something experienced
in the past, but about an image that is in the mind: 'We are asked
about sensible things and we answer by speaking of our images of
them.'[47] Don Ferrari focuses even more sharply on the problem
involved here:

'The important point to notice here is that this image or copy
[of the thing which was perceived in the past] is always a
presently existing thing. It is, in fact, *a presently existing image of
a past object of consciousness*' (emphasis his).[48]

The consequence of this is, as Ferrari points out further, that I do
not have any real access to the past anymore:

'If all I ever reach in memory is a copy or image of what I

have experienced in the past, then my present contact with
the past is completely severed. I cannot now know anything
of the past; I can only know those present images which
past experiences have left in my memory. But, since I cannot
know the past apart from those images – I cannot know the
sunrise as it actually was, apart from the present image I now
have of it – I cannot claim to know that the images
correspond to my past experiences. In other words, I cannot
know that they are images at all. They may be mere
imaginations.[49]

Thus, according to this image-theory, I could not know it to be a
true theory; for I would not be able to know whether these mental
pictures are really images of past things, which is taken as starting
point of the theory.

Augustine does not seem to address this difficulty. He appears
to have never attempted to solve it. The main reason for this may
lie in the fact that, apart from his general theoretical description
of recollection, he in reality has a much more adequate conception
of this act shown by various side remarks throughout his writings.
It is not an uncommon historical phenomenon that an author clearly
sees and points at a reality, even though his theoretical explanation
and interpretation of it does not do full justice to the datum in
question.

In the following, I will try to show why Augustine was misled in
his account of recollection, but also to what extent he had a much
more adequate understanding of the matter. Such a discussion will
open up the way for a less corporeal conception of memory which
meets Augustine's basic intention of showing the incorporeality of
the soul to a greater extent than his own theory.

Memory is an enormously puzzling phenomenon. It is under-
standable why Augustine was so deeply amazed at it. It has characteristics that, at first glance, seem to be irreconcilable; for instance,
the thing recollected is, on the one hand, immediately given to me;
yet, on the other hand, in its reality it is usually not present at all:
I recollect St Peter's Basilica in Rome and it is vividly present to
me, though in reality I am far away from it. To explain this and
similar apparently opposite features is an extremely difficult task,
due to the intricacy of the subject matter as such. This is certainly

one reason why Augustine's (and many others') explanation of memory does not fully meet the phenomenon, though he clearly saw it.

Augustine saw that when we recollect something, in a sense we see again an object which we perceived in the past. When he asks Evodius whether he could still remember the city of Milan with its size and character – Augustine wrote the *De Quantitate Animae* in Rome probably after a trip to Milan – Evodius answers that there is nothing he remembers more vividly and completely. So Augustine concludes that, even though he does not see the city with his eyes as he did before, he still sees it in or with the mind (*animo vides*).[50] Here he clearly points out that what he sees in memory is nothing but the city of Milan itself, though in a quite different way than he saw it in the past. Also, when contemplating the immense objects we can remember, Augustine relates that we see them in our memory as if they were outside (*quasi foris viderim*), meaning that we perceive them themselves (which are really outside of us) by looking into our memory.[51]

If this is so, why then does Augustine explain the recollected object not to be the outside thing as such, but a mental image of it, which leads to the untenable consequences mentioned above?

A main reason seems to lie in the fact that Augustine is looking for a way how to account for what one might call the incorporeal presence of the object of recollection. Obviously, these *things* we remember remain really where they are; they are certainly not contained in memory as real corporeal objects.[52] As we have already seen with imagination, memory, too, could never hold in itself these immense objects as *real*. But how are they in memory?

For understanding Augustine's reasoning it is instructive to see how he thinks other objects of recollection, apart from outside bodies, to be present in memory. In his major treatment of memory (*Conf.* X, 8–25), Augustine distinguishes between four basic kinds of memory contents (*quae continentur memoria*):[53] (1) the images of corporeal beings (X, 8); (2) 'ideal entities' (*rationes*), that is, what is known in the arts and sciences (X, 9), numbers (X, 12), and the concepts of happy life, truth, God (X, 20); (3) past acts of mine, such as how I learned something (X, 13), how I distinguished between true and false in learning (X, 13), how I remembered and forgot something (X, 16); (4) psychic experiences, such as a past joy or sadness, and a past fear or desire (X, 14). All these things are present in memory, but in different ways, according to Augustine. While the corporeal beings, as we saw, are present in memory through their images, the ideal entities and the past acts of mine are *themselves* present in memory (*per praesentiam* X, 17; *nec eorum imagines, sed res ipsas gero* X, 9). In the case of psychic experiences, Augustine is himself not certain whether they themselves or their images are contained in memory (*utrum per imagines an non, quis facile dixerit?*) (X, 15).

In the light of this classification one striking feature of Augustine's view of memory becomes apparent, namely the fact, as was pointed out before, that he conceives of memory as a kind of storehouse containing these various entities; he describes it as a sort of container, though not a corporeal one.[54] Consequently, what is contained in it can itself only be incorporeal and cannot be perceivable through the bodily senses. As clearly given in experience, when we remember we do not *see* through the eyes.

Since Augustine was quite aware of this state of affairs, there was no problem for him to locate past *psychic* acts (perhaps also past experiences) and ideal *incorporeal* entities[55] in memory in the manner of self-presence. However, bodies can obviously not be contained in memory as real objects, for which reason Augustine had to find a way of determining how they could be incorporeally present in memory. The most plausible solution to him, then, was to say that bodies are in memory in the form of their incorporeal images.

There is a second main reason why Augustine held this image-theory of memory with respect to corporeal objects of sense. This reason is again based on a valid insight into the nature of memory which, however, gets falsely explained in terms of this theory.

Augustine distinguishes between two classes of objects of recollection:[56] those objects that are recollected as linked to a past experience, and those that are not. For the first class, Augustine gives the example of a voice that was heard in the past and that, having left a trace of it, is somehow re-heard in recollection, though the actual voice itself is no longer sounding (*vox inpressa per aures vestigio, quo recoleretur, quasi sonaret, cum iam non sonaret*). In this case, the object of recollection implies a reference to the past as past.

This form of recollection is distinct from recollecting those objects that, though present in memory, are not explicitly linked to the past. Augustine mentions here the knowledge of literature (*litteratura*), of rhetoric (*peritia disputandi*), and of the kinds of questions (*genera quaestionum*) that can be asked, for instance, in a dispute. Though these various types of knowledge must have been acquired in the past, they are usually recalled from memory without any reference to this past act of acquiring them. As Augustine says, they themselves are present in memory without claiming to be the images retained in memory of an object experienced in the past;[57] they do not as such imply an immediate link to the past itself.[58]

Augustine develops his image-theory of memory primarily in regard to past acts of experiencing externally perceived bodies, which are acts that do imply a reference to the past (the first class of objects of recollection). And in recollecting these past acts, it really seems that the immediate object of the recollection is an image of the thing experienced in the past. I recollect this thing the very same way as I saw it in the past. I re-perceive it from the very same point of view as in the past, explains Augustine:

> For we can only remember as many corporeal species as we have perceived, how great they were and such as they were when we perceived them, since the mind absorbs them into the memory by means of the bodily sense.[59]

And giving an example he says:

> I remember (the sun) as just as large as I saw it. For if I remember it as greater or as less than that which I saw, then I no longer remember what I saw, and, therefore, I no longer remember it at all. But because I remember, I remember it just as great as I saw it.[60]

This feature strongly suggests the object of recollection to be an image of the thing perceived in the past; for it is just the same view I have on the thing when I presently recollect it, as I had in the past.

Also, as one might add, it is only I myself who can recollect the thing under this particular aspect. Nobody else could remember it this way. Consequently, the object of recollection is in a unique sense *my own* object. It can, therefore, not be the real thing outside of myself, as it seems, since this is a publicly accessible object. Everyone could perceive it; but only I can perceive the object of my recollection. Does this mean, then, that, despite our criticisms, the image-theory is nevertheless the correct explanation for the phenomenon under discussion?

It seems that the major reason why Augustine adopted the image-theory lies here. He saw this image-like character of the object of recollection so clearly that he drew the conclusion that what I recollect can only be an image of the real thing perceived in the past. However, what he does not seem to have considered for his theory – though, as I want to show, he is implicitly aware of it – is the fact that there are various meanings of image confused in this reasoning. Let me briefly point out the most important of these senses in order to uncover the confusion more clearly.

A first sense of image refers to the aspect or point of view under which a corporeal object outside of myself is perceived. Every object of sense is given to us in a concrete perspective being relative to the conditions and the place from which we look at it. This aspect of the object can in principle be shared by anyone who perceives the object exactly from the same point of view.

Secondly, image can mean that particular aspect of an object that is given in recollection. Like the first sense of image, this aspect could also be shared in principle, namely when one and the same object, having been perceived by various people under the same perspective, is now being recollected. However, what can *not* be shared in this recollection is the perspective that only I myself have of the object recollected. For this aspect is accessible exclusively in and through the recollection of my own individual act of originally perceiving it. Nobody else can have this particular image, since it is 'stored' in memory insofar as it is implied in my original perception, that is, *as my* image. The objective determinations of this object, however, i.e. its essential nature as such 'lying behind' my particular perspective, remain transcendent and 'publicly' accessible. Unlike the specific aspect, its being and nature is in no way dependent on and co-constituted by the act of being perceived.

Thirdly, a completely different meaning of image refers precisely to those products of imagination that we discussed in the preceding section. Though images in this sense might be taken from real objects outside of us, as such they are freely formed and shaped by ourselves. They are not the images (aspects) *of* an object, but the outcomes of subjective acts of imagination, that is, purely mental entities.

It seems that it is a confusion primarily of these last two meanings of image that led Augustine to explain the object of recollection to be a mental image, rather than the real thing itself perceived under a particular point of view.

That these two meanings of image, viz., the aspect under which a thing is given in recollection, and the mental entity as product of imagination, can easily be confused is due to two main reasons.

On the one hand, both realities meant have certain features in common. Both of them are in a sense my own; the aspect is *my* aspect of the thing being constituted by myself perceiving it, and the mental entity is even more clearly my own fiction. Thus, both are dependent on myself. Furthermore, both are directly perceived, and not inferred or concluded to, and that by myself alone. Again, they both imply a reference to real things outside of myself: the aspect, in that it is the aspect *of* a real thing; the mental entity, in that it is often taken from real things. However, and that is again common to both the mental entity and the aspect as perceived in recollection, the present act of perceiving these two realities is not directed at the real thing standing in front of myself *hic et nunc*; for the aspect that is perceived in recollection is of a thing that is no longer *really* present to me, and the mental entity was never a really real thing at all.

On the other hand, in actual experience these two realities are very much interrelated and can often not be distinguished in concrete cases. For instance, I recollect the view I had when I saw St Peter's Basilica in Rome. The more this recollected experience lies back in the past, the more difficult is it to sort out, from the whole picture presently given to me, the real aspects of the Basilica seen, i.e. real memories, and later products of my imagination. Often, especially in recollections of the distant past, I am quite unsure whether I really remember something that I saw, or whether I merely imagine something on the basis of a real memory or perhaps on the basis of what someone else told me about this thing. This becomes quite obvious, for instance, when in the process of re-reading a novel I realize how much my imagination has shaped and added on to the story. Or as Augustine points out, the images that we make up of future actions, events and hopes and that we reflect upon as if they were present, are taken from the abundance of things that are given in memory.[61] We form images out of 'memory material,' which includes our past acts of perceiving real things under particular aspects. These two meanings of image (viz., the aspect under which a particular thing is perceived in recollection and the mental product of my imagination) are often so closely related to each other in lived experience that they can hardly be distinguished and appear to be identical.

Even though Augustine seems to have fallen prey to this confusion in his theoretical explanation of memory, at other places he describes the essential difference between the objects of imagination and those of recollection with his characteristic sharpness. The object of recollection, as we have already seen, is fixed in its content; I recollect the object as I experienced it in the past. When Augustine points out this feature of recollection, he immediately contrasts it with the object of imagination, which in its content can be multiplied and varied innumerably and altogether infinitely (*innumerabiliter atque omnino infinite multiplicantur atque variantur*).[62] Being 'free' from the determinations by the real world, these images are receptive to any kind of formation.[63]

In an even more revealing passage of *De Genesi ad Litteram*, Augustine keenly distinguishes between these two meanings of image:

> Even when we do not see anything with the eyes of the body, we still mentally regard corporeal images, whether true ones (*veras*) as we see the bodies themselves and hold them in memory, or fictitious ones (*fictas*) as the power of thinking (*cogitatio*) was able to form. For there is a difference between us thinking of Carthage that we have gotten to know (*novimus*) and us thinking of Alexandria that we do not know.[64]

Here Augustine calls the object of recollection even a *true* image, precisely because it exactly corresponds to the view one had of the real thing itself. And this fixed, true aspect of the thing, which in his example is the city of Carthage that he has seen and knows quite well, is completely different from the fictitious image that he can form of the city of Alexandria that he has never seen. Though he has a generic idea of what a city looks like (as opposed to a mountain or river, etc.) drawn from previous experiences of cities, the image he makes up for himself of a concrete unknown city has evidently another character than that view he once had of a city that is now present in memory.

How could this difference, clearly given in experience, be characterized? What is it that accounts for it? It is interesting to see that in *De Magistro*, which Augustine wrote roughly 25 years before finishing *De Genesi ad Litteram*, he states that he does not see how one could call memory-images true. They are simply images contained in memory that do not as such have any relation to the real world. Yet, already at that time, he was aware of a specific characteristic proper to memory-images alone. For he says that we carry them as proofs (*documenta*) of the things that we perceived before. For us, they contain an implicit reference to something we really perceived once.[65]

The question that immediately arises is how Augustine can, on the one hand, rightly maintain that what we see in recollection somehow claims to be our past view of a real thing, while, on the other hand, he holds that what we see in recollection is a (presently existing) image that cannot even be known to correspond to a particular past reality. This question can even more forcefully be posed in the light of another observation Augustine makes. When explaining how we can become certain that a person's name, which we had forgotten and now remember again, really is his name, Augustine points out the following: we remember with certainty that this is his true name because we used to think of him in connection with his name. Even if a third person told us his name, we would not simply believe him (*credimus*) as if we learned something new from him, but we would still try to recollect his name from our own memory. And only in so recollecting can we approve (*recordantes adprobamus*) that this name really is as it was told us.[66]

What Augustine is saying here is basically that there is a form of certain knowledge implied in recollection which is different from the belief in the truth of another person's account. Though both my recollection and the account of someone else refer to the very same fact, viz., the name of this particular person, the kind of certainty I have of the correctness of this fact is completely different in each case: in one case, I base my certainty on the credibility and truthfulness of this third person; in the other case, I base my certainty on my own powers of cognition and recollection. I am aware that in recollecting I am somehow in touch with the real past objects (which are, in this case, my past experiences of connecting the name with this particular person); the recollection claims really to get at what I once experienced in the past. Even though I might be mistaken in my remembrance (due to forgetfulness, imaginations, repressions, and certain other confusions involved), the decisive point under discussion is that the experience of attaining certainty about the real fact in question on the basis of my own acts of recollection is essentially different from that of being certain because of my belief in someone else telling me the truth.

Though Augustine is quite aware of this experientially given difference, in his image-theory of memory he seems to overlook it. For in saying that the direct object of recollection is a mental image and not the thing itself perceived in the past, he in fact replaces this conscious awareness of really attaining to the past thing by a blind belief in the 'truthfulness' of an image and of an unconscious process of image formation (which, as we saw, is for Augustine the source of memory-images).[67] The very kind of indirect certainty that Augustine sees to be different from the immediate certainty of grasping reality in recollection, would have to be assumed, thus, if the image-theory were correct. For, in that case I would simply recollect an image, trusting and believing it to correspond to a past reality.

This experiential awareness of really seeing a past reality itself in recollection, which Augustine himself acknowledges, is the strongest indication that the image-theory does not do full justice to the phenomenon. It seems clear that what we recollect is the past thing itself. But how is that possible since this thing is no longer really present?

It seems that it is the most adequate way of explaining this apparently paradoxical structure of recollection to say that we see the past thing *by* 're-living' our very experience through which we saw this thing in the past. Using the term 'reproduction,' E. Husserl expresses it thus:

I recall the illuminated theater of yesterday, i.e. I perform a

'reproduction' of the perception of the theater; thus, in this
representation the theater comes before me as a present one
and this is what I intend, though I understand this presence
as belonging to the past, compared to the actual presence of
the present perceptions.[68]

If we really recollect, we go back into our past life, and in 're-
producing' or 're-performing' the very acts we performed in the
past, we now see again exactly what we saw that time and under
exactly the same point of view. That is why the object of recollection
has this image-like character: I see it from exactly the same angle
and perspective as I saw it in the past.

It is precisely this 're-living' of my past acts that Augustine has
in mind when he says:

> There also (in the huge hall of my memory) I meet myself
> and recall myself – what, when, or where I did a thing, and
> how I felt when I did it.[69]

I transport myself, so to speak, into my past life; I 're-experience'
what I experienced at that time, which also includes 're-experiencing' the feelings and affections that accompanied these past acts
of mine.

Yet, as Augustine keenly observes, these affections are not 're-
experienced' in the same fully conscious way as they were experienced in the past. Memory, Augustine says, holds these affections
not in the manner in which the mind has them when experiencing
them (*non eo modo, quo eas habet ipse animus, cum patitur eas*), but
in a manner that is proper to the power of memory alone. For, as
he goes on explaining, I can be happy while I recollect past sorrows;
and I can be fearless in remembering past fears, and vice versa.[70]

What this means, then, is that we 're-live' our past acts and
affections in a way in which they do not fully 'fill out' our actual
present consciousness. For in happily recollecting my past sorrow,
I am somewhat affectively aware of the specific quality of that
sorrow; I 'feel' it again, yet *while* my present conscious being is
'filled' with happiness. Here we find a peculiar mixture of experiencing at the same time an actually present state of mind together
with a past affection in a way in which the latter is, as it were, ' "one
step removed" from the present center of our consciousness,' as

Ferrari puts it.[71] The past act is 're-experienced,' but not in the manner in which I experience a present act.

Thus, re-experiencing or re-living here means neither the performance of a *new* present experience, even if this might be a perception of the very same object that I perceived in the past, nor a re-performing of a past act in the literal sense of really going back in time. For in both cases (if the latter were possible), I would perform an actual experience which would lack precisely this peculiar distance to the past characteristic of recollection. Rather, in re-experiencing a past act I again experience this identically same act, but *as* a past act. In this sense, recollection combines the present with the past: the same past act is presently recollected (re-experienced) as past.

This characteristic distance of the past act in the act of re-experiencing it can also be seen through the fact that this past act (and, in the case of a past perception of a thing, also this thing itself that is re-perceived through this act) stands somehow in front of myself. I 'look' *at* it in recollection, and I can even control it in a peculiar way. Augustine describes this control I have over my memories very beautifully in almost poetic language:

> When I go into this storehouse, I ask that what I want should
> be brought forth. Some things appear immediately, but
> others require to be searched for longer, and then dragged
> out, as it were, from some hidden recess. Other things hurry
> forth in crowds, on the other hand, and while something else
> is sought and inquired for, they leap into view as if to say,
> 'Is it not we, perhaps?' These I brush away with the hand of
> my heart from the face of my memory (*a facie recordationis
> meae*), until finally the thing I want makes its appearance out
> of its secret cell.[72]

I can freely recall memories, placing them in my sight; I can interrupt them; I can drive them away; and in looking at them, I can be more or less attentive, trying to see them more clearly; I can judge them to be true or false memories. All these acts are *presently* performed *while* I re-live the past act. They are performed with respect to the past act *insofar as* I re-live it right now.[73]

This suggests that besides the re-living of the past act, recollection also includes a present perceptual gaze at this past act which

is linked to or implies many of the other present acts just
mentioned. Indeed, when Augustine explains why we can recollect
at all, he points out two things. First, the will to remember a past
thing at all arises from some 'part' of this event that I have already
remembered. For instance, he says, when I wish to remember what
I ate yesterday evening, I have already remembered either *that* I
ate yesterday evening; or if I do not yet remember this, I have
certainly remembered that something happened at that time.
Secondly, the will to remember arises from those things that are
thence shown through recollection by the act of looking at the
recollected object (*eis quae inde per recordationem cernendo expri-
muntur*); that is, Augustine says, it arises from the combination of
something that we have remembered with the vision that thence is
performed in the gaze of our thinking, when we remembered (*et
visionis quae inde facta est in acie cogitantis cum recordati sumus*).[74]

What Augustine is saying here is that we can only wish to
recollect something if we have some vague prior remembrance of
what we want to recollect. Only then can we direct the gaze of our
thought toward the object to be recollected; and in so doing, we
visualize the object, which, in turn, can motivate a greater desire
to recollect it more vividly and clearly.

This act of looking at the recollected object is certainly a present
act directed at this object. It is not implied in the original act as
such (which is precisely its object). And yet, the re-living of this
past act, being essentially involved in recollection, could not be
performed without such vision of the act. As Augustine points out,
only because we look at the act can we really remember (or re-
live) it in recollection. These two, the re-living and the vision of
the past act, appear to be two elements of the act of recollection.
The reason why sometimes they can hardly be distinguished lies
in the fact, as Ferrari explains, that 'in the characteristic trans-
porting of ourselves back to the past experience, and in the reliving
of it phase by phase, the accompanying (present) perception of the
experience is really a part of the act of reliving it.'[75] In re-
performing a past perception, for instance, which includes the re-
perception of the same past object, I at the same time have the
present perceptual awareness of the modes, feelings, affections,
that were accompanying this past perception. Only in re-living this
act can I direct my present attention to these accompaniments as

elements of this act. Thus, recollection can be described as the joint activity of both the re-living of, and directly looking at, a past experience.

In this discussion, it should have become evident that Augustine's theoretical account of memory is not fully adequate to the reality in question, but that he nevertheless sees and points out features of memory that he could not explain in terms of his own theory, features that clearly belong to the phenomenon as it is given in experience.

Now the important question for our general context is: Can recollection be performed by a bodily entity? And could memory be conceived of as something like a (bodily) container into which one enters in recollecting? If not, there must be an incorporeal subject in man performing these acts.[76]

For Evodius, Augustine's interlocutor in *De Quantitate Animae*, it is even ridiculous to doubt whether memory belongs to the body: 'Can we believe or think that a lifeless body remembers?'[77] Yet, in the light of modern computer technics it could be objected that bodies also do have a 'memory' with a storing and retrieving faculty. Therefore, it might be assumed that recollection need not necessarily be an act of an incorporeal being (soul).[78]

However, it is not difficult to see the great difference between a 'computer-memory' and its 'acts of retrieval,' on the one hand, and man's recollecting or re-living of his past, on the other hand. For a computer does not in any way go back into its past re-experiencing its 'acts' the way it 'performed' them. The reason for this does not only lie in the fact that it is incapable of experiencing anything at all; but a computer also lacks this peculiar relation to the past that we found in man's recollection. What is stored in the computer is not 'past material' given as past (at least not to the computer); but its 'retrieval' is nothing but the making explicit to us of what, in a special mode of conservation, is presently contained in it. The unique distance to the past, characterized by the fact that a *past* act is re-experienced and thereby made *present* in the peculiar manner described above, is completely missing.

Above all, a computer does not in any way re-experience a past *reality* itself. In retrieving the information stored in it, the computer, so to speak, remains imprisoned in its own immanence. Yet, as we tried to show, man's recollection is precisely not of a 'memory-immanent' image, but is a re-perception of the past object itself. In really recollecting, man *transcends* the realm of his own products of imagination, going beyond what is 'stored in him' by reaching out again to the reality itself that is given as past. Actual recollection implies a real transcendence of one's own immanence towards reality – an act that cannot be performed by a computer.

In fact, such an act of transcendence essentially presupposes a subject that is not only incorporeal, but that possesses rational features. For the attaining to the past object itself is accompanied and 'verified,' as we discussed above, by an experiential *certainty* (of attaining it) that is structurally quite distinct from the *belief* in the 'truthfulness' of a memory-image regarding its exact correspondence to reality. This certainty, which for its very occurrence presupposes rational abilities, is given even in those cases in which I am *uncertain* whether or not I recollect the past object correctly. For even such uncertainty as to the particular determinations of the object recollected implies the certain awareness of being really in touch with a past reality, and not with its image. By re-perceiving in recollection St Peter's Basilica in Rome, I am aware of really perceiving it itself again, even though I may not exactly remember all of its details. On the other hand, I may even gain a *new* understanding of the Basilica on the basis of my recollection, precisely because in re-living the original act of its perception I now 'see' *it* again, as it were, with different eyes. I may see in it new dimensions of value and of beauty, though I recollect the very same object.

Indeed, there are many possible modes and points of view under which a past object can presently be recollected. I can have good or bad feelings about this object, which would correspond to recollecting it in an approving or rejecting attitude; I can still agree with my past motives for seeing it, or, through a process of maturation, I have come to another opinion about it; I can happily dwell in a past experience, or I may prefer to forget it soon. These and other attitudes towards the past can obviously not be found in a computer, but reveal a subject with rational qualities.

It should also be pointed out that even the recalling of those memory-contents that, as distinguished above,[79] do *not* imply a link to the past, is different from a computer's retrieval, though the latter might appear more similar to it than to the re-experiencing of the past just discussed. For instance, in recalling the knowledge of a fact in history, without re-experiencing the original act through which it was acquired, I perform many acts that are essentially foreign to a computer. First of all, I have the free intention to recall this fact; it is an exercise of my own free will through which I endeavor to place it in my sight. Again, there are acts involved of knowledge and of judging whether or not the fact recalled is the one I wanted to recall. There is a peculiar certainty resulting from the 'fulfillment' of my intention of recalling. And I can brush away those facts that come forth from memory without being called for, as we saw in Augustine's beautiful description.[80] Evidently, only a rational being, and no computer, is able to recall in such a way.

Likewise, there are many reasons why a fact *cannot* immediately be recalled. I may have a 'bad memory' for a specific *kind* of facts, such as for numbers, names or historical facts; I may recall more readily what I read, or what I heard; throughout the course of time, I may have simply forgotten something that was unimportant for me; or I may have repressed what was displeasing. In none of these ways, however, is a computer hindered from retrieving the information stored in it.[81]

But above all, the recalling of a fact from memory implies a peculiar transition from habitual to actual consciousness, about which more will be said later in the context of analyzing Augustine's notion of *memoria sui*. Man's recalling is a *conscious* 'rendering actual' of what is present in a quite different mode of consciousness. Such a transition cannot be compared to a computer's making explicit of what it conserves in its proper (electro-magnetic) manner.

From all these considerations it becomes manifest that it is merely in a very vague analogous way of speaking that a computer can be said to have a 'memory.' For the full experience of remembering and recollecting, as it is given to man, cannot be attributed to a body, but presupposes a performing subject that is incorporeal, and also bearing rational (spiritual) features.

Furthermore, it is not only not a bodily organ in us that performs acts of recollection, but it is also not a part of our body that we enter into in recollecting. For obviously, memory in the sense of my re-livable past experiences, as well as in the sense of the facts known and held in 'habitual consciousness,' is no body at all. It is not experienced as being spatially extended and divisible into parts, nor as being located at a particular place of the body. On the contrary, the experience of memory is as such completely detached and independent from any feeling of the body from within. It is given as of something other than the body.[82] Therefore, to speak of memory in bodily terms (as Augustine frequently does, and as is so hard to avoid in the use of language) is merely to give rise to materialistic misconceptions of it. Augustine himself sees this danger implied in employing corporeal images for the reality of memory, when in one place, where he wants to say that the sciences we have learned also have their place in our memory, he immediately corrects himself: *quasi remota interiore loco, non loco*,[83] that is, they have their place in memory (metaphorically speaking), but no real physical place. Memory in reality does not have corners, cabinets and shelves as a real storeroom does.

And yet, one could still raise the objection that memory is nothing but our brain, and that each memory-content is stored in a specific part of the brain. For it is empirically certain that the destruction of particular brain-cells affects a (partial or complete) loss of memory. However, this objection is based on a confusion of the 'categories' of 'identity' and 'condition.' The (true) fact that memory is affected by damages of the brain does as such not show the identity of the two at all.[84] For the brain could simply be the bodily *condition* for memory (just as the destruction of a painting, and thereby of its beauty, is no proof for the identity of the material substratum and the beauty of this painting). That this is indeed so becomes manifest precisely from our preceding analyses which tried to show that (human) memory cannot be found in, and be identical with, the operations of a computer (or of other bodies, such as the brain), but that it presupposes an incorporeal subject with rational abilities. This conclusion remains valid, notwithstanding the fact that the correct functioning of the brain conditions the possibility of memory (in fact, of all other spiritual acts of man), at least in this life. For if it can be shown that man has an immortal soul and that memory might continue after death (to assume which is not at all improbable), the brain would not be presupposed for memory as such, but only insofar as man lives in the constitution of his present state of being, that is, in the union of body and soul.[85] In this context, however, a deeper unfolding of these extensive problems cannot be offered.[86] For our purpose, the central point is to realize that the valid observation of the dependence of memory on the body does not disprove the argument to be made, namely that memory is of a completely different, spiritual nature.

Augustine even goes so far as to call memory the mind itself. For using a 'modern' argument from the 'ordinary language approach,' he points out that when we want someone to commit something to memory we say, 'Keep this in mind'; and when we forget something we say, 'Something slipped my mind.'[87] These colloquial expressions suggest that memory belongs to our spiritual nature. Indeed, in memory Augustine sees the seat of our mind (*sedem animi mei*), because it is in and through memory that the mind can remember itself.[88]

To reflect on memory as somehow the ground of one's own self-identity in time, however, will be reserved for a later discussion.[89] Here it was our main goal to show this spiritual reality of memory that, as Augustine marvels in a very famous passage, in a completely incorporeal and unextended manner 'contains' the whole universe:

> Great is this power of memory, exceedingly great, O my God – a large and boundless inner hall! Who has plumbed the depths of it? Yet it is a power of my mind, and it belongs to my nature. But I do not myself grasp all that I am. Thus the mind is far too narrow to contain itself. But where can that part of it be which it does not contain? Is it outside and not in itself? How can it be, then, that the mind cannot grasp itself? A great marvel rises in me; astonishment seizes me. Men go forth to marvel at the heights of mountains and the huge waves of the sea, the broad flow of the rivers, the vastness of the ocean, the orbits of the stars, and yet they neglect to marvel at themselves. Nor do they wonder how it is that, when I spoke of all these things, I was not looking at them with my eyes – and yet I could not have spoken about them had it not been that I was actually seeing within, in my memory, those mountains and waves and rivers and stars which I have seen, and that ocean which I believe in – and with the same vast spaces between them as when I saw them outside me.[90]

If memory and the act of recollection are clearly understood, they cannot but be attributed to the soul. Neither a computer, nor any part of our body, is capable of holding its past in this manner. To do so is essentially reserved for the soul alone.[91]

(C) Distentio animi

Though in his lengthy discussion of memory Augustine is primarily concerned with the act of recollection, that is, of explicitly going back into and re-living one's past, there are passages in which he seems to refer to a similar, yet different phenomenon. Particularly, in his fundamental and classic investigation of time in Book XI of his *Confessiones* and in his descriptions of acts of hearing, speaking, singing,[92] acts that are in special ways related to temporally extended objects, Augustine makes reference to another form of memory that, though being called by the same name of *memoria*, is quite distinct from recollection as discussed in the preceding section. For he seems to mean here not an explicit retrieval of memorial content of the distant past, but a non-intentional retaining of the *immediate* past which he closely relates to an anticipation (*exspectatio*) of the *immediate* future.

For our main purpose of arguing, together with Augustine, for the incorporeal nature of the soul this discussion is very important, in that it reveals a peculiar relation to time that, as we will try to show in the following, is not found in bodily entities. By bringing to light these retaining and anticipating faculties, therefore, further evidence shall be gained for the existence of an incorporeal subject (soul) in man.

An explication of this peculiar mode of relating to time should be introduced by a brief description of the nature of time.[93] Let me give a summary of the basic results of Augustine's investigations into this subject, which continue to be foundational for all subsequent research.[94]

Time, Augustine says, is a deeply puzzling enigma (*implicatissimum aenigma*).[95] The more one tries to penetrate and explain it, the more one is perplexed by its strangely peculiar nature, though there is hardly any word that is more familiar to us than time.[96]

One such perplexing problem concerns the question as to how and where what is contained in time *is*. All that was in the past *is* no longer (*praeteritum iam non est*); all that will be in the future *is* not yet (*futurum nondum est*).[97] Therefore, it seems that only that which is in the present can really *be*. But what does it mean to be in the present? What does the present mean at all? We could speak of the year in which we live as the present. However, what is present is not the year as a temporally extended whole, nor its months, days, hours, minutes or seconds, since each of these could further be divided into ever smaller extensions of time;[98] and only what is actually present is distinct from the past and the future. Thus, only that can be called the present that can no longer be divided into even the smallest parts of moments (*minutissimas momentorum partes*);[99] for if it, as an extended stretch of time, were still temporally divisible, it could be split into past and future moments.[100] Present, therefore, does not have any space (*praesens autem nullum habet spatium*).[101] It is like a temporal moment that flies so fast from the future into the past that it cannot extend into any duration.[102]

Yet, how can that which is not temporally extended in any way be called time? Above all, how can we say that the present *is* at all, since the reason of its being a temporal present is precisely that it will not be?[103] For it is only because the present immediately passes over into the past that it can be called a *temporal* moment, since a perpetual present would no longer be time, but eternity.[104] This transitive character, therefore, belongs essentially to the present; it accounts for its being a moment in time. And yet, a temporal being (that is, a being existing in time) actually *is* only in the present, since the past is no longer and the future is not yet.

There appears to be a real paradox implied in the structure of the present moment of time. On the one hand, it is in this temporally unextended moment that an object contained in time really *is*; in it time itself is in a sense most actual, as only the present has the power of 'realizing' temporal being. On the other hand, this moment of the present is the most feeble and unstable moment of time, since, due to its essential transition into the past, it *is* only insofar as it will immediately not be.[105] Thus, Augustine wonders whether one should not rather say that time *is* only insofar as it tends toward non-being (*tendit non esse*).[106]

It may, however, be added that there are two different senses of 'being in time' that should not be confused here. On the one hand, a temporal being *is* only in the unextended present moment, because this moment alone is able to give *reality* to what is not yet prior to its being no longer. Only in the present, a being contained in time is real. Before this moment 'it' *is* not; and after it, 'it' is no longer a real, but a 'past being.' Certainly, this *'non esse'* of the past cannot be complete nothingness, since the past does have some kind of 'being'; otherwise, it could neither bear properties, such as being unchangeable, nor could it be searched for. History as a science would be meaningless, just as the distinction between true and false judgments about past facts. Therefore, Augustine's remark concerning the non-being of the past should be interpreted as meaning that a 'past being' *is* no longer in the sense in which alone what is present really is.[107]

On the other hand, the term 'being in time' may also refer to the fact that the temporal object *is* one and the same throughout the changes in the modes of time. Ontologically speaking, there is no break between an object as present and as past; it is the same being that *is* at one time, and that is no longer at another time. This ontological endurance of the identical being, without which a temporal being could not *be* at all as this one being, is precisely the condition for the possibility of its switching its temporal states, and thus its modes of being (reality) in the sense just mentioned. For if the transition from present into past meant an actual change of being, as if after each present moment a completely new being would come into existence, there could never be 'past being' remaining identically the same; in each temporal moment, ontologically distinct beings would have to be created that exist solely in the present. Obviously, this is not the case in reality. Thus, Augustine's point that temporal being *is*, insofar as it tends toward non-being, is to be understood in the sense that it is the same being, ontologically speaking, that endures the temporal changes, thereby passing from actual reality into a state of being no longer.

This transitional character of time, flying from what is not yet, through what lacks any temporal duration, to what is no longer,[108] poses the question of how and where the present time is measured. We often speak of shorter and longer periods of time that have passed by. But in which 'space' of time have we measured this passing time?[109] It could not have been in the future, since what is not yet cannot be measured; nor in the present, since what is without temporal extension cannot be said to be shorter or longer; nor in the past, since what has passed by can no longer be measured in its temporal duration.[110]

This measuring of periods of time leads Augustine to direct his attention more closely to the inner *experience* of time. He uses the example of hearing the Ambrosian verse '*Deus creator omnium.*' This verse consists of alternately shorter and longer syllables. But, Augustine asks, how do I know them to be shorter and longer when hearing this verse? Obviously, I have to juxtapose a shorter syllable to a longer one, or vice versa, measuring the one in comparison to the other. But how can this comparison be made if they do not sound at the same time, but subsequently to each other? How can I use the shorter syllable as measure for the longer one, if the former has already passed by as soon as the longer comes into being? And how can I measure the longer one itself, if it needs to have passed by and to have reached its end before it can be measured as this whole stretch?[111] It seems that the experience of temporal objects is only of those that are no longer, or more precisely, of those that have presently been experienced, but have passed away in their actual being. Does this mean, then, that in measuring these periods of time I measure something that does not even exist anymore? Is that not an intrinsic impossibility?

It is clear that, though these syllables *are* no longer really (since only what is present *is*), they must still 'be' in some form, since it is a fact of manifest sense-perception (*sentitur sensu manifesto*)[112] that I experience one syllable to be shorter (or longer) than another one, and since I cannot measure what does not exist.[113] Thus, Augustine comes to the conclusion that the only explanation is that I do not measure these temporally extended syllables themselves which do not exist any longer, but only something of them that remains fixed in my memory:[114] *In te, anime meus, tempora metior.*[115]

What Augustine is here referring to is the unique phenomenon of the lived experience of time, or rather, of temporally enduring objects – an experience which, unlike these objects themselves, is characterized by a certain extension of the present. While the object perceived (the syllable) 'contains' a sequence of unextended temporal actualities of the present 'now' that 'fly' from the future into the past, our experiential awareness of this enduring object is an 'extended actualization of the present'; for each present moment of the object 'lives on' in us, extending our mind, as Augustine puts it, employing the expression '*distentio animi.*'[116]

In order to substantiate this assertion and to clarify its exact meaning for our purpose of showing the incorporeal nature of the soul, we must penetrate and analyze more deeply these peculiar acts of perceiving temporally extended objects.

We can use as a starting point Augustine's example of hearing spoken language.[117] When we listen to someone talking to us, we perceive an object, consisting of sentences, words, syllables, and even of unexpressed residues, that unfolds temporally. We do not perceive a whole sentence at the same time, since its beginning and end 'are' at distinct temporal moments. Rather, what in each moment is actually present to us to be perceived is a tiniest part of the sentence; in fact, considering that both our act of perceiving and the sentence perceived, as objects in time, *are* actually and really only in unextended temporal moments (though remaining one and the same beings throughout the changes in the modes of time), what we perceive in each *present* moment is merely a temporally unextended section of the whole sentence, since we can only perceive what really *is*. And yet, as is clear from common experience, we do perceive the whole sentence, which perception is presupposed, for instance, for understanding the meaning 'attached' to it as this whole.[118] But how can this enduring perception be explained if all we presently perceive are unextended, actually real, parts of the sentence? To this problem Augustine presents the following solution:

> Since even the shortest syllable begins and finishes, its beginning sounds at another time than its end. It is therefore stretched out in an interval of time, however small that may be, that is, it stretches out from its beginning through its middle to its end. Thus, our reason finds that temporal spaces can like local spaces be infinitely divided; and therefore, the end of a syllable cannot be heard with its beginning. Consequently, we can say that in hearing even the shortest syllable we do not hear anything, unless our memory assists us, so that, at that temporal moment at which no longer the syllable's beginning but its end sounds, that movement of it remains in the mind which had come into being when its beginning sounded.[119]

Since the beginning and the end of even the shortest syllable, which must be infinitely divisible into temporal 'spaces,' sound at different times, they together cannot be heard simultaneously. Therefore, in order for us to hear at all, our memory has to help us in that those movements of speech that *are* no longer are yet retained through it in our mind (*maneat ille motus in animo*) when we perceive what subsequently follows. These immediately past moments must somehow be kept in memory in order that the whole syllable and sentence can be heard. For since the second syllable cannot sound at the same time as the first one, it cannot be heard at the same time;[120] rather, it is heard after, and yet 'on the basis of,' the perception of the latter. Though this is no longer a presently performed perception, it still forms the background necessary for perceiving the whole sentence. And it is only because this first syllable is kept in memory that we can know the second one to be second, and that there are two syllables at all.[121]

In modern philosophy, this form of memory that was referred to perhaps for the first time by Augustine, has been further analyzed under the name of retention particularly by Husserl,[122] and recently by Ferrari.[123] Both of them emphasize the fact that there is a genuine perception of the *whole* temporal object (for instance in perceiving the *melody* of a series of tones), but that this perception consists, on the one hand, of presently actual perceptions and, on the other hand, of the retentions of these perceptions. It is therefore an act that presupposes these two kinds of consciousness of the enduring object.[124] Retention is thereby conceived of as a perceptual awareness of the immediately past that 'holds the just-past perception in the mind in its full perceptual character'.[125] It could be described as a 'memorial extension' of a past perception both in the sense of being a perception of an object that no longer really *is* but merely is past, and in the sense that no additional act of recollecting, re-performing, or retrieving is presupposed (which is precisely the main difference between recollection and retention as two 'faculties' of our memory).[126] As such a perception of the immediately past, retention follows upon the original perception, modifying the latter in that it achieves a gradual ' *"Abklingen" der Urimpression*' (a 'dying away' of the original impression);[127] that is, the original perception 'extends' into its retentions, gradually losing its experiential givenness in the perceiver, and thereby falling into the background of what is actually and really experienced as happening in him, viz. the *present* original acts of perception. This gradual 'dying away,' as well as the lack of any deliberate retrieving of the past into the present (as happens in recollection) leads Ferrari to attribute the uniqueness of retention to the fact

> that the retentional awareness is a *fully perceptual awareness of the object, in the absence of any present perception.* We 'see' the object, vividly and in its absolute particularity, but we do not perform this 'seeing.' At least, we *no longer* perform it (emphasis his).[128]

In other words, I actually *live* only *in* the actually performed acts of perceiving the *present* phases of the object; nevertheless, I still also presently perceive its immediately past phases without consciously living, that is, actualizing my conscious subject *in*, this perception, which would be indicated by the unreflexive concomitant awareness of myself *as* performing this act.[129] In this lack of consciously lived actualization, Ferrari points out, retention is similar to the knowledge of facts that is stored in memory without being thought of presently.[130] Here the 'paradoxical structure' of retention becomes manifest in that it keeps a genuine perception in the mind without being an actually lived perception that is accompanied by the simultaneous awareness of myself as its performing subject.

This memorial retaining of the immediately past plays an important role in our daily common life; in fact, without it regular life seems to be impossible. As Augustine says:

> Each conversation, each sweet singing, indeed each bodily movement in our actions would collapse and perish, and no continuation could be achieved, unless the mind keeps in memory (*memoriter*) those movements of the body that have been performed, joining them to those that will follow in the action.[131]

All our acting implies and presupposes the retaining of the immediately past phases of these actions. I could, for instance, not utter a single sentence, would I be aware only of what is presently in my mind in each moment of my speaking. It is hardly possible to imagine what it would mean for us to forget each present moment immediately after it has passed by, or to have to recollect explicitly each single past phase. If this were the case, a continuous flow of action would be impossible, not only because it would constantly be interrupted in each temporal moment, but also because the necessary basis of what immediately follows would be taken away. For, as Augustine points out in the quote cited above, the immediately future phases of our actions are joined in our mind to what has passed by, building on and continuing them. The experienced continuity of our actions implies that we must have some pre-awareness of the immediate future 'on the basis of' our awareness of the immediate past. If such a pre-awareness would be missing, each moment, immediately following on the present moment, would be experienced as an unexpected surprise.

In order to show more clearly the givenness of such a pre-awareness and its dependence on the past, one could refer to a variety of cases in which it is experienced as being in a particular way modified by past experiences. For instance, in the flow of listening to a piece of music, my pre-awareness of what is to follow immediately upon the presently performed moment is shaped by my past knowledge of that piece. If I have heard this piece many times before, so that it is still fresh in my memory, my anticipation of its immediately future phases will be very much 'fulfilled' without any element of surprise. However, even in this case, it still makes an experiential difference as to whether I know this piece from listening to its performances, from playing it by myself, from studying its score, or from conducting it. Depending on the specific background, my pre-awareness will be modified in a particular manner. Again, I might have listened before to different performances and interpretations of the same piece, so that my present expectation of the immediately following may remain unfulfilled and be 'disappointed' (which as such is not at all a negative feature, being rather capable of increasing the aesthetic enjoyment). And even if I had never heard the piece at all, I would still have some pre-awareness, though less 'content-filled,' during its performance because of my general experience of melodies and harmonies in music.

It should be clear that what is meant here by pre-awareness or by the anticipation of the immediate future is distinct from the explicitly intentional pre-conception of the future. I can make plans and have ideas about the future; I may have some foresight of what will still happen;[132] prophets have the gift of seeing future events.[133]

In all these cases the future is rendered an explicit object of our thinking. We 'look' at it intentionally. However, pre-awareness in the sense described above cannot be conceived of in the same manner, since an explicit directedness at each immediately following future moment is not only practically impossible, but would also destroy this very flow of action that our pre-awareness is meant to achieve.[134]

The difference between these two kinds of relating into the future can also be seen in acts of reciting poems and songs. Augustine emphasizes very strongly that in doing so, we pre-conceive in thought (*praevideremus cogitatione*) what we have stored in memory; it is primarily memory, not foresight, that enables us to recite them.[135] Nevertheless, though taken from memory, the poem to be rendered is pre-thought before, and during, its being recited. My anticipation is explicitly directed at it as a whole (*in totum exspectatio mea tenditur*).[136] I pre-conceive of it as of this whole poem that is then to be recited phase by phase. But *while* I actually recite it, I am also aware of its immediately following parts that I am supposed to say without constantly directing my intentional gaze at them; if I did, the actual flow of my presentation would inevitably be interrupted. Thus, we find here both kinds of anticipation of the future united in one act: I explicitly pre-conceive the whole poem or more or less longer phases of it, and I am non-intentionally aware of the immediately following moments of my recitation. Though distinct, both unite and interact in this one act, for which they are presupposed.

In our previous section on imagination we have already seen Augustine distinguishing between the pre-conception of an act *before* it is being performed, and the anticipation of the very next moments *during* its performance.[137] There we also expressed our doubts as to whether Augustine is right in assuming also the latter to be always directed at some mental image. Whereas this may perhaps be true in some sense for the intentional expectation of the more distant future, the immediate future, which, like the retention of the immediate past, is not aimed at in the flow of our actions through additional acts of explicit attention, appears to be given much more directly without mediation by any images. Here lies its uniqueness as this peculiar anticipation, in that it is *non-*

intentionally directed at a future object itself (viz. this immediately following part of an action), and not at its image.[138]

This discussion of our retaining and anticipating faculties has brought us closer to understanding Augustine's notion of *distentio animi*.[139] By that he means to express this peculiar 'extendedness' of our mind, this 'stretching out' of it both into the future and into the past.[140] And with it he also finds an explanation of our experience of time as consisting of shorter and longer phases, despite the actual present being a temporally unextended moment. For, as Augustine says, the mind anticipates (*exspectat*), is attentive (*attendit*), and remembers, or more precisely, retains in memory (*meminit*), so that what it anticipates passes through what it is attentive to into what it retains in memory (*ut id quod exspectat, per id quod attendit, transeat in id quod meminerit*).[141] This process of the future becoming past by going through the present attentiveness,[142] which is experienced as a continuously flowing whole, strongly suggests speaking of the mind as 'stretched out' in time. Our experience of time is marked by the continuous awareness of the future passing through the present into the past. All three modes of time, or rather, of what is contained 'in' them, are in a special way embraced and unified in the one experience of time, which, therefore, appears to be temporally extended.[143] Though only what I am actually attentive to in my perception is presently given, the past remains present through memory, while the future is given through anticipation.[144] The experienced present extends itself, encompassing both its immediate past and future.[145]

What then is the significance of this *distentio animi* for our main interest in showing the incorporeality of the soul? Is there any meaning in discussing these retaining and anticipating faculties within the context of arguing for the soul not being a body?[146]

The answer is easily given. For if these faculties can be shown to be really given in man (which precisely is what we attempted to do in this section), they can also be seen to presuppose a subject that is essentially distinct from a corporeal entity. For a body is by nature incapable of relating to time in this very peculiar manner. The subject of which these faculties are to be predicated must be of an incorporeal nature; as Augustine says, to be presently aware of past, present, and future is possible only for the soul and for no other being.[147]

However, in order to justify this conclusion the specific sense in which the soul, unlike any body, 'extends' itself beyond the present moment through its retaining and anticipating faculties has to be clarified. For there are other senses of relating to time which are common to both corporeal and incorporeal beings.

As we have discussed earlier, a temporal being is actually real exclusively in the present moment; in the future it is not yet, and in the past it is no longer. But it is identically the same being that endures these changing modes of reality. Ontologically speaking, there is no change of being in its passing from the future through the present into the past. In this respect, all beings that are contained in time are alike: all of them, including our body and our soul, *are* exclusively in the present now, yet remaining ontologically identical throughout the temporal flux.

However, the decisive difference between the body's and the soul's relating to time lies in the fact that a body is restricted to this more ontological relation to time, while the soul is able to go beyond itself, in the present moment stretching out into the future and the past. Though it is real, like a body, only in the present, enduring as ontologically identical being, yet through the *distentio animi* it 'extends' beyond the present now in a way compared to which a body is rather imprisoned in time.[148]

We deal here with two fundamentally distinct dimensions of relating to time. On the one hand, there is the ontological dimension of 'being' and enduring in time in which body and soul, as temporal beings, share. On the other hand, there is the completely new additional dimension of extending into and encompassing both future and past *in* the present moment. While any body is limited to the first dimension, the soul, due to its retaining and anticipating faculties (*distentio animi*), realizes both of them. In fact, in the soul the latter essentially presupposes the former building upon it. For if the soul were to change in its being after each present now, it would be incapable of extending itself into future and past, since 'it' would simply not have any future or past but merely present. Without its ontological identity, thus, the *distentio animi* would be impossible.

Hence Augustine can hold that the *distentio animi* is only found in the soul. A body is simply lacking this peculiar relation to time.[149]

Furthermore, also the sense in which the soul is 'extended' is completely different from a body's spatial extension. For not only is a 'spatially extended soul' a contradiction in terms, as we tried to show in Chapter 1, but the 'extension' of the soul into past and future is also not spatial at all. We do not occupy a larger space when anticipating the future and retaining the past; it is not as if we became more voluminous in experiencing time. Rather, it is a genuine 'extending,' however, not in a spatial, but in a temporal sense. Though like a body being actually real only in the present, and therefore being capable of performing acts only in the present, the soul in a real sense transcends the present now 'extending' itself, not in space but in time. In this sense, no body can be extended. Even the spatio-temporal moving of bodies, that, from one point of view, could be seen as a temporal extending (since it is a moving extension *in time*), is certainly quite different from the *distentio animi*. For this moving in time essentially presupposes locomotion, which is in no way implied, nor possible, in our transcending the actually present moment. Unlike a body, the soul does not move locally, but only temporally.[150]

And yet, one may refer to the reality of potentialities occurring in various realms of *living* beings, and object that with them we find another *distentio* of the present into the future, which would disprove Augustine's argument that the *distentio animi* exists solely in the soul. For a seed, for instance, anticipates the future in the present in that it has the determinate tendency of becoming a tree, just as a baby possesses all the potentialities for becoming an adult.[151] Does this inner, present finality towards future actualization, clearly given apart from the human soul, not constitute a transcendence and an 'extension' of the present similar to the *distentio animi*?

A close comparison of these two strikingly similar phenomena, however, not only reveals their specific difference, but even throws the peculiarity of the *distentio animi* as a uniquely mental 'attribute' into greater relief. For this inherent finality is still located on the ontological dimension of a being's 'being in time,' as distinguished above, which can at best be seen from the fact that it is a *determinate* inclination to an actualization characteristic of its nature. A particular state of future being is ontologically anticipated in the present, and is being actualized in the continuous flow of time. But this is precisely distinct from the soul's *exspectatio* of the immediate future, which, as we saw using the example of listening to a piece of music, is open to receiving various kinds of modification. It is constantly changed according to our particular background. In fact, this *exspectatio* accompanies and is implied in basically all forms of our acting: in our speaking, singing, perceiving, walking, etc. It is, thus, not linked to a specific ontological reality (action) which it is ordained to realize; as such it is not 'content-filled' at all. In the light of this peculiar independence and universality it becomes more manifest that the *distentio animi* constitutes a new dimension of relating to time, as was argued above, presupposing, yet going beyond that of (ontologically) *being* in time as a concretely determined being. And this new dimension that cannot be found in potentialities, is precisely man's *conscious* relating to time. Man has an *awareness* of the immediate future, which is implied in the variety of his actions independent of their specific nature. He is capable of transcending time consciously in and through his actions, regardless of their particularity.

In Chapter 3, we will more elaborately discuss this 'universal' predicate of consciousness. Here it may still be mentioned that the givenness of this additional dimension of relating to time in man is one decisive reason why a retaining of the immediate past in the present moment is also lacking in the finality of a potency. For due to its groundedness in the ontological dimension of a being, the latter is also incapable of 'extending' itself into the past in the manner of the *distentio animi*. Despite its (ontological) ordination towards the future, it remains imprisoned in the flow of time.

Thus, the kind of extension that is implied in the *distentio animi* is not only different from any spatial extension found in bodies, but also from a potency's ordination toward future actualization. It is a 'temporal extension' that essentially presupposes an incorporeal subject, indeed a subject that possesses the unique 'attribute' of consciousness. To realize this dimension of relating to time is reserved exclusively for the soul.

2   Man's cognitive faculties

The preceding arguments for the incorporeality of the human soul took their starting point in certain imaginative and memorial faculties of man. We saw how Augustine tried to argue from them to a performing subject that cannot be a body. In the course of this discussion, we also got some positive understanding as to the nature and the abilities of this subject. Particularly, certain acts of imagination and the act of recollection revealed this subject (soul) not only to be incorporeal, but also, to a certain extent, to have features characteristic of a rational being.

This line of reasoning shall be taken up in the following in that we want to present and unfold those arguments of Augustine for an incorporeal soul in man that are based on his rational faculties, particularly on his ability to know.

Augustine reflected extensively on the nature and the kinds of knowledge. From his early period of writing he was occupied with the question of whether man can with certainty attain to reality itself, as it is given independently from himself. He went through phases of doubt struggling with the threat of scepticism, until he finally became convinced of the possibility of knowing something as it is in itself.[152] It is not surprising, thus, that the theme of knowledge plays an important role in Augustine's philosophical thinking.

However, as our main concern is to give further evidence, on the basis of knowledge, of an incorporeal soul in man, Augustine's epistemology cannot be discussed for its own sake at any great length. An adequate treatment of its various aspects and gradual developments would go far beyond what is intended in the following.[153]

One major restriction is that in this section we will discuss Augustine's view of only two kinds of knowledge, namely sense-perception and the intellectual cognition of eternal reasons, leaving aside, for instance, knowledge based on the testimony of others in faith (*De Trin.* XV, XII, 21), that of my own self (*De Trin.* X) (which will be central to Chapter 3), or that of God insofar as he can be known by reason (*De Lib. Arb.* II, II, 5 – II, XV, 39). Even though these and any other form of knowledge could in principle be used for showing the incorporeality of man's soul, following Augustine's primary concerns we will be concentrating on those of his arguments based on sense-perception and intellectual cognition. The basic structure of these arguments to be developed can hypo-thetically be stated thus: if man can know in these ways, he must have an incorporeal, indeed rational, soul.

(A) Sense-perception

In the twelfth book of *De Genesi ad Litteram*, Augustine has a lengthy discussion of what he calls the three kinds of vision (*tria ista genera visionum*): the corporeal, the spiritual, and the intellectual vision. He describes their characteristic differences, using the example of the sentence, 'Love your neighbor as yourself,' as it stands written in the Bible. The letters of this sentence are seen with the bodily eyes, which seeing is a 'corporeal vision'; the neighbor to whom this command may be applied is generally represented by means of images, and this implies a 'spiritual vision'; the nature of love (*dilectio per substantiam suam*), however, is perceived in neither of these ways, but by the mind (intellect) alone, a perception which is an 'intellectual vision.'[154] (One might mention here a fourth kind of 'vision,' namely the understanding of the meaning of this sentence both as such and as a command directed at me, which is not at all identical with the perception of its letters or with the insight into the nature of love as such.) All these visions occur (to various degrees) when reading this one sentence, and they occur, Augustine says, in one and the same soul.[155]

Here we find *in nuce* what shall be developed in more detail in the following, with the exception of the second, the 'spiritual vision' that was analyzed in the previous section on imagination. Let us turn first to the 'corporeal vision,' that is to sense-perception, and see how Augustine argues from it and from acts that are implied in or based on it to the incorporeality of the human soul.[156] These arguments will in a sense be more important than those based on intellectual cognition, since sense-perception involves bodily organs, a fact which could easily suggest it to be nothing but an act of the body. Therefore, to show that *even* sense-perception as a psycho-physical act cannot be performed by a corporeal being will give much greater force of conviction to the thesis in question that knowledge implies an incorporeal subject (soul).[157]

Augustine describes the act of sense-perception, best exemplified by the ocular vision which takes place in the most excellent of the five senses,[158] as being 'born' by both the thing seen and the one seeing it.[159] The thing alone could not produce a sense-perception, nor could we speak of a sense-perception without anything *of* which it is; we always perceive *something*. This process, Augustine says, is constituted by the one who sees in that he 'contributes' to it the sense of the eyes and the intention of looking at and beholding the thing (*aspicientis atque intuentis intentio*), while the sense-information is imprinted on him by the visible thing, which is what is commonly called vision.[160] The act of sense-perception (in sight) thus consists of both an ocular sensing with or through the eyes, together with the intention of perceiving and even intuiting the thing on the part of the subject, and the 'giving information about itself' to the perceiving subject on the part of the thing seen.[161]

In this last respect, sense-perception is distinct from knowing something on the basis of inference. When, for instance, we see smoke, we really sense it (*sentimus*). However, the fire that we do not see, we know to be its underlying cause, not directly, but on the basis of perceiving the smoke (*ex eo*).[162] In this case, the fire is not immediately grasped through the senses; I do not see what this particular fire looks like. Rather, I infer its existence from my knowledge that smoke must always be caused by a fire. In sense-perception, on the other hand, the thing perceived stands immediately before my eyes, and it itself informs me about what and how it is as this particular thing.

This object of sense-perception is seen to be outside of us and to be contained in space, which, as we saw Augustine arguing in Chapter 1, makes its perception possible.[163] Or, to be more specific, the object of sight is contained in space, while the object of hearing is divided by time.[164] In either case, the object is something exterior to us which is perceived by a sense of the body.[165]

From the five bodily senses, that are the senses of seeing, hearing, smelling, tasting, and touching,[166] Augustine distinguishes a certain interior sense (*sensum interiorem*) to which whatever the bodily senses perceive is referred.[167] It is also through this interior sense which, according to Augustine, man shares with the animals, that he determines whether the object perceived is to be shunned or desired.[168]

What Augustine seems to have in mind here is a certain interior faculty that is, so to speak, the one focal point of all the impressions received from the various senses. This one inner sense is equally present in all bodily senses, so that it can somehow unify and integrate into a coherent experiential whole whatever 'sensible messages' are referred to it by the senses at each given time. It seems that if man were lacking such a central faculty and if he could only be aware of what one bodily sense reports to him at a time, daily life would practically be impossible. For in most of our activities, we rely on sense-data gained by more than one sense, unified into one whole sense-*experience*. And on the basis of this unified sense-experience, we sometimes react to a concrete thing, shunning or desiring it, perhaps even in the form of an 'automatic' reflex. In this respect, the inner sense jointly presides over all bodily senses (*omnibus [sensibus] communiter praesidet*),[169] because it moves them to shrink from, or to adhere more closely to the thing perceived.

There is another function that Augustine ascribes to this inner sense in relation to the bodily senses. The inner sense, Augustine says,[170] not only perceives what is reported to it from the bodily senses, but it also experiences these senses themselves in their act of perceiving something. He proves this assertion by giving the following example. In order for us to see through the eyes, we must have the awareness that they are open and are directed at the thing to be perceived. This awareness of the eyes themselves must be given in the act of perception. Otherwise, we could not exert any control over them which, as we will see, is essentially implied in sense-perception, such as the moving of the eyes (*movet oculum videns*).[171]

This sensitive awareness of the eyes cannot be attributed to the eyes themselves through which we perceive only bodily realities outside of them; as eyes, they cannot sense themselves from within.[172] For this reason, Augustine ascribes this sensitive power to the inner sense. For it is the same subject 'in' me that perceives through the senses and that, in the very same act, has this sensitive awareness of the senses themselves.

At this point, the question can be raised whether this inner sense may be an interior organ of our body (perhaps the brain) or another bodily sense. Is Augustine right in 'locating' the inner sense not in the eyes as the sense of sight (nor in any other bodily sense-organ), but interiorly in the soul itself (*ille enim sensus in oculis est, ille autem in ipsa intus anima*)?[173] If so, it would reveal an incorporeal subject (soul).

In the final section of our first chapter, we saw how Augustine argued for the incorporeality of the soul on the basis of its feeling the body from within. The basic thrust of this argument was that only an incorporeal subject can be present in the various locally distinct parts of the body simultaneously as one and the same subject. For a body can be present exclusively at one place at a time without being split into parts.

A similar reasoning can be applied to the inner sense as that power by which we perceive outside reality *through* the bodily senses. For not only does sense-perception imply the inner awareness of the senses themselves, as we saw, which is nothing but a concrete instance of an interior body-feeling; but it is also one and the same subject that perceives simultaneously through the five senses being located at different places on the body: the sense of sight is somewhere else than that of hearing, which is again spatially distinct from that of smelling and tasting; and the sense of touching outside reality is even located throughout the whole body.[174] But if the inner sense were attributed to a part of the body (the brain), it could not at the same time be 'present in' all these five locally distinct senses through which it perceives exterior objects. As a body, it would have to move from one sense to another, since it can be located only at one place at a time, or it would have to split itself so as to be present with its various parts in each single sense. In this way, for instance, our nervous system is diffused throughout the whole body in that in each bodily organ, spatially separated from the others, a multitude of the millions of nerves is found which together make up this one system. However, if it is clear that the many sense-data of so different kinds (that is, of objects seen, heard, smelled, etc.) are reported to the same subject in which they are unified to one sense-*experience*, it is also clear that this subject perceives through the senses as one whole subject that is not divided among the parts of the body as is the nervous system. As Augustine says, it is one soul that does everything, in the ear that it hears, in the eye that it sees.[175] And when he remarks that 'in your body you hear at a different place than where you see, but in your soul you hear where you see,'[176] he means precisely that, while the single sense-perceptions occur through different bodily senses, their performing subject is one and the same, being common to all of them.[177]

Though we will later argue more explicitly for the simplicity of the soul, especially on the basis of self-experience in the sense of *se nosse*,[178] it should be evident that the simultaneous presence at a variety of spatially distinct locations, implied in sense-perception, is essentially impossible for a part of our body; it requires a subject (soul) that is and remains one indivisible individual entity.[179]

But furthermore, as one could add, this inner sense, or rather the subject of which it is predicated, is not even given as being located at a particular place of the body. Unlike the bodily senses or the single nerves, this 'unifying center' is not perceived with reference to a specific bodily part. Precisely because it is incorporeal, it cannot have a fixed localization in the body, and consequently, it cannot be experienced as such.

Though this line of reasoning might have given enough evidence to understand that no bodily organ could be the one performing subject that perceives through the senses, Augustine goes further pointing out essential features of sense-perception that can only be accounted for by an incorporeal subject (soul).

When we perceive through the senses we have a control over them in at least two different ways.

First, we can deliberately direct our senses to, and avert them from, the thing to be perceived. As Augustine puts it, by a movement of the body the will can separate the bodily senses from the bodies to be sensed, so that we may not perceive them. For instance, we close our eyes or look away when we do not want to see something; we spit out something that we do not want to taste; or we draw our body away in order not to touch something.[180] Though Augustine refers to this active control over the senses also with respect to hearing and smelling, it seems that we have a much less direct control over the ears and the nose than over the other senses. Particularly the ears seem to be the most passive senses in that they cannot deliberately be closed from within (as the eyes can), being receptive to every noise. This control over the sense-organs, thus, seems to be given to us to a lesser and greater extent, depending on the particular sense in question.

Secondly, there is a power implied in sense-perception that Augustine calls the intention of the mind (*intentio animi*).[181] This faculty can again be understood in basically two ways.

On the one hand, *intentio animi* is the desire to perceive a certain thing (*videndi appetitus*)[182] through the senses. As Augustine explains, it is the mind itself that seeks those things that are sought by the bodily senses, since it directs the senses to what is to be perceived.[183]

This intentional will as initiating cause of a sense-perception, as one might call the intention of perceiving a certain thing, does not lie in the bodily senses, but in the subject that perceives through them; it is certainly an act of *myself*, and not of my eyes. Augustine proves the point by showing that even a blind man, that is someone whose bodily organs of sight have been extinguished, could still experience in himself the effort of perceiving something through the eyes. This fact indicates that a certain desire to see remains intact (*manet quidam videndi appetitus integer*) whether or not it can be realized in an actual act of seeing.[184] Consequently, the intention (*intentio*) in this sense of the term cannot be predicated of the eyes, but of the soul alone.

It may also be mentioned that we can find here one deeper meaning of Augustine's 'active theory of sensation' which has often been discussed.[185] What Augustine has in mind when stressing the active part the soul plays in sense-perception is this intention of doing something (*intentione facientis*) in and through the body. It is the soul that is the agent of sense-perception, governing the body, which, in turn, makes these operations easier or more difficult, depending on how much it co-operates with the soul;[186] for instance, the better my ears, the more fulfilled is my intention to hearing music. Sense-perception implies this mutual co-operation between the intention of the soul and the bodily sense-organs.[187]

There is a second meaning to Augustine's term *intentio animi*. While the first meaning, that is, the intention of perceiving by which the senses are also directed to the thing to be perceived, *precedes* the actual sense-perception,[188] intention in the second sense of the term is rather an element of this act itself. It is the fixing of the mind's *attention* to the thing being perceived: *voluntas animi quae rei sensibili sensum admovet, in eoque ipsam visionem tenet*.[189] The very act of sense-perception implies an attentiveness on the part of the subject without which the thing could not really be perceived. Augustine gives various examples in which the senses are fixed on the thing to be perceived, but in which the mind is not attentive. He relates that very often it happened to him that when he was reading through a page or a letter, he had his attention centered on something else. Though his eyes were applied to the letters, he in fact did not read anything at all, so that he had to read it again.[190] Also, he says, man can sometimes be so absorbed in a mental activity that he averts himself from everything that is present to his open eyes. He might be walking somewhere, having forgotten where he came from or where he wanted to go, though his eyes are perfectly healthy. His mind is simply diverted.[191]

These examples show that the eyes (or any other sense) could not perceive something 'on their own,' without the mind paying its attention through them. 'As such, our senses, the windows of our body, are open in vain, whenever he who is attentive through them, is absent' (*fenestrae enim frustra patent, quando qui per eas attendit absens est*).[192]

One might add that in paying attention to a thing, for instance, through the eyes, there are many other things in our visual field that are 'half-intentionally' co-given. When we see a building, we at the same time also see the surroundings of this building, even though this does not stand in the focal point of our attention. What is given to the senses is usually a huge field of sensible data of which we choose a particular object by being especially attentive to it, perceiving the rest of them on the periphery of our conscious attention. This holds equally for those data given to a particular sense, as well as for those given to various senses at the same time. We have the power to pay more or less attention to whatever is presently given to our senses.[193]

Closely related to this attentiveness to the thing perceived is another amazing feature of sense-perception that again could not be accounted for by the bodily senses alone. The senses of sight and hearing, Augustine says, raise a question worth marvelling at: how can the soul perceive (*sentiat*) where it does not live, or how can it live where it is not?[194] (The same question could as well be asked at least with respect to the sense of touch, if not with respect to all sense-perceptions.)

Augustine explains the question by using an example from sight. I see the stars and the sun in the sky, which certainly are very far away. Now I could not see anything if I were not alive; and I live 'in' my body until death. How then can I see something outside of my body that is so far away, if I live only in my body? If seeing presupposes living, it seems that I can see only where I live. Or is it perhaps, Augustine wonders, that, when seeing the sky, I live in the sky, since sense cannot be without life? Or do I see something without living there, since, even though I live in my body, I see things in places outside of my body, touching them by my sight? Do you see, Augustine asks Volusian, the addressee of his letter, how many mysterious secrets there are (*quam hoc sit latebrosum*) in a sense so well known to us: *miratur hoc mens humana, et quia non capit, fortasse nec credit* (the human mind wonders at this; and since it cannot grasp it, it perhaps does not believe it).[195]

Augustine argues in a similar way in *De Quantitate Animae*.[196] After showing that the eyes do not see themselves[197] (that is, they do not see at that place where they are), Augustine concludes that they can see only where they are not (*omnino non posse [videre], nisi ubi non sunt*).[198]

Though this way of expressing the problem is rather startling and could be very misleading (as to suggest that the soul is 'outside' the body of a living man, which opinion Augustine thinks some very learned men have held),[199] the central insight is an important one. What Augustine is referring to here and what is so difficult to express is the fact that in sense-perception man, though ontologically remaining 'in' his body, transcends himself by reaching out, so to speak, to the thing outside of himself (or to its appearance). Man still lives in and experiences his body from within (which is, for instance, shown by the inner experience of pain in the eyes that can be felt when looking directly into the sun). And yet, in a sense he goes out of himself, 'touching' the outside thing itself. In sense-perception, man gets in real contact with the beings outside of himself, precisely because he transcends the boundaries of his body.[200]

Augustine is so clearly aware of this phenomenon,[201] that he uses it as an argument for the fact that sense-perception implies an *incorporeal* soul. For since a bodily part, such as the eyes, can be receptive (*patitur*) for something only at that place where it is, but since we can through the eyes experience things outside the eyes, these experiences could not be given without the soul. The bodily eyes could not transcend themselves in this way; they always occupy their proper place in space. Consequently, the soul that perceives these outside objects through the eyes precisely where they are (or where they appear to it), cannot be a body contained in place (*nullo loco animam contineri*); for no body could account for this transcendence given in sense-perception.[202]

One could however object to Augustine that corporeal entities also, such as mirrors or even the eyes themselves, reflect exterior objects in a 'self-transcending' manner. Why then should the transcendence characteristic of sense-perception exclusively presuppose an incorporeal subject?

It must be admitted that, if transcendence were merely an entity's being in contact with outside reality given at a distance, Augustine's argument would not be cogent, as the objection rightly brings out. However, there are two completely different kinds of transcendence at stake here – a difference that can best be seen when the transcendence of sense-perception is understood in the light of Augustine's discussion of the *intentio animi* presented earlier. For both this transcendence as well as the intending and attending to the object are indispensable elements of the same act of sense-perception, mutually presupposing each other: I cannot pay attention to an object without being in contact with it having transcended myself toward it; and I cannot transcend myself toward it without having intended it. The way in which I am related to an object in sense-perception is, for this reason, essentially different from the way in which, for instance, my eye-balls may reflect the same object.

My eye-balls do not have the intention to reflect the object. They do not pay any attention to it varying in degrees of full or 'half-intentionality.' Above all, they do not *know* the object at all, nor their own mirroring it. The *cognitive* relation of 'reaching out' and grasping the object, which is implied in sense-*perception*, as well as the becoming aware of oneself as perceiving it, are completely missing. In fact, not even we ourselves are aware of the fact that the thing we perceive through the eyes may at the same time be reflected by them.

These hints should suffice to make evident that the intentional contact with an object essentially implied in the transcendence of acts of sense-perception is quite foreign to a body's mirroring of the same object. In sense-perception, I transcend myself 'actively' in an intentional, cognitive manner.

From this it becomes clear why Augustine argues from the transcendence characteristic of sense-perception to an incorporeal subject. For this kind of transcendence is neither found in the bodily sense-organs, nor in any other body, as also the attentive will could not be predicated of a stone or of whatever body that is seen;[203] the act of sense-perception implies an attentiveness that is proper to the mind alone (*solius animi est haec intentio*).[204]

Though this argument ultimately presupposes results to be gained later in the section on man's free will, the main point that is to be brought out is that sense-perception reveals features that cannot be accounted for by the bodily senses alone, but that must be of a different incorporeal subject (soul) acting in and through them.

The same conclusion can be reached when we consider acts that might be implied in or based upon sense-perceptions, acts that Augustine attributes to man's reason. A brief discussion of some of these acts will yield further evidence not only of the fact that sense-perception presupposes an incorporeal subject, but that this subject must also possess rational features.

It is to our reasoning faculty (*rationantem potentiam*), Augustine says, that whatever is received from the senses of the body is referred to be judged.[205] Because of my reason, I know *why* the oar dipped in water appears to be broken though it is really straight, and why it is perceived in this manner through the eyes. The sight of the eyes can merely tell us that it appears to be so, but it cannot make any judgment about it.[206] What we see through the eyes is a broken oar; that this is a deception and in reality not really such, however, we know only through processes of reasoning based on other sense-data and on the knowledge of certain laws of optics. Therefore, Augustine points out that in all corporeal visions the testimony of the other senses and, above all, that of the reasoning faculty of the mind itself is to be employed, so that whatever is true in this class of things may be found as much as it can be found.[207] In another context, he speaks of a certain power in us of going beyond the images given to our mind from the bodily senses (*vi quadam qua supergreditur omnem phantasiam, quam volutat animus haustam de sensibus corporis*).[208] He seems to refer here to our 'common sense'[209] on the basis of which we usually know right away whether what we perceive is a really existing thing or merely a deceptive appearance of it.

Even though Augustine is fully aware of the possibility of being deceived in sense-perception, in his mature writings he defends the evidence of the senses as not being absolutely certain, but trustworthy. Though we might sometimes be deceived by the senses, we are even more wretchedly deceived if we think that they are never to be trusted, he says.[210] In fact, practical life would seem to be completely unlivable if we would not as a rule trust our senses to be perceiving the outside things as really existing.

Yet, it remains true that the senses as such could not decide about the truth of what they perceive.[211] On the basis of my sense-perceptions alone, I could not know whether what I perceive is a thing itself or its appearance. But I do know with certainty that the thing *appears* to the senses this way, that it is given *to* them under this aspect. Indeed, I should rather accuse my eyes of false information, Augustine says, if the oar dipped in water *appeared* to be straight, rather than broken; for then, they would not perceive what is to be perceived in such cases.[212] This knowledge of how and why things should appear to the senses this way is not gained through the senses themselves. Instead, it presupposes a subject with rational abilities – a subject that is able to perform acts of judgment.

Besides the act of judging the validity of a particular sense-perception, Augustine mentions other acts that are implied or based upon knowledge through the senses, but that could not be performed by the senses alone.

There is, for instance, Augustine's distinction between seeing (*videre*) and comprehending through seeing (*videndo comprehendere*). Seeing here means the sensing of what is directly present (*id videtur quod praesens utcumque sentitur*). The comprehending, however, refers to the totality of the thing seen (*totum autem comprehenditur videndo*). What Augustine means is that I comprehend (or better grasp), for instance, a ring as one whole being standing in front of myself, while I see merely what is directly present to my sight, that is, a very particular aspect of it. I do not see its back, though I grasp it as having a back. Both acts, Augustine says, can be called vision; however, the comprehending (grasping) refers to the gaze of the mind (*obtutum mentis*), while the seeing refers to the corporeal eyes (*corporales oculos*), since they can perceive only that aspect that is directly given to them.[213] It is obvious why Augustine attributes these two acts to two different subjects. For to comprehend an object *as* one three-dimensional whole is not only to go beyond what is immediately present to the senses, but is to perform an act of *knowledge* that cannot but be performed by a rational subject. The senses as such could not grasp and know that there is more to an object than what they directly perceive.

Another act distinct from, but implied in, sense-perception is the *understanding* of what I hear. There are two things involved in an act of hearing, Augustine points out, namely the hearing proper (*auditus*) and the understanding (*intellectus*).[214] Imagine, he continues, a man who knows Latin, but does not understand what is said (in Latin). This man *hears* the same words and syllables as someone else present. Yet, while the latter may understand their meaning, these words do not bring about anything in the heart of the former (*in corde ipsius nihil genuerunt*).[215] (As the context reveals, the term 'heart' is used here with reference to the intellectual or rational power of man.)

One could even distinguish three different cases here in order to show how rational features can be implied in acts of hearing. There is, first of all, the case in which I hear someone speaking, yet understanding neither the language nor, consequently, its meaning. Though it is an actual act of sense-perception, it still lacks a rational comprehension. Secondly, I may understand the language and the general meaning of the words being used; but I do not grasp the 'point' of the whole passage or speech. Beyond the hearing of the word-sounds, I do have a rational understanding, however, not of the particular content to be expressed through the language, but merely of the language as such. Thirdly, the most 'fulfilled' sense-perception is given when I grasp the speech on all three levels: on the level of word-sounds, of the language being used, and of the content to be expressed. Again, it is clear that these acts of comprehension go beyond the actual sense-perception through the ears. Though implied and built on the latter, they are of a completely different, rational nature. For they presuppose abilities that cannot be found in the senses themselves, such as the knowledge and understanding of languages and of specific terms in one's own language, or the comprehension of the subject matter in question. To perform these and similar acts is obviously reserved for a rational being.

Another interesting act that Augustine at times refers to is the phenomenon of recognizing spiritual states in other persons through their bodily expression. The lips, the face, the eye-brows, the eyes, the hands are often means (*media*) and signs (*signa*), he says, through which we can grasp something of the mind of others. Though they are bodily, they express something spiritual.[216] It is obvious that, while the seeing of another's bodily features is a proper act of sense-perception, the grasping or intuiting of what they may express presupposes very different rational and emphatic faculties. It is a form of penetrating into the 'interior' of another, compared to which the bodily senses merely reach the 'outside.' Such understanding intuition clearly requires an incorporeal subject with rational faculties.

All these acts, though based on perceptions mediated through the senses, cannot be accounted for by them alone, nor by any other bodily member, such as the brain, which could not even relate to the outside of the body in this manner. Instead, they reveal a performing subject (soul) that must be incorporeal possessing also rational abilities.[217]

Augustine refers explicitly to the soul as to the 'I,' the one spirit (*unus ego animus*), that acts as subject in all sense-perceptions.[218] It is I who see through the eyes, who hear through the ears, who smell through the nose, etc., and that in such a way that I can see only through the eyes, hear only through the ears, smell only through the nose, etc. Each bodily member has its own specific function, though one common life (spirit) lives in all of them (*officia diversa sunt, vita communis*).[219]

Sometimes Augustine designates this rational subject that perceives through the senses as someone inside: *aliquis intus qui per oculos videat*.[220] Our eyes do not see, but someone sees through them. This someone inside Augustine also calls the inner man (*homo interior*), who is the one subject of the bodily senses and to whom, as to the one knowing (*uniformiter scienti*), all sense-perceptions are reported.[221] This subject cannot be a part of the body, but must be something incorporeal.[222]

Hence, even the mysterious phenomenon of sense-perception which implies corporeal elements, reveals, when closely analysed, an incorporeal, indeed rational (spiritual) nature in man,[223] says Augustine: our sensual vision is mingled with something spiritual (*visio quae fit in sensu habet admixtum aliquid spirituale*).[224]

(B) Intellectual cognition of eternal reasons

Having seen how Augustine argues that even the act of sense-perception, which presupposes bodily organs, implies an incorporeal subject with rational abilities, our intention in the following is to reach the same goal on the basis of man's acts of grasping eternal truths. The argument to be developed is meant to show, first, that man is able to know some objective reality outside of himself without the help of the senses, and secondly, that this knowledge by nature presupposes an incorporeal and rational being (mind) as its performing subject.

However, it is clear that the scope and purpose of the present discussion does not allow for a complete treatment of Augustine's epistemology of the eternal reasons, such as of his refutation of scepticism, his reinterpretation of the Platonic doctrine of ideas, his theory of illumination, or his analysis of the nature of truth. Though important topics in themselves, they shall merely be outlined insofar as they shed further light on the rational incorporeality of man's soul.

Augustine distinguishes two basic modes of cognition. Whatever we grasp by thinking, he says, we grasp either through the sense or through the intellect (*cogitatione capimus, aut sensu aut intellectu capimus*).[225] Besides sense-perception, Augustine clearly acknowledges a form of knowledge in which the intellect itself can immediately and directly grasp reality.[226] He commonly calls this intellectual knowledge the *cognitio intellectualis*,[227] being characterized as the contemplation of eternal things (*contemplatio aeternorum*) – an act resulting in wisdom (*sapientia*).[228]

In order for us to understand the nature of this act, and above all, to see that and why an incorporeal subject is necessarily presupposed for it, let me briefly point out Augustine's conception of the eternal reasons as the proper object of this form of knowledge.

In *De Libero Arbitrio*, Augustine gives some examples of such reasons or ideas. He mentions the numbers and the laws governing them,[229] for instance those that result from their being infinitely many;[230] he speaks of moral norms, such as living justly, subduing the lower to the higher, giving everything its due;[231] he refers to the laws of beauty (*pulchritudinis leges*) in the light of which we experience the beauty of things outside of us.[232] In *Contra Academicos*, Augustine formulates the principles of non-contradiction and of excluded middle (not in an elaborate 'scientific' form but by means of examples).[233]

All these and innumerable other laws and principles either are themselves reasons (*rationes*) or are grounded in them.[234] But what does Augustine mean by them? How does he characterize their essential nature?

For answering this question, the most revealing and comprehensive, and also the most influential, text of Augustine's is found in *Quaestio XLVI, De Ideis*.[235] The essential passage reads as follows:

> The ideas are certain principal forms (*principales formae*) or stable and immutable reasons (*rationes*) of things which themselves are unformed and therefore eternal and, always remaining the same (*eodem modo sese habentes*), are contained in the divine intelligence. And though the ideas never come into existence nor pass away, it is nevertheless said that everything that can and does come into existence and pass away is formed according to them. The soul, however, is unable to contemplate (*intueri*) them unless it is rational, and this with that faculty by which it excels, namely the mind and reason itself, that is, with its face, as it were, or its interior and intelligible eye.... Since these reasons of all things, both created and to be created, are contained in the divine mind in which nothing can be unless eternal and immutable, and since Plato called these principal reasons of things ideas, they are not simply ideas, but true ideas (*ipsae verae sunt*), since they are eternal and remain immutably the same. It is through participation in them that whatever is exists, however it is. But among the things that are created by God, the rational soul surpasses all and is closest to God, as long as it is pure; and as much as it clings to Him in love, it is overshowered and illumined by Him with that intelligible light, and so it perceives, not through the corporeal eyes but through its foremost faculty by which it excels, that is, through its intelligence, these reasons, the vision of which makes it most happy.[236]

The reasons are the principal immutable forms of things. Their nature cannot be changed. That is why they are eternal. For instance, the ratio of one to two, or that of two to four remains *always* such (*semper talis est*); it was not truer yesterday than today, nor will it be truer tomorrow or after several years; this ratio cannot not be (*nec poterit ista ratio non esse*).[237] In this sense, the ideas always remain in the same manner.[238] They always had and always will have the very self-same being (*idipsum esse semper habuerunt, semper habitura sunt*).[239] They did not come into being, nor will they pass away.[240] And for this reason, they are contained in the divine mind of God, since only in God can what is eternal and immutable exist,[241] and since, as one can add, whatever is eternal and immutable cannot but be contained in God.[242]

In this way of being essentially unchangeable, the eternal reasons, though clearly distinct from the sensible contingent things that cannot remain themselves for even an instant of time,[243] are not unrelated to the latter. On the contrary, they are essentially *ordained* towards the really existing world in that whatever exists is formed and shaped according to them.[244] As ideal 'essential plans,' the eternal reasons are participated in by the changeable things of this world rendering them not only what they are, but that they are at all.[245] For without participating, for instance, in the fundamental laws of being, such as the law of non-contradiction, a thing could not *be* at all. Similarly, a thing is chaste or eternal or beautiful or good or wise only because it participates in the nature of chastity itself, of eternity itself, of goodness itself, of wisdom itself, which are natures that are *not*, like these concrete things, subject to corruption, ugliness, evilness.[246] They themselves remain unchanged, while what participates in them can, because of its mutability, be formed according to them to various degrees of perfection. In this sense, then, Augustine holds the ideas to be the stable causes (*causae*, or *causae exemplares* as later terminology will call them) of all unstable things,[247] the immutable grounds (*origines*) of all mutable things, and the eternal reasons (*rationes*) of all non-rational and temporal things.[248]

Yet, Augustine goes further pointing out that the ideas are not only the reasons (essential plans) of things, but that they are themselves true (*ipsae verae sunt*),[249] that is, that they are also eternal *verities*.[250] Since truth, as Augustine shows in the *Soliloquia*, cannot not be − for even if truth perished, it would still be true that truth perished −,[251] it must be eternal as are the ideas. For as chastity as such does not die when a chaste man dies, so truth does not die when true things die.[252] Therefore, the eternal reasons are so essentially related to truth that they can themselves be called true.[253]

For our purposes it is important to see whether and how these *rationes*, which for Augustine are the proper object of the *cognitio intellectualis*,[254] can be known, and, above all, whether the subject of this knowledge could be some bodily members of ours, for instance the brain-cells. Our aim will be to show, following Augustine, that only an incorporeal rational soul can possibly be the performing subject of such acts of knowledge.

These ideas, Augustine says, are present to the gaze of the mind in a certain incorporeal light of its own kind (*in quadam luce sui generis incorporea*).[255] As the eyes of the body perceive whatever is given to them in a corporeal light,[256] so the mind beholds (*intuetur*) the ideas, to which it is attached in a marvellous incorporeal, that is, non-spatial way (*miro quadam eodemque incorporali modo, scilicet non localiter*),[257] in this interior light of truth (*in illa interiore luce veritatis*) by which the inner man is illumined.[258] Augustine calls this light also the light of the eternal reason in which the immutable truths are beheld (*lumen rationis aeternae, ubi haec immutabilia vera conspiciunt*).[259] They are luminously made manifest to man by God, the inner teacher.[260]

This theory of illumination, briefly presented, has subsequently been interpreted in various ways.[261] It is neither our task here to unfold the theory in the light of its historical origins and developments and to evaluate its interpretations critically, nor to show that Augustine's view does not as such imply an ontologism, and that illumination can be understood as a phenomenon distinct from any supernatural inspiration through grace. Rather, for our purposes it suffices to see that in the act of grasping an eternal truth there is a kind of luminosity which, as Augustine himself admits, is easily experienced, but which to explicate is impossible.[262]

What Augustine has in mind seems to be basically the experience of evidence that 'flows' from the understanding of an intrinsically intelligible truth. In grasping its intelligibility and essential meaning (*ratio*), it 'identifies' itself to us as being true, giving us the luminous awareness that it is really such as we comprehend it.[263] In this sense, the eternal ideas (and ultimately God in whom they exist) shine into us, in Augustine's terminology, as we become partakers in the light of the truth itself (*particeps veritatis*).[264] And, above all, it is in this light of truth, in which we participate through the experience of evidence, that we attain certainty, or more concretely, that we attain to most certain truth (*certissima veritas*).[265] If we gain an insight into such an unchangeable eternal reason, we understand that it must necessarily be such as it is. The fact that three times three equals nine is necessarily true, even if the human race is snoring, Augustine says.[266] Grasping its intrinsic necessity, we become certain that this fact must truly be such as we understand it; it cannot be otherwise. It makes itself evident to us through its intelligible light in which we know it with certainty.[267]

However, Augustine does not want to say that we have this most certain knowledge with respect to the fullness of truth in all its depth. Quoting the word of Paul, '*ex parte scimus*' (1 Cor. 13, 9), Augustine states that our knowledge in this life in which our soul is still pressed down by the body, is rather limited.[268] We can merely attain to elements of the whole truth. Yet, when we do have an 'intellectual vision' of a truth, we cannot be deceived. For either we understand this fact, and then it is true; or, if it is not true, we do not understand it (*aut enim intelligit, et verum est; aut si verum non est, non intelligit*).[269]

There are two *kinds* of error that Augustine distinguishes in order to bring out this point more clearly: to err in what one sees (*in his errare quae videt*), and to err because one does not see (*errare quia non videt*).[270] The first kind of erring can happen in sense-perception, viz., in the case of seeing a thing that in reality is not *as* it is seen; here one is deceived about the thing itself. But this kind of error cannot occur in the act of intellectually understanding eternal ideas. For these are either (intellectually) seen, and if so, they are seen in their truth as what they are; or they are not seen.[271] If I, however, claim something to be, without seeing it that way, I commit an error. I maintain something to be true, without having beforehand grasped its truth.[272]

Now could it possibly be assumed that such an intellectual act of understanding a truth with luminous certainty can be performed by a corporeal being? Could it perhaps be my blood, my physical heart, the multitude of brain-processes taking place in my brain-cells, or some other part of my body that gains these certain insights into the eternal ideas?

It is surely possible to think of a body being illumined by a light.

Any corporeal entity that is exposed to the sun would be an example. Yet, the kind of illumination that Augustine has in mind as an element implied in the act of intellectual cognition cannot be interpreted as a being lit up of one of my bodily organs. I gain insights into eternal truths independently of, and without any effect on, the brightness and darkness of my bodily members. However Augustine may ultimately explain this experience of illumination in intellectual cognition, it can only be an incorporeal and a spiritual phenomenon unlike any light effect in the physical world.[273] For being involved in acts of understanding proper, indeed, in acts of understanding necessary eternal truths with absolute certainty, this kind of illumination cannot be received by a body which, as is clear and will become more obvious in the following, is by nature incapable of grasping any intelligible truth (in fact, of grasping anything at all).

Furthermore, the impossibility of assuming a bodily organ to be the performing subject of acts of intellectual cognition can also be seen through another act that Augustine discusses at length, and that is implied in this intellectual vision. In grasping a certain truth, we are also aware of its *iniudicabilitas*. What Augustine means by this term is the fact that the eternal unchangeable verities cannot be judged according to some higher standards of truth. We find them to be such as they are, being unable like inspectors to correct or judge them, on the basis of exterior criteria, that they *ought* to be as they are, or that they *ought* to be different (better, more beautiful, more perfect, truer) than they are (as is the case with contingent beings).[274] For, as Augustine explains, this would imply that they could be otherwise, which is essentially impossible.[275] There is no higher measure (*modus*) of perfection and truth that could be imposed on them; they necessarily have their own measure in themselves, because of which they cannot be judged to be true in the light of another criterion outside of themselves.[276]

But it is precisely in the light of the eternal truths that we can judge sensible, temporal things. When we, for instance, say that something is not as white as it ought to be or that someone is not as gentle as he ought to be,[277] or when we praise the beauty of bodies, we do so in the light of what Augustine calls the immutable and true eternity of truth (*incommutabilem et veram veritatis aeternitatem*).[278] Because these truths are unchangeable and contain the highest criterion of their truth and perfection within themselves, we rightly judge all inferior things according to them (*secundum veritatem de inferioribus recte iudicamus*).[279] And we judge these things, which we perceive sensibly, to be better, the closer they are to them,[280] in a way in which the eternal ideas themselves cannot be judged. Thus, Augustine summarizes what he means by the injudicability of the eternal ideas in his characteristically brief, but precise manner: '*nullus de illa iudicat, nullus sine illa iudicat bene*' ('Nobody passes judgment on them, but nobody judges well without them').[281]

Regarding the question of what it is 'in' us that grasps this intrinsic injudicability of the ideas and that perceives and judges sensible things in the light of them, it again seems evident that this cannot be a part of our body. For, just as those acts discussed in the preceding section, that are based on sense-perception without being performed by the senses or any other bodily organ alone, this perceiving of the changeable objects of sense *in the light of* higher measures of truth and perfection also goes far beyond the abilities of our bodily members. For it presupposes the capability of *understanding* these measures themselves *as* injudicable, and of applying them to sensible reality. Obviously, only rational souls (*nos et omnes animae rationales*)[282] can perform such judgmental comparison of these two realms of being, viz. the timeless unchangeable world of ideas and the contingent changeable world of flux shaped according to them, in a concrete act of sense-perception.

Perhaps the deepest and most characteristic feature of intellectual cognition, which, for this reason, is also the most cogent indication that an incorporeal subject is performing it, is what could be called, following Augustine, its receptive transcendence. Let me quote the marvellous passage from *De Vera Religione* which contains in a sense the culminating point of Augustine's insight into the nature of the intellectual cognition of eternal reasons:

> Do not go outside; return within yourself. In the inward man dwells truth; and if you find your mutable nature, transcend also yourself. But remember in doing so that you must also transcend yourself even as a reasoning soul. Reach out for that from where the light of reason is enkindled. What does

every good reasoner attain but truth? Because truth does, of course, not reach itself by means of reasoning, but is precisely what those who reason desire to attain. See there a harmony than which there can be no greater, and unite yourself with it. Confess that you are not what it is: it does not seek itself, but you reach it by seeking, not in space, but by a disposition of mind, so that the inward man may unite himself with the indwelling truth in a joy that is not low and carnal but supreme and spiritual. . . . Reasoning does not create truth but discovers it. Before it is discovered it abides in itself; and when it is discovered it renews us.[283]

The grasp of truth, first of all, requires the returning within oneself, the recollection of oneself. For, as Augustine states, truth dwells in the inner man, that is, in the soul that is not absorbed in the sensible world of flux through the body, the outer man.[284] Recollection is an indispensable presupposition for any search of truth. But going within ourselves we find that we are mutable by nature and cannot be the source and ground of eternal truth.[285] Therefore, we must transcend ourselves (*transcende et teipsum*) to that source which enkindles our reason. Intellectual cognition implies the transcending of our nature, and the reaching out to and direct grasp of the truth itself; we understand that something is truly the case because we find it itself being such. Indeed, we must also transcend our own reasoning in the sense that we cannot make up the truth we grasp. Truth does not become truth through a process of reasoning. We do not create truth, but discover it. For before we find it, it abides in itself, waiting for us (*manet*); and when it is discovered it renews us, filling us not with low carnal pleasure, but with highest spiritual joy.

Because of their unchangeable nature, the eternal truths are not formed by our reasoning; we have to discover them. Transcending ourselves, we must go *to* them directly and receive from them the knowledge of what they are in themselves. And in this transcendent eternal mode of being, they are receptively accessible to all of us at any time. There is not 'my truth' or 'your truth'; but truth is common to all who want to see it in its hidden, but public light (*secretum et publicum lumen*).[286] Truth is to be discovered by each one of us (without becoming our personal possession), since it is common to all who know.[287] The cognition of the eternal truths, then, could be best described as a transcending act of discovery.[288]

The central question imposing itself now, viz. whether the performing subject of such acts of intellection could be conceived of as being a body, shall be answered, following Augustine, in two steps, first, by showing, in comparison to sense-perception, the lack of any bodily 'mediator' in these acts and thereafter, by arguing directly against the possibility that our bodily organs account for the receptive transcendence implied in them.[289]

From the various features that distinguish the intellectual cognition from sense-perception and that reveal the former's lack of bodily elements, only two shall be mentioned as being pointed out by Augustine.

First of all, sensible objects are given only to a very limited number of people at a time. Precisely because they themselves, as well as the bodily senses presupposed for their perception, are located at a particularly determined place in space and time, they are accessible exclusively to those men that are spatially and temporally close to them. However, as we just saw, there is a spatial and temporal universality to the eternal ideas in the sense that they can in principle be grasped by anyone at any time. As Augustine remarks, someone understands justice in the East, and someone understands justice in the West; though they are bodily separated, the gaze of their minds is directed at one and the same justice.[290] Thus, the commonality of truth that Augustine strongly emphasizes could not be maintained if intellectual cognition would imply bodily 'mediators.' It must be an act of an incorporeal subject alone.

Secondly, unlike sensible things, the eternal reasons are not only not placed in the spatio-temporal order; they are simply not corporeal at all. The objects of intellectual cognition are not contained in space, they are not separated from each other by spatial intervals, they are not smaller in part than in their whole;[291] in a word, these intelligibles are present to the visions of the mind in their incorporeal nature (*in natura incorporali sic intellegibilia praesto sunt mentis aspectibus*).[292] From this it follows that they must be known in a different way than corporeal beings, since, as we argued in Chapter 1, only the latter are accessible to perception through the bodily senses. Only what possesses the marks of corporeality is known sensibly, for which reason, to use Augustine's

example, we do not see (in the sense of sense-perceiving) mathematical figures.[293] But since we do have an understanding grasp
of them, we must perceive them, without the senses, by our intellect
(rational soul) itself.[294]

Yet, it is not only the lack of any bodily mediation that, even
more clearly than the case of sense-perception, reveals the
performing subject of intellectual cognition not to be a bodily organ
(brain). For also the kind of transcendence that, as we tried to show
above, is essentially implied in intellection, cannot be accounted for
by a body. For a transcending grasp of these immutable reasons
also means a transcendence of the temporal order into the 'realm
of eternity.' *Transcende tempus*, Augustine says when admonishing
us to search for the truth, since in it there is no past and future,
but only present.[295] And in his famous account of the mystical talk
he had with his mother at Ostia, he beautifully describes the ascent
from the meditation of temporal beings to the contemplation of the
eternal, which is beyond any passing of time.[296] In understanding
an eternal verity, man is in contact with what is timeless. Though
being ontologically present in time as one and the same being
underlying its constantly changing phases, in the intellectual
perception of truth he goes beyond this temporal order;[297] being
and remaining in time, he cognitively reaches into eternity.[298]
However, for a body, which is essentially 'imprisoned' in the ontological dimension of being in time,[299] this kind of transcendence is
simply excluded. Though it does participate in the eternal reasons
in being formed according to them, it is incapable of 'entering'
into eternity, and this, in such an 'active' cognitive manner. In its
ontological dependence on these reasons a body remains in the
temporal contingent world of flux. But man, as a temporal being
sharing in this dependence ontologically, is able to transcend his
very self *cognitively* by reaching out into the realm of timeless truth.
It is evident that such an act of transcendence and of understanding
cannot be performed by a part of his body, but requires an incorporeal subject with rational features.

Furthermore, one could add that though my bodily organs might
be able to produce mental images or constructions of thought, as
could happen when drugs and other stimuli are being used to affect
our actual state of mind, a transcending act of grasping an eternal
truth could never be interpreted as product of such physical

processes. For if it were the outcome, for instance, of certain changes of brain-cells, it would not yield any knowledge of a truth *as it is as such*, precisely because it would itself be *produced* in an arbitrary, non-rational manner. Such an 'act' could not make any claim to the truth of its knowledge, since it would simply not be the knowledge *of* something. The receptive transcendence which, as we saw Augustine arguing above, is essentially implied in the intellectual cognition, would be completely lacking; in fact, it would even be substituted by the 'mechanisms' of purely irrational processes.[300] As Augustine states, this act of grasping an unchangeable transcendent truth, of understanding its intrinsic necessity, of receiving from it the knowledge of itself, can only be performed by the soul, that is, only by the rational soul: *anima vero negatur eas [rationes] intueri posse, nisi rationalis*.[301] No body can sense the life of wisdom, to use Augustine's figurative way of speech, but the rational mind (*mens rationalis*); for not even any soul (*anima*) can sense wisdom, as animals too have a soul without being able to perform this act.[302]

Though it is not our topic to enter into a discussion of animal-souls, it should be evident that the cognition of the eternal reasons can only be an act of the rational soul (mind). Indeed, as Augustine says, this desire to understand what is true and best is the highest vision of the soul, beyond which it has nothing more perfect, more noble, and more right.[303]

3   Man's free will and power over his body

We cannot close our presentation of Augustine's discussion of those faculties of man that presuppose an incorporeal soul possessing rational abilities, without having dealt with what could be considered man's most characteristic rational faculty: his free will. In a sense, this power is even more central to man as a rational being than that of knowledge. For it is in and through his free willing that man determines and shapes himself, being able thereby to become what he is meant to become, and to reveal his most inner being by entering into contact with the world actively and morally responsibly.

In Augustine's thought the power of free will plays a decisive role. In fact, Augustine has been called a philosopher of freedom,[304] and rightly so, since he was one of the first great thinkers that paid attention to and analyzed this central faculty of man,[305] thereby having gained an understanding of it that in its profundity was, and still is, directive for any further investigation. Augustine was particularly occupied with three main problems concerning man's free will: the problem of the harmony between God's foreknowledge of future events and man's freedom (which implies the question of predestination),[306] the problem of the relation between grace and free will, and the problem of evil.

Without discussing his solutions to each of these problems, we want to employ in this section his way of showing man to be free and his descriptions of the nature of freedom, in order then to ask the question of whether free will could be attributed to some bodily member of ours. If not, we can eventually draw the conclusion that man's power of free willing also reveals an incorporeal, indeed rational, subject (soul) 'in' him.

Augustine begins his well-known refutation of the position of Cicero, namely that to admit a foreknowledge of God would be to jeopardize man's freedom, by relating the latter's insistence on the reality of a free will in man. If all that happens were determined by fate, Cicero had argued, there would be nothing in our own power and no freedom of will; and, as Augustine continues expressing Cicero's thought:

> if we grant that, says he, the whole economy of human life is subverted. In vain are laws enacted. In vain are reproaches, praises, chidings, exhortations had recourse to; and there is no justice whatever in the appointment of rewards for the good, and punishments for the wicked. And that consequences so disgraceful, and absurd, and pernicious to humanity may not follow, Cicero chooses to reject the foreknowledge of future things.[307]

Having had an acute awareness of law and justice, Cicero was so convinced of the existence of man's freedom that he denied God's foreknowledge of the future (which he wrongly thought to imply an efficient cause exteriorly determining man's actions). If human life is to have any legal and moral meaning at all, he argued, man must be free.

As we just said, it would go too far to present Augustine's

response to the difficult question addressed here by Cicero. But it is clear that Augustine was equally certain of a free will in man. In fact, at another place he points out that he knows himself as having a will with the same certainty with which he knows himself to be alive.[308] And elsewhere, he charges all those, who through silly talk want to do away with the fact that the soul has been given the power of free decision, with being even so blind as not to see that they themselves utter these 'vain and sacrilegious' opinions with their own free will.[309]

But what makes Augustine so certain that we have a free will, apart from the fact that its non-existence would have consequences destructive for any moral and legal order?[310]

He first of all observes that it is most certain that nobody but he himself wills (or does not will) when he is willing (or not willing) (*cum aliquid vellem aut nollem, non alium quam me velle ac nolle certissimus eram*).[311] It is I myself, and only I myself, who wills whenever I will something. I feel (*sentio*) firmly and intimately (*firme atque intime*) that *I* have this will and engender or act through it when I will.[312] I feel that when I will, it is not someone who 'wills me,' somehow from the outside;[313] rather, I feel it to be my spontaneous action, in the sense that it is I myself who brings it about.[314] (Only later, in the light of Augustine's discussion of *se nosse*, we will be able to understand more clearly what exactly is meant by the term feeling [*sentire*] in this context, and how the awareness of my willing essentially implies the awareness of *myself* as really existing subject performing it.) Indeed, Augustine even goes as far as to say that the will is in a sense the only thing that he could call his own (*quid autem meum dicam prorsus non invenio si voluntas qua volo et nolo non est mea*).[315]

There is something deeply seen in what he expresses here. The will is in a sense my truest self, the proper 'I,' because it is the will that is most directly in my power. There is nothing so immediately given to me (*nullo intervallo*) in my power over it, as my will, as soon as I will (*mox ut volumus*).[316] Because of the will, I in a unique sense possess myself as able to determine myself instantaneously: I as subject determine myself as object. This is precisely the uniqueness of the will that it is one and the same ontologically identical being, namely I myself, that is both subject and object of its own willing.[317] Hence the peculiar immediacy implied in our willing.[318]

From this fact of having a most direct power over myself in and through my will it also follows, secondly, that all I willingly do is done by nobody but myself. When I willingly determine myself to perform an act, there is no other efficient cause of this act than I myself.[319] As Augustine points out, human wills are the causes of human works.[320] For, as he continues a little later, we do many things that, if we were not willing, we would for this reason not do, – a fact pertaining primarily to our willing itself which we cause to be, since it *is*, if we will, and it *is* not, if we do not will; for we would not will, if we were precisely unwilling.[321] In this sense, one could speak of the 'auto-causality' of the will in that there can be no cause of the will prior or exterior to the will itself.[322]

If our will were not in our power, Augustine argues, it were not a will at all: and precisely because it is in our power, it follows, thirdly, that it is *free* in us.[323] A will without being free is no will.[324] It belongs necessarily to the nature of the will to be free, as Augustine explains:

> So also, when we say that it is necessary that, when we will, we will by free choice, in so saying we both affirm what is true beyond doubt, and do not still subject the free will itself thereby to a necessity which destroys liberty. Our wills, therefore, exist, and do themselves whatever we do by willing, and which would not be done if we were unwilling.[325]

If I do something willingly, I do so by my own free choice (*libero arbitrio*), that is, as exclusive cause of my actions I choose to do this act freely, independent of any outside determining force. My 'auto-causality' as such implies freedom.[326] And it is this undetermined free exercise of the will that conditions the possibility of being responsible for my actions and being guilty in the case of sinning (*voluntarium et ob hoc culpabilem esse*).[327] Since I am free, nobody but I myself is responsible for my willing, and thus, also for my making bad use of it in sinning. The power of free will is the cause of my sin (*causam peccati mei*), Augustine affirms.[328] For though we always have a free will, it need not always be good;[329] we can freely choose to do evil, even for the sake of doing evil.[330]

Thus, the reality of my free will is given to me through the very experience of myself as willing something. If I honestly reflect upon myself I must realize that I have the power of determining myself freely, that is, without any determination from the outside.[331] (That this self-experience is also indubitably certain will be discussed in the section on the *se nosse*.)

Yet, the question of the extent of our freedom still remains. For is not there a multitude of things that we cannot do, even if we want to do them? And are we not in our acting often dependent on exterior influences determining us in one or another way? What exactly is it, then, that we are free to do, and how far does our determining power reach? To answer this question will prove to be decisive for our primary purpose, namely to show the will to presuppose an incorporeal and rational subject.

We have already seen Augustine making the distinction between willing (*velle*), resp. not willing (*nolle*), and doing (*facere*) on the basis of willing.[332] Both are 'functions' of the same will. But the manner in which they are exercised is different in each case. Let me try to shed some more light on the problem by analyzing a very revealing, well-known passage of the *Confessiones* in which Augustine describes a peculiar conflict of will that seized him right before his conversion:

> The mind commands the body, and the body obeys. The mind commands itself and is resisted. The mind commands the hand to be moved and there is such readiness that the command is scarcely distinguished from the obedience in act. Yet the mind is mind, and the hand is body. The mind commands the mind to will, and yet though it be itself it does not obey itself. Whence this strange anomaly and why should it be? I repeat: The will commands itself to will, and could not give the command unless it wills; yet what is commanded is not done. But actually the will does not will entirely: therefore it does not command entirely. For as far as it wills, it commands. And as far as it does not will, the thing commanded is not done. For the will commands that there be an act of will – not another, but itself. But it does not command entirely. Therefore, what is commanded does not happen; for if the will were whole and entire, it would not even command it to be, because it would already be.[333]

In this text, Augustine juxtaposes two ways of willingly doing something (*facere*): the volitional moving of our body, and the spontaneous bringing about of spiritual acts in our mind itself (in Augustine's concrete case, the actual step of converting). He speaks of the peculiar 'monster' (*unde hoc monstrum?*) that the body obeys the will more easily than the mind itself;[334] for one would think that a self-command of the mind is exercised with greater ease than the commanding of a completely different nature, which the body is.

For our purposes, it is worth investigating this inner conflict of the mind, in order to understand the 'functions' and the freedom of the will more clearly. In the light of this investigation, we will then be able also to analyze our freedom with respect to the other kind of volitional doing that Augustine mentions, the moving of our body. Both of these discussions will eventually serve as foundation of our main argument that man's free willing cannot be performed by a part of his body.

The inner state of mind that Augustine is describing is characterized by two voluntary 'movements' opposing each other 'in' the same mind. On the one hand, there is the self-command of the mind (*imperat*) that it should will (*velit*) to do the step of conversion; the mind commands itself, and it could not do so unless it were willingly doing so (*non imperat, nisi vellet*). On the other hand, this command given by the will is not carried out by the will, though both of them are of the same mind (*nec alter est nec facit tamen*). The mind willingly gives a command to itself, but its own will resists its being put into practice. This opposition leads Augustine to draw the conclusion that the will does not will and, for this reason, does not command entirely (*ex toto*), but merely insofar as it is willing actually to do what it commands itself; for otherwise, there would be no need for a command preceding the volitional carrying out of the act to be done, since in this case, viz. when the will would be whole (*plena*), the will to command and the will to carry out the command would coincide.

Augustine explicitly warns against inferring from this duality of the will that there are two contrary minds made of two contrary substances in man;[335] for as is clear from inner experience, it is one and the same 'I' (mind) that, on the one hand, wills and that, on the other hand, does not will.[336] But how is this inner conflict to be explained? How can I will something without being willing to carry it out?

Interpreting Augustine's observations, one finds in them an

example of an opposition between the two 'functions' of the will mentioned above: the willing proper (*velle*) and the volitional doing (*facere*). The former refers to the inner decision made with respect to a certain action: I decide to do this act (in various degrees of determination and resoluteness) having the intention (the will) to carry it out. In this sense, I command myself saying an inner 'yes' to my doing the act. However, this willing intention is certainly not identical with its actually being carried out. For the latter requires an additional act of the will, often after quite an interval of time, through which the intention is realized. While the former can be characterized as an expression of my volitional attitude towards the action in question, the latter means my active causing of this action to become real. Both 'functions' issue from my own will; yet, as such they need not coincide. If they do, however, I will 'wholly,' to speak with Augustine, since in my actual doing my intention receives that fulfillment that it 'desires' (wills) to bring about.[337]

It is primarily (*primitus*) our willing in the sense of having the intention to do something, Augustine points out, that is in our free power and that most properly possesses the features of a free will discussed above.[338] For while the actual carrying out of a decision may be weakened or jeopardized by factors that are not under our direct control, such as the inner and outer temptations that hindered Augustine from making the final step of converting, the act itself of willing to do so is freely brought into existence by myself at any time I want. Though I may for various reasons be hesitant and irresolute actually to *will* something at all, I am still free to perform this act of willing, since such irresolution is subject to my own free self-determination; I am free to strengthen my will and to determine myself as to whether or not I should perform a certain act, having always the choice to say an inner 'yes' or 'no' to my doing this act.[339] In this sense, Augustine speaks of the approving or disapproving as pertaining to the will proper (*consentire vel dissentire propriae voluntatis est*).[340] And it is also this free inner attitude towards a possible action that is the primary root of sin. For if a man had the intention to do an evil action, but was for some reason hindered from actually carrying it out, he would indeed be a sinner, Augustine argues, precisely because it is the decision to do so that lies directly in his free power and that, for this reason, he is primarily responsible for.[341]

Now in order to approach our main question of whether such acts of willing, in the proper sense of having the intention to do something, could be performed by a part of our body, we have to understand that, though a body may be capable of exercising a certain power over itself, it is essentially unable to have this kind of free self-determination that we find in our own willing.[342] There are very common cases in which bodies 'act' on themselves, such as in an explosion, in watches or other mechanical and atomic devices, and, above all, in the growth of *living* beings (plants, animals and human bodies); however, in none of these cases do we find this power being caused by a free intention of the body to act this way. An explosion is not brought about in the body because it wills to explode; rather, it 'acts' on itself 'from the outside,' that is, not by its *inner* willing intention to do so. It performs a '*facere*' without a free '*velle*.' Even the inner life-principle of living bodies is not *free* to affect their growing at the time it wants. Like a body, it is not aware of its own free choice of exercising such power over a body, precisely because it does not have this choice. It is not a subject that *willingly* determines itself, out of its own free decision. In this sense, Augustine argues that a stone does not have the power to stop its falling to the ground, while the mind is not moved from something superior to something inferior (in sinning) without its own consent of the will (*voluntarius*).[343] Though this comparison could be misleading in suggesting that man would be able willingly to stop a fall from a high place, what Augustine has in mind is primarily the fact that a stone is determined exclusively by 'exterior' forces lacking the 'inner' volitional power over itself that is given to man,[344] for which reason it is also not responsible for its moving, and therefore unable to sin. Whoever denies this, Augustine exclaims, is not only more stupid than a stone, but simply insane.[345]

Even though, as we mentioned earlier, the full certainty of myself as freely willing an act is to be gained only through the form of self-knowledge that Augustine calls *se nosse* and that will be discussed in the following chapter, it is still clear that this kind of free self-determination given in our inner experience cannot be accounted for by a part of our body. It must be a completely different incorporeal subject (the soul) that is the efficient cause of our acts of free willing; as Augustine points out, it is a subject that itself governs, while bodies *are* governed (*regunt enim animi, reguntur corpora*).[346] Since bodies, as we argued above, do not have the power of determining themselves *freely*, they cannot be the agent of our acts of free will, to which they are rather subjected. In fact, Augustine goes even as far as to say that bodies should not be counted among the efficient causes at all, since they can only affect what the wills of spirits (*spirituum voluntates*) do with them, that are not only those of human spirits, but also those of angels and ultimately that of the absolute Spirit, God Himself.[347]

The same conclusion is to be drawn from analyzing the other kind of volitional doing (*facere*) referred to above, viz. the spontaneous moving of our own body. As Augustine relates, man's power of ruling his body is often taken to be an indication of something stronger in him than the body, which was thought to be the mind.[348] He might think here primarily of Plato's argument in the *Phaedo*.[349]

In order to sketch out and unfold the argument, it is necessary to pinpoint more exactly that form of body-movement that alone gives evidence of an incorporeal subject. For not only can it be impossible for us to move our body or parts of it at all; but also the brain and certain bodily reflexes may have a moving effect on our body. Hence the question of which kind of governing the body can only be performed by the soul.[350]

In the first place, Augustine makes the distinction between *velle* and *posse*, that is, between the will to move the body, and the ability to do so.[351] For men may want to carry out something through their body, he points out, yet be incapable of doing so because they lack the members required, or because they are hindered by chains or by paralysis.[352] Again, some parts of the body move without our volitional causation, such as the pulsations in the veins,[353] while other members can only be moved by some men but not by all.[354] Man is not given absolute power over his body,[355] a fact analogous to his incapability, discussed above, of spontaneously bringing about spiritual states at any time, though the respective obstacles are certainly quite different.

However, there is a form of moving the body, or certain parts of it, that is affected by an exercise of the will, such as when we volitionally move our legs in walking, our mouth in speaking, or our hands in writing.[356] In this case, as Augustine points out, we act through the members of the body in a manner that implies the preceding of an inner word (*verbo apud nos intus edito*); for no one willingly does anything (*aliquid volens facit*) that he has not previously spoken in his heart.[357] Augustine explicitly refers here to that moving of our body that is caused by an act of willing proper (*velle*), which, as we discussed above, is characterized by the free intention of saying an inner 'yes' in regard to the action to be performed: I spontaneously move my body because I freely will to do so.

It should however be remarked that there are various degrees of willingly acting on or through the body. We may do many things merely from habit without having made the full decision to carry them out prior to their performance. Or we may gradually learn to move certain parts of the body in a special way, as in playing piano, so that the moving effort of our will will always be more decreasing, etc. Yet, it remains true that the more the bodily action is preceded by my free willing intention to perform it, the more is it 'stamped' to be a free act of *mine*. For being primarily in my power, it is the will to do so, and not the movement as such, that renders it an expression of myself, whereby my willing, however, presupposes the knowledge of my ability to perform the respective bodily movement; for, obviously, I can only have the full intention to do a certain action, if I know that I am able, at least in principle, to bring it about.

Now concerning our central question as to whether this form of free volitional moving of the body is performed by some bodily organ of mine, we find that, apart from the fact argued for above that a body cannot be counted among the efficient causes acting freely, the actual intention of the will to move the body is itself also no bodily movement at all. Though our body is moved locally, which is the proper way for bodies to move (*localiter enim moveri corporis proprium est*), the very effort of the will through which this movement is caused, is not locomotion.[358] The volitional commanding and governing of the body itself obviously does not move from one place to another but is an incorporeal motion (*incorporeus motus*) which, for this reason, cannot be of a body;[359] it must be of the soul that does not spatially fill out the body, as water fills out a sponge, but that is joined to the body in wonderful manners (*miris modis*), on the basis of which bond it moves the latter in space.[360] This is precisely the peculiarity of the act in question that an incorporeal being, the soul, affects through a *spaceless* command of its will a *local* movement of the body.[361]

Thus, also the free volitional governing of our body reveals a cause that cannot issue from some bodily organ of ours, but that must be predicated of the soul,[362] indeed of the rational soul.[363]

Though we do not want to enter here into the question in which sense the spontaneity of animals may also be considered a kind of willing,[364] man's free self-determination, as it is given in inner experience and as we tried to unfold in its different aspects and dimensions, can only be that of a rational being, and of no body or irrational soul, Augustine says.[365] The reality of a free will is precisely a central characteristic of what it means to be rational.

In conclusion, we can, with Augustine, come to the understanding that the acts of our will essentially presuppose an incorporeal subject (soul) that is also rational. If we pay close attention to what occurs in us when we will we may eventually arrive at Augustine's own definition of the will: *Voluntas est animi motus, cogente nullo, ad aliquid vel non amittendum, vel adipiscendum* (the will is a movement of the soul, being in no way forced, either for not losing or for attaining something).[366]

In this chapter, we tried to show how Augustine argues for the incorporeality of the human soul on the basis of fundamental faculties of man, viz. on the basis of certain imaginative and memorial faculties, of his cognitive faculties of sense-perception and cognition of eternal reasons, and of his free will and power over his body. All the acts performed through these faculties reveal a subject that cannot be a body, but that must be of an incorporeal nature, possessing rational abilities.[367] Even though a discussion of the simplicity of the soul is reserved for Chapter 4, we did get some understanding that this subject is the one single soul, I myself, acting through these various faculties. My soul, therefore, is something spiritual (rational) and incorporeal by far excelling the nature of my body, as Augustine summarizes the results of our investigation:

> The nature of the soul is more excellent than the nature of
> the body, excelling it by far; it is something spiritual,
> something incorporeal, something similar to the substance of

God. It is someone invisible who reigns the body, moves the members, directs the senses, prepares the thoughts, performs the actions, holds the images of infinite things.[368]

CHAPTER 3

Knowledge of the self as showing the 'conscious spirituality' of the soul

In our previous analyses we have gained with Augustine some understanding as to how the soul is by nature distinct from any corporeal entity, including our own body. We say that there are experiences and acts in man that do not bear bodily predicates, and that man possesses faculties and powers that essentially presuppose an incorporeal subject (the 'I' or the 'inner man') to be their performing agent. Indeed, we saw that this subject possesses rational features, which investigations took us a step further in our endeavour to get more positively at the nature of this mysterious being in man that Augustine calls soul.

Augustine's most direct and perhaps most convincing arguments for an incorporeal soul in man, however, are those deriving from man's immediate knowledge of himself. For in these arguments, the starting point is not taken from acts or faculties of man which implicitly or indirectly show man to have an incorporeal nature. Rather, these arguments are based on the direct inner experience man has of himself. They presuppose his immediate insight into himself. In this sense, the arguments to be developed in the following are most positive in that they try to take their starting point directly in the grasp of the soul itself. And it is in this way that the question of what the soul is, rather than what it is not, may also be answered more adequately. For precisely by studying man's cognitive relations to himself his soul will manifest itself not only as being incorporeal, but also as possessing the peculiar 'predicate' of consciousness, which, together with the rational abilities analyzed above, is meant to constitute the 'spirituality' of his soul (mind).

Before entering into the discussion, one introductory remark should be added. Augustine develops these arguments based on man's self-knowledge primarily in his classic work *De Trinitate*. As the title of this work indicates, it is in the first place a theological treatise on the doctrine of the Trinity. Yet, this theological outlook does not in any way invalidate the purely *philosophical* insights to be found in this work. For Augustine's method consists precisely of philosophically showing the analogies to the Divine Trinity in man that would to an extent illuminate this incomprehensible mystery revealed in faith. Inspired by the revealed doctrine of the Trinity, he tries *by reason* to find images in man that might help us to a better understanding of this doctrine, as he himself writes: *desideravi intellectu videre quod credidi*.[1] His remarkable and highly original discussion of the various 'trinities' in man, therefore, cannot be considered a fideistic drawing out of theological premises, but is a genuine contribution to philosophical anthropology, a contribution that has indeed rarely been surpassed.[2]

Without even attempting to give a systematic presentation of these 'trinities' Augustine discovers in the 'inner' and the 'outer' man,[3] our attention shall in the following be drawn to one aspect of the 'trinity' *mens-notitia-amor*. For it is in this context that Augustine not only investigates man's knowledge of himself, but that he, by the same token, explicitly argues for the spiritual incorporeality of his soul.[4]

Even though it seems to be very obvious and self-evident that man knows himself, a closer analysis of this fact will prove it to be an extremely complex and puzzling phenomenon. In our procedure, therefore, we will try to uncover step by step the various self-conscious relations of man that Augustine discusses. In this way, it will gradually become more evident that none of these relations can be explained in materialistic terms, but that all of them essentially presuppose a spiritual subject (mind). Thus, the following lines of reasoning are to be seen as complementing each other, contributing various elements to the one well-known Augustinian *cogito*-argument for the incorporeal spirituality of the human soul (mind).[5]

1   The unique self-presence of the mind to itself

In order for us gradually to grasp the structures of man's self-knowledge, we should begin by pointing out a very basic feature of the mind, as that subject that performs these self-conscious acts, a feature often referred to by Augustine: its unique immediate self-presence to itself. Though this discussion will later have to be developed and modified in the section on *se cogitare*, and above all, in the section on *se nosse*, at this point it will provide some insight into the conditions for man's possibility of knowing himself, and it will be at the basis of a first (preliminary) way of showing the underlying subject of his self-knowledge not only to be incorporeal, but to be spiritual.

It is a remarkable question, Augustine says, to investigate where the mind goes when it wants to find itself.[6] Most of the time, the mind goes out of itself into the exterior sensible world, so much so that it becomes unable to distinguish bodily things from itself, considering also itself nothing but another body.[7] Or, as Augustine laments elsewhere, men go forth to marvel at the great wonders of nature, but themselves they pass by.[8] However, what is so in the mind as the mind itself?[9] What is so present to the mind's cognition as itself?[10]

This immediate presence of the mind to itself, Augustine explains, is manifested whenever it is said to the mind: 'Know Thyself.' For in the very same moment (*eo ictu*) in which the mind grasps the meaning of the word 'Thyself,' it knows itself as being referred to, for no other reason than that it is present to itself.[11]

Augustine elaborates on this unique immediacy of the mind's self-presence by comparing it to the manner in which sensible things, as well as their mental images, are present to the mind:

> For the mind is more interiorly within, not only than those
> sensible things which are evidently without, but even than
> their images which are in a certain part of the soul that also
> the beasts have, though they lack the intelligence which is
> proper to the mind. As the mind, therefore, is within, it goes
> in some way outside of itself when it directs the affection
> of its love towards these sensible things which leave their
> footprints, as it were, in our mind because we have thought
> of them so often. These footprints are, so to speak, impressed

on the memory when the corporeal things which are outside
are so perceived that, even when they are absent, their images
are present to those who think of them. Let the mind,
therefore, know itself, and not seek itself as if it were absent;
let it fix the attention of its will, by which it formerly
wandered over many things, upon itself, and think of itself.
So it will see that there never was a time when it did not
love itself, and never a time when it did not know itself.[12]

Obviously, the mind is much more interiorly present to itself
than sensible bodies which are manifestly without. Yet, Augustine
argues that even the images of corporeal things which are held
within the mind are less present to itself than itself, and this for
various reasons.

First of all, these mental images of bodies which, according to
Augustine, are like footprints (*vestigia*) impressed on the memory
in the cognition of the corresponding outside bodies,[13] have an
'ontological status' that is different from that of the mind. For while
the mind is a real entity in and of itself, as we will discuss more
fully in Chapter 4, these images precisely presuppose a mind for
their actual existence; without a mind, they could not exist at all
as such images. They are beings in and of the mind (*entia rationis*,
as the Scholastics said), but not the mind itself.[14] Consequently,
these images, though in the mind, are not in the same way present
to it as it is to itself. For the mind is not present to itself as to its
own image (even though, as we will see later, there is a sense in
which this can also be the case), but by a certain interior presence
that is not feigned but real (*quadam interiore non simulata sed vera
praesentia*);[15] indeed, it is present to and *in* itself[16] in a sense in
which these images must still be seen to be outside of itself.

Secondly, the mind is more interiorly (*interior*) within itself than
these images which are merely in a certain part of the soul (*in parte
quadam animae*), which is that part, Augustine explains, that the
beasts also have.[17] He seems to refer here to that aspect of the
soul that is closely related to sense-perception, which faculty the
animals share with man, though in a less rational manner, according
to Augustine.[18] This 'extroverted' aspect of the soul that contains
its images is not 'on the same level' as that wherein the mind is
present to itself. For the mind is much more deeply within itself,

so to speak, at the center and at the very core of its being where only itself, and no image of something, not even of itself, can be present to itself. This becomes especially manifest from deeply existential acts, such as of deliberate self-determination, of important decisions, of hope, of despair. Even though such dimensions of depth in the mind's self-presence are not always consciously actualized, the fact that we do become aware of them at times reveals their ontological givenness. Again, also in this (second) sense, images are not 'within' the mind but 'without.'

Thirdly, Augustine points out that, in order for the mind to have images within itself, it first has to go out of itself; for forming an image of a thing, it precisely must first perceive this thing that exists really outside of itself, by transcending itself to it. Yet, there is no need at all for the mind to leave itself in order to become present to itself, as if to its mental image. As it is truly within itself, its knowing contact with itself does not go 'through' related acts of perceiving extra-mental reality, as is implied in the inner perception of mental images, even in that of false images of itself; rather, in self-knowledge the mind is cognitively present to *itself*, that is, to itself alone.

From this real, immediate presence of the mind to itself it follows, fourthly, that there never has been, nor that there ever will be, a time when the mind does not know itself (*numquam se nescierit*).[19] Since it is really present to and in itself, incapable of being outside of and apart from itself, Augustine thinks, it must also have a *constant* cognitive relation to itself, that is, it must always 'know' itself in a very special sense.[20] However, with respect to mental images it would evidently be false to say that we always had a particular image in our mind of which we could never not know. For, first of all, there are so many images that 'come and go' in our mind, so that, by the very dynamism of our thinking, a particular image is usually not kept for a long period of time. And secondly, even if an image is stored in our memory, thus being in some way present to us for a longer time, it will usually be changed and reshaped by our imagination to such an extent that it would be hard to consider it the very same image. All these and other changes are excluded from this form of continuous inner self-'knowledge' that Augustine sees to be implied in the mind's undestroyable self-presence.[21]

But there is still another, fifth, reason that one could add in order to show that the mind is more intimately present to itself even than to its own images. For these mental images can be shared by many minds in the sense that one and the same outside thing could, in the form of its image, be present to all minds that conceive of it. The mind, however, due to its unique self-presence, has an awareness of itself that is exclusively its own. Nobody else can share in this immediate contact I have to myself when I, for instance, make a decision, rejoice, suffer. Such acts as my own acts are *really* experienced only by myself. Since it is I myself who rejoices, I alone live in and experience this act truly. Though there are forms of empathy in which the inner experiences of other (real or fictional) persons are 'co-felt' *as if* we would ourselves experience them, we are clearly aware in these acts of empathizing that they are not our own personal experiences, as they are still given to us somehow 'from the outside.' In fact, not even God, the absolute omniscient Being, could share in this immediate experiential awareness I have of myself (which becomes manifest particularly in experiences of evil, such as in hatred, in despair, in the experience of conscience). Here I realize that only I myself experience myself *realiter*, in the strict sense of the term. This does not mean, however, that only I myself know of everything that is happening in me. Though other human beings are by nature limited in gaining cognitive access to my inner being, this is not at all to be excluded for a super-human spirit possessing greater powers of discernment. In this sense, we will later see Augustine saying that God is closer to me than I to myself, knowing me better than I do.[22]

Thus, man is present to himself in an intimacy and a privacy that cannot be compared even with the manner in which mental images are given to him. In fact, one could say that this unique intimacy is possible only in man's relation to himself; for in this way he is present to nothing but himself, and nobody but himself is present to himself in this way.[23]

It may be interjected here that this intimate closeness we have to ourselves, this inevitable self-possession that excludes any possibility of 'getting rid of ourselves' is also of deep personal and existential importance. Augustine brings out this point in the very moving description of his emotional state of mind after having lost his most beloved friend. Not finding any peace and rest of heart, he tries to escape from himself, realizing, however, that this is impossible: where could my heart flee from my heart? Where could I flee from my own self?[24] Man is inalienably related to and 'bound up' with himself, a fact that in some cases might become a cause of great personal suffering.

Now posing the question of the spiritual incorporeality of the mind in the light of its uniquely immediate presence to itself, we may present the following arguments, not explicitly developed by Augustine, but clearly implied.

First of all, the fact that the mind, and only the mind, is *really* present to itself, excludes its being a body. For, as Augustine points out, bodies are always given to us as being outside of us (*manifeste foris sunt*).[25] The mind goes somehow outside of itself (*quodam modo exit a semetipsa*)[26] when it comes in contact with sensible matter (as well as with all other reality, one should add, such as plants, animals, other minds, that *is not* itself). There is always a certain distance between the mind and a body presented to it. As we saw in the section on sense-perception, as perceiving subject the mind transcends itself in order to attain to its object standing at an ontological distance.[27] In this, the object of sense-perception is much 'less' present to the mind than its own mental images that in their being are dependent on the mind. But if even the latter, compared to the mind's presence to itself, are still to be seen as being 'outside' the mind, as we argued above, much more so are all corporeal objects of sense at a distance to the mind. For since it is identically the same mind that is present to itself, there is absolutely *no ontological* distance between it and itself (which does not mean that there could not be a *cognitive* distance between the real same mind as subject and object of its own self-knowledge, as we will see in the following section). With this immediacy, then, the mind is and can be present only to itself, and to no mental image, much less to a corporeal entity. It must therefore be incorporeal.

Secondly, we saw that the exclusive self-presence of the mind to itself accounts for the privacy of its inner life that cannot really be shared in from the outside. However, there is nothing in the nature of a body that would render it perceivable to only one person. In principle, a body is cognitively accessible to anyone. It is a public entity. Consequently, the intimate privacy implied in my own access to myself could not be accounted for by a corporeal being. I alone am aware of myself really from within, and nobody else can share in this experience, while many people, for instance, could look at my body from without. In fact, many central organs of mine, such as the millions of my brain-cells, are only given from without, being perceived, if at all, mostly by other people. Thus, since only one and the same mind has this unique access to itself, and since bodies are as such 'publicly' accessible, the mind cannot be a body.[28]

Even though it will be investigated more fully in the section on Augustine's notion of *se nosse*, one might also mention here, thirdly, that the fact of the mind not only being ontologically identical with itself, as any other being, but also being conscious of its self-identity in this uniquely intimate manner, shows that it cannot be a body. Cognitive self-awareness presupposes a being that, compared to lifeless matter and even to man's animated body, possesses a radically new kind of life: consciousness. This will reveal itself to be a uniquely *spiritual* phenomenon that cannot be found in matter.

Yet, as has become manifest during the course of the present discussion, for showing the conscious spirituality of the mind more clearly, there is the need to develop the insight into the unique self-presence of the mind, particularly in the light of the different *kinds* of self-knowledge to be analyzed successively in the following. In this way, we will see the complexity of Augustine's central argument for the mind not only as an incorporeal, but as a spiritual being, taken from man's cognitive contact with himself.

2 Self-reflection *(se cogitare)*

A first most explicitly cognitive way for man of knowing himself is through acts of self-reflection (*se cogitare*). With these acts, we encounter a most amazing and puzzling phenomenon: man placing himself in front of himself, becoming both subject and object of his own thought. Let me try to unfold Augustine's description of this most peculiar act in order to show the impossibility of its being performed by anything but a spiritual subject (mind).[29]

In a well-known passage, Augustine expresses his amazement at the act of self-reflection, stressing the unique power of thought (*cogitatio*) that becomes manifest in it:

> But so great is the power of thought that not even the mind itself may place itself, so to speak, in its own sight, except when it thinks of itself. And consequently nothing is so in the sight of the mind, except when it is thought of, as not even the mind itself, by which is thought whatever is thought, can be in its own sight in any other way than by thinking of itself. But how it is not in its own sight when it does not think of itself, since it can never be without itself, as if itself were one thing and its sight another thing, I am unable to discover.[30]

The mind is capable of knowing itself by placing itself in its own sight – a fact clearly given from inner experience. Indeed, Augustine says, so great is its own power of thought that it is not only able to put itself in front of itself, but that it *must* do so in order to know itself clearly and explicitly. Even though it could never be without itself (*sine se ipsa numquam esse possit*) since, as we saw, it is most intimately and really present to itself, it can gain an explicit, conceptual knowledge of itself only through this act of 'looking' at itself. This is precisely the greatness of our faculty of cognitive thought that only through it can we know something, even if this is our own self.

But how is it possible that the mind, being always within itself, does not always think of itself? Does this self-cognition perhaps not pertain to its nature, being merely present in it at times? How can we *not* always be in our own sight (which we certainly are not), since we are always 'with ourselves,' and since our faculty of reflection seems to belong to the very nature of our mind?[31] This Augustine is unable to determine.[32]

The act of self-reflection (*se cogitare*) can only be understood in the light of our previous discussion of the real self-presence of the mind. For the peculiarity of this act lies in the fact that one and the same identical reality (the mind) is at the same time both subject and object of its act of knowledge: I as knowing subject know myself as object known.[33]

We find here the unique case where the mind has a knowledge that is neither of a lower essence than itself, such as a body, nor of a higher essence, such as God, but that is entirely on a par with, equal to, and identical with the mind itself (*par omnino et aequale atque identidem*).[34] As, according to Augustine, the value of knowledge is determined by the rank of the object known, the mind's knowledge of itself cannot surpass itself, since it is the mind itself that knows and is known (*non se superat notitia sua quia ipsa cognoscit, ipsa cognoscitur*).[35]

In fact, Augustine even extends this subject-object identity to the *act* of self-knowledge itself, claiming that the terms 'knowing' and 'known' are not only referred to the mind as the performing subject of its self-knowledge (*notitia*), but also to this very *notitia* itself:

> And although self-knowledge (*notitia*) is referred to the mind as knowing or as being known, in respect to itself it is also spoken of both as known and as knowing; for the knowledge by which the mind knows itself is not unknown to itself.[36]

Both the mind as well as its acts of knowing itself can be said to be knowing and to be known; both are subject and object of self-knowledge.

This conclusion, however, which seems strongly motivated by Augustine's Trinitarian speculations, requires some clarification in order not to be misunderstood. For while the act of self-knowledge can itself certainly be known by the mind (though it should be made clear, which Augustine does not do in this context, whether it is known through a subsequent act of reflection [*se cogitare*] or in the way of *se nosse* to be discussed later), this act can in no way be said to 'know' in the same sense in which the mind itself knows. For obviously, an act of knowledge itself does not know either itself or the mind. It is the mind as subject of all knowledge that knows *through* its act, as Augustine himself points out: *notitia qua se mens ipsa cognoscit*.[37] In this sense, one cannot speak of an act of knowledge to be knowing, since only a mind knows strictly speaking.[38]

However, there is a completely different sense in which an act of knowledge can also be said to be knowing, that is, to be a 'subject' of knowledge. And this is what Augustine seems to have in mind here. For one reason for Augustine's marvelling at the power of cognitive thought is that the mind cannot know (*cogitare*) anything, not even itself, without its faculty and the respective acts of *cogitatio*. It is only in and through its acts of knowledge that it is capable of knowing something at all. Therefore, besides the mind as the primary, strictly knowing subject, its acts of knowledge can be seen to be 'secondary' agents of its knowledge. Only in this quite different and very specific sense is it true to refer also to acts of self-knowledge as both knowing and being known.

Even though the reflection on our *acts* plays an important role in our personal life, such as in the examination of conscience, in the following our attention will focus exclusively on this act of *self*-reflection which is performed, for instance, whenever the mind is told: 'Know Thyself' (*Cognosce te ipsam*).[39] Following Augustine, this act shall first be compared to other acts of knowledge that imply some means of mediation, by which procedure further light will be shed on the immediacy of this knowing contact the mind has with itself. Thereafter, it shall be analyzed in the light of the question of whether a body could possibly be its performing subject.

Augustine contrasts the act of self-reflection explicitly to three other acts of knowledge. Though they certainly do not constitute a complete listing of the numerous ways in which man can know reality, they are nevertheless quite well-chosen for our purposes here.

The first kind of knowledge contrasted by Augustine with self-reflection refers to things that we know, or rather believe, on the basis of what we have been taught about them, as when we know the Cherubim and the Seraphim to be certain celestial powers.[40] We have never seen them directly, as they are absent from us; and yet, we do know of them through what we have learned on the testimony of others (*quae testimonio didicimus aliorum*).[41] In daily life, this belief in others is a very common form of knowledge. Through it, we learn about distant parts of the earth, about history, about when and where we were born. And it would be most absurd, Augustine stresses, to reject all this as false, merely because it is not certain knowledge.[42] Nevertheless, this form of knowledge is different from self-reflection, as the latter obviously does not imply any trusting reliance on someone else. It is a most immediate direct perception of oneself.

Secondly, Augustine distinguishes self-reflection from acts that try to grasp the inner being of *others*. He observes, for instance, that the will of another man is given to us neither through sense-perception, nor through understanding, except if he reveals it to us by some corporeal signs, in which case, however, we believe rather than understand.[43] As was pointed out above, each man experiences himself and his acts in a uniquely intimate privacy which excludes any immediate being shared in by someone else; I cannot see the will of another person *as* it is seen by himself.[44]

However, as Augustine suggests, there are ways of sharing in another's experiences 'from the outside.' The other can reveal his will and thoughts to me, so that I may in a sense co-experience them. Or I may 'perceive' his internal experiences insofar as they are expressed in his body. For instance, as Augustine mentions at another place, many movements of our soul are recognized in our eyes;[45] likewise, through another's facial expression his inner state of anger may be intuited.[46] In these cases, we somehow gain a direct insight into another person's interior life through the medium of his body. Such bodily expressions become often the motivating cause of our compassion, grief, resentment, and similar feelings for others.[47]

Yet, it is evident that this intuiting and sharing in another's experiences is quite different from the experience of our own inner being. For not only do we merely believe, rather than understand with certainty, that another has these experiences (which is distinct from the knowledge of ourselves, as we will see in the following sections); but they are also still mediated to us by certain bodily signs and expressions, which is excluded precisely from our own *immediate* self-reflection. I reflect upon myself in an immediacy that cannot be compared to how another's inner life is given to me: though mediately perceivable, it is as such hidden from me and cannot be grasped directly.[48]

Thirdly, Augustine contrasts the act of self-reflection with the manner in which we see our own face and our eyes. This act, of all three acts mentioned, bears the closest similarity to self-reflection, since it consists in the perception of the very same perceiving organ. Yet, compared to self-reflection there is a decisive difference: our eyes cannot see themselves, unless a mirror is placed in front of them.[49] As it belongs to the nature of the eyes to be located at a fixed part of the body, in their vision being directed to what is outside,[50] they are able to perceive other eyes, but never themselves directly.[51] This fact can be applied to all five bodily senses since it is obvious that none of them can be perceived by itself or by another sense (*manifestum est quinque istos sensus nullo eorum sensu posse sentiri*).[52] (According to Augustine's theory of the senses, the five bodily senses cannot perceive each other, but are perceived by the 'inner sense' [*sensus interior*], that in turn cannot perceive itself either, but is perceived by reason [*ratio*], which alone is aware of itself.)[53]

Though Augustine does not explicitly explain why the senses cannot reflect upon themselves, it is clear that this is grounded in the fact that our sense-perception is a psycho-*physical* phenomenon implying bodily elements, viz. the sense-organs. They, as any other corporeal entity, are by nature incapable of completely turning over themselves, as will be shown below. Our senses could thus be said to be absent from themselves in that epistemological sense in which the mind is precisely present to itself.

However, the difference between self-reflection and knowledge through the senses can still more clearly be grasped when self-reflection is compared to the manner in which the eyes do see themselves, namely by looking in a mirror. In this way, it will also become manifest that only an incorporeal, indeed only a spiritual, subject is capable of immediately reflecting upon itself.

It is in no way to be thought, Augustine states, that the mind knows itself, as it were, in a mirror.[54] We cannot, from the way in which we see our eyes, infer to the manner in which we reflect upon ourselves. Augustine does not argue very much to prove his point, as it seems to be quite evident to him. But in the light of certain theories of knowledge, particularly in the light of Marxist epistemology according to which the adequacy between our knowledge and the objects known is explained in terms of mirror-reflections causally produced in our brain by the objects,[55] it becomes of pressing importance that we unfold Augustine's insight more fully.

When I look in a mirror, perceiving my own face, in fact I do not see my face but merely a reflected image of it.[56] The mirror itself obviously does not contain my real face. Therefore, what I directly look at in the mirror is not the same as what someone else sees when looking at me – that is, my real face. In self-reflection, however, the situation is completely different. As we have seen above, the mind, when reflecting upon itself, knows itself *really*, and not merely an image of itself. It is not as if the mind were a mirror constantly reflecting itself, by means of which image alone we would have cognitive access to ourselves. Rather, the mind knows itself *really* and in such a direct manner that any mediating means (besides the very acts of self-knowledge themselves) is to be excluded essentially.[57]

Furthermore, each image in a mirror is reversed. I do not see my face as anyone else sees it, except when the mirror-image is again reflected by a second mirror. But it is absurd to assume such a reverse perception with respect to the mind's knowledge of itself. I reflect upon myself as I am really, not in reverse.

Again, there are many possible deceptions due to using a mirror as means for knowledge. A mirror can be distorted in such a way that it does not exactly reflect its object as it really is. Augustine himself refers to the fact that smaller mirrors – and this would include the retina – project a smaller image of an object than exists in reality;[58] or a mirror-image might have a different proportion than does the real object. For this reason I can never be completely sure whether what I see in a mirror is really an exact or a somewhat distorted image of my face. Clearly, deceptions of such a kind cannot occur in self-reflection. I do not see myself spatially bigger or smaller depending on how accurately an inner mirror works. (In an analogous spiritual sense, I may have certain false images of myself, which, however, are not due to an alleged mirror in me that, without my free interference and responsibility, just happens to reflect me distortedly, but which have quite different, personal and moral, origins.)

Besides these structural differences between knowledge by means of a mirror and self-reflection, there are certain intrinsic contradictions implied in the (Marxist) attempt to explain all knowledge in terms of mirror-reflections.[59] If our mind knew reality in the same way as a mirror reflects corporeal objects, it would not only be unable to know incorporeal and spiritual realities, which would imply the essential impossibility of self-reflection, but it could not even know itself as a mirror, which is precisely what is presupposed for stating this theory. For a mirror obviously cannot reflect itself and the images contained in it. We could thus never know this theory to be true, since we would not even be able to know ourselves as a mirror. One of the basic fallacies underlying this mirror-theory of knowledge seems to lie in overlooking the fundamental difference between two relations: the relation obtaining between a mirror and the real object reflected in it, and the one obtaining between a perceiver and the mirror-image. For the latter is a real conscious act of knowledge that implies the self-transcending intentional 'having' of an object as it is in itself,[60] whereas the former constitutes a case of an 'automatic' causal relation that lies completely outside the specifically conscious realm of being. If our knowledge were reduced to the former relation, we would not be able to know anything in itself, not even ourselves.

Without going into further detail, let it suffice here to point out with Augustine that the mind when thinking of itself (*se cogitare*) does not, like the eyes, perceive itself by means of a mirror. Self-reflection is a much more immediate form of knowledge in which the mind itself, and not its image, is grasped.[61]

Augustine mentions further absurdities that follow from viewing the act of self-reflection as analogous to sense-perception or to certain phenomena occurring in the material world.

In a beautiful passage[62] he points out that when the mind reflects upon itself it does so not by one part of itself seeing another part of itself (*numquid ergo alia sua parte aliam suam partem videt*), as the eyes, being parts of our body, do not perceive the body as a whole, but merely some of its members. Ocular vision (and in different ways any other sense-perception) is by nature limited in that the eyes can perceive only those parts of a thing that are directly present to them. If the whole object is to be seen, they must wander around it, directing their vision at its various aspects. There could never be a complete perception of an object in the sense that all of its parts were seen from one point of view without change of place.[63] However, when the mind thinks of itself it does not merely perceive parts of itself as if approaching itself from various spatial directions. It does not change its position in order to see itself as a whole; nor does it place itself at various spots in order to be seen by itself. For if it has wandered away from itself in order to be seen, where will it remain in order to see (*si conspicienda migravit, conspectura ubi manebit*)? Because of its real presence to itself, the mind cannot perceive itself like a bodily object that, standing at a distance, is given to it only under one aspect at a time; rather, the mind reflects upon *itself*, that is on itself as a whole, and it does so, not by leaving and wandering around itself, but by immediately 'bending back' upon itself.[64]

Though we will more explicitly discuss later the indivisible wholeness of the mind which is experienced in self-reflection, it might be added here that the act of self-reflection also can not be explained in terms of certain 'reflections' that occur in the realm of bodies. A piece of paper, for instance, can be folded so that it 'bends back' upon itself. However, in this case, some parts of the paper merely come into contact with *other* parts of it. For a corporeal being it is essentially impossible to cover itself up completely in that all of its parts were present to each other. But precisely this is given in the act of self-reflection in which the mind is present to itself wholly and completely. It is one mind that, not by a part of it, but as a whole reflects upon itself completely – a phenomenon that cannot even be imagined, much less explained, by means of corporeal analogies.

Finally, Augustine argues that in self-reflection the mind cannot be assumed to be doubled. It is not as if it is one mind, being *in* itself, that thinks, and another mind, standing *before* itself, that is thought of (*in se sit conspiciens ante se conspicua*).[65] This is found in sense-perception as well as in 'reflections' by means of a mirror. Self-reflection, however, constitutes the unique case in which one and the same ontologically identical being, the mind, is both subject and object of its act of knowledge. Certainly, one can distinguish these two *epistemological* functions of the mind within self-reflection; in this sense, and in this sense alone, the mind can be said to be doubled into knowing subject and object known. Nevertheless, it is clearly the very same mind that reflects upon itself, a condition even presupposed for its epistemological duality.[66]

From these considerations the following conclusion can be drawn with Augustine. The act of self-reflection (*se cogitare*), being manifestly given from inner experience, reveals, when carefully analysed, a uniqueness of essential structure that is found neither in perceptions implying bodily senses nor in purely corporeal phenomena. This amazing act in which the same identical subject looks at *itself* and not at its image separately standing before itself, in a way that, unlike the manner in which bodies are given in sense-perception, implies actual wholeness (as opposed to the partiality of aspects) and real immediacy, cannot be explained by spatial movements, but must be an incorporeal conversion (*se cogitat non quasi per loci spatium sed incorporea conversione*).[67] No corporeal being could be the subject of this act. Hence, Augustine's argument developed in this section can be summarized thus: since the mind knows itself (*cogitat se*) in a way in which no body could bend back upon itself, it cannot *be* a body or a part of it. In fact, in the light of our previous discussion of knowledge and anticipating the results to be gained in the section on *se nosse*, we may say that this subject of self-knowledge must be spiritual in the sense of both being rational and being conscious. For like any act of knowledge, to know oneself explicitly presupposes rational abilities; and such incorporeal reflecting upon oneself can ultimately be accounted for only by a self-conscious subject. But to draw this conclusion requires further arguments to be developed in the following.

3 The mind's absolute certainty of itself – the cognition of the *ratio aeterna* of the mind as such

Perhaps the most well-known and most influential Augustinian proof for the spiritual incorporeality of the mind is based on Augustine's so-called *si fallor, sum* argument. Long before Descartes' celebrated *cogito, ergo sum*, Augustine had already anticipated his essential insight in an even deeper and more extensive form. Due to his profound analysis of human consciousness, Augustine was able, perhaps more than Descartes, to see the ontological conditions for the indubitable certainty the mind has of itself. And as this argument is brought up in various works throughout Augustine's literary career, it is not hard to imagine that it must have played an at least equally important role in the development of his thought and convictions as was the case with Descartes.

For both thinkers the discovery of the *cogito* was of decisive significance both philosophically and existentially. Indeed, it seems that Augustine employs this argument to a greater extent than does Descartes; for it comes up in at least three important areas of his thought: most prominently, in his refutation of scepticism by his demonstration that in knowing myself most certainly I in fact know truth (*De Vera Religione, De Civitate Dei*), then as the starting point of his famous *veritas*-argument for the existence of God (*De Libero Arbitrio*), and in his discussion of the spirituality of the soul (*De*

Trinitate). As our principal interest, however, is neither to compare the similar philosophical insights as well as the methodological place of the *cogito* in Augustine's and Descartes' thought,[68] nor to present a systematic treatment of the development, elaboration, and application of this argument within Augustine's work, we will concentrate in the following on this absolute certainty of oneself insofar as it can be used to show the spiritual incorporeality of man's soul.

Among the various arguments for the spirituality of the soul that Augustine develops in *De Trinitate* from the fact of man's self-knowledge, the one to be presented in the following is most elaborately treated. No doubt, Augustine considered it a central proof for overcoming any materialistic conception of the soul. Let me therefore try to unfold this argument step by step, uncovering its ontological ground in the structure of man's consciousness, and thereby safeguarding it from possible misconceptions.

Augustine's basic procedure in this argument is to bring to light what we *know* about ourselves with certainty and to reject everything that we merely believe ourselves to be. In this way, he tries to show that, in case of conflict, the mind can only be what it for certain knows itself to be, and that it cannot be what it merely assumes itself to be. This absolute certainty which Augustine finds in the mind's awareness of itself, thus, is employed as the key element of the present argument.

Before discussing the nature of the mind, Augustine briefly distinguishes between thinking (*putare*) and knowing (*scire*).[69] The former is meant to refer to the kind of uncertain knowledge that is based on individual assumptions, conjectures, opinions; the latter is to designate an absolutely certain knowledge that cannot be shaken even by doubts and deceptions. This general epistemological distinction goes back at least to Plato,[70] and had been used by Augustine for his refutation of scepticism already in his early dialogues, particularly in *Contra Academicos*.[71] In the present context, however, Augustine applies this distinction directly to the mind's self-knowledge, raising the question of what it knows about itself with certainty. And he puts forth, as a thesis to be proven in the course of the argument, that when the mind considers itself, for instance, to be air, then it thinks (*putat*) that it is air which lives and understands in man, but it knows (*scit*) that it *itself* lives and understands; it does not know itself to be air, but thinks of itself so (*aerem autem se esse non scit sed putat*).[72] In other words, a materialist who regards his 'soul' to be some body, merely thinks such, while he knows for certain that it is he himself who thinks so.

That the former thought is merely an assumption can be shown from the fact that men generally had doubts and different opinions on what it is that lives, remembers, understands, wills, thinks, knows, and judges in us. Some thought it to be air, others to be fire, or the brain, or the blood, or atoms, or a fifth body unknown to Augustine;[73] again others thought it to be the arrangement of the body's organs. All of them, however, share in the same uncertainty as to what exactly the mind is. They just endeavour to put forth various opinions and conjectures, attempting to give some account of the nature of the mind.[74] Yet, despite this uncertainty, Augustine points out, every man knows for sure that *he* lives, understands, and performs all these other acts. This is not even doubted by those who differ in their opinion on whether this subject is a spirit or a body, and which type of body; all know with certainty that *they* understand, exist, and live (*omnes tamen se intellegere noverunt et esse et vivere*).[75]

In the following, this last thesis needs to be argued for in greater detail in order that the conclusion of the mind's spiritual incorporeality may eventually be drawn from it, according to Augustine's underlying principle: to remove from the mind what it thinks itself to be, and to consider only what it knows for certain (*secernat quod se putat, cernat quod scit*).[76]

The question of certainty, of gaining infallible knowledge of a truth that can no longer be doubted, has occupied Augustine's mind from the early period of his writing.[77] Already in *De Beata Vita* (386),[78] Augustine asks the doubting Navigius whether he thinks that he knows anything at all. Upon the hesitant response of the latter, Augustine continues asking him whether he knows that he is alive. Receiving as answer a firm 'yes,' Augustine replies by asking him whether he also knows that he has a body. Again, Navigius answers in the affirmative. Thus, Augustine assures his interlocutor that he can at least be certain of the fact that he consists of body and life.[79]

In a similar way, in the *Soliloquia* (387) Augustine (that is, his *ratio*) convinces himself that he must know for certain that he exists

and that he thinks. Though he does not know how he knows that
he exists, or whether he is a simple or a composite being, or
whether he is moved or not; *that* he exists and *that* he thinks he
knows to be true.[80]

The insight that I may be uncertain of everything else, but not
of my own existence and life, has been developed and elaborated
on by Augustine in his more classic, mature writings.

In the *De Libero Arbitrio*, this thought comes up at two different
places. In the first one, Evodius poses the problem to Augustine
of whether any being that lives knows of its life. To this Augustine
responds that knowledge presupposes reason which the animals
lack; even though they live, they do not know of it. Consequently,
Augustine states, not every being that lives knows that it lives,
though everything that knows that it lives lives necessarily (*non
omne quod vivit scire se vivere, quamquam omne quod se vivere sciat
vivat necessario*).[81] (Evidently, Augustine does not mean to claim
that we live *because* we know ourselves as living, as if our life were
constituted by our knowledge. His point rather is that, since we
know ourselves as living, we must live necessarily. For precisely in
order to have this certain knowledge of our living, we must live.)

At the second place, Augustine continues this line of reasoning.
If it is certain to you that you exist, Augustine explains to Evodius
– and in this certainty you cannot even be deceived, since for you
to be deceived your existence is presupposed – it must also be
certain that you live, as was shown above. Asking Evodius therefore
whether he understands (*intelligis*) that these two facts are most
true (*verissima*), Augustine, upon receiving an affirmative answer,
reveals to him that he thereby knows also a third fact, viz. that he
understands. Of these three things – his existence, his life and his
understanding – he must be so certain that he cannot even be
deceived about them.[82]

What in the last text is merely mentioned as a remark on the
side, namely that existence is the condition for the possibility of
deception, is brought out in much greater detail in what probably is
the most precise and most well-known presentation of the argument
under discussion, in *De Civitate Dei*:

> For we are and know that we are, and we love to be and to
> know that we are. Moreover, in these three things I have

mentioned, no falsity similar to truth disturbs us; for we do not come into contact with these by some bodily sense, as we perceive the things outside of us, such as colours by seeing, sounds by hearing, smells by smelling, tastes by tasting, hard and soft objects by touching, of all which sensible objects it is the incorporeal images resembling them, which we turn over in thought and hold in the memory, and which excite us to desire these objects. But, without any delusive imagination of appearances or phantasms, I am most certain that I am, and that I know it, and that I love it. In respect to these truths, I am not at all afraid of the arguments of the Academicians, who say, What if you are deceived? For if I am deceived I am. For he who does not exist, cannot be deceived; and for this reason, I am, if I am deceived. And since I am if I am deceived, how am I deceived in believing that I am? For it is certain that I am if I am deceived. Since, therefore, I, who would be the one deceived, would have to be, even if I were deceived, I am certainly not deceived in my knowledge that I am. And consequently, neither am I deceived in knowing that I know. For, as I know that I am, so I know this also, that I know.[83]

Here again, Augustine first refers to the absolute immediacy in which we are aware of our own existence. Unlike 'outside' sensible things which are perceived by means of the senses or by the mediation of mental images stored in memory, my existence is most immediately given to me. I do not know myself as existing on the basis of some 'instrumental causes.' Instead, this knowledge is as immediate as the mind is present to itself. And it is precisely this which accounts for the fact that I am most certain that I am, and that I know that I am most certain of my existence; for, as Augustine points out more explicitly elsewhere,[84] this knowledge (that I exist and that I live) is not seen with the eye of the flesh, as are sensible objects that are presented to us from without (*obiciuntur extrinsecus*) and that, for this reason, are potentially delusive for us. The kind of deception, therefore, that is intrinsic to the 'structure' of sense-perception is as such excluded from the knowledge of my own existence.

Yet, Augustine goes on wondering (in *De Civitate Dei*) whether there is any kind of deception at all that would jeopardize the certainty I have of my existence. Though I cannot be deceived in this knowledge on the grounds of false sense-information, could the Academicians (the sceptics) not object that I might be deceived in some other way, whatever this may be? Against this charge Augustine presents his famous insight: even if I am deceived, I am (*si enim fallor, sum*).

The back-bone of this argument lies in the fundamental fact that being deceived (in whichever way) necessarily presupposes existence, and that the knowledge of one's being deceived implies the knowledge of one's existence. *If* I know that I am deceived (which knowledge cannot be gained, though, *while* I am deceived), I must necessarily know that I exist; for without existence, I could neither be deceived, nor know of it. This is why Augustine can say that, since I am if I am deceived, I cannot be deceived about the fact that I am; because for a deception about that to occur, my existence is presupposed. By nature, it requires an existing subject that is to be deceived.[85]

One might generalize the crucial insight underlying the argument by stating that any mental activity essentially and necessarily implies the knowledge of the existence of its performing subject. Any mental act as such presupposes an existing mind, so that the knowledge of such an act necessarily reveals the existence of the performing mind. This existence, as will be argued for more fully in the subsequent section, is *not inferred* to from the experience of these acts. Without performing a deductive argument, I become aware of my real being *immediately* in and through the knowledge of my acts. This fundamental metaphysical and epistemological fact is exemplified by Augustine with respect to other mental acts and states.

Again with reference to possible objections by the Academicians, Augustine shows that our dreaming in sleep also requires an existing and living subject. It is no cogent charge against the certainty of my own existence to point out that I may merely dream that I live, whereas in reality I may not live at all. For, evidently, sleeping and seeing in dreams are states only of someone who lives (*et dormire et in somnis videre viventis est*).[86] Therefore, even if I became aware of my existence as a living being only in a dream, I still knew for certain that this is a knowledge not of something dreamt, but of a fully *real* fact. For dreaming necessarily presupposes living.

It is a completely different, empirical question whether one is able to perform acts of knowledge in dreams. Augustine suggests that sleep deprives only the senses of their faculty of perception, in order that the body may be restored from its labours, but that it leaves to the mind its power of sensing and understanding.[87] At another place, however, he clarifies his view stating that our reason and intellect also can be dormant in the soul or be more or less active, though the human soul as such is never anything but rational and intellectual.[88] Independently of whether or not this is a correct explanation, the fact that a man's dreaming in sleep implies his living is indubitably certain. He might not actually think of this fact in the dream; if he did, he would know it with certainty.

Augustine mentions another objection against this certainty that might be brought forth by a sceptic:[89] he could say that I am perhaps insane without knowing it, and that I am mistaken in the knowledge that I live, as similar errors are common in the case of mentally disturbed people. However, Augustine retorts, even he who is insane, lives (*qui furit vivit*); insanity presupposes life. An insane person might not know this essential truth; he might not even be aware of his own existence. And yet, as long as he is insane, he still lives. Thus, Augustine concludes, the knowledge that I live cannot be jeopardized by a thousand kinds of fallacious appearances (*mille fallacium visorum genera*), since he who is deceived, lives.[90]

The most developed passage, however, in which Augustine shows what is essentially and necessarily implied in an act of the mind, is found in *De Trinitate* in his analysis of the act of doubting, which act could be directed at our own existence. For after stating, as we saw above, that people have doubts as to whether the mind is a body, and what kind of body, Augustine applies this same doubt to man's self-knowledge:

> Who would however doubt that he lives, remembers,
> understands, wills, thinks, knows, and judges? For even if
> he doubts, he lives; if he doubts, he remembers why he doubts;
> if he doubts, he understands that he doubts; if he doubts,
> he wishes to be certain; if he doubts, he thinks; if he doubts,

he knows that he does not know something; if he doubts, he judges that he ought not to consent rashly. Whoever then doubts about anything else ought never to doubt about all of these; for if they were not, he would be unable to doubt about anything at all.[91]

Without elaborating on these various elements that are essentially implied in an act of doubting,[92] in the present section I want to draw attention to one important feature of this indubitable certainty we have of our existence – a feature that emerges quite clearly in this passage.

While in the previous texts quoted from Augustine the main emphasis was laid on proving that *I* must exist if I can perform a mental act, in this passage Augustine implicitly shows that we deal here with general essential laws that are universally valid for any concrete person. The fact that my doubting implies that I live, remember, understand, will, think, know, and judge, is not something that is true exclusively in my own case. Rather, I can understand that *whoever* doubts something should not doubt any one of these acts, without the existence of which he could not doubt anything at all (*quisque igitur alicunde dubitat de his omnibus dubitare non debet quae si non essent, de ulla re dubitare non posset*).[93]

What Augustine is analysing here is the general nature of doubt as such. It belongs essentially to the nature of doubt that the one who doubts lives, that he remembers why he doubts, that he understands that he doubts, that he wants to be certain, that he thinks in doubting, that he knows that he does not know something, that he judges that it is better not to consent without further reflection. If therefore someone truly doubts, these various acts must necessarily be implied in his doubt; otherwise, he does not doubt at all. In addition to the certainty I have of my own life, memory, understanding, etc., while I am doubting, I also understand with certainty that, since doubt as such essentially presupposes these acts, everyone who doubts is in the same way certain of himself. In fact, one could even say that the certainty I have of myself in doubting is to be attributed to the evidence from both the immediate concrete awareness of myself as a living, understanding, doubting subject, and the knowledge of the general nature of doubt insofar as it is applied to myself; for the latter is 'verified' by the particular existential awareness I have of myself in doubting. Both sources of certainty in a unique way 'interact' in the case of my own personal doubting: I know my own existence both from the inner awareness of my act of doubting as well as from the insight that any doubt as such presupposes an existing subject.[94] (In the following section, we will come back to this point when analyzing in greater detail the particular awareness of myself.)

Augustine further illuminates the difference and the relation between these two forms of knowing the human mind and its acts by distinguishing between what we specifically know of a concrete mind and what we know about the nature of the mind as such through the study of our own mind (*scire possumus quid sit animus consideratione nostri*).[95] In a very revealing passage, Augustine describes this difference between concrete empirical and abstract general knowledge of the mind:

> When the human mind, however, knows itself and loves itself, it does not know and love something immutable; each individual man, attentive to what is going on within him, speaks in one way when he expresses his own mind, but defines the human mind in a different way by a special or general cognition. Therefore, when anyone speaks to me about his own mind, as to whether he understands or does not understand this or that, or whether he wishes or does not wish this or that, I believe what he says; but when he speaks the truth about the human mind, either specially or generally, I recognize it and approve.
>
> It is, therefore, obvious that what a person sees in himself is one thing, for another does not see this but believes what the speaker tells him; but what he sees in the truth itself is another thing, for another can also behold the same thing; the former is changeable in time, while the latter remains steadfast in its unchangeable eternity. For it is not by seeing many minds with our bodily eyes that we gather, on the basis of their similarity, a general or special knowledge of the human mind; but we contemplate the inviolable truth, whence we can as perfectly as possible define, not what each man's mind is but what it ought to be in the light of the eternal reasons.[96]

The decisive differences between these two forms of knowing the human mind can be summarized thus. What I know particularly of my own or someone else's mind, such as whether or not he understands a particular thing, is something changeable in time, while my understanding of the human mind as such is of something abiding in immutable eternity (*alterum mutari per tempora, alterum incommutabili aeternitate consistere*). For the nature of the mind as such remains unchangeably and timelessly the same, whereas the specific events occurring in a particular mind are constantly varying throughout the course of time.

Furthermore, I merely believe (*credo*) someone telling me about his present interior state of mind. As I do not have an immediate access to his inner life, I can neither verify nor falsify what he tells me about himself. (I am certainly aware of the concrete happenings in my own mind; but nobody else has such a direct grasp of them.) However, when he talks to me about the human mind generally, I am able to recognize (*agnosco*) the same truth and to approve (*approbo*) of it. For this is known in the truth itself (*in ipsa veritate*) which is directly accessible to both of us. Augustine makes it explicitly clear that this general knowledge of the mind is not gained inductively on the basis of observing many minds and seeing their common nature. Rather, we behold (*intuemur*) its inviolable truth (*inviolabilem veritatem*) in the eternal reasons (*sempiternis rationibus*) in the light of which we understand how a concrete mind is to be, if it is a mind at all.[97]

The general nature of the mind, thus, is one of these eternal verities that we discussed in a previous section.[98] There we saw Augustine arguing that we perceive the *rationes aeternae* in an intellectual vision not mediated by the senses, and that we perceive all things which are made according to them in the light of their immutable and ideal nature. In the same way, with the eye of the mind we behold in that eternal truth also the form according to which we are (*in illa igitur aeterna veritate ... formam secundum quam sumus ... visu mentis aspicimus*).[99] We see ourselves and any other mind as participating in this universal form, so that we can, from the study of our own minds, attain to a knowledge of other minds, if what we discovered in us is not a part of our empirically changeable nature, but belongs to us *essentially*. Therefore, in knowing for certain that *my* doubting necessarily presupposes *my* existence, I also understand that this must be the case in each person; for it belongs to the very nature of both the mind and doubt that an actual act of doubting must be performed by an existing mind.

Moreover, Augustine points out (in *De Vera Religione*) that whoever understands that he is doubting, understands with certainty something that is *true*, namely that he is doubting. He is certain, therefore, of a truth (*de vero ergo certus est*). And by this very same knowledge, he also overcomes his doubt as to whether there is truth as such (*utrum sit veritas*). For since he knows one true fact with certainty, he also knows that truth exists, since nothing is true unless it is true through truth (*nec ullum verum nisi veritate verum est*).[100] Hence, in knowing our own doubting as a true fact we do not only gain an understanding of the general essential relation between a mind and its acts, but we also realize that this one true fact shatters any doubt as to the existence of truth as such; for whatever is true must 'contain' truth in order to be true.[101]

Though this argument alone would suffice to uproot any sceptical doubt about truth, Augustine refers still to another, more formally logical argument for the existence of truth based on the indubitable certainty I have of myself. He shows that in knowing my own existence as true, I implicitly know an innumerable number of true facts, since the knowledge that I exist implies the knowledge that I know that I exist, and so *ad infinitum*. This infinity of truths which are most certain (*certissime*), cannot possibly be comprehended and expressed by myself. They are necessarily implied in the one certain knowledge I have of my existence, without me thinking and stating them.[102]

On the basis of this certainty we have of ourselves Augustine develops an argument for the incorporeality of the mind that has since become perhaps his most celebrated one:[103]

> The mind however is certain about itself, as is clearly shown
> from what we have already said. But it is by no means
> certain whether it is air, or fire, or some body, or anything of
> a body. It is, therefore, none of these things. And it belongs
> to that whole which is commanded to know itself, to be certain
> that it is none of those things of which it is uncertain, and

to be certain that it is only that which alone it is certain of to be.

For the mind thinks in this way of fire, as it thinks of air and any other bodily thing; but it can in no way happen that it should think that which itself is, in the same way as it thinks that which itself is not. For it thinks all of these through an imaginary phantasy, whether fire, or air, or this or that body, or that part or combination or harmony of the body; nor is it said to be all of these, but one of them. But if it were any one of them, it would think this one in a different manner than the rest, that is, not through an imaginary phantasy, as absent things themselves or something of the same kind are thought which have been touched by the sense of the body; but it would think it by a kind of inward presence not feigned but real (for there is nothing more present to it than itself), in the same way as it thinks that it lives, and remembers, and understands, and wills. For it knows these things in itself; it does not imagine them as if it had touched them outside of itself by its sense, as corporeal things are touched. And if it adds nothing from these thoughts to itself, so as to have an opinion of itself as of something of this kind, then whatever still remains to it, that alone is itself.[104]

Here we get a sense of the sharpness and enthusiasm with which Augustine deals with philosophical problems. Discovering basic underlying principles, he rigorously draws out their conclusions with admirable clarity.

One such principle on which the whole argument rests is expressed in the seemingly tautological statement that the mind is certain that it is only that of which alone it is certain to be (*idque solum esse se certa sit quod solum esse se certa est*). This does not mean that the mind is merely what it knows of itself, as if it had a full comprehension of itself (an objection to be posed at the end of this section). Rather, it means that the mind can only *be* the being which it knows itself to be with certainty, and not a being about which it has merely an opinion. Hence, in analyzing what is essentially implied in such certain knowledge and in excluding from it what is only assumed, Augustine is able to show conclusively what the mind is, or at least, what it cannot be.[105]

As we saw Augustine arguing throughout this section, in self-knowledge the mind knows itself to be existing, living, understanding, with a certainty that is stronger than any possible deception and doubt; for even if it were deceived and doubted its own being, it would necessarily have to exist (and to perform all those acts that are essentially implied in doubt). This it knows with indubitable certainty that *it*, that is, the mind itself, must exist and function as the performing subject of all its acts, of whatever kind they may be.

However, as to the *nature* of this 'something' (the mind) that it knows to exist, the mind is uncertain. Whether it be fire, air, or some other body or bodily organ, people have different opinions. There is no absolutely certain knowledge that it is, let us say, the brain; for this 'knowledge' could immediately be doubted, without the act of doubting as such testifying to its truth. Instead, these opinions on what the mind is are gained through an imaginary phantasy (*per phantasiam imaginariam*). Men think and imagine it to be this or that body. In the same way as they have before their minds the images of those bodies which they have once perceived sensibly, so they have in them the various assumptions about what may be the nature of the mind.[106]

Yet, as Augustine formulates another principle similar to that about certainty just mentioned, it can in no way happen that the mind thinks that which itself is, in the same way as it thinks that which itself is not (*neque ullo modo fieri posset ut ita cogitaret id quod ipsa est quemadmodum cogitat id quod ipsa non est*). In other words, the mind cannot *be* that of which it thinks in a different way than it thinks of itself. And it thinks of its nature to be fire, air, brain, or another body, as Augustine just showed, by some imaginary phantasy, which is further proven by the very fact that people have *various* opinions on the nature of their minds. For as all minds think of themselves in the same way, and as each man has only one mind, people would necessarily have to agree that the mind is one specific kind of body, unless these opinions really are the results of imaginary thinking. For otherwise, the very variety of views of the mind could not be explained.

In reality, however, the mind thinks of itself, as Augustine summarizes his discussion of the real self-presence of the mind which we presented earlier, by a certain interior presence that is not feigned but real (*quadam interiore non simulata sed vera prae-sentia*); for nothing, not even its own images, is more present to itself than itself. Consequently, the fact that *it* lives, remembers, understands, wills, the mind knows most immediately, since it is the same mind, being most truly present to itself, that knows these acts being performed by itself.

From these considerations the conclusion of the mind's incorpor-eality can be drawn in two ways: (1) since the mind, being really present to itself, thinks of itself most immediately, while it thinks of its alleged bodily nature through some imaginative represen-tations, it cannot *be* a body – according to the principle that it cannot be that of which it thinks in a different way than it thinks of itself; (2) since the mind, due to its real self-presence and due to its knowledge of the general nature of the mind as such, is indubitably certain of the fact that *it* exists, lives, understands, etc., but since it merely believes (*putat*) that it is a body, it cannot itself be a body; for the mind, being certain of *itself*, cannot be that of which it is uncertain. Therefore, it can only be itself, and not a corporeal being. Thus, Augustine concludes, when the mind subtracts from itself all images and thoughts in the light of which it has formed opinions about itself, and considers only what it truly knows of itself, then whatever remains to it of itself, that alone is itself (*quidquid ei de se remanet hoc solum ipsa est*).[107]

With this conclusion, Augustine fulfills the maxim underlying his philosophy of mind, indeed his entire philosophy as such: to look at the reality in question as it is given to us truly, and to reject all conceptions of it that are derived from sources outside of itself.[108] If we apply this method to the study of the mind, we will understand that it cannot be a corporeal entity.

And yet, there are a number of objections that could be raised against Augustine's reasoning. One could, first of all, ask whether those people that (rightly) hold the mind to be incorporeal think such to be the case on the basis of opinions and mental imaginations that are also as uncertain as any materialistic view of the mind. The very distinction between the manner of thinking of oneself and that of thinking of one's nature, which was employed to reject any assumption of the mind being some kind of body, could thus be suggested as disproving the incorporeality of the mind; for the latter would be just as well founded on an assumed opinion.

Similarly, when we reflect upon what we actually know about our nature we find that there are immense mysteries in us. Augustine, in answer to a certain Vincentius Victor who had accused him of his expressed ignorance about the origin of the soul comparing him to the cattle, devoted a considerable portion of his book on this question[109] to showing that there are many more things about man that we cannot comprehend. We do not know the exact structure of our body; we do not know how the pulsations in the veins are affected or why we can move some bodily members without being able to move others; we do not fully know the powers of our own memory, understanding, will – which ignorance Augustine uncovers by using some interesting examples.[110] Though we are most certain (*certissimi sumus*) *that* we remember, understand, will, we are entirely ignorant of *what* these acts are and what their corresponding faculties are capable of;[111] still, it is we ourselves that we cannot comprehend (*nos sumus, qui nos comprehendere non valeamus*), though we are certainly not outside of ourselves (*certe non sumus extra nos*).[112] If then our own nature is a great question to us,[113] how could we know our mind to be incorporeal, or even spiritual, merely from the certain fact of our existence? This spiritual incorporeality could as well be one of those characteristics of our nature that are ultimately incomprehensible to us.

Also in the light of the fact that, as Augustine marvels, God is more intimately present to me than I myself (*interior intimo meo*), knowing me better than I do,[114] could it not be possible that only God knows what my mind really is and that this knowledge is not accessible to me? He alone has a grasp of my true nature, while my own self-knowledge is not only limited, but is also subject to the various opinions, and in fact deceptions, I have of myself.[115]

In fact, could the objection, under the influence of Kant[116] or the later Husserl,[117] not be pushed so far as to claim the complete impossibility of us grasping our own self *as it is*? If it is true that what I know in self-reflection to be myself is an '*Erscheinung des innern Sinnes*' and not the real 'I' existing as such, as empirical psychology makes us believe, and that the actual 'transcendental I' is as such beyond our experience and not knowable,[118] then the very basis of Augustine's argument is destroyed. Under this assumption, I would not be certain of *myself* as really existing, but only of an appearance of myself; I would not attain to my own reality, but I would merely be certain of having an image of myself that is co-constituted by the structure of my subjectivity. I could thus never know whether *I* am an incorporeal spiritual subject, or just a kind of body. My actual, really existing 'I' would simply be unknown to me.

These objections reveal the need for a deeper uncovering of the grounds on which the argument under discussion is founded. In order to do so, we have to ask Augustine whether he can provide for a faculty or a feature of the mind that, despite the objections, would show both that man does know himself most certainly as being incorporeal and indeed spiritual, and that this knowledge is really of *himself* as he is in himself.

4 Inward self-awareness *(se nosse)*

In the last section reference was made to an incompleteness implied in Augustine's argument for the spiritual incorporeality of the mind as it was presented from the indubitable certainty that the mind has of itself. Man's self-knowledge is imperfect, in that he is unable to understand his own nature fully and in that he is inevitably open to various deceptions about himself, having images of himself that do not necessarily correspond to what he truly is.[119] Nay, it has even been claimed that man does not know his own real 'I' at all. In the light of these observations and doubts, the validity of Augustine's argument needs to be re-investigated in the attempt to ground it eventually on a firmer footing.

(A) Augustine's analysis of 'se nosse'

In the introductory line of his argument quoted in the preceding section, Augustine states that the certainty the mind has of itself has clearly been shown from what he had already shown previously.[120] This reference goes back to the very beginning of his discussion of self-knowledge in Book X of *De Trinitate*. There, in Chapter 3, Augustine tries to show that the mind does have some kind of knowing awareness of itself, even if it is ignorant and still in search of itself (as to its actual nature). The basic structure of this argument is presented here since it is fundamentally significant for our problem of man's self-certainty.

Augustine takes his starting point in the question of what the mind loves when it seeks to know itself while it is still unknown to itself.[121] In other words, how can man's desire (love) to know himself, which presupposes his ignorance of himself, be accounted for, since the very fact of having the desire shows that he must have some knowledge of himself; for obviously, and as Augustine points out, it is most certain that nothing can be loved unless it is known.[122] Thus, Augustine raises the question of the possibility of the love for self-knowledge. He considers various explanations, until he eventually succeeds in finding a most peculiar form of self-knowledge that resolves this seemingly paradoxical problem.[123]

A first possible explanation is that the mind desires to know itself because it knows and has heard of the beauty of other minds; from them it has formed an image of itself so that it is known to itself generically (*genere ipso sibi nota est*).[124] However, to know a generic image of the beauty of minds as such, is not identical with the concrete *self*-knowledge that is presupposed for its desire to know itself, precisely because the former is of an image taken from the knowledge of other minds, and not of itself.[125] But why is it that the mind can know other minds without knowing itself, since nothing can be more present to itself than itself?[126]

Before Augustine directly addresses the importance of this unique self-presence of the mind for the problem under discussion, he investigates further possibilities of explaining the fact of the mind's desire to know itself in a state of being ignorant of itself.

The mind may see in the reason of the eternal truth (*in ratione veritatis aeternae*) how beautiful it is to know itself, desiring to realize this knowledge in itself.[127] Yet, this explanation also does not account for the fact that in desiring to know itself the mind must have a knowledge of *itself* (and not of eternal verities about itself), though it is very remarkable, Augustine states, how it does not know itself while knowing how beautiful it is to know itself.[128] (In the preceding section, we touched on the intimate relation between the knowledge of the general nature of the mind and its concrete self-knowledge.)

Or does the mind desire to know itself, Augustine continues, because it has some kind of secret remembrance (*quandam occultam memoriam*) of being destined to a final blessedness which it believes that it can reach only by knowing itself? But in this case again, the desire for knowing itself is not based on an actual self-knowledge but on an interior orientation to happiness, which might be given in the mind without the former.[129]

Finally, approaching his central point Augustine wonders whether it could be the case that the mind when loving to know itself does not love itself, which it does not yet know, but loves knowing itself (*non se quam nondum novit sed ipsum nosse amat*). But if so, is it possible to love (and to know) the *knowing* of itself without knowing itself?[130]

In a very revealing way, Augustine then argues, first, that the mind does know its own knowing (which is presupposed for loving the knowing of itself in a state of being still in search of itself), and secondly, that precisely in knowing its own knowing it knows itself:

> But where does it know its own knowing, if it does not know itself? For it knows that it knows other things, but does not know itself; therefore, it also knows what knowing is. How then does that which does not know itself, know itself as knowing something? For it does not know another mind as knowing, but itself. Therefore, it knows itself. Thus, when it seeks to know itself, it already knows itself as seeking itself. Therefore, it already knows itself. Hence, it cannot be altogether ignorant of itself, since it certainly knows itself, insofar as it knows that it does not know itself. But if it does not know that it does not know itself, then it does not seek itself in order to know itself. And, therefore, the very fact that it seeks itself clearly shows that it is more known than unknown to itself. For it knows itself as seeking and not knowing, while it seeks to know itself.[131]

From the fact that the mind knows that it knows other things it follows that it also knows what knowing is. For, as Augustine states elsewhere, one could not even say that one knows or does not know without knowing what it is to know.[132] But if the mind knows its own knowing, is it possible that it does not know itself?

Addressing this question Augustine shows that it is precisely in knowing its own knowing that the mind knows *itself* as knowing. For it does not know another mind as knowing, but itself (*neque enim alteram mentem scientem scit sed se ipsam*). The very fact that it knows its own knowing (of something) implies the knowledge of *itself* as knower. And the same holds for seeking to know itself, which Augustine used as his starting point. For in so doing, the mind knows *itself* as seeking to know itself. Though being ignorant about itself (since otherwise it would not seek to know itself), it knows itself insofar as it knows *itself as* not knowing itself. In seeking to know itself the mind knows itself as seeking and as not knowing (*novit enim se quaerentem atque nescientem dum se quaerit ut noverit*).[133]

We find here a most peculiar form of *self*-knowledge that is based on the awareness that in performing an act of knowledge, indeed even of seeking to know my own nature, I know *myself*, and no other self, as performing these acts: I am aware of myself *as* being their performing subject.

Augustine explicitly distinguishes this form of inward self-awareness from the direct grasp of myself in self-reflection: it is one thing not to know oneself, and another thing not to think of oneself (*aliud sit non se nosse, aliud non se cogitare*).[134] I may not think of myself reflexively (*se cogitare*), but this does not mean that I do not know myself inwardly (*se nosse*). In a very peculiar way, I am aware of myself as performing subject of my acts during their performance, in a manner quite different from how I directly reflect upon myself.

Though Augustine does not further elaborate on the distinctness, and the relation, of these two kinds of self-knowledge, in the light of both our earlier discussion of the act of *se cogitare* and the present argument for the givenness of such inward self-awareness (*se nosse*) it is not difficult to develop this point. For in introducing his argument presented above Augustine distinguishes precisely between the explicitly thematic understanding of the mind (*se cogitare*), which, for the sake of the argument, he assumes not to be given but sought for, and the *se nosse*, which is also found precisely in the absence of the former. Because *se nosse* is *not* an actual 'bending back' upon myself, in which act I am both subject and direct intentional object of the same act of explicit cognition, it is independent of whether or not the implicit intention for self-*knowledge* is 'fulfilled.' Rather, it is the very fact that I perform an act at all, whether it is an act of actual knowing or seeking to know myself, that provides the basis of the self-awareness in the sense of *se nosse*. For in and through performing such an act I am aware of myself as performing it; in fact, I am aware of both *my act* of seeking to know, or actually knowing, myself and of *myself as* doing so. Hence the difference and the relation between these two forms of being related to oneself. (Certainly, the experience of *se nosse* is not exclusively given in acts of self-knowledge [*se cogitare*]. For obviously, I am aware of any act that is performed by myself in this peculiar inward manner.)

Before addressing the question of the significance of this inward self-awareness (*se nosse*) for Augustine's argument for the spiritual incorporeality of the mind presented in the preceding section, it may be illuminating to give a sketch of the most subtle phenomeno-logical elaboration and development of this aspect of Augustine's anthropology known to the present writer, in K. Wojtyla's book *The Acting Person*.[135] For in this way, the phenomenon of *se nosse*, with which Augustine deals more as a presupposition of his argu-ment than as a direct object of philosophical analysis,[136] may be better understood, especially with respect to that 'quasi-intentional' cognitive manner of being related to oneself that is found in it. For this reason the following excursion into Wojtyla's thought seems permissible in our general context.

(B) *Excursion into Wojtyla's notion of consciousness*

Within the main intention of Wojtyla's book, viz. to understand man as a personal being through or by means of his conscious, free actions, the analysis of human consciousness plays an important role. It is in and through consciousness that man becomes aware of his actions and of himself. But how is this becoming aware of his inner being to be explained? How are we conscious of ourselves even before we explicitly reflect upon ourselves?

Wojtyla begins his analysis of consciousness by distinguishing between 'conscious acting' and the 'consciousness of acting': 'one is used attributively, when reference is made to conscious acting; the other is employed as a noun, which may be the subject, when the reference is to the consciousness of acting'.[137] We may say that the attributive usage of 'conscious' refers to the fact that the person is consciously present in his acts. They become part of his consciousness, which they as conscious entities immanently and constitutively presuppose and imply. The person *lives* them consciously as constitutive 'parts' of his actual conscious life.

Distinct from this consciousness as immanent constituent of the person's act is the consciousness *of* acting. In this sense, consciousness is used as a noun and means the person's consciousness of his acts as well as of himself as their performing agent:

> Indeed, man not only acts consciously, but he is also aware of both the fact that he is acting and the fact that it is he who is acting – hence he has the awareness of the action as well as of the person in their dynamic interrelation.[138]

Thus, both senses of consciousness interrelate in that man is conscious *of* his acts as they, in turn, imply himself as living them; only because they are parts of his conscious life can they be known both as his *acts* and as *his* acts.

It is the consciousness in the substantival (noun related) sense through which we are aware *of* our acts and *of* us acting, that is of special interest for our purposes in this context.

Wojtyla distinguishes two functions this consciousness (as a noun) fulfills with respect to conscious acts, prior to and independent of any explicit self-knowledge through reflection. The first function consists in what he calls the 'reflecting' or the 'mirroring' of our conscious acts as they are being performed by us. Consciousness in this function acts in a manner analogous to a mirror, reflecting our conscious activity 'from within.' Through consciousness we are aware of ourselves living a conscious act and of this act itself. This awareness is given, Wojtyla points out, as preceding, accompanying and succeeding the act.[139] What he seems to mean is that we can be aware of an act in three ways: by our anticipation of the act *before* it is performed, by the present awareness of it *while* it is being performed, and by the enduring experience of it *after* its performance. As we have, within the context of discussing Augustine's *distentio animi*, already dealt with the peculiar relation consciousness has to time, we will concentrate here on the function of consciousness as mirroring conscious acts *during* their performance.

The mirroring of our conscious acts while they are being performed is not to be understood strictly in terms of the mirror-phenomenon occurring in the material world. We have already seen why the act of explicit self-reflection cannot be explained in the light of corporeal mirror-reflections. In a similar way, this accompanying consciousness of our acts also does not perform its reflecting function simply like a mirror, but 'in its own peculiar manner [it] permeates and illuminates all it mirrors,'[140] and it '*interiorizes* in its own specific manner what it mirrors, thus encapsulating or capturing it in the person's ego.'[141]

Wojtyla seems to point here at the fact that this inward awareness we have of ourselves performing our acts is not a mere 'reflection' somehow happening 'automatically.' This awareness implies rather a *conscious* 'having' of our acts in which we are aware of them *in the light* of our general state of consciousness (as when we perform an act 'in good or in bad conscience'), and in which they are kept and stored in consciousness. Unlike a mirror, consciousness reflects a conscious act in the light or against the background of our ongoing conscious life; we become aware of this act within the broader context of our general state of consciousness. And this awareness is not only given to us in the performance of our acts, but it is also 'interiorized' in consciousness in a manner in which no image is kept in a mirror. A mirror reflects what is momentarily present to it without storing it in any way; however, the accompanying awareness of our acts is kept in consciousness, which is manifest from the fact that we can explicitly 'bend back' upon it subsequent to its actual performance, as we will discuss shortly.

But the conscious contact that is realized in the mirroring function of consciousness is not identical with the manner in which we are commonly related to an object of knowledge. Usually, the object known stands over against us; we 'look at' it intentionally and frontally, having it put, so to speak, in the focal point of our attention. When we are aware of ourselves and of our acts through the mirroring function of consciousness, however, we are conscious of these objects not directly and explicitly (intentionally), but inwardly in a 'quasi-intentional' manner. For this accompanying awareness of ourselves as performing conscious acts is not an explicitly cognitive relation to ourselves, as when we render ourselves an object of direct self-reflection. On the other hand, through the mirroring function of consciousness we are given to ourselves in a manner analogous to an intentional conscious relation; for we (and our acts) are reflected by consciousness *as if* we were its object standing somehow over against it. This 'quasi-intentional' distance between consciousness and the objects reflected by it (viz. ourselves, our acts) accounts for the fact that consciousness is able to perform some cognitive function in its mirroring; for since the subject-object relation, essentially implied in any knowledge, is in a peculiar way still preserved in it, we are able to gain some cognitive, though not explicitly conceptual, understanding of ourselves and our acts. As Josef Seifert says in explaining Wojtyla,

> consciousness in the substantival sense has some sort of 'cognitive function' and implies a getting acquainted with our conscious acts *as if* they were objects of our consciousness, without them, however, being actually objects over against our consciousness.[142]

The second function of consciousness that Wojtyla terms the reflexive function fulfills a quite different, though complementary, task. While in the first, the refle*c*tive, function our conscious being (as being reflected) assumes the position of an *object* that is known of through consciousness in this peculiar 'quasi-intentional' manner, the second function of consciousness allows us to experience our acts *as our own* acts. The distance that enables the former to gain some cognitive awareness *of* ourselves and our acts during their performance, is now bridged by this most intimate experiential awareness of ourselves as *subject* of our acts: 'Consciousness allows us not only to have an inner view of our actions (immanent perception) and of their dynamic dependence on the ego, but also to *experience these actions as actions and as our own*' (author's emphasis).[143]

In the performance of our acts, not only do we have, prior to any *explicit* self-reflection, a preliminary knowing contact with ourselves and our acts (in which they are in some quasi-intentional fashion *objects* of knowledge), but we also experience ourselves most inwardly as the *subject* performing our acts. Consciousness reflecting ourselves and our acts as objects (first function) now reveals them to us as belonging to our own subjectivity (second function); they are not simply its (neutral) objects, but are experienced as our own subjective acts. Thus, the quasi-intentional cognitive subject-object duality implied in the first function is overcome in that the object is experientially manifested as being or as belonging to the same subjectivity as the subject in a completely 'distanceless' manner.

This inward experience of ourselves *as subject* is closely related to consciousness in the adjectival sense, mentioned above, as immanent constitutive element of our conscious acts; indeed, it seems to imply the latter. For it is precisely in living our own acts consciously (adjectival sense) that we experience ourselves as subject of these acts, due to the second, reflexive, function of consciousness. Our lived presence *in* our acts is the condition for our becoming aware of *ourselves* 'in the role' of subject of our acts. By interiorly experiencing ourselves and our acts, consciousness (in its second function) reveals to us the subjectiveness of what it reflects as part of our own personal being.

It is through this inward awareness of ourselves as subject that we truly experience ourselves as an 'I,' as the ego that not only *is* the subject of its acts (ontologically), but that is also aware of itself being this subject:

> To *be* a subject (suppositum) and to *experience* oneself as a subject are two completely different dimensions. Only in the latter one do we encounter the reality proper to the human 'I.' Precisely in making up this second dimension of the personal subjectivity of man, consciousness plays a key constitutive role. One could also say that because of consciousness the human suppositum becomes and manifests itself as the human I.[144]

The experience of myself as subject of my acts, thus, reveals to me my real personal 'ego-ness': I experience myself as an 'I,' as the subject that performs my conscious acts. Still, the question remains how Wojtyla sees the two functions of consciousness as well as consciousness as the immanent constitutive of our acts to be related to self-knowledge (*se cogitare* in Augustine's terminology). How do they depend on or presuppose each other?

Self-knowledge is understood by Wojtyla in the same Augustinian sense that we discussed earlier, namely as the act of explicitly 'bending back' upon oneself, placing oneself in one's own sight. This act, though unique with respect to its identity of subject and object, is as intentional as any other act of knowledge: I grasp myself as an intentional object standing over against myself. And as such an explicitly intentional act, self-knowledge (like any *conscious* act) implies the conscious presence of myself *in* itself as its constitutive element. I consciously live my act of self-knowledge which therefore is also mirrored by consciousness through its reflec-*t*ive function. Like any other conscious act, I know also the act of self-knowledge during its performance in this peculiar manner. And due to the reflexive function of consciousness I am aware that this act is really *my* act, and that it is really *myself* who performs it. Though I am consciously (intentionally) directed only at myself as object of self-knowledge, I am inwardly aware (through the two functions of consciousness) both of this act of self-knowledge that implies myself as subject gazing at myself as object, and of myself as performing this act of self-knowledge and as being thought of in this act. In this sense, self-knowledge (the conscious act) can be seen to precede its being mirrored by consciousness in that it is presupposed for the latter.[145]

Yet in another sense, self-knowledge follows on the functions of consciousness. For I can 'objectivize,' that is, make an object of explicit self-knowledge, what has been reflected by consciousness. Since consciousness, as was pointed out, does not simply mirror my acts, but interiorizes them as *my* acts, I am able to place them (as they are 'contained' in consciousness) directly in my own intentional gaze:

> When man is conscious of his acting, he also knows he is acting; indeed, he knows he is *acting consciously*. He is aware of being conscious and of acting consciously. Self-knowledge has as its object not only the person and the action, but also the person as being *aware* of himself and *aware* of his action. This awareness is objectivized by self-knowledge.[146]

However, as the relation between consciousness and its object (myself, my acts) is not fully intentional, but 'quasi-intentional,' I cannot 'extend' this relation into explicit self-knowledge; rather, a new act is required *subsequent* to their being mirrored by consciousness. It is precisely what consciousness *has* mirrored that I reflect upon.

Thus summarizing Wojtyla's analysis we find that I am inwardly aware of my conscious acts and of myself as living and performing them. Even though I do not intentionally 'bend back' upon myself in the performance of these acts, I am cognitively aware of them in this quasi-intentional manner 'from within' (first function of consciousness), and I experience them as *my* acts being performed by myself (second function). This experiential awareness is always given whenever I perform a conscious act, that is, whenever I as conscious subject live *in* the act.

(C) Answer to objections and restatement of Augustine's argument for the spiritual incorporeality of the mind

These elaborations may have shed further light on the kind of self-awareness that Augustine means by *se nosse*, that is, that according to which we know ourselves *as* knowing (or *as* seeking to know) something, without explicitly thinking of ourselves (*se cogitare*). And it is in virtue of this inward knowledge that Augustine can maintain the indubitable certainty we have of our own existence,[147] and can argue from that for the spiritual incorporeality of the mind.

When Augustine, in response to the possible sceptical charge that we might still be deceived in, and may doubt, the immediate givenness of our own existence, retorts that even deception and doubt testify to this existence, he invites the sceptic precisely to *perform* a conscious act, that of self-deception and of doubt, trying to lead him thereby to realize that it is *he* who is deceived about himself and who doubts. The act of doubting, if it is to be a *real* doubting, presupposes him as its conscious subject; otherwise, there would be no doubt at all. And it is only a really existing subject, something that is not, let us say, an imagined literary figure or a 'dream-person,' that can really doubt. For to doubt something really, that is, to perform a real conscious act of doubting, is possible only for a real subject. A novel-figure that 'exists' merely in the mind of its 'creator' cannot really doubt, nor perform any other act of actual thinking; if it did, it would be a real person and not an element of someone's imagination.

This essential law that real acts of doubt (or actually performed acts in general) imply a really existing subject is verified by the *experience* of my own personal doubting. The sceptic who accepts Augustine's challenge and doubts that he exists, realizes in the very act of his doubt that it is really *he* who doubts and that this 'he' really exists; for *he* doubts *really*. In performing the act of doubting his own existence, he becomes aware, with indubitable certainty, of the very existence that he doubts, however in a quite different way. For the fact that he does not exist is thought of (*cogitari*) in the sense that it is a direct object of his thinking; it stands before his mind in some intentional distance, presenting itself as an object to be considered and deliberated about. However, his act of doubt and deliberation itself is not known to him by being directly reflected upon, but inwardly through what Augustine calls *se nosse* and what Wojtyla has described in his discussion of the two functions of consciousness. For this reason, the former can be doubted, while the latter, viz. the act of doubt itself implying the performing subject, is known with certainty.[148]

Thus, in addition to his intellectual insight that a real conscious act must be performed by a real subject, in and through the concrete actual performance of such a conscious act he also *experiences* himself as such a real subject. He is in actual contact with a reality that does not stand before his mind in an intentional cognitive distance, but that he knows most immediately to be real: himself. One could say that man in the very performance of a conscious act becomes experientially aware of his own actualization of reality, of his own being really real. This awareness is not thought of, but is indubitably given in this unique manner of *se nosse*.[149]

In a previous section on the self-presence of the mind to itself we have already seen how Augustine argues that there can be nothing more present to the mind than itself, and this to itself alone. Now we have to understand that it is this self-presence that is the ontological ground and the condition for the possibility of *se nosse*, through which the former becomes experientially manifest; or, as one could even say, *se nosse is* the mind's self-presence insofar as it is consciously experienced.

The real self-presence of the mind to itself that Augustine refers to, is given only in my immediate inward experience of myself as performing subject of my acts. For even when I intentionally reflect upon myself (*se cogitare*) I am related to myself in some cognitive distance that as such allows for the possibility of being deceived. I may not think of myself as I really am, but merely of an image I have formed of myself; I may variously change my mind about myself depending on my moods and feelings, etc. The cognitive (non-ontological) distance between subject and object of self-knowledge as such 'gives room' to potential self-deceptions, conditioning the possibility of aberrations from the true reality of the object (self) to be known. In this sense, self-knowledge is never fully certain for man.[150]

Yet, there is a sense in which self-knowledge does attain to indubitable certainty, namely precisely when it is the thematic explication of the experience of *se nosse* (as well as of the certain grasp of the eternal verities about the mind discussed previously). For in this case, it subsequently 'objectivizes' an experience that essentially excludes the possibility of deception. Because *se nosse* does not imply the cognitive distance characteristic of *se cogitare*, realizing instead the most immediate real contact I can have to myself, I cannot consciously 'escape' my *real* self. Any such attempt implies the reality of *myself*, since the more I doubt and think about the possibility of being deceived about myself, the more do I become aware and certain of *myself* as doubting such. When self-knowledge, therefore, is based on *se nosse*, which is what underlies Augustine's statement 'I know that I exist,'[151] it itself 'participates' in the certainty implied in the latter. In fact, in this case both forms of relating to myself interact in that self-knowledge renders thematically *cognitive* the 'quasi-intentional' relation of *se nosse*, thereby itself becoming indubitably certain; both complement each other, together achieving the possibility of an explicitly thematic, and absolutely certain, self-knowledge.

It is in the light of these clarifications that the objections against the certainty of self-knowledge mentioned at the end of the preceding section can be answered, and thus the way cleared for a more cogent restatement of Augustine's argument for the spiritual incorporeality of the mind based on this certainty.

(1) It was objected that there are many things in me that I do not and cannot comprehend, as for instance the exact power of my memory or the actual strength of my will, and that this ignorance would jeopardize the certainty of self-knowledge. To this objection it can now be responded that it is precisely not a supposed certainty of explicit conceptual knowledge of the self and of its faculties that is maintained (which, as the objection rightly points out, is not given to man); rather, the self-certainty in question is gained in a completely different manner of experience, in the manner of *se nosse*. For this experience, which could subsequently be rendered explicitly cognitive, manifests the *reality of myself* with indubitable certainty.

(2) Also the mysterious fact that, as Augustine says, God is more interiorly present to me than I to myself, is no charge against this self-certainty. For even though God does know me better than I myself, since He possesses an absolute immediate grasp of the very depths of my being,[152] He *cannot* share in the inward experience I have of myself as performing subject of my conscious acts. In *this* way, I *alone* am able to experience myself really. For on the one hand, this follows from the facts that, as Augustine points out, the mind knows (*novit*) nothing as it knows that which is present to itself, and that nothing is more present to itself than it is to itself.[153] On the other hand, it becomes also clear when one thinks of our 'negative' feelings; for certainly, God cannot actually and really have the experience, for instance, of being desperate, evil-minded, hateful, or of an evil (or good) conscience, in the same manner as I do. In this manner, I alone am aware of *my* experiences. (This is not to suggest a lack of cognitive powers on God's part; rather, it is to emphasize and to throw into greater relief the irreplaceable individuality of the mind which is experientially made manifest in *se nosse*, as we will see more fully in Chapter 4.)

(3) Finally, with respect to the idealistic claim that what is given to us in inner experience as 'I' is an appearance of the inner sense while the real 'transcendental' I is unknowable to us, Augustine provides sufficient insight into the nature of man for showing that such a position is untenable, if it means to imply that the 'real I' is never given in any inner experience. For certainly a full cognitive grasp of ourselves in our ultimate dimensions is not given to us (as it is given only to God), which is a consequence of our being limited in our knowing powers. However, the claim that the object of self-experience is an appearance, and not a reality in itself, can be rejected on the grounds of the faculty of *se nosse*, and this in basically two ways.

First, though it is certainly possible, as we pointed out earlier, that self-knowledge in the sense of self-reflection (*se cogitare*) can have as its object images and appearances of the self, *that* to which these images appear can itself not be an appearance of something. For in order to be an appearance at all, a *real* conscious subject is presupposed *to* whom it appears, that is, a subject that precisely does not have this very weak mode of being proper to an appearance, viz. the 'heteronomous existence' of being exclusively *as* object of consciousness (in which weak sense, however, even an appearance can be considered to have reality), but that *is* really ('autonomously'), being as conscious subject the condition for the possibility of any appearance. Without it, there can be no appearance of the self, as Kant assumes. And it is precisely this real subject, I myself, that I am aware of, through the experience of *se nosse*, *as* that to whom something appears. Precisely in having an appearance of myself (Kant's starting point), I know *myself* as really existing; for without being real, I could not have such an appearance, and I could not know of my appearance without knowing (in the sense of *se nosse*) of my real self as that subject to whom it appears. This awareness must necessarily be implied in the awareness of having an appearance. We find the same thing – *ceteris paribus* – in the act of doubting, analyzed above.

Secondly, if I know of myself as *having* an appearance, it follows from what we just pointed out that the awareness *of* myself (*se nosse*) cannot be that of an appearance, precisely because I myself am no appearance. In fact, it seems that the 'quasi-intentional' object of *se nosse* could never *be* an appearance, but only a *really* 'autonomously' existing subject. For the experience of *se nosse* is possible at all exclusively in the very act of performing a conscious act which presupposes the reality (not the appearance) of the performing subject. I can only be aware of myself *as* performing an act (*se nosse*), insofar as I am really existing; if 'I' were merely an appearance, there would be no experience of *se nosse*, which there certainly is.

Thus, it seems from these two considerations that Kant and other idealistic thinkers see only one kind of cognitive relation man has to himself, viz. direct self-reflection (if not even this is denied as in Fichte), on the basis of which alone their conclusions can validly be drawn. However, they apparently fail to grasp this, in a sense, more fundamental form of self-awareness that Augustine terms *se nosse*. For when this is seen and experienced in its full importance, there can be no doubt that through it I am in contact with my really existing self; for, to summarize the argument, even if I doubted whether 'I' might be an appearance, I would be aware of really myself actually doubting. In doubting *really*, I know myself as really, not apparently, existing.[154]

It may be added here that the reality of a free will in man is also revealed in a special way through this faculty of *se nosse*. For since during the performance of my acts I am aware of myself really, also in acts of willing I experience my *real* self as their performing subject, and this with the same indubitable certainty with which I am aware of myself as performing other acts.[155] And if this act of my own real willing is analyzed, it reveals that this 'real I' wills freely in the sense that it possesses a determining power over itself that is experienced as most truly *its own*, and not as a determination 'from without.' In acts of willing, I experience myself (*se nosse*) as the subject bringing about these acts spontaneously 'from within myself,' as it were, as their creator. Thus, through the experience of *se nosse* I become aware of the freedom of my will.

On the grounds and in the light of these investigations of this unique kind of self-awareness (*se nosse*), Augustine's argument for the spiritual incorporeality of the mind presented in the preceding section can more forcefully be restated. As we have seen,[156] Augustine arrives at the conclusion that the mind cannot be identical with a body in basically two ways. First, due to the fact that the mind is aware of itself most immediately in a manner quite different from the way in which it thinks of its alleged corporeal nature, viz. by means of images and representations as intentional objects of its acts of deliberation, the mind cannot *be* a body; for it cannot be that of which it thinks in a different way than it thinks of itself. Secondly, because the mind is indubitably certain of itself as performing subject of its acts while they are being performed, whereas it merely believes and wonders whether it is a body and, if so, of which kind, it follows that it cannot be a body; for the mind, being certain of itself, cannot be identical with that of which it is uncertain. Or, to put the argument more simply, because the mind possesses a kind of self-awareness that is given to it only with respect to itself, and not with respect to any corporeal entity, it cannot be corporeal.[157]

In *De Genesi ad Litteram* Augustine presents basically the same argument in a somewhat shorter version:

> What does it (i.e. the mind) still search for, if it knows itself as searching? For if it did not know itself, it would not be able to know itself as searching for itself; but this accounts only for the present. However, it also searches to find out

about itself what happened in the past, as well as what will happen in the future. At last now, it may therefore give up the idea of being a body; for if it were such something, it would know itself as such a thing – it that knows itself more than the heaven and the earth which it knows through the eyes of the body.[158]

Starting from the insight that the mind knows itself even though, or precisely when, it is still searching for its real nature, since it knows *itself* as searching for itself (*quaerentem se novit*), Augustine argues that it should abandon the assumption of being a body; for if it were a corporeal entity, it would know itself as such a thing (*quia si aliquid tale esset, talem se nosset*). In other words, if 'I' were a bodily organ, then I would, in acts of knowledge, of searching to know, or in other conscious acts, have to be aware of that organ *as* performing these acts, and could not think of that organ merely as an object of my mind. Indeed, there would have to be a bodily organ in me that would perform these acts in the awareness of itself as performing them.

That this cannot be the case can also be seen from the fact that the manner of experiencing my body (*sentire in corpore*)[159] is quite different from the way in which I am given to myself in the experience of *se nosse*. Though my body, too, is usually given to me inwardly accompanying my general conscious life, it is not experienced as subject of my conscious acts. Not only are some of its parts not even known consciously 'from within,' but only as objects of exterior investigation;[160] but even those members that can be felt 'from within' are not known *as* performing subject(s) of my conscious acts. While in *se nosse* I am aware of myself, that is, of an object that is given not as distinct from, but as identical with, myself as subject of this awareness, the inward experience of my body clearly implies the awareness that what is experienced is not 'I myself' as performing subject of my conscious acts, but is precisely something that *I* am conscious *of* as being distinct from 'myself': my body.

Again, due to this experientially given distinctness and lack of immediacy, the inward feeling of my body, that is, not the feeling *qua* feeling (which is another conscious act) but *qua* feeling the actual reality of my body, is also not as indubitably certain as my own self-awareness. For the knowledge of the existence of my body is not warranted to me in the same way and with the same certainty as I know that *I* exist, since I could in principle doubt whether I have a body or whether it is merely an appearance, without this act of doubting essentially implying the real existence of my body. Precisely because my body is not the performing subject of my conscious acts, I cannot become aware of it through the experience of *se nosse*, which is what grounds the indubitable certainty I have of *my* existence.[161]

Moreover, the inward feeling of my body presents itself as a unified experience of a *variety* of its members, viz. of those that are accessible to being experienced 'from within.' Though the usual body-feeling is *one* inward experience of my body as a whole, unless special attention is paid to a particular part of my body, or unless a particular part 'forces itself' upon my conscious awareness, e.g. in pain, this feeling is the 'unified result' of various experiences of the single members of the body. And these members are given not only as being many, but also as being spatially located 'in' the body, so that the whole unified body-experience implies the awareness of something extended in space. Such an awareness, however, is completely foreign to the inward experience of myself as subject of my acts. For, as will more fully be argued for in the section on the individuality of the mind, this subject is experienced as one simple whole that does not consist of constitutive parts being distinct and separable from each other. Its experience, therefore, is not in need of being 'unified' from those of various partial 'I's,' but is of one single subject: I myself. And this subject is given in the performance of my conscious acts neither as spatially extended, nor as located at a specific part of my body. In performing an act, I am not aware of 'myself' being placed somewhere in my body, as when I feel a pain in my leg. Though I *am* in a way contained in space *insofar as* I am united to my body that fills out and is located at a particular place in space, as subject of my conscious acts I do not occupy a fixed spot in or on my body.[162]

Thus, the inward awareness of *se nosse* is essentially different from that of feeling my body 'from within.' I do not experience myself as I experience my body, not to mention any outside body. This self-awareness is a unique experience that is possible exclusively with respect to 'I myself' (my mind).

This insight, it seems to me, lies at the bottom of Augustine's argument, presently under discussion, that the mind cannot be a body; for if it were, it would know itself *as* a body, which it evidently does not.[163] In fact, analyzing this kind of self-awareness, not only does one discover the lack of corporeality in its object (that is I myself), but, above all, one gets a *positive* awareness of the actual nature of this self (mind).

In the experience of *se nosse* I am most immediately in contact with a reality that is conscious, indeed self-conscious. It is a subject that possesses a 'quality' which is unique and irreducible to anything else. This 'quality' of consciousness, of having the ability to be meaningfully aware of some other reality as well of itself – a 'quality' that deserves genuine philosophical wonderment and amazement – is found uniquely in my own subject (I). Only with regard to myself, and to no other reality, do I experience the phenomenon of self-consciousness (which is not to suggest that I am the only conscious being).

Furthermore, this experience implies the awareness of a *real* subject that is conscious: I myself. *I* as a real being am conscious; consciousness is not a subject in and of itself. (This point as well as the question of the relation between mind and consciousness will be more extensively discussed in a subsequent section on the mind as substantial subject of its conscious acts.)

In fact, as Augustine argues, in the experience of this conscious reality (the mind), I also become aware of it being a *substance*. In knowing itself in the sense of *se nosse*, the mind knows its own substance; and since it is certain about itself, it is certain about its own substance (*quapropter dum se mens novit substantiam suam novit, et cum de se certa est de substantia sua certa est*).[164] The substantiality of the mind (the I) is given in the inward experience of myself as the really existing subject of my conscious acts. *I* am experienced as real and as the underlying single 'bearer' of my acts, which is basically what substantiality means, as we will see more fully in the following chapter.

And it is this conscious 'I,' the mind or soul, that Augustine calls a *spiritual* substance (*animus quae substantia spiritalis est*).[165] The mind is not only not a body, but it is positively characterized by 'spirituality,' a term which is meant to express what is experientially encountered in *self*-awareness during the performance of one's conscious acts.[166]

Thus, the experience of self-awareness (*se nosse*) provides a clue in showing and understanding the mind to be spiritual. Its incorporeality, therefore, is of a spiritual (self-conscious) kind, a fact which gives even stronger evidence of its distinctness from the body.[167]

5 The mind's perpetual self-knowledge (*memoria sui*)

Mention has already been made of the fact that Augustine refers quite often to a form of self-knowledge that, under the name of both *se nosse* and *memoria sui*, he contrasts to explicit self-reflection (*se cogitare*). For our general purpose of discussing the spiritual incorporeality of the human mind this discussion of Augustine's is of interest for two main reasons. On the one hand and from a historic point of view, it rounds up a picture of the different forms of self-knowledge treated in Augustine. On the other hand, such a discussion is interesting, thematically speaking, because it provides additional insight into man's spirituality, particularly with respect to a 'sub-conscious' dimension of his mind. Thus, the following presentation may give a more complete view of Augustine's contributions to a philosophical psychology of man from the point of view of his self-knowledge.

When referring to the distinction between *se cogitare* and *se nosse*, Augustine at times explains their difference by using an analogy from memory. If someone does not think of himself (*se cogitare*), Augustine points out, this does not mean that he does not know himself (*se nosse*); for to think of something and to know something are two different things. A man who is skilled in many sciences is not ignorant of grammar when, not thinking of it, he thinks about the art of medicine.[168] It is possible that a man, thinking of something else, knows something that he is not thinking of.[169] Something is in his mind that is not in his present thought.[170]

This 'part' or faculty of the mind to which is attributed all knowledge that is not presently being thought of is memory: *memoriae tribuens omne quod scimus etiamsi non inde cogitemus*.[171] To it pertains whatever knowledge of a thing is present in the mind while it is not actually thought about.[172]

Using as an analogy this quite evident fact that our knowledge of something is kept in memory while we are presently engaged in something else and that such other mental occupation does not as such cancel out these memory-contents, Augustine expounds the two forms of self-knowledge in question. After explaining the act of reflexive self-thinking (*se cogitare*) as an incorporeal conversion, as was explicated in a previous section, he argues that, even when the mind is not in its own sight in this way, it still knows itself as if it were to itself a memory of itself (*tamen noverit se tamquam ipsa sibi sit memoria sui*).[173] The mind possesses an inward knowledge of itself (*se nosse*) that is given to it in a manner similar to what is contained in memory. As the mind knows certain things that it does not presently think of, so it also knows itself, without actually reflecting upon itself. Its self-knowledge is not begotten when it beholds itself as understood by its own thinking, as if it had previously been unknown to itself; but it was known to itself as things are known that are contained in memory (*ita sibi nota erat quemadmodum notae sunt res quae memoria continentur*).[174]

It seems that Augustine slightly oscillates here in his use of the term *memoria*. On the one hand, he refers to it as to a cognitive power that yields to the mind some pre-reflexive knowledge of itself; in this sense, *memoria sui* stands for *se nosse*. On the other hand, *memoria* is employed in the more common sense of that 'part' of the mind in which knowledge, in this case *self*-knowledge, is stored. Hence, the epistemological and ontological connotations of the term.

However, it might be that Augustine deliberately does not distinguish between these two meanings of *memoria*, for the simple reason that they coincide in the case of such pre-reflexive self-knowledge. For if the mind is in cognitive contact with itself inwardly before any thematic cognition of itself in self-reflection, it seems that it must also 'know' itself constantly in the sense of being always present to itself in some cognitive fashion. (It is not even interrupted by states of sleep or loss of actual consciousness, because, as we will see shortly, this form of the mind's knowing contact with itself is 'located' according to Augustine on a 'sub-conscious' level.) There is therefore no need for a 'storing faculty,' as this function is contained in and taken up by this ongoing cognitive self-presence of the mind. Unlike the common case where knowledge of some other reality is stored in memory, but where memory itself does not possess its own cognitive function by which this knowledge could constantly be 'kept alive,' *memoria sui is* both self-knowledge (*se nosse*) and, due to its constancy, 'storing' faculty.

This interpretation is also supported by another definition of *memoria* given by Augustine. In response to the question of whether memory is not exclusively concerned with the past, Augustine contends that even in a present thing, which the mind is to itself, that by which it is present to itself is not unreasonably to be called memory (*in re praesenti quod sibi est mens memoria sine absurditate dicenda est qua sibi praesto est*).[175] Memory (*memoria*) is that faculty of the mind by which it is present to itself, which implies both its ontological and, as a consequence, its epistemological self-presence, in that it is one and the same mind that is related to itself in some cognitive manner. Hence the mind's perpetual knowledge of itself (*se nosse*) which is due to its inalienable identity with itself.

Augustine often refers explicitly to this constant pre-reflexive self-knowledge, which he relates also to interior self-love, self-understanding, and self-remembrance.[176] It belongs essentially to the human mind, he argues, that it never ceases to remember itself, to understand itself, to love itself (*sic itaque condita est mens humana ut numquam sui non meminerit, . . .*).[177] These perpetual relations to itself are referred to by Augustine also as to the inner memory of the mind (*interiorem mentis memoriam*), the inner understanding, and the inner will, all three of which always being together at the same time from the moment when they began to be, independently of whether or not they have been thought of.[178] The mind knows itself as long as it lives; and since it lives eternally (*sempiternum*), its knowledge of itself remains always with itself, though it does not eternally think of itself.[179] (As Augustine explains in the context of this passage, the term *sempiternum* is not to denote the eternity that God alone possesses. It should more properly be rendered by immortal.)[180]

What Augustine has in mind here may be differentiated into two kinds of cognitive relation to oneself (*memoria sui*): an 'habitual' self-awareness distinct and independent of actual self-reflection (*se cogitare*), and a perpetual 'sub-conscious' self-'knowledge.' Let me try briefly to unfold these points.

When Augustine, in distinguishing between *se cogitare* and *se nosse*, uses the analogy of memory,[181] he refers to a form of self-awareness (*se nosse*) that is similar to the way in which memory-contents are present to the mind, viz., being known without constantly being thought of in actual recollection. In the same manner, Augustine points out, I am known to myself without constantly thinking of myself. There is an 'habitual' *self*-awareness that accompanies my conscious life independent of my *actual* conscious engagements. In this respect, this self-awareness seems to be structurally identical with the one that we discussed in the preceding section on *se nosse*. But what we now see Augustine adding to this discussion is the fact that *se nosse* can be given to various degrees of actuality. For, as we saw above, in the manner of *se nosse* I am fully conscious of myself as performing subject of my acts *actually*, and, as we see now, this self-awareness can be given merely 'habitually,' as it were, in the background of my presently actual consciousness. Just as an act of recollection renders actually conscious what is 'contained' in memory, so the 'habitual' self-awareness (*se nosse*), accompanying my conscious acting,[182] is the more actualized the more consciously I perform a particular act. In this sense, *memoria sui* can be characterized as the less actual, that is 'habitual,' form of *se nosse*, which is nevertheless experienced consciously.

Still there seems to be another kind of self-knowledge that Augustine refers to by the term of *memoria sui*, particularly in the context of discussing the mind's perpetual interior self-love, self-understanding, and self-remembrance.[183] In this context he seems to think that I have a cognitive relation to myself that, so to speak, slumbers in the darkness of my 'unconsciousness' without myself being able to 'awake' or actualize this knowledge. As Michael Schmaus explains:

> When Augustine speaks of inner *memoria, intelligentia* and *voluntas*, he has in mind the deepest level of the soul which the brightness of consciousness has not yet illuminated and where thought does not yet detect differences. . . . He again calls *memoria* the realm in which this unconscious life of the mind is performed in its threefold form, so that both the *meminisse* proper as well as the unconscious *intelligere* and *velle* are functions of the *memoria*.[184]

By *memoria sui* Augustine seems to mean here a form of cognitive self-contact that is neither actually nor 'habitually' conscious, but that is to be 'situated' on an 'unconscious,' or rather 'sub-conscious,' dimension of the mind.[185] The mind 'knows' itself without being in any way *consciously* aware of itself from inner experience. Through this *memoria sui*, it is constantly related to itself in some cognitive manner, uninterrupted by the changes of what happens in its (awakened) consciousness. Unlike *se nosse*, it cannot be actualized by a more conscious (actual) performing of its acts. It is a dimension of the mind that is hidden from or 'behind' consciousness (hence 'sub-conscious'), on which level the mind nevertheless is able to 'know' itself in some way. For this reason, Martin Grabmann contends that with this teaching of *memoria* Augustine has introduced into psychology the notion of unconsciousness.[186]

However, it remains an open question how Augustine arrives at this notion of *memoria sui*. For since it means an 'unconscious' or 'sub-conscious' dimension of the mind 'lying behind' actual consciousness, it can precisely not be known through fully conscious inner experience. But we do know of it, he contends, though the marvellous way in which we, as it were, know what we do not know, viz., what is implied in our *memoria*, is mysterious even to him (*id nos nescio quo eodem miro modo si potest dici scire nescimus*).[187]

Perhaps Augustine was strongly motivated by his Trinitarian speculations. Perhaps he thought that it belongs essentially to the nature of a spiritual (self-conscious) being, inalienably related to itself, to be known to itself constantly, if not consciously, at least 'sub-consciously.'

Whatever his approach may have been, the fact that *memoria sui* in both senses discussed can only be attributed to the mind and not to the body is undeniable. 'Habitual' *se nosse* as well as this 'sub-conscious' self-'knowledge' essentially presuppose the reality of a spiritual being that is capable of being conscious to various degrees of actuality and 'awakeness.' Evidently and as a consequence of our argument in the preceding section, this is by nature excluded for a body.

Concluding we can say that through his treatment of *memoria sui* Augustine has not only shed further light on the essential distinctness of mind and body by pointing at a 'sub-conscious' level of the former, but he has also thrown into greater relief what it means for man to have a spiritual mind. This summarizes the results of the arguments based on altogether five structurally different forms of self-knowledge that were treated in the present and in the preceding chapter: the knowledge of the general nature of the mind as such, the intentional self-reflection of the 'present self' (*se cogitare*), the intentional recollection of the 'past self' (*recordari*), the 'quasi-intentional' awareness of the self during the performance of its acts (*se nosse*) to various degrees of actuality, and the perpetual 'sub-conscious' self-knowledge (*memoria sui*). On the basis of these forms of self-knowledge we tried to show how Augustine argues not only for the incorporeality of the mind, but, above all, tries to lead us to see it positively as a spiritual being. In fact, we saw briefly how Augustine concluded to this spiritual reality as to a substance. Following this line of thought it will be our goal in the subsequent chapter to determine the exact meaning of this substantiality of the mind and of the specific relation obtaining between a spiritual substance and its acts (accidents). This discussion will eventually lead to a concluding statement on the nature of man as consisting in a unique substantial union of the essentially distinct substances of mind and body.

CHAPTER 4

The mind as a spiritual substance

The mind is a spiritual substance (*animus quae substantia spiritalis est*).[1] This definition, which implies also its being an incorporeal,[2] an invisible,[3] a living,[4] and a rational substance,[5] is not merely stated by Augustine without further reflection. As we have already seen at the end of our section on *se nosse*, Augustine concludes to the substantiality of the mind from this unique form of experiencing my own self. For in becoming aware of myself as the really existing subject performing my conscious acts, I experience myself precisely as a substance: I am aware of myself being the really existing 'bearer' of my acts.[6] This relation of subsistence obtaining between myself and my acts, such as doubting, remembering, understanding, etc., is acknowledged, Augustine says, even by the materialists who think these acts are grounded in some kind of a body. Even they rightly see that acts must be in a subject (*in subiecto esse*).[7]

But what does Augustine mean by substance? In virtue of which essential characteristics can he speak of the mind as a substance at all? In fact, why does he refer to the mind as a more proper substance than the human body?[8]

For approaching these questions, a brief terminological sketch of Augustine's use of the term *substantia* is in order. This will be followed by a more systematic investigation of those basic characteristics of the mind that justify its being called a substance more properly than is a body. In this manner, we will be able both to refute those conceptions of the mind which, as mentioned earlier, consider the mind not a self-subsisting entity but a kind of harmony or epiphenomenon of the body,[9] and to give further evidence of the essential distinctness of mind and body which, as shall be shown, accounts for the unique substantial unity that man is.

1 Augustine's notion of substance

Mention has already been made of the fact that Augustine's terminology is usually not very precise and strictly defined. Due to his amazing ability of grasping and penetrating into phenomena, he often appears to be drawn to employ a variety of terms in order to throw the datum meant most adequately into relief. This lack of a 'scientific' technical language becomes manifest in his usage and application of the term *substantia*.

Unlike Aristotle, whose *Categories* he was familiar with and seems to have been influenced by,[10] and unlike Thomas Aquinas as well, Augustine never presents a systematic discussion of terms such as 'substance,' 'accident,' 'category,' 'quality,' etc., though he does refer to the realities signified by means of examples.[11] Nevertheless, there are places and contexts in his work from which a more precise meaning of these terms, particularly 'substance,' may be gathered.

For Augustine *substantia* is usually synonymous with *essentia: essentia quam substantia solet intellegi.*[12] However, the term *essentia* seems to be employed in at least two very different senses, only one of which is the equivalent of *substantia*. For, on the one hand, Augustine speaks of *essentia* as of the nature of the thing that is (exists), as when he refers to the ancients as equating the terms *essentia, substantia,* and *natura,*[13] or when he himself explains that what is meant by *natura* can also be called *substantia,*[14] or when he points out in his Trinitarian definition that the *una essentia* (the one nature) of God is in Latin also rendered *una substantia*, while the Greek term for substance, ὑπόστασις, is generally translated by the Latin *persona*, applying to the three divine persons.[15] In this sense, *substantia* and *essentia* are synonymous notions referring to the nature, the whatness, of a being.

On the other hand, Augustine explains the meaning of *essentia* as derived from *esse: ab eo quod est esse dicta est essentia.*[16] What he is referring to here is the being itself that is: *essentia*, in this second sense, is for Augustine what is 'be-ing,' that is, that which is the subject of (the act of) *esse.*[17] Only because a being *is*, and for no other reason, it is called *essentia.*[18] Its existence (*esse*) is the metaphysical reason for its being a 'something' at all.[19] The same is said by Augustine of substance: that which is not a substance *is* not at all; substance therefore is something that is.[20]

In this second sense of *essentia* as the subject of *esse*, the reality meant by *essentia* or *substantia* can, in special cases, be referred to also by *persona*. Though Augustine speaks primarily of the divine Persons as substances,[21] he also refers to man as a substance and a person; man is a substantial and a personal being.[22]

What this statement means we shall investigate in the following with respect to man's mind. For it is mainly the mind that Augustine, not without deeper reasoning, calls a substance, and that primarily accounts for what we as men are, namely human substances (persons).[23]

There are basically three characteristics that Augustine ascribes to the mind as a substance or person: its being the subsisting bearer (*subiectum*) of its acts,[24] its being single and individual,[25] and, as such an entity, its being really real as subject of *esse* (reality).[26] All of these characteristics[27] shall be shown as given in the case of the mind; in fact, they shall be shown as given there in a more perfect manner than in the case of any body. Thus, our aim in the following is not only to argue for the substantiality of the mind, but also to show this substantiality to be superior to that of the body, in a way that, though again revealing their essential distinctness, will eventually throw their unity into greater relief.[28]

2   The mind as subject of its conscious acts and of consciousness as such

The first characteristic that Augustine attributes to a substance and from which it derives its name is the fact that a substance is the subsisting bearer of accidents or qualities. Itself standing on its own, a substance is that to which those things cling for support that, in order to be at all, require an underlying subject. Augustine exemplifies such a relation of subsistence with respect to corporeal entities. A body is a substance, he points out, when it underlies qualities that essentially presuppose itself as their subsisting bearer, such as color or form.[29] As such, these qualities cannot exist on their own; they are by nature attributed *to* an underlying subject. For this reason, the color and the form of a body are themselves not substances, but are *in* a substance (*non substantiae sunt sed in substantia*).[30] Without the body, they would not exist at all. On the other hand, the subsisting body itself is in its being independent of having this or that color. For it to be a body, it is in no need of possessing a specific quality; if its particular color or form ceases to be, it would not be deprived of its being a body, since it does not belong to its essence to retain this or that form or color (*non hoc est ei esse quod illam vel illam formam coloremne retinere*).[31]

Thus, in the light of this first characteristic of substantiality that is to be called a substance which, itself existing *per se*, serves as the subsisting bearer of things (qualities, accidents) that, existing *per aliquid*, essentially require to be grounded in some underlying subject. The very term substance expresses this relation of subsistence.[32]

The question to be posed now is whether and in which sense also the mind can be called a subsisting bearer of its acts. For it seems evident, even to the materialists, as Augustine observes, that these acts cannot exist on their own, but must be in a subject (*in subiecto esse*).[33] Acts of knowledge, doubt, love, memory, are essentially to be predicated *of* a subject performing them.[34] But how is this relation to be understood in comparison to the substance-accident relation obtaining in corporeal entities? Is there a difference and, if so, could this subject of our acts still be called a substance in the light of the mark of subsistence as the first fundamental characteristic of substantiality?

When in the section on *se nosse* we tried to show, following Augustine, the reality and spirituality of a mind 'in me,' our starting point was taken precisely from the experience of my conscious acts, particularly that of doubt. Analyzing this act, we found that in its performance I am aware (through the experience of *se nosse*) not only of the act itself, but also of *myself* as that real subject performing this act. This subject, as was argued, cannot be a part or organ of my body, but must be a completely different, spiritual, being: the mind ('I,' self). This central insight was gained, thus, from the experience of its being the performing subject of my conscious acts. And it is to this relation obtaining between the mind and the acts it performs that we must pay attention in discussing the question of whether and in which sense the mind can also be seen to be the subsisting bearer (substance) of its acts.

At various places, Augustine explicitly points out that man's conscious acts are not self-sufficient entities, but belong to *me*, the one person, who acts through them:

> These three, memory, understanding, and love are mine, not their own (*mea sunt, non sua*); they do what they do not for themselves, but for me, nay rather, I do it through them. For I remember by memory, understand by understanding, and love by love.[35]

I in a sense actualize myself in my acts. They do not perform themselves, as if my memory, understanding, and love were independent subjects in me living and acting on their own. Rather, these acts, though being distinct from each other in their specific nature,[36] are all performed by one and the same subject: the 'I.' I live in each of my acts; they are *my* acts. Their diversity is unified through the fact that it is the same subject that actualizes itself in them. In this sense, Augustine can say that these acts *are not* man, but that he, the one person, *has* them in his mind.[37] Their relation to the 'I' or mind cannot be one of identity (i.e. of *being*), since in their multiplicity and essential inability to 'perform' themselves, they are clearly distinct from the mind. It must, therefore, be a relation of subsistence in which the mind *has* them in some sense: the question is, in which sense.

At one place, Augustine argues explicitly that the manner in which knowledge and love are in the soul cannot be compared to the way color, shape, or other accidents inhere in a body:

> We are also reminded at the same time, if we can in any way visualize it, that these (i.e. knowledge and love) exist in the soul; they are, so to speak, so folded within it that, when unfolded, they are perceived to be numbered substantially, or, what is the same thing, essentially. They are not in the soul as in a subject, as color, or shape, or any other quality or quantity are in the body. For anything of this kind does not extend beyond the subject in which it is. Thus the color or the shape of this body cannot be of another body. But the mind can also love something else besides itself by the same love by which it loves itself. Similarly, the mind does not know itself alone, but also many other things.[38]

The basic difference that Augustine sees between the relation of bodily accidents to their underlying subject and that of mental acts to the mind lies in the fact that a bodily accident is specifically related to this one body. The color or shape of a particular body is an accidental determination precisely of this body alone; only this body is colored or shaped in this way, and not another one. There obtains an 'introverted' relation of an accident determining its subject. Though ontologically presupposing the latter, the bodily accident, in turn, determines its bearer, that is, its bearer alone. Its proper function as an accident is exclusively exercised 'inwardly.' In contrast, knowledge or love exist in the soul (*in anima exsistere*)[39] not exclusively with respect to the soul itself, but also with respect to other objects outside of it. By the same love by which it loves itself, Augustine says, it can as well love other things. Certainly, as far as their ontological status is concerned, these acts, like bodily accidents, are as well grounded exclusively in one and the same subsisting subject; as 'qualitative characteristics' of this subject, however, they are also 'extroverted,' reaching beyond their underlying subject.

Yet, it should be objected to Augustine that there are also bodily accidents that extend to the outside. For instance, the heat and the light of a fire, the radiance of a piece of gold, or the fragrance of a rose, are real accidents predicated of a particular subject; however, they are also 'extroverted,' determining their surroundings in a special way.

In the light of this objection one could develop Augustine's thought by pointing out that it is not so much the mere fact of relating to the outside which distinguishes a mental act from a bodily accident, but rather the *manner* of this 'extrovertedness,' which is conditioned by the greater unity of the mind with its acts. For the acts of knowing and loving outside reality, like conscious acts in general, 'participate' in the substantiality of their performing subject in a way that is not found in bodily accidents. Each act can be seen as a special manifestation of its subject as substance, in that as mental act it could not be what and how it is without its 'bearer.' The act 'I know' is not some kind of being (accident) having its own proper characteristics, like a color, fragrance, heat, etc.; one could rather say that this act *is* the subject insofar as it is knowing. A conscious act is so united to its underlying substantial bearer (subject) that this certain (qualitative, non-ontological) independence of bodily accidents from their substance is completely foreign to it.[40] And thus, in acting 'towards the outside,' it is this 'mind-act *whole*' that enters into the intentional relation, in a manner compared to which those bodily accidents that do affect their surroundings do so much more 'on their own.' It is not the fire as such that warms the air, but the heat as its accident.

This greater unity of the mind with its acts may be one reason why Augustine continues his argument by stating that love and knowledge are not in the mind as in a subject, but are themselves substantial as the mind is.[41] They do not inhere in the mind like a bodily accident inheres in its bearer; rather, Augustine thinks, they 'participate' so much in the substantiality of the underlying performing subject that they can themselves be considered substantial.[42]

In a similar way, one could add, the mind-act unity accounts also for a difference to bodily accidents in the manner of their relating 'inwardly.' For accidents, such as shape or color, determine their underlying substance in a particular way; they are added to it 'from the outside.' Though they are ontologically dependent on their bearer, they, in turn, 'act' upon the latter, shaping and forming it. In contrast, acts of knowledge, love, and of other faculties, cannot be described as accidental determinations which are added to the mind. They do not inhere in the mind in this sense. Even though they also determine the mind, for instance, in rendering it knowledgeable through acts of knowledge, they do so in a quite different manner. For it is not really the act as such that exercises this determining function; but it is the mind itself that, acting in and through its acts, shapes itself. I gain knowledge, because I am the one that is present in my act of knowledge. In fact, one could say that I fully become *myself* only in and through my acts. Since *I* live and actualize myself in them, I also express and 'shape' myself through them. It is not difficult to see how inadequate, and even false, it would be to speak of my love as of something accidentally attached to 'myself' from the outside.[43]

This most intimate closeness between the mind and its acts, structurally quite different from that between a bodily substance and its accidents, is thrown into even greater relief when one asks the question of how not only (conscious) acts, but consciousness as such relates to the mind, that is, to the substantially underlying subject (person) of these acts. Is consciousness ontologically identical with the mind, or is it somehow 'attached' to it, and if so, in which sense?

Augustine does not address this question explicitly, but the answer to be proposed seems to be in accord with his most basic convictions on the nature of the mind. For if the mind is a real substantial being, as we saw Augustine arguing in the section on *se nosse*, and if it is clear from common experience, and from Augustine's notion of *memoria sui*, that there are various forms of unconsciousness and of more or less partial loss of consciousness, it cannot be, as Descartes' notion of *res cogitans* suggests, that consciousness belongs necessarily to the mind, as if man would always be actually conscious. Rather, consciousness must be something that belongs somehow in the category of accident (in a very broad sense). For consciousness is to be predicated *of* a mind; only a mind as ontological subject can, but need not always, be conscious. Though it is not constantly actualized, however, consciousness is an essential constituent of the person's 'ego-ness,' to use Wojtyla's terminology. Through it, not only does man become 'inwardly' aware of himself as being a real, unique subject, an 'I'; but his 'ego-ness' is even ontologically constituted by his consciousness. For it is precisely *in being conscious* that the person actualizes his most true self, that he 'awakens' to that state of his being in which he, as this concrete subject, is enabled to enter into a unique, conscious, relation to the world, thereby rendering and manifesting himself as this specific ego.[44] Without consciousness, that is, without actualizing myself in and through my consciously performed acts, I would not be an 'I' in the true sense; I would be just another 'sleeping' entity like any corporeal being.[45]

Consciousness, thus, as that element of our acts that renders them precisely conscious, must, on the one hand, be seen as something distinct from the person (mind), in that he is not always conscious; but on the other hand, it is so closely related to the person that it is, in the particular sense just outlined, identical with the person, constituting and revealing his most real self ('I'). Perhaps, it could be described best as the 'awakened' fully actual state of the person (mind).

This peculiar relation of both identity and distinctness obtaining between the person and his conscious state of being, can be grasped also from inner experience. As has already been mentioned, there are various degrees of awareness and of qualitative determination implied in the experience of my conscious acts 'from within.' I can live my acts more or less consciously; of some of them I may be aware just 'peripherally,' while others involve myself as being 'awakened' to fully actual consciousness.[46] Or, as Augustine observes, in the moments of transition from awakeness to sleep and vice versa, I may have the peculiar experience of not being myself, even though I am always identical with myself experiencing these transitions solely as *mine*.[47] These gradations of awakeness given in inner experience testify to the fact that I (the person or mind) am both 'behind' my consciousness as well as 'in' it; for I actualize *myself* in and through consciousness in these various degrees of awakeness: as ontological bearer, I am the subject of consciousness as of an 'accident'; as awakened subject of my conscious acts, I am essentially constituted by the latter. Both of these aspects form part of the peculiar relationship of the mind to consciousness as to its awakened state of being.

Such a conscious awakening and self-actualizing can evidently occur only within the realm of spiritual beings. Only a being that possesses the unique 'attribute' of self-consciousness can realize the peculiar substance-accident relation given in the mind's relation to its acts. Any 'sleeping' corporeal entity, including our own body, is restricted to bearing just a specific kind of accident, and this in a quite different manner than the mind bears its acts, as was pointed out above.[48] A body is essentially unable to 'switch' from lesser to more awakened states of consciousness and vice versa, a fact which again manifests its distinctness from spiritual and conscious beings.[49]

The conscious awakening we have in mind here, however, must not be confused with another kind of 'awakening' that takes place also in the non-spiritual world. For in a sense, the developing and actualizing of a seed also, for instance, can be seen to be a certain awakening. Augustine sometimes expresses his marvel at the amazing phenomenon that a whole tree grows out of a tiny grain of seed which already contains in a unique potential manner its structure or form (*ratio*).[50] The same process occurs in the growth and development of man's body;[51] and in fact, there is a similar awakening also on his spiritual level. For man's mind, Augustine says, is never anything but reasonable and intellectual, even though his reason or intelligence is sometimes dormant, or appears to be smaller or greater at other times.[52] During infancy it lies, as it were, asleep in the mind, as if it were nothing, being destined, however, to be awakened and exercised as years increase, so as to become capable of knowledge and science, fit to the perception of truth and the love of the good.[53]

What Augustine is referring to here can be seen as another kind of awakening of the mind: the growth and actualization of its rational powers essentially belonging to it, at least potentially. An infant is not yet able to enter into a meaningful, rational relation to the world, and to grasp intellectually the meanings and reasons of things. However, these powers usually awaken gradually to ever fuller actualization, both 'on their own,' and through our active exercise of them. Each man is called to activate and to unfold these potentialities that lie dormant in his mind.

Without going into greater detail regarding, for instance, the kind of potency here at stake and the manner of its actualization, it should be pointed out that this form of spiritual awakening is distinct from, though related to, the conscious awakening of the mind in its acts. For the former occurs, so to speak, on the ontological level of the mind, in that the mind's being and nature grow to a fuller actualization of what is potentially given in it. In contrast, the conscious awakening of the mind goes in a completely different direction, precisely because it occurs exclusively on this unique conscious level. While the former could be described as an 'interior' awakening of the mind, which in a similar manner takes place also in the non-spiritual realm of being, the latter is also 'exterior' in the sense that the mind actualizes itself 'into' its own 'accident,' namely consciousness. As was mentioned above, this conscious awakening implies both the identity and the distinctness of mind and consciousness, which peculiar duality is foreign to the former, more ontological, kind of actualization.

Again, as a consequence of this 'exteriority,' the mind 'switches' more often from an unconscious to a conscious state. During each course of a day there are usually times of more or less conscious awakeness. Such a fluctuation, however, is not given in the awakening of man's rationality. Since this belongs much more to the ontological reality of the mind, it is not directly subjected to its constantly changing state of consciousness. Though there are also increases and decreases of man's rational development, they usually occur in more extended periods of time.[54]

Yet, despite their distinctness, these two forms of spiritual awakening interact and complement each other, and this, as it seems, in basically two ways. On the one hand, the mind's actualization in consciousness is a decisive presupposition of its rational awakening; for even though there are aspects of the latter that seem to grow 'naturally,' especially during childhood, it is in and through consciousness that man is aware of these rational potentialities, thereby using and perfecting them. In a state of 'unconsciousness,' man could not bring his rationality to a fuller actualization; only when consciously awakened is he able to contribute his proper share to its unfolding. On the other hand, the degree of rational awakeness determines the 'quality' of man's conscious acts, precisely because what actualizes itself in consciousness is the mind being rationally awakened to a certain extent. An infant's conscious acting is characterized much less by meaningfulness and reasonability than that of an adult, even though the latter too need not always actualize himself to his fullest extent, since, as was pointed out, there are various degrees of the mind's self-actualization in its acts. Yet generally, the possibility of using his rational powers, to the extent of their awakeness, is always given to man.

This comparison of the two forms of mental awakening[55] should have thrown the peculiarity of the mind's conscious actualizing into greater relief. It is precisely not an immanent 'interior' unfolding of potentialities; but it is a unique awakening in which the mind in a sense goes out of itself into its 'accident,' consciousness, thereby, however, really actualizing *itself*.

And it is this peculiar relation that reveals the mind not only to be distinct from a bodily substance, but also to be able to realize much more perfectly the first characteristic of substantiality, that is, to be an underlying subject of 'accidents.' For the mind does not merely serve as ontological bearer of its acts; rather, as their performing subject, it is present and lives *in* them consciously. They are not 'attached' to it determining it 'exteriorly,' but they *are* in a sense itself in its conscious actualization. As such, they are much more closely related to the mind, and in a completely different manner, than a bodily accident to its bearer.[56] In this, then, the mind can more properly be seen to be an underlying subject (substance), since it both bears, and consciously lives in, its acts, rendering itself much more indispensable for them than a body for its accidents.

3   The individual oneness of the mind

Augustine does not explicitly point out that a substance in general is characterized by individuality. However, he does speak of the nature of the human mind as of a certain single thing,[57] and of the person as of something singular and individual (*aliquid singulare atque individuum*).[58] And, as will become clear in the following, this individuality is attributed to the mind precisely because it is a substance as the real subject underlying its acts. In fact, we will see that the kinds and degrees of individuality found in the mind throw its substantiality into even greater relief. For only a being that realizes the characteristics of substantiality mentioned above to the extent the mind does, can possess individuality at all in the most proper senses to be pointed out. It should become evident, therefore, that individuality (oneness, simplicity, singleness) belongs essentially to the mind as to a substance, indeed, that it belongs to it more properly than to any corporeal entity.[59]

Among the various senses of the term 'individual oneness' applied to the mind (person) there is one more fundamental meaning in Augustine that shall first be discussed more extensively, namely the individual wholeness of the mind. For the fact that the mind is one in the sense of not being constituted by parts into which it could be divided, but that it is a simple indivisible whole – this fact is the ontological presupposition of all other kinds of oneness to be pointed out thereafter.

(a) Augustine argues for the indivisible wholeness of the mind in the context of his discussion of *se nosse*. As we analysed in a previous section, his starting point in this discussion lies in the question of how it is possible that the mind does have a knowing awareness of itself, even if it is ignorant and still in search of itself as to its actual nature. How is it that it knows itself while it is unknown to itself? Before Augustine solves this problem, as we saw, by distinguishing between *se cogitare* and *se nosse* as two distinct kinds of self-knowledge, he investigates the possible solution of claiming that the mind consists of parts of which one is known while the others are unknown. If it is granted that the mind can be ignorant of itself, but that it must, by that very fact, also be known to itself, could one not conclude that the mind knows itself in part and does not know itself in part (*an quod ex parte se novit, ex parte non novit*)?[60] Directly responding to this 'solution' Augustine develops the following argument against the assumption that the mind can be divisible into parts:

> What shall we, therefore, say? That the mind (*mens*) knows itself in part, and does not know itself in part? But it is absurd to claim that it does not know as a whole what it knows. I do not say that it knows as a composite whole (*totum*), but what it knows it knows as a whole (*quod scit tota scit*). When it, therefore, knows something of itself which it cannot know except as a whole, it knows itself as a whole. But it knows itself as knowing something, nor can it know something except as a whole. Therefore, it knows itself as a whole.[61]

This argument needs to be unfolded step by step. Its starting point lies in the fact that whatever the mind knows, it knows as a whole, that is, as a subject that is essentially one. Each act of knowledge presupposes a single, whole subject performing it. (Augustine's clarification that the term 'whole' [*tota*] in reference to the mind as performing subject of its knowledge may not be interpreted in the sense of *totum*, that is, in the sense of a whole as the sum-total of parts, will better be understood in the light of another passage to be discussed below.)[62]

It is a fundamental fact of inner experience that the performing subject of my knowledge and of all other acts is one simple being. As we saw in our presentation of Augustine's discussion of *se nosse*, in knowing myself as performing an act (*se nosse*) I know myself as one 'I.' The experience of *se nosse* precisely implies the awareness that it is one and the same subject ('I') that underlies all those acts that are truly *mine*. Though being 'materially' distinct from each other, my acts share in the same 'predicate' of 'being mine,' because it is the same 'I,' and not a variety of 'I's,' that performs all of them.[63] In this sense, Augustine here speaks of the mind knowing as a whole (subject) whatever it knows. (Let us also recall the unique phenomenon, discussed in Chapter 1, of feeling the various, locally distinct parts of the body at the same time, a phenomenon which cannot be explained unless it is performed by the same undivided subject.)[64]

The second step of Augustine's argument consists of the hypothetical premise that the mind, which can know only as a whole (subject), must also know itself as a whole (as object of its knowledge), *if* it knows something about itself. For if it is really itself about which it knows something, it must also know as a whole what it knows in knowing itself as an object. In other words, if I *as subject* of my self-knowledge experience myself as one, I must experience myself as one also *as object* of my self-knowledge, if it is really myself I know.

The third step, then, is to refer to the actual fact, developed above, that the mind does know itself as subject of its knowledge (including its self-knowledge) through the experience of *se nosse*. From this it follows, fourthly, that the mind knows itself as a whole also as object of its self-knowledge. For since as a whole (subject) it knows really *itself*, it must know itself also as a whole (object), precisely because it is identical with itself. Hence, the idea that this apparent paradox, of the mind knowing itself in not knowing itself, could be solved by assuming the mind to consist of parts some of which are known while others are unknown, manifests itself as unacceptable. The mind is given as something simple that cannot be split into parts.[65]

In a similar way, Augustine goes on arguing that the mind knows itself also as a living and as an understanding whole. It is one mind that lives and understands, so that when it knows itself, through *se nosse*, as living and understanding, it knows itself as one whole.[66] Again, he shows at length that the mind, in seeking to know itself, also knows itself as a whole, an argument that can be left out here because of its similar logical structure. So Augustine can come to the conclusion that, whenever the mind is spoken of, it is spoken of as a whole (*cum enim ea ipsa dicitur, tota dicitur*).[67]

In order to grasp more clearly the exact meaning of this 'wholeness' of the mind, Augustine rejects possible materialistic misconceptions according to which it might be explained. Could one not say, for instance, that the mind is one whole composed of its knowledge and love? As a body is made up of parts into which it

can be divided, could not the mind also be thought to be a whole
(*totum*) constituted by its acts and faculties as by its parts?[68]

In his response to this question Augustine reveals his acute
awareness of essential distinctions. For he shows that the relation
between a whole and its constitutive parts is essentially different
from that between the mind and its acts, resp. their corresponding
faculties, such as its knowledge and love, which he discusses with
respect to the mind itself.

A whole that is composed of parts cannot be embraced by one
of its parts (*nulla pars totum cuius pars est complectitur*);[69] that is, no
part of a whole can contain the whole in itself, since as part it must
always be smaller than the whole. However, when the mind knows
or loves itself, Augustine points out, it knows itself as a whole, that
is perfectly (which is not to be understood in the sense of a
complete all-comprehensive knowledge of oneself which Augustine, as we saw, rejects explicitly); its knowledge extends to the
whole of itself (*mens vero cum se totam novit, hoc est perfecte novit, per
totum eius est notitia eius*).[70]

The mind's knowledge is not restricted to knowing only its
own knowledge, which it would have to, according to materialistic
principles, were it a constitutive part of the mind. Instead, in self-
knowledge the mind is able to 'embrace' the whole mind, including
its other faculties, such as its love, understanding, memory.[71] If my
knowledge had the same relation to the mind as, for instance, my
finger has to the whole body, it could not extend beyond itself
encompassing the whole. Consequently, the mind cannot be
composed of its faculties as of its parts.

Yet, Augustine continues by objecting against this answer as
follows. Could one not say, then, that, just as one drink is made up
of wine, water, and honey which, when mixed together, are found
throughout the whole drink, so also the mind as a whole consists
of its faculties and acts, since they too interpenetrate each other?[72]

In answer to this objection, Augustine points out that the three
liquids making up the one drink are not *of* one substance, even
though the one substance of the drink is brought about by them.[73]
They cannot be predicated of the same underlying subject, not
even of the drink itself. For it is they that constitute the drink,
instead of the drink being their subsisting bearer. Furthermore,
these three components of the drink each lose their specific charac-

teristic essence which delimites the one from the other. Unlike, for instance, water and oil which do not completely mingle because they retain their specific nature, these three liquids constitute the drink in such a way that they can no longer be distinguished from each other. There is, therefore, no real relation between them, properly speaking, since a relation presupposes at least two distinct entities.

Applying this analysis to the mind in relation to its self-knowledge, self-love and other acts, Augustine makes the same point that we treated in the preceding section, viz. that these acts are necessarily of one and the same substance.[74] It is one and the same subject, the 'I,' of which, as their performing 'bearer,' these acts are to be predicated.[75] Therefore, not only do they not constitute me, as three liquids constitute a drink; they also retain their proper nature and activity, in that they are distinct from and indeed relate to and comprehend each other: I can love my knowledge or know my love, as Augustine develops in a lengthy passage.[76] These specific relations would be impossible were these acts intermingled like liquids having lost their own proper nature and function.

It becomes clear that the mind is not a whole in the sense of being constituted by its acts and faculties. Rather, as their underlying subject it is a being that, unlike any divisible body, has everything that it possesses simultaneously as a whole (*omnia quae habet in uno simul habentem*).[77] In spite of the innumerable variety and diversity of conscious acts, they are performed by one and the same simple mind that is nowhere divided (*in una nusquam dispertita mente*).[78]

Thus, oneness in this first sense of being a simple indivisible whole is much more perfectly realized in the mind than in a body. For, as we just saw and as we argued for in greater detail in the first chapter, a body is an essentially manifold being consisting of a multitude of non-identical parts into which it could be divided. For this reason, a body cannot only not be the performing subject of my acts,[79] but it is also less properly called a substance than the mind according to the principle that oneness is a criterion of substantiality.[80]

It should, however, be added that Augustine draws a clear distinction between the simplicity of the mind and simplicity in the sense of unchangeable oneness that is found only in God. Implicitly rejecting certain tendencies in Plato of absolutizing the human soul,[81] Augustine strongly emphasizes that the mind is not simple in the sense of being immutable. Only the absolute, divine substance, God, is most truly simple (*verissime simplex*), since in Him there is no difference between His knowledge and His being, but both are one (*utrumque unum*).[82] In this sense, in which simplicity implies unchangeability, the mind is not a simple, but a manifold nature (*non simplicem sed multiplicem esse naturam*). However, in comparison to a body, Augustine states, the mind is certainly more simple (*simplicior*), since it is not extended in space and therefore not divisible into parts.[83]

To be sure, the use of the comparative form of simple, '*simplicior*,' does not posit a hierarchical gradation of various degrees of one and the same kind of simplicity, from matter to mind and on to God. As is clearly implied in Augustine, simplicity in the sense of indivisibility into parts is not a lower degree of the absolute unchangeable oneness of God, though being presupposed by the latter. As an exclusively divine predicate, God's simplicity cannot be shared in by contingent beings to a lesser degree, since every creature is mutable (*omnis autem creatura mutabilis*).[84] One could rather speak here of two *kinds* of simplicity: actual indivisibility and absolute oneness of being and nature. For in this conception, the simplicity of the mind in the sense of real indivisibility and wholeness is not jeopardized by the fact that the mind is by nature mutable and contingent, precisely lacking the divine simplicity. In fact, the essential mutability of man's conscious life reveals even more the simplicity of his mind, since it is one and the same mind (the 'I'), and not various non-identical parts of it, that performs and experiences these numerous acts and changes in his consciousness.

Though this indivisible simple wholeness is a fundamental ontological feature of the mind presupposed for all other kinds of its simplicity, as we will shortly discuss, in many other ways it is less important and less characteristic of the individual oneness of the human mind (person). For there are still various senses in which Augustine's expression of the one person that each individual man is (*una persona, id est singulus quisque homo*)[85] can be understood, each revealing him as essentially superior in individuality, and thus in substantiality, to any corporeal being. Let me try to point out the most important of these senses of oneness to be found in man's personal mind, explicitly mentioned by or virtually contained in Augustine. Such a discussion will also bring to light even more clearly the impossibility of explaining the simplicity of the mind in materialistic terms.[86]

(b) One can speak of the oneness of the mind in the sense that there is only one mind 'in' each man. This sense of oneness does not necessarily follow from the fact that the mind is an indivisible whole, though it presupposes the latter. For it could still be thought that man consists of various (whole) souls, as a trialistic position may assume. However, if human mind refers to the conscious, rational self, the 'I,' that is experienced as performing subject of my acts, it is clear that this subject, without denying various levels of 'animality,' higher 'spirituality,' or of awakeness in it, is given as numerically one.[87] I experience only one self 'in me:' *ego ipse certe unus sum*, says Augustine.[88] It is one human person that is the subject of his various acts;[89] and each man consists of only one such mind, since there are as many minds as there are men.[90] Yet, in no sense at all, one can add, could it be said of a bodily element, or even of an ultimate material particle (as an entity that, like the mind, is not actually divisible),[91] that it is the only one man consists of. His body is precisely composed of an uncountable number of living cells and particles; though each of them may be an indivisible whole, it is certainly not the only one 'in' a man. The reason for this lies primarily in the fact that such a particle, though actually indivisible, still lacks the positive simplicity of the mind as the spiritual (conscious and rational) subject of its acts. For it is this positive simplicity that alone renders it capable of constituting, together with the body and its parts, the one human being. One mind suffices, so to speak, for a man, while he requires a multitude of cells and particles on his bodily side.

(c) This numerical oneness of the mind reaches a new dimension in the light of the fact that the mind endures in time as one and the same ontologically identical subject. This fact does not seem knowable directly through inner experience. For I do not possess an absolute certainty in the awareness of my own past as really *my* past (as opposed to those memories that are based on the experiences of others or on the products of my imagination), not to mention of my very early past. However, considering the 'structure' of certain acts man is able to perform, the mind's temporal endurance becomes clearly manifest. For instance, the act of recollection as analyzed in a previous section cannot be explained unless it is one and the same mind that re-experiences in the present what it itself experienced in the past, which is particularly obvious, for example, from the experience of presently repenting an earlier wrong-doing.[92] Or the experience of *distentio animi* is only to be accounted for, as we pointed out, because it presupposes the ontologically identical reality of the same mind enduring through temporal changes. Augustine himself argues for the identity of the mind in time on the basis of his notion of *memoria sui*.[93] Mentioning the temporal priority of memory-contents to those acts by which they are recollected, he tries to show that such priority cannot be predicated of the mind in relation to itself because of its constant self-knowledge (self-understanding, self-love):

> But when knowledge is begotten, and that which we have
> known is placed in the memory and is again seen by
> recollection, who does not see that the retention in the memory
> is prior in time to the sight in recollection, as well as to the
> combining of both of these by the will as a third? But again
> it is not so with the mind. For it is not adventitious to itself,
> as if to the mind already existing, there were to come from
> somewhere else that same self not already existing; or as if
> it did not come from somewhere else, but in the mind itself
> already existing, there was born the mind itself not already
> existing, just as there arises in the mind which already existed,
> the faith which did not exist; or as if the mind sees itself,
> as it were, set up in its own memory, after it has learned to
> know itself by recollection; just as if it were not there before
> it knew itself, since from the moment that it began to be, it
> has certainly never ceased to remember itself, never ceased
> to understand itself, and never ceased to love itself, as we have
> already shown.[94]

This difficult text can only be understood in the light of our previous discussion of *memoria sui* as a perpetual 'sub-conscious' self-'knowledge' of the mind. The actual givenness of this form of self-contact, Augustine here argues, shows the mind to be and to remain the same ontologically identical reality throughout time. For this self-'knowledge,' uninterrupted by all conscious changes, belongs to the very nature of each mind as mind from the very beginning of its being. Therefore, if it is given, it must always be given in one and the same mind, that is, in this one ontological reality that does not exist prior to itself as if 'coming' to itself either 'from without' or 'from within' or through recollection. As Augustine explains, unlike knowledge that is stored in memory and that precedes its being recollected, the mind itself is not adventitious to itself in time, as if to itself as an already existing being the same self which has not yet existed were to come from somewhere else (*quasi ad se ipsam quae iam erat aliunde eadem ipsa quae non erat*). If it exists, it exists as itself and does not 'receive' itself 'from without.' Similarly, it does not 'receive' itself 'from within,' as if in itself as the already existing mind, the mind itself were born which did not exist before, as faith or any other mental activity is born in the existing mind. And the mind does not come to itself the moment it recollects itself and sees itself in its own memory, as if it did not exist prior to its own self-recollection. Thus, if and as long as the mind exists, it must exist as this one ontologically identical reality throughout time.

However, one may wonder whether oneness in the sense of such temporally enduring identity can be affirmed also with respect to the human body. Certainly, as *my* body, it remains the same throughout time, precisely because it is and remains united to the same mind ('I'); yet, as an ontological reality exchanging its *constitutive* elements every seven years and always incorporating into it new 'life-material' through nutrition and growth, the body rather seems to be a constantly re-constituted entity that is never strictly identical with itself. Unlike the mind that as the same spiritual subject underlies its constantly changing acts and states of consciousness, the body is in its very being, and as this concrete body, an always 'new' entity, strictly speaking. Also in this time-related sense, then, the mind reveals a higher degree of oneness than the body.[95]

(d) Each human mind (person) is not only one in the numerical sense mentioned above, but it is also one absolutely speaking in the sense that there is one and can only be one person in the world that is 'I myself.' This does not mean that I am the only person in the world, which would be a metaphysical solipsism; rather, it means that only one mind is truly 'I,' realizing, so to speak, the idea of my characteristic 'self-ness,' namely I myself. Though it is true that, in virtue of the universally valid principle of identity, *any* being is absolutely one and unique, the mind, in addition, is also *aware* of its own uniqueness and irreplaceability. Its self-identity as well as its unrepeatable individuality, which ground and account for its being numerically one (*quia unus homo iam singulus homo est*),[96] are consciously experienced and become manifest not only from its awareness of being always self-present and never separable from itself, as discussed earlier, but also from genuinely existential acts. For instance, in love the beloved is seen as a singular unrepeatable person that could not be replaced by someone else. Likewise, the fact that I give someone a particular *name* shows his unique singularity. Above all, specifically religious experiences reveal the unrepeatable individual uniqueness of each man, as when he becomes aware of what it means to stand before his Creator, Judge, and loving Father – constantly recurring themes in Augustine, especially in his *Sermons*, his *Expositions of the Psalms*, and in his *Confessions*. All these experiences imply the awareness that I myself, and likewise any other person, am something unique in the world, asking to be taken seriously and responded to as this one person for whom there can never be a substitute.[97]

But where in the material world could such a uniqueness be found? A particle of matter, though it is (*qua* being) self-identical, is perhaps the least unique being whatsoever; among the myriads of particles, each one could probably be replaced by any other one. Above all, none is conscious of its own self-identity at all. And even on the level of more complex organic structures and bodies, no comparable unrepeatable uniqueness is given. For bodily organs can be replaced by those taken from another human body. Indeed, even the human body as such (*Körper*) seems to be in principle replaceable by that of someone else. Only the lived body (*Leib*) can be seen as unrepeatably unique, precisely because it 'participates' in the uniqueness of the human mind with which it is intimately united.[98] It is not the body *qua* body, but *qua* united to this unique mind, which possesses the mark of unrepeatable individuality. Again, also in this (fourth) sense of oneness the mind is more perfectly one than a body.[99]

(e) All the kinds of oneness mentioned so far reveal the mind to be one also in the sense of being clearly delimited from other beings. Each person is, as this unique being, fundamentally distinct from any other person (which does not exclude, but rather conditions, the possibility of interhuman relations, as we shall shortly discuss). This is not only manifest from a consideration of what it means to be one in all the senses already referred to; but it can also be seen from the fact that the mind is somehow a 'self-sufficient' being possessing faculties and powers that are exclusively its own. It is obvious that when I will, love, enjoy, or know something, I perform these acts through my very own faculties. Everyone beholds wisdom, Augustine says, with his own mind, neither with mine, nor with yours, nor with that of someone else (*unus quisque id [i.e. sapientiam] nec mea nec tua nec cuiusquam alterius, sed sua mente conspiciat*).[100] I am essentially incapable of using the mind and faculties of another man.[101] Certainly, I may ask him for his help or advice, thereby making use of his mental powers. An immediate employment of his faculties, however, as if I were really present in the other, is obviously impossible. Because the mind does not consist of replaceable parts, and because it is, as one unique being, ontologically distinct from any other mind, it cannot enter into a mutual exchange of mental powers.

This insight also leads to a rejection of an Aristotelian conception of the mind (νοῦς) as of 'an independent substance implanted within the soul,'[102] at least as it has been interpreted by Averroes as referring to a universal intelligence common to all members of the human species.[103] Even though Augustine does not seem to have been familiar with such a view,[104] he would certainly have opposed it: it is the one nature of the mind (*una mentis natura*), he says, that embraces our intellect and action, our counsel and execution, our reason and reasonable appetite.[105] There is no 'part' of our minds which belongs to some general human intelligence. All faculties are predicated and used by one and the same mind.[106]

Surely such an exclusive 'self-sufficiency' and ontological delimitation from others cannot be found on the corporeal level. Each body seems open to taking into itself various elements from the outside, as, in the case of my own body, I could in principle incorporate into it the blood, cells, or certain organs of others, or many artificial means. In this, it appears much less clearly demarcated from other bodies. In fact, one could even state the general rule that the more an entity is unique in its being and nature (the fourth sense of oneness), the more is it delimited from other beings. The body of one man, for instance, is much more distinct from that of another man, than two grains of sand are from each other. Thus, as a consequence of its greater uniqueness, the mind surpasses any corporeal being also with respect to that kind of oneness by which it is characterized as this clearly demarcated being.

(f) The unique self-embracing oneness of the mind could be further amplified by another form of oneness. All the acts I perform with my faculties bear the characteristic stamp of being '*my* acts.' The more a person realizes and fulfills his nature as this unique *individual* in the world (the fourth sense of oneness), the more will all his actions become an expression of his own subjective *individuality*. There will be a peculiar quality attached to his acts that characterizes them as *his*, and nobody else's (similar to the style or the hand-writing peculiar to a person). This particular individuality or subjectivity that permeates each man's being and acting follows from his being an ontologically unique single person. Because he is one in all senses discussed so far, he is capable of attaining this unrepeatably unique quality that cannot be found apart from himself. As a consequence, it is clear that, like the forms of oneness mentioned above, so also oneness in the sense of individual subjectivity cannot be given in a body, at least not to the extent to which it is found in each human mind (person).

(g) Finally, another feature following from all the kinds of oneness already referred to shall be pointed out. As a unique clearly delimited being, each mind (person) is also one in the sense of being essentially incapable of being 'fused' with another mind or with any other being in order to constitute a new 'individual' whole. It cannot give up its unique being and nature by becoming a part of a greater whole in mingling with another entity. Though Augustine argues explicitly only against a conversion of a human mind into a body, into an irrational animal, and into God,[107] he clearly implies also the impossibility of any 'fusion' of individual minds (persons), especially in his long philosophico-theological treatise on the revealed mystery that the Divine Trinity consists of really individual (not fused) persons in one nature.[108] However, if one thinks of corporeal entities, there is nothing in a concrete body that would by nature exclude its fusion with another body. Not only liquids, but also solid pieces of matter could in principle be melted into each other, and this could happen both on the level of inorganic lifeless bodies and on that of our own 'lived' body. A corporeal being simply does not possess such an individual uniqueness that would render its union with other bodies impossible. Also in this sense, then, the mind is and *remains* one, preserving its individuality as this single being in a manner essentially different from a body. It is as such incapable of becoming a part of something else.

Yet, one might object to this reasoning as implying a solipsistic conception of the human being in which he is excluded from entering into interhuman relations and becoming part of greater communities. Without going into an argument and a discussion here of the ontological foundation and status of communities,[109] this objection can briefly be responded to on the grounds of two main points, which shed even further light on the specific kind of the mind's oneness here at stake: (1) A genuine community or a relation of love does not come into being through a *fusion* of two or more people. Unlike two metals that are melted into each other, losing their specific characteristics, each member of a community is to maintain his truly unique being and nature. For only in this case can a genuinely spiritual union be established (which might find its physical expression, as in spousal love) that is not only structurally quite different from, but incomparably deeper than, any 'fused union' on the material level. Man's individual oneness, therefore, does not exclude his becoming a member of communities; on the contrary, it is just this which is presupposed by the latter.[110] (2) A community cannot be explained on strict analogy with corporeal wholes. For it *is not* the sum-total of its constitutive parts (its personal members) as is a body, nor is it the totality of organs united by an 'immanent life-principle,' as is our bodily organism. Rather, a community is something built upon its members (*Überbau*) that grows out from their interpersonal relations. As such, it has a quite different metaphysical status and nature than its grounding members, for the simple reason that a community is not a real individual person. In contrast, the relation between a corporeal whole and its parts remains, so to speak, on the same (corporeal) level. Bodies that are united still remain bodies. Likewise, a whole organism is a 'living entity,' just as its constitutive organs. Thus, what is excluded in the case of human beings is a union in the sense of bodily fusion. A 'being part' of communities, however, is in no way rendered impossible by man's peculiar oneness. A community is a completely different kind of a whole, which presupposes precisely the preservation of the uniqueness of its members.

Still, another critical question could be raised with respect to this last form of oneness, viz. resistance to being absorbed into a greater whole. If this feature truly holds for the mind, how then can it be united to the body, constituting the one nature of man? How can man be called a composite of mind and body, as Augustine strongly maintains,[111] if the mind resists being a constitutive part of a whole?

An answer to this crucial problem shall be proposed in the final chapter within the larger context of discussing how the substantiality of the one man consisting of mind and body can be maintained in the light of the essential (substantial) distinctness of these two components. At this point, it has to be left open as to whether this last kind of oneness is given in the mind in every respect, or with a very special restriction: with respect to its being a constitutive part of man.

Instead, it should be pointed out how all these senses of oneness or simplicity are realized in the mind to the same full extent, as it were, residing on the same ontological level. A corporeal being possesses one of these kinds of oneness to a degree that, in many cases, is independent of the degree of another kind, as an ultimate particle, for instance, is far more simple in the sense of indivisibility than the human body, but much less simple as far as its uniqueness and individuality is concerned. By contrast, the human mind not only surpasses any body in all these senses of simplicity; it also realizes in itself these different kinds to the same full degree. Because all of them are grounded in and follow from the same indivisible and uniquely unrepeatable reality of the mind, as we pointed out, they 'reveal' the individuality of the mind (in its various aspects) to an equally high degree. There is something about the nature of the mind as a spiritual being that renders it metaphysically incapable of becoming 'one among many'; 'from within itself,' it is ordained to being one and unique. Though Augustine does not present an explicit discussion of these points, they seem clearly to be implied in, and can logically be drawn out from, what he means when speaking of the person as of something single and individual.[112]

If individual oneness is a fundamental characteristic of substantiality, it follows that the mind, in the light of this criterion, can also be called a substance more properly than the body. Not only is it a more perfect subsisting 'bearer' of its acts than a body of its accidents, as we tried to show above, but as such a conscious subject it is also one and individual in various senses, and in each of these senses it is more properly one and individual than any body could be. For this reason, it deserves the designation 'substance' more adequately than the body. That the same conclusion can also be drawn from applying to the mind the third characteristic of substantiality, viz. to be really real as subject of *esse*, shall be shown in the next section.

4   Man's mind is more real *(esse)* than his body

At the beginning of the present chapter we pointed out that Augustine derives the term *substantia* or *essentia* from the verb *esse*: something is a substance or an essence if it *is*, that is, if it is the subject of being (*esse*). To be real, thus, is a further feature of substantiality. However, *esse* (reality) or, in later terminology, the act of being, is, as such, an analogous notion. According to Augustine, there is a hierarchy of *esse* established by God: to some beings He gave a more ample, to others a more limited *esse*, so that He ordered the natures of beings (*essentiarum*) in degrees.[113] As one could say, some beings are by nature more real than others; they are more deeply grounded in reality, actualizing it to a greater extent.

Our task now is to ask what is this hierarchy of real being, and particularly, where in it are the mind and the body to be placed. This discussion will not only make manifest that in the light of this third characteristic of substantiality also the mind is more properly a substance than the body, but it will also show that the mind can for this reason not be a harmony or epiphenomenon of the body, as certain theories mentioned by Augustine hold.[114]

In the *Confessiones*,[115] Augustine develops a hierarchy of real being in a brief description of his personal ascent to God, the absolute and most real being. As to the lowest degree of reality, he there refers to the phantasms of those bodies that do not even exist (*phantasmata corporum, quae omnino non sunt*), such as those empty fictions (*figmenta inania*) the Manicheans presented to him as God. More real than these fictions are the images of really existing bodies, which, in turn, are surpassed in their degree of reality by the existing bodies themselves (*quibus certiores sunt phantasiae corporum eorum, quae sunt, et eis certiora corpora*). But even more real than corporeal entities is the soul which is the life of bodies (*melior vita corporum [anima] certiorque quam corpora*). In this, the soul as a living being is surpassed only by God.[116]

It is not difficult to see that the image of a body is much less real than the body itself, precisely because it is not a real body. Certainly, as image it is real in some sense; but compared to the autonomously existing being of the body, which really *is* a body, the image possesses a much different kind, and much lower degree, of reality than the actual body. A similar conclusion can with Augustine be drawn also with respect to the mind and a body.

Augustine specifies his statement of the superiority of life over any 'dead' bodily entity regarding different kinds of life.[117] Among beings that are created by God and that, as living beings, rank above those that do not have life, he points out, those that are sentient rank higher than those that lack the capacity of sensation (*praeponuntur sentientia non sentientibus*), as trees are surpassed in being by animals. And among those that have sensation, the intelligent rank above those that have no intelligence (*praeponuntur intellegentia non intellegentibus*), as men are higher than animals. Even among intelligent beings, he holds, there is the hierarchical distinction and superiority of those that are immortal, such as the angels, over those that are mortal, such as men (*praeponuntur inmortalia mortalibus*).[118]

This hierarchical structure of God's creation is one according to the order of nature (*ista praeponuntur naturae ordine*).[119] It is based upon the degree of reality and value *intrinsic* to a being. For Augustine explicitly distinguishes between the value a being has in and of itself because of its rank in the hierarchy of being (*quid per se ipsum in rerum gradibus pendat*) and the value that is attributed to a being because it is desired by our needs and appetites (*necessitas [seu voluptas cupientis] autem quid propter quid expetat cogitat*).[120]

Whereas the latter may change according to the measure of its being desired by various people and in various situations, the former is grounded in the very nature of the being itself; it is something that belongs to a being in itself, and not in its relation to the appetite of another, or the utility of something else. Therefore, in the order of intrinsic value, a being maintains the same axiological rank, as long as it remains this same being, while this hierarchy may be inverted in the order of 'relational value,' as men, for instance, generally prefer to have bread in their house than mice, and gold than fleas, as Augustine remarks.[121]

But why is it that Augustine thinks man as an intelligent being is much higher placed in this hierarchy, established by the degree of reality and value intrinsic to a being,[122] than non-intelligent living beings, and above all, than bodies?

The answer can be found if we think of what it means to be intelligent, that is, to have a rational and a spiritual mind, which primarily accounts for the superior position of man excelling the whole kingdom of animals.[123] For, with respect to physical power and other bodily faculties, man is inferior to most animals, as they often have healthier and more tenacious limbs, are faster and more agile in their bodily movements.[124] But, as Augustine continues, man is able to dominate and to tame them in a way in which no animal could subject man to itself, even if it did away with a multitude of men by the kind of superiority peculiar to it.[125] And this ability is not something that, though specifically human, belongs to a lower level of his being, such as his ability to joke or laugh,[126] but it is grounded in what is highest in man: his rational and spiritual mind.[127]

Throughout our analyses in this work, we encountered faculties of man that essentially presuppose a spiritual and a rational subject. By them, man is capable, for instance, of transcending himself and entering into meaningful cognitive contact with the world and other persons, of acting on the world freely and in a morally responsible way, of knowing and determining *himself* in a fully awakened, conscious manner. Man is not a 'sleeping,' self-enclosed entity that, like a stone, is 'in itself' being wholly dependent on and subjected to exterior forces. And as we saw in the preceding section, as such a conscious, spiritual, personal being each man is also absolutely unique and irreplaceable. Compared to a body, and even to animals, man is much more fully, much more centrally, a part of the real world. In a sense, he *is* a real world in and for himself. And this is precisely what in Augustine's eyes gives him a degree of reality and of value that is in principle superior to anything that does not have a mind.[128] Man's mind is not only better and more potent than any body,[129] Augustine goes even so far as to say that, as God excels any creature, so also the mind excels any corporeal creature in the dignity of its nature.[130] For what among creatures could be greater, he marvels, than the understanding life (*vita intellegens*), which is the mind, or what could be less than a body?[131] Indeed, even if a soul has fallen by sinning (*peccatrix anima quocumque ceciderit*)[132] and has suffered a degradation and defect in its natural ornament, it will still surpass without doubt the dignity of all bodies,[133] not only of its own body which is a part of the corporeal universe, but also of the collective body of the whole universe itself.[134] There is something that remains essential to its nature and that it cannot lose: its dignity as a person.[135]

Thus, we find after Augustine that also with respect to the third characteristic of substantiality, namely being really real, man's mind is more properly a substance than his body. In virtue of its rational and spiritual nature, it is placed much higher in the hierarchy of being (*esse*) than any body (or animal). In fact, we also find the three characteristics of substantiality interpenetrate and depend on each other: by being the one (unique, individual) subsisting subject of its spiritual acts the mind achieves this superior position in reality.

These considerations, finally, allow for a more forceful response to those theories that claim the mind to be a harmony (*temperatio*) or epiphenomenon of the body.

Though Augustine refers to such theories,[136] he does not seem to have argued against them to any greater extent.[137] However, in the light of his discussion of the mind's spiritual substantiality and in the light of the subsequent development of his thought,[138] we may make the following points.

First of all, there is a certain plausibility to the assumption that the mind inheres the body in the manner in which a color, harmony or beauty is attached to a corporeal bearer. For both the mind as well as a beauty are *in*corporeal entities, as such lacking essentially bodily characteristics. In Chapter 1, we mentioned the fact of such incorporeal aspects of matter. However, this similarity should not lead us to overlook the essential difference between the two, which is plainly obvious from the fact, among other facts, that these incorporeal aspects are not spiritual data which are *consciously* performed 'from within.' A beauty is not 'lived' by a conscious subject.[139] This alone shows that the mind and its acts cannot simply be seen on analogy to bodily epiphenomena.

Secondly, being ontologically dependent on its substance, an epiphenomenon of a body does not have the kind of power over its bearer that the mind can exercise over the body. Already Plato points out against Simmias that we are able to command bodily movements and to resist the passions of the body.[140] And Augustine mentions the fact that we can turn away from the bodily senses in the perception of intelligibles, as disproving this theory of soul as *temperatio* of the body.[141] One could list many more acts performed with respect to our body, such as speaking, walking, singing, etc., that could not be accounted for if the mind were like beauty dependent on the body.

Thirdly, the most cogent refutation of any epiphenomenalistic theory can be developed precisely on the basis of the present discussion of the spiritual substantiality of the mind. For if Augustine is right in arguing the mind to possess a higher degree of reality (*esse*) than the body, and if it is acknowledged that any accident is *qua* accident dependent on, and thus inferior in reality to, its underlying substance, it follows logically that the mind cannot be an accident (epiphenomenon) of the body. The superior substantiality of the mind as a *spiritual* substance renders its inhering in a body (or any other being) metaphysically impossible. Itself being a substance of this kind, the mind cannot but 'stand in itself.'[142]

Summarizing the results gained in this chapter we can with Augustine conclude that the mind as one individual reality being the performing subject of its acts is, for these reasons, a substance;[143] in fact, as such *spiritual* substance it realizes the characteristics of substantiality to a higher degree than any body. Therefore, it cannot be an epiphenomenon (accident) of the latter.

And yet, one final question remains to be posed: Does the recognition of the spiritual substantiality of the mind not have to lead Augustine to a fatal dualism in which the unity of man is destroyed? If mind and body are acknowledged to be distinct substances, to different degrees of perfection, is man thereby not split into two separated parts and thus compromised in his essential oneness? An answer to these crucial questions will be reserved for the concluding chapter.

CHAPTER 5

The unity consisting of mind and body

The question whether Augustine's view of the substantiality of the mind logically leads to a destruction of the unity of man presents itself as even more pressing in the light of his strong affirmation that man is one being consisting of soul *and* body.[1] In fact, Augustine considers this unity itself (that is, man) a substance.[2] Are these two contradictory positions, or is it possible to reconcile the substantial distinctness of soul and body with the view that man, himself being a substance, *is* the union of these two parts?[3]

This problem is as such not peculiar to Augustine, but pervades the whole history of philosophy. From Plato a tension can be observed between, on the one hand, an emphasis on the unity of man and, on the other hand, a stress on the distinctness and duality of the components of which he consists, body and soul. The former is generally attributed to the Aristotelian-Thomistic tradition, the latter to the Platonic-Augustinian tradition, though, as often is the case, these generalizations do not do full justice to the thought of at least the main representatives of these traditions. For not only is Augustine fully aware of the oneness of man, but Thomas Aquinas also speaks of man as consisting of soul and body as two distinct substances.[4] Nevertheless, it is true to say that in either tradition there is a different emphasis in regard to the nature of man.[5]

The approach to be taken in the following attempt to show a way of reconciling these two points of view is based on the assumption that the *kind* of unity man is essentially presupposes the distinct substances of body and soul. Only and precisely by holding an anthropological dualism can the substantial oneness of man be explained and accounted for.[6]

1   Man as a psycho-physical being

At various places throughout our work, we saw Augustine pointing out and investigating phenomena that can be accounted for only if man is seen to be a composite of a corporeal and a spiritual substance. For these phenomena are to be 'situated' neither in the soul alone, nor in the body, but precisely in that whole that is constituted by *both* of them in their essential distinctness: man. To recall them briefly will reveal man to be a reality that is unique with respect to each of his constitutive parts, possessing properties that neither the soul nor the body possesses in and of itself.[7]

Most prominently, in our section on the 'lived' body we saw Augustine describing the unique phenomenon of *sentire in corpore*. The soul is sensitively present in the various, locally distinct parts of the body not by some part of itself, but as one and the same whole soul, which can simultaneously have 'full' sensations of even the smallest spots all over the body. This amazing fact, clearly given from inner experience, is used by Augustine, as we analyzed, as the basis of an argument for an incorporeal (spiritual) soul 'in' the body. Indeed, it is precisely the unity of a spatially extended corporeal being with an incorporeal simple being that accounts for this experienced fact. Neither two bodies, nor two souls alone could bring about such *sentire in corpore*. It essentially presupposes the *composite* reality that man is.

Again, the very datum of a '*lived body*,' indeed of a body that, as we found in following Augustine, is amazingly fitted to the soul expressing its dignity by being erect and acquiring a 'preciousness by participation,' proves that it is united to a spiritual soul (mind). For only a body *as* a constitutive part of *man* can be lifted up from the mere material level (*Körper*) and become such a unique reality of a human 'lived' body (*Leib*).[8]

Furthermore, in our section on sense-perception we saw how Augustine tries to show that there is an incorporeal, spiritual subject performing acts through the *bodily* senses. Sense-perceptions by nature consist of a spiritual and a corporeal 'side'; if one of them is lacking, they cannot be performed. In fact, the variety of the different kinds of sense-perceptions, such as seeing, hearing, etc., can only be explained by the various bodily organs involved, since the performing subject (soul) is the same in all of them. Thus, both the very occurrence of the act of sense-perception as such and its specific forms reveal it to be a psycho-physical phenomenon.[9]

Moreover, the act of freely moving our body 'from within' discussed earlier manifests the unity of body and soul in man. For, as we saw, the volitional governing itself of the body is a *spaceless* motion of a spiritual subject (soul) affecting a *local* movement of bodily members. Such an act can exist only in the *composite* being of man.

Finally, we briefly mentioned Augustine's references to the datum of facial expressions (in the section on *se cogitare*). Our body is not only expressive of the soul as such by being erect; our face and eyes particularly are also the media through which psychic states and experiences can be expressed.[10] We may gain a direct access to another's interior life through his bodily expressions. Clearly, this phenomenon again presupposes the intimate unity of a spiritual and a corporeal being; it can neither be found among bodies alone, nor among 'body-less' spirits, but only in man.

All these and many other relations that could be established between body and soul,[11] reveal man to be a whole that consists of the two distinct realities of a spiritual and a corporeal substance, but that, at the same time, constitutes a new reality having its own specifically unique (human) nature as one psycho-physical being.[12] Man as this one composite being can be understood only if the distinctness of his two constitutive elements is clearly grasped.[13]

The peculiarity of this kind of unity that man is may become further manifest when one compares it to the way corporeal beings unite in order to constitute greater wholes. In this manner, too, the question left open at the end of our previous section on individual oneness may find an answer, namely whether the soul can also be called one in the sense of not allowing itself to be a part of a whole.

As we pointed out in that section, any corporeal being is in principle open to being fused with other bodies. Because of their lack of a specifically determinate uniqueness and irreplaceability in and of themselves, they are more easily united with and added to greater bodily wholes, into whose 'prevailing' particularity they get absorbed. The single parts of bodies seem in principle exchangeable, without the whole changing its particular character. Yet, they are not absorbed into it in that they became parts of a completely different being. The whole body still remains a body possessing, like its parts, corporeal properties.

But precisely the opposite holds true for the unity of body and soul in man. The composite whole that man is precisely does not remain on the same 'essential level' as its parts; man as a psychophysical being, as we saw, has a nature in and of himself which, by presupposing a corporeal and a spiritual being, is unique to either of them. And these two components are exclusively unique in the sense that my soul is and can be united only to my body. Certainly, as a corporeal being my body (*Körper*), like any other body, consists of exchangeable elements; however, as *my* body (*Leib*) united to *my* soul it belongs exclusively to myself as this one man. If my body were united to another soul (theoretically assuming such a possibility), a completely different man would come into being. Each man consists of two irreplaceably unique parts. There is nothing in man, Augustine says, pertaining to his substance and nature, except body and soul.[14] There is such a deep ordination towards each other that a man would not be what he is without these two constituents that are exclusively his own.[15]

This fact of the two components of man belonging exclusively to himself – a fact that is not found in bodily wholes – suggests, furthermore, that the part-whole relation in man runs, as it were, in the opposite direction than on the corporeal level. For in a body the whole determines the specific character of the parts that are absorbed into it according to their proper place and function; their own 'individuality' is changed into what they are *as* parts of this whole. One and the same piece of stone, for instance, receives a quite different character depending on the mosaic of which it is a part. Man, however, as composite of body and soul is what he is because of his parts, among which precisely the soul occupies the primary place. Not only does my soul form and 'individualize' my body rendering it *my* 'lived' body, but it also accounts primarily for my individuality as this one man. My concrete nature as man is 'consequential' to my constitutive parts, and not vice versa as in matter. And since it is the soul that is most properly individual, my concreteness as man 'follows' primarily from its being my central constituent.

It becomes evident that the body-soul unity is structurally quite different from those unities found on the corporeal level. Its specific peculiarity cannot be conceived in terms of bodily fusions. In this respect, then, the soul can also be called one in the sense of not allowing itself to be a part of a greater whole, that is, when such union is seen on analogy with the way corporeal beings unite. But it is not one (in this same sense of oneness) absolutely speaking, since it constitutes, together with the body, the one human being. In this it is a part of man.

It would, however, be wrong to assume that the soul as part of man is thereby jeopardized in its substantiality. On the contrary, this is rather thrown into greater relief. For though it is in one sense less perfectly substantial than the whole man, precisely because it is merely part of him while he himself, incapable of becoming part of a new substantial being, possesses also this kind of oneness, the soul is still the primary element accounting for man's substantiality. Man is a substance because of his soul which is a substance. In this sense, Augustine calls the mind the principal part of man, as it were, the head of the human substance.[16] He himself as composite being is what he is primarily in virtue of his spiritual substance.[17] This is what gives him his particular place in the hierarchy of being. And this is what renders him a *personal* being,[18] whereby the term 'person,' correspondingly, refers primarily to his soul, and secondarily to man himself as consisting of soul and body.[19]

Thus, accepting and synthesizing Augustine's thought one could describe man as a psycho-physical reality that in order to be this one concrete being essentially presupposes the distinctness of its two components, body and soul, and that is a person primarily in virtue of its spiritual substance. Man is one *because* he consists of these two elements.[20]

And yet, the question immediately poses itself: *How* is this unity possible? How can an invisible, incorporeal, spiritual substance be joined to a corporeal one? Where is the connecting link, and how are they kept together? It seems that without answering these questions sufficiently Augustine's position is untenable.

2   The mystery of the unity of man

The problem of the exact connection of body and soul in man is as such distinct from, though clearly related to, the main question of our work, viz. as to the essential (substantial) distinctness of body and soul. While this latter question concerns the 'whatness' of both body and soul as well as the *fact* of their constituting the one man, the former treats the actual 'how' of their union. The difference of these two questions needs to be emphasized strongly for both historical and systematical reasons. For not only has the actual manner in which body and soul unite been explained quite differently by thinkers who hold basically the same view on their natures, as becomes manifest especially in the body-soul 'solutions' of various dualistic thinkers,[21] but it also seems to be the case that man's rational powers of understanding are different with respect to each of these questions. While the whatness of body and soul and the fact of their relation can be investigated rationally (which is precisely what we tried to do in our work), the 'how' of their relation, that is, the 'bond' of their unity, seems to go beyond our rational comprehension. Body and soul as two essentially distinct substances *are* united to constitute the one man, but we do not know how. Augustine explains his position thus:

> The manner in which spirits are joined to bodies and become living beings (*animalia*), is thoroughly marvellous and cannot be comprehended by man – but this is precisely what man is.[22]

However, the knowledge of our ignorance in this specific case may not lead to a total rejection of the results of our analyses thus far. For, as Augustine strongly admonishes elsewhere, one should not give up the evidence for a thing already gained with certainty as a result of encountering a fact about the same thing that one is unable to explain by reason.[23] It would be irrational to reject a piece of evidence found to be true solely because we do not see how we can reconcile it with another piece of evidence; yet it would likewise be irrational – or rather rationalistic – to claim an evidence where such is not given. That the 'how' of the body-soul unity cannot immediately be explained is no reason for the alleged need of finding 'solutions' that appear as 'philosophical constructions,' nor is it a justification for the denial of the *fact* of this unity altogether. Rather this incomprehensible 'how' may be seen as an indication of the actual existence of 'natural mysteries,' or apories, that lie beyond the limits of man's knowing powers.[24]

It was Augustine's greatness as a philosophical thinker to be conscious of such rationalistic temptations. He was capable of being simply amazed at mysteries in being, discovering their existence, but willingly acknowledging that their 'ultimate how' is not accessible to human reason.[25] On the basis of this attitude he was led to conceive of the unity of body and soul in man as constituted in a very mysterious manner:

> If we were only souls, that is, spirits without any body, and if we dwelt in heaven and had no knowledge of earthly animals (*terrena animalia*), and were told that we should be bound to earthly bodies by some wonderful bond of union, and should animate them, should we not much more vigorously refuse to believe this, and maintain that nature would not permit an incorporeal substance to be held by a corporeal bond? And yet the earth is full of living spirits, to which terrestrial bodies are bound, and with which they are in a wonderful way implicated.[26]

This 'natural mystery' of the unity of man[27] could more readily be acknowledged if it is seen as an analogy to other unities found both in the natural and supernatural realm of being (if we may leave for a moment the purely philosophical context and turn to those mysteries the actual existence of which is not known rationally but is accepted on the basis of faith in revelation). For instance, the deepest union between two persons in love presupposes these two individuals that become 'one soul';[28] but who would want to say *how* this unity is actually constituted? Even more inexplicable to man is the analogous unity of Father and Son in the Divine Trinity that is believed in faith.[29] Similar to the union of body and soul in man is also that of the human and the divine natures in the one person of Christ, both of which Augustine compares in a longer passage, even contending that the former is a greater mystery since in it an *incorporeal* nature is united to a *corporeal* one while in the latter the *incorporeal* nature of the Word of God is united to an *incorporeal* human soul having a body (*animae habenti corpus*) the occurrence of which union seems more readily possible.[30] Whether or not this reasoning is tenable,[31] the comparison as such is illuminating for our purposes, though it shall not be decided here whether Augustine's conception of the unity of man can on the basis of this passage be termed 'hypostatic.'[32]

One may make reference here to a principle operating in reality in the light of which these and similar 'unities' could be placed in proper perspective. It might be called the principle of 'unity in and through duality.' There are beings that exist as 'unified consequence' of two essentially distinct realities, whereby the actual bond of unity, though known to be existing, remains hidden to us in its 'ultimate how.' Applying this principle one can with Augustine say that man *is* a mystery,[33] a mystery, however, that is rationally known to consist in the unity of the two distinct substances of body and soul.[34]

Afterword

An intended goal of our work was to throw into greater relief the richness of observations and analyses to be found in St Augustine's philosophy of mind. Employing the 'introspective method' as only very few thinkers have, Augustine gained an understanding of man's 'inner being' that, as should have become evident, in its originality and sharpness of insight has rarely been equalled. The multitude of observations regarding the various mental faculties, elaborated on in Chapter 2, and the investigation of the complex problem of the mind's relation to itself, treated in Chapter 3, especially revealed the 'handwriting' of a psychological genius. But also the more metaphysical reflections on the nature of bodies, including the human body (Chapter 1), on the substantiality of the mind (Chapter 4), and on the composite nature of man (final Chapter), showed Augustine to us as a thinker with an acute awareness of the inexhaustible aspects and particularities of being. For these reasons, the decision to choose Augustine as a historical source of a systematic-phenomenological study in philosophical anthropology seems to have been justified by our results.

Furthermore, the wealth of insight found in Augustine provided a most fertile ground for realizing the main purpose of our work, viz. to show, against any materialistic conception, the incorporeal and spiritual substantiality of the human soul. After a brief characterization of what it means to be corporeal, it was our principal task to bring to conceptual clarity, following Augustine, that which is given in inner experience, and to ask whether this also bears the marks of corporeal beings. The structure of the argument, thus, consisted in two steps: the identification and description of 'inner data,' and the subsequent investigation of whether or not they are corporeal. In thus developing arguments that were either explicitly elaborated by Augustine or virtually contained in his work, we were allowed to gain an insight not only into the incorporeality, but also, positively, into the (rational, conscious) spirituality of man's soul. This insight could further be deepened by the discussion of the kind of being the soul has, that is, to be a substance, which eventually led to a brief 'synthesizing' statement of the nature of man as unity of body and soul.

Certainly, the questions discussed do not exhaust a philosophical anthropology. There are many further problems regarding man that would require extensive philosophical research, such as the question of the origin of the human soul and of evolution, the question of the historicity and personal development of man, the question of the various interpersonal relations obtaining between men and constituting communities, the question of the meaning of man's life, and, above all, the question of whether there will be a life after death. Yet as important as these questions may be, they all presuppose what we tried to show in this work: man as a being consisting of body *and* soul. This is the cornerstone on which all further reflections, in fact all meaning in human existence rest. If just one reader will have become convinced of this fact, that man does have a soul which is spiritual, our work will have fulfilled its purpose.

Notes

Introduction

1 Surveys on the various approaches to Augustine can be found, with corresponding literature, in Carl Andresen, ed., *Bibliographia Augustiniana* [Darmstadt: Wissenschaftl. Buchgesellschaft, 1962), Franz Körner, *Das Sein und der Mensch. Die existenzielle Seinsentdeckung des jungen Augustins* (Freiburg/München: Alber, 1959), pp. 1–40, Alfred Schöpf, *Augustinus. Einführung in sein Philosophieren* (Freiburg/München: Alber, 1970), pp. 9–20.

2 Cf. *Conf.* I, 1: 'inquietum est cor nostrum, donec requiescat in te.'

3 *Conf.* III, 6: 'O veritas, veritas, quam intime etiam tum medullae animi mei suspirabant tibi.' *Tract. in Ioh.* XXVI, 5: 'Quid enim fortius desiderat anima quam veritatem.' See Joseph Geyser, 'Die erkenntnistheoretischen Anschauungen Augustins zu Beginn seiner schriftstellerischen Tätigkeit,' *Aurelius Augustinus* (Festschrift der Görresgesellschaft hrsg. von Martin Grabmann und Joseph Mausbach) (Köln: Bachem, 1930), p. 71: 'Only with inner emotion can one read the beautiful words in which Augustine says that he thinks he must owe it to the prayers of his pious mother that he had such a passion for the knowledge of truth.' See also John Mourant, 'St Augustine's Quest for Truth,' *NSchol*, 5 (1931), 206–18, Josef Rief, 'Liebe zur Wahrheit. Untersuchungen zur Ethik des jungen Augustinus,' *ThQ*, 141 (1961), 281–318.

4 This is particularly manifest from his early Cassiciacum-dialogues and from his letters.

5 Discussions of Augustine's arguments for the spiritual incorporeality of the soul are found in the following works: Martin Ferraz, *De la psychologie de saint Augustin* (Paris: Durand, 1862), pp. 41–69, Theodor Gangauf, *Metaphysische Psychologie des Hl. Augustinus* (Augs-

burg, 1852), pp. 158–82, Etienne Gilson, *The Christian Philosophy of St. Augustine*, trans. L. E. M. Lynch (New York: Random House, 1960), pp. 44–8, Martin Grabmann, *Die Grundgedanken des Hl. Augustinus über Seele und Gott* (Köln: Bachem, 1916) pp. 51–60 (perhaps still the best short survey of the various arguments), Wilhelm Heinzelmann, *Über Augustins Lehre vom Wesen und Ursprung der menschlichen Seele* (Halberstadt, 1868), pp. 14–23, Guido Mancini, *La Psicologia di S. Agostino* (Napoli: Ricciardi, 1919), pp. 65–86 (with comparisons to Plotinus), James Morgan, *The Psychological Teaching of St Augustine* (London: Elliot Stock, 1932), pp. 102–23 (surprising lack of the arguments from *De Trinitate*), Jean-Félix Nourrisson, *La philosophie de Saint Augustin* (Paris: Didier, 1866), pp. 165–98, W. O'Connor, *The Concept of the Soul According to St Augustine* (Washington D.C., 1921), pp. 48–56, Joseph Storz, *Die Philosophie des Hl. Augustinus* (Freiburg: Herder, 1882), pp. 104–16, Wilhelm Thimme, *Augustins erster Entwurf einer metaphysischen Seelenlehre* (Berlin: Trowitzsch, 1908) (treats only the arguments from *De Quantitate Animae*), Leopold Wittmann, *Ascensus. Der Aufstieg zur Transzendenz in der Metaphysik Augustins* (München: Berchmans, 1980), pp. 248–51.

6   See note 7 and *Conf.* IV, 15. Cf. Grabmann, *Grundgedanken*, pp. 49–50.

7   *Solil.* I, II, 7: 'A. Deum et animam scire cupio. R. Nihilne plus? A. Nihil omnino.' Also *De Ord.* II, XVIII, 47: 'Cuius (i.e. philosophiae) duplex quaestio est, una de anima, altera de deo.'

8   *Conf.* III, 4. Cf. Körner, *Sein und Mensch*, pp. 68–75.

9   *Conf.* V, 7.

10 On Augustine's relation to the Manicheans see Kurt Flasch, *Augustin. Einführung in sein Denken* (Stuttgart: Reclam, 1980), pp. 27–55, and Anna Escher di Stefano, *Il Manicheismo in S. Agostino* (Padova: CEDAM, 1960), pp. 56–82.

11 *Conf.* VII, 20. See Willy Theiler, *Porphyrios und Augustin* (Halle: Niemeyer, 1933), p. 3: 'It may not be inferred from the plural form, *Platonici*, that Augustine knew other Platonic writers through their works besides Porphyry and Plotinus, as he was interpreted by Porphyry.' Augustine knew Porphyry in the translation of Marius Victorinus (*Conf.* VIII, 3).

12 *Conf.* VII, 1.

13 *Ibid.*

14 *Ibid.*

15 *Conf.* V, 10: 'mentem cogitare non noveram nisi eam subtile corpus esse, quod tamen per loci spatia diffunderetur.'

16   See Peter Brown, *Augustine of Hippo* (Berkeley and Los Angeles: Univ. of California Press, 1967), p. 85.

17   *Conf.* V, 14: 'Tunc vero fortiter intendi animum, si quo modo possem certis aliquibus documentis manichaeos convincere falsitatis.' And in a later work Augustine states: 'Animam vero non esse corpoream non solum me putare, sed plane scire audeo profiteri' (*De Gen. ad Litt.* XII, XXXIII, 62).

18   Brown, p. 86: 'The story which Augustine tells in the *Confessiones* of his dilemmas in dealing with this problem is one of the most dramatic and massive evocations ever written of the evolution of a metaphysician; and his final "conversion" to the idea of a purely spiritual reality, as held by sophisticated Christians in Milan, is a decisive and fateful step in the evolution of our ideas on spirit and matter.'

19   Cf. Karl Jaspers, *Die großen Philosophen* Bd. I (München: Piper, 1957), p. 326: 'Augustine's way of thinking is characterized by a fundamental feature that in its fruitfulness has not been exhausted: he makes present original experiences of the soul. He reflects on the wonders of the self-presence of our being.'

20   This seems to be the prevailing method used in the studies of Augustine's anthropology, as in Alois Dempf, 'Die Menschenlehre Augustins,' *MThZ*, 6 (1955), 21–31, Erich Dinkler, *Die Anthropologie Augustins* (Stuttgart: Kohlhammer, 1934), Heinzelmann, *Augustins Lehre*, Mancini, *La Psicologia*.

   For further literature on Augustine's sources see Jakob Barion, *Plotin und Augustinus. Untersuchungen zum Gottesproblem* (Berlin: Junker und Dünnhaupt, 1935), pp. 13–52, Charles Boyer S.J., *Christianisme et néo-platonisme dans la formation de Saint Augustin* (Paris: Beauchesne, 1920), Fulbert Cayré, *Initiation à la philosophie de Saint Augustin* (Paris: Desclée de Brouwer, 1947), pp. 61–92, G. M. Manser, 'Augustinus' Philosophie in ihrem Verhältnis und ihrer Abhängigkeit von Plotin,' *DT*, 10 (1932), Nourrisson, *La philosophie* Vol. II, pp. 92–152, Robert O'Connell, *St Augustine's Early Theory of Man* (Cambridge, Mass.: The Belknap Press of Harvard Univ. Press, 1968), Robert O'Connell S.J., 'The Plotinian Fall of the Soul in St. Augustine,' *Tr*, 19 (1963), 1–35.

21   The so-called 'existential method' was introduced by Franz Körner in his book *Das Sein und der Mensch* and adopted, for instance, by Leopold Wittmann. It means an interpretation of Augustine's thought in the light of his personal life and existential struggles.

22   *De Doctr. Christ.* II, IX, 14 and II, XI, 16.

23   Anton Maxsein, *Philosophia Cordis. Das Wesen der Personalität bei Augustinus* (Salzburg: Müller, 1966).

24   Alfred Schöpf, *Wahrheit und Wissen. Die Begründung der Erkenntnis bei Augustin* (München: Pustet, 1965), pp. 25–9. 'Whoever wants to deal with Augustine's works must attempt to think through the trains of thought expressed in them and then judge whether they are true or false, i.e. he must himself perform the act of philosophising proper by trying to realise the insights in himself. The study of Augustine must be like a dialogue. Augustine's insight must become one's own, his searching must become one's own concern, his errors, however, must become the object of critique. But the central point and criterion in this intellectual exchange must be truthfulness' (p. 25).

25   Schöpf, p. 25.

26   *De Trin.* XIV, VII, 9: 'Id agunt et litterae quae de his rebus conscriptae sunt, quas res duce ratione veras esse invenit lector, non quas veras esse credit ei qui scripsit sicut legitur historia, sed quas veras esse etiam ipse invenit sive apud se sive in ipsa mentis luce veritate.' Contrary to the *CC*-edition, which has *duce veritate* in the last line, I accept Migne in this case.

27   *De Mag.* X, 33: 'Ita magis signum re cognita quam signo dato ipsa res discitur.' See the whole context where Augustine excellently shows that true learning means not the perception of words, but the grasp of the things themselves signified.

28   Gilson, p. 269, O'Connor, p. 38.

29   *De Trin.* I, III, 5.

30   Brown, p. 123. Cf. also Rudolph Berlinger, *Augustins dialogische Metaphysik* (Frankfurt, Klostermann, 1962), pp. 14–15: 'In almost all his works, Augustine lets the truth which he has grasped appear as in the many colors of a prism, and lets it take shape under ever new aspects of the problem.'

31   *De Trin.* V, VII, 8: 'Quamobrem non est in rebus considerandum quid vel sinat vel non sinat dici usus sermonis nostri sed quis rerum ipsarum intellectus eluceat.'

32   *De Trin.* V, VII, 8: 'Hoc exemplis planum faciendum est.'

33   *De Mag.* XIV, 45: '. . . illi qui discipuli vocantur, utrum vera dicta sint, apud semetipsos considerant, interiorem scilicet illam veritatem pro viribus intuentes. Tunc ergo discunt.' Gilson beautifully describes Augustine's view of the teacher-student relation: 'Masters merely explain, with the help of words, the disciplines they profess to teach; then those who are called students search within themselves to see if the things their masters tell them are true. To the extent of their abilities, they conduct this examination with their eyes fixed on the truth within and in this way are instructed, establishing for themselves that the things told them are true. Who then is the real master? Is it

the teacher? As far as the truth is concerned, the teacher is in the same position as his student: he is not so much "teaching" as "taught." The real master is that Truth which belongs neither to teacher nor student but is common to both and present in both; the Truth which instructs them both in the same way and thus brings them necessarily to agree' (p. 74).

34 *Lib. de Videndo Deo (seu Ep. CXLVII)*, 2: 'Nolo auctoritatem meam sequaris, ut ideo putes tibi aliquid necesse esse credere, quoniam a me dicitur.'

35 *De Quant. An.* VII, 12. James Morgan rightly observes that Augustine does not rely on, and hardly cites, authorities, neither those who oppose him, nor those who support him such as those great names as Plato and Plotinus (*The Psychological Teaching*, pp. 104 ff.).

36 *Contra Ep. Fund.* 2: '. . . cum quo labore verum inveniatur et quam difficile caveantur errores.'

37 *De Vera Rel.* XXV, 47: 'Nam ipsi rationi purgatioris animae, quae ad perspicuam veritatem pervenit, nullo modo auctoritas humana praeponitur.' See *ibid.* XXIV, 45.

38 *De Trin.* II, prooem: 'Magisque optabo a quolibet reprehendi quam sive ab errante sive ab adulante laudari.'

39 *De Trin.* I, III, 5. Cf. *Tract. in Ioh.* XVIII, 7: 'Mores perducunt ad intellegentiam.'

40 *De Trin.* I, II, 4.

41 *De Trin.* V, I, 1: 'Ab his etiam qui ista lecturi sunt ut ignoscant peto ubi me magis voluisse quam potuisse dicere adverterint quod vel ipsi melius intellegunt vel propter mei eloquii difficultatem non intellegunt, sicut ego eis ignosco ubi propter suam tarditatem intellegere non possunt.'

42 See, for instance, Klaus Bernath, *Anima Forma Corporis* (Bonn: Bouvier, 1969); Anton C. Pegis, *At the Origins of the Thomistic Notion of Man* (New York: Macmillan Co., 1963); Josef Pieper, *Tod und Unsterblichkeit* (München: Kösel, 1968), pp. 45–66. In Chapter 5, however, we will briefly have to touch on the Thomistic conception of the oneness of man.

43 *De Trin.* I, III, 8: 'Proinde quisquis haec legit ubi pariter certus est, pergat mecum; ubi pariter haesitat, quaerat mecum; ubi errorem suum cognoscit, redeat ad me; ubi meum, revocet me.' See *ibid.* III, prooem. 2.

44 *De Trin.* I, III, 5.

45 Cf. Fred Lord Townley, *The Unity of Body and Soul. The Value of the Body in Christian Teaching and Modern Thought* (London: Unwin Brothers Limited, 1929), p. 102: 'He [i.e. Augustine] appears to have

been the first of the Fathers to insist on the conception of soul as spiritual substance, and also to apply the term "extension" to matter as indicating its distinctive attribute.'

46   *Conf.* IV, 14: 'grande profundum est ipse homo.'

47   *En. in Ps.* XLI, 13: 'Si profunditas est abyssus, putamus non cor hominis abyssus est? Quid enim est profundius hac abysso?'

48   *De Trin.* V, I, 2: 'Quod nos ipsi in interiore homine sumus scientia comprehendendis laboremus nec sufficiamus.'

49   Cf. Morgan, p. 91. For studies in this area we may refer to August Brunner, *Der Stufenbau der Welt* (München: Kösel, 1950), Hedwig Conrad-Martius, 'Die "Seele" der Pflanze,' in *Schriften zur Philosophie* I, ed. Eberhard Avé-Lallement (München: Kösel, 1963), pp. 276–362, Helmuth Plessner, *Die Stufen des Organischen und der Mensch* (Berlin-New York: de Gruyter, 1975), Bertram Schuler, *Pflanze-Tier-Mensch* (München/Paderborn/Wien: Schöningh, 1969), Josef Seifert, *Leib und Seele* (Salzburg: Pustet, 1973), pp. 71–115.

50   *Sermo LII*, VI, 17; *ibid.* VII, 18; *Tract. in Ioh.* XXIII, 10; *De Trin.* X, IX, 12: 'Cognosce te ipsam.' *En. in Ps.* CII, 2: 'Quid est anima tua? omnia interiora tua.' Cf. Friedrich Seifert, *Seele und Bewußtsein* (München/Basel: Reinhardt, 1962), p. 41: 'Augustine is the most powerful example of what renders "psychology" possible in the important sense of being liberated from all historically conditioned conceptions: the absolutely compelling power of pure inner perception.'

51   *De Gen. ad Litt.* VII, XXI, 30: 'iam non possit inveniri nomen, quo proprie distinguatur ista natura, quae nec corpus nec Deus est nec vita sine sensu.'

52   Nevertheless, a brief survey of the most common terms for soul employed by Augustine is in order, so that they may be understood in a broad general meaning. There are basically four concepts occurring in his writings:

(1) *anima* (soul). This term is the most comprehensive one used by Augustine for soul. For it means both the principle of life animating the bodies of men and of animals (*anima corporis vita est*) (*Tract. in Ioh.* III, 4), as well as the rational and intellectual soul of man (*anima rationalis vel intellectualis*) (*De Trin.* XV, I, 1). It is the *anima* that has seven levels (*gradus*) according to its functions and potentialities in man (*De Quant. An.* XXXIII, 70–76). It seems to comprise everything in man that is not corporeal.

(2) *animus* (soul). Augustine took this term from Varro in whose natural theology it means the highest level of the soul where the intelligence resides (*De Civ. Dei* VII, 23). It refers to the human soul

as a rational being, in which sense it is synonymous with *mens* (*De Trin.* XV, I, 1; *De Civ. Dei* XI, 3).

(3) *mens* (mind). Most often used by Augustine especially in his 'psychological' studies of *De Trinitate*, *mens* is what excels in the human soul as *anima* (*De Trin.* XV, VII, 11; V, I, 2; XIV, VIII, 11); for it is the rational intelligence of man (*rationalis intellegentia*) (*De Trin.* X, V, 7), that faculty where his *ratio* and *intellegentia* (or *intellectus*) are 'situated' (*De Lib. Arb.* I, I, 3; I, IX, 19). It is the human soul properly speaking insofar as it is able to understand and to know wisdom and truth (*De Trin.* XII, III, 3; *Tract. in Ioh.* I, 18). As such, Augustine calls it the head of the human substance (*caput humanae substantiae*) (*De Trin.* VI, IX, 10).

(4) *spiritus* (spirit). Augustine briefly defines this term thus: *omnis mens spiritus est, non autem omnis spiritus mens est* (*De Trin.* XIV, XVI, 22). It means the same as *mens* and *animus* (*De Civ. Dei* XIV, 2), but not exclusively; for *spiritus* can also be predicated of God, of the animals, analogously even of the wind, as Augustine accepts from Scripture (*De Trin.* XIV, XVI, 22). And apart from man's rational power, *spiritus* refers also to his faculty of forming mental images (*visio spiritualis*) which ranks lower in the soul than the former (*De Gen. ad Litt.* XII, XXIV, 51).

Cf. also Gilson, pp. 269–70, note 1; and O'Connor, pp. 38–9.

53 *Sermo LII*, VII, 18: 'Quid habet anima tua? Intus commemora, recole. Non enim quod dicturus sum, id posco ut credatur mihi: noli acceptare, si in te non inveneris.'

CHAPTER 1   *The lack of bodily properties in the soul*

1   *De Trin.* X, VII, 9: 'Itaque alii sanguinem, alii cerebrum, alii cor (non sicut scriptura dicit: "Confitebor tibi, domine, in toto corde meo", et: "Diliges dominum deum tuum ex toto corde tuo"; hoc enim abutendo vel transferendo vocabulo dicitur a corpore ad animum), sed ipsam omnino particulam corporis quam in visceribus dilaniatis videmus eam esse putaverunt. Alii ex minutissimis individuisque corpusculis quas atomos dicunt concurrentibus in se atque cohaerentibus eam confici crediderunt. Alii aerem, alii ignem substantiam eius esse dixerunt. Alii eam nullam esse substantiam quia nisi corpus nullam substantiam poterant cogitare et eam corpus esse non inveniebant, sed ipsam temperationem corporis nostri vel compagem primordiorum quibus ista caro tamquam connectitur esse opinati sunt.'

2   Cf. *De Civ. Dei* VIII, 5, where Augustine attributes most of these views to figures in the history of philosophy: 'ut Thales in umore,

Anaximenes in aere, Stoici in igne, Epicurus in atomis, hoc est minutissimis corpusculis, quae nec dividi nec sentiri queunt, et quicumque alii, quorum enumeratione inmorari non est necesse, sive simplicia sive coniuncta corpora, sive vita carentia sive viventia, sed tamen corpora, causam principiumque rerum esse dixerunt.'

3   Anaximenes, *Fragment 2*: 'Just as our soul, being air, holds us together, so do breath and air encompass the whole world' (cited from Frederick Copleston S.J., *A History of Philosophy* [Garden City, N.Y.: Images Books, 1962 –] Vol. I, 1, p. 42.

4   Cf. Copleston, I, 2, p. 136 on the early Stoa: 'The soul of man . . . is part of the divine Fire which descended into men at their creation and is then passed on at generation, for, like all else, it is material.'

5   See the opinion of Simmias in Plato's *Phaedo*, 85e–86d.

6   *De Trin.* X, VIII, 9: 'Nam de quinto illo nescio quo corpore quod notissimis quattuor huius mundi elementis quidam coniungentes hinc animam esse dixerunt.' See also Aristotle, *De Anima* I, 2 where he gives a survey of the views of the soul present at his time, and Quirin Huonder, *Gott und Seele im Lichte der griechischen Philosophie* (München: Hueber, 1954).

7   See the quote in note 2.

8   *De Trin.* I, I, 1: 'Quorum nonnulli ea quae de corporalibus rebus sive per sensus corporeos experta notaverunt, sive quae natura humani ingenii et diligentiae vivacitate vel artis adiutorio perceperunt, ad res incorporeas et spiritales transferre conantur ut ex his illas metiri atque opinari velint.'

9   *De Trin.* X, VIII, 11: 'Sed quia (mens) in his est quae cum amore cogitat, sensibilius autem, id est corporalibus, cum amore assuefacta est, non valet sine imaginibus eorum esse in semetipsa. Hinc ei oboritur erroris dedecus dum rerum sensarum imagines secernere a se non potest ut se solam videat; cohaeserunt enim mirabiliter glutino amoris. Et haec est eis immunditia quoniam dum se solam nititur cogitare hoc se putat esse sine quo se non potest cogitare.' Cf. *De Trin.* X, VI, 8, *De Quant. An.* III, 4, *Ep. CXXXVII*, II, 4.

10   Cf. Josef Goldbrunner, *Das Leib-Seele-Problem bei Augustinus* (Kahlmünz: Laßleben, 1934), p. 23: 'When man in his striving gets entangled in the objects of the sensible world and yields to practical materialism, then theoretical materialism follows with psychological necessity.'

11   Martin Grabmann, *Grundgedanken*, p. 51: 'In these thoughts of Augustine there is also a serious warning addressed to our time. Is not the materialism and sensualism of modern philosophy and literature the theoretical echo of a one-sidedly material culture, of having given up

in practice ideal values and goals, of an unlimited distraction and alienation which leads by itself to an exclusive preoccupation with material gain and sensual pleasure?' See note 14.

12 This holds particularly for the theories mentioned in note 14. Cf. Karl Popper's review of the history of the mind-body problem in Karl R. Popper and John C. Eccles, *The Self and Its Brain* (Springer International, 1977), pp. 148–210. See also Josef Seifert, *Das Leib-Seele-Problem in der gegenwärtigen philosophischen Diskussion* (Darmstadt: Wissenschaftl. Buchgesellschaft, 1979), and Beda Thum, 'Theorien des Bewußtseins,' in *Geist und Leib in der menschlichen Existenz*, ed. Görres-Gesellschaft (Freiburg/München: Alber, 1961), pp. 60–75.

13 *Tract. in Ioh.* CXI, 2: 'Abscedat ab animo omnis imaginum corporalium cogitatio; quidquid menti occurrerit longum, latum, crassum, qualibet luce corporea coloratum, per quaelibet locorum spatia vel finita, vel infinita diffusum, ab his omnibus, quantum potest, aciem suae contemplationis vel intentionis avertat.' Cf. *ibid.* XL, 4.

14 This reductionistic temptation engendered by the amazing impact that physical science has exercised on the modern mind, is most prominently felt in the so-called mind-brain identity theory according to which statements about mental states are strictly identical with those about neurophysiological events, not with respect to their sense but with respect to their *referent*. See, above all, the articles by Feigl, Place, Smart, and Armstrong in *The Mind-Brain Identity Theory*, ed. C. V. Borst (Bristol: Macmillan, 1970). Similarly, the (philosophically naive) attempt to substitute rational operations of the conscious mind by 'stimoceivers' implanted in the brain in order to build up a 'psychocivilized society' (see José M. R. Delgado, *Physical Control of the Mind. Toward a Psychocivilized Society* [New York, Evanston, London: Harper & Row, 1969]), seems strongly motivated by an exuberant 'faith' in the alleged powers of modern science. Also the various forms of epiphenomenalism – from Huxley's assertion that 'our mental conditions are simply the symbols in consciousness of the changes which take place automatically in the organism' (cited in *Body, Mind, and Death*, ed. Antony Flew [New York: Macmillan, 1964], p. 205), to Gilbert Ryle's behaviourism that reduces 'mind' to the 'doings' and dispositions of bodies (see his *The Concept of Mind* [London: Hutchinson, 1949], pp. 116 ff.), and on to the theses of dialectical Marxism according to which mind is nothing but the product and function of matter (cf. its more detailed presentation, with corresponding literature, in Josef de Vries, *Materie und Geist* [München: Pustet, 1970], pp. 75–85) – all these theories appear greatly inspired,

at least in part, by the increasing exploration of material structures and processes.

For this reason, Augustine's exhortations as well as his arguments for the spiritual incorporeality of the mind to be developed in our work are implicitly applicable also to many 'modern' anthropologies. (See note 86, Chapter 2 notes 350,367, Chapter 3 note 163). For it is the same issue yesterday and today that is to be studied here.

15 *De Trin.* X, VII, 9: 'non cum eis vocabuli quaestione pugnandum est.'

16 *De Nat. et Orig. An.* IV, XII, 17: 'Ac primum scire vellem corpus quid esse definias. Si enim non est corpus nisi quod membris carnalibus constat, nec terra erit corpus nec caelum nec lapis nec aqua nec sidera nec si quid huiusmodi est; si autem corpus est quicquid maioribus et minoribus suis partibus maiora et minora spatia locorum obtinentibus constat, corpora sunt etiam ista quae commemoravi: corpus est aer, corpus est lux ista visibilis.'

17 For Augustine not only men but also the animals bear flesh: 'et quidquid carnem gerit et homo non est' (*Sermo CL*, IV, 5).

18 This definition appears again and again in Augustine's work. Cf. *De Trin.* X, VII, 10; *De Civ. Dei* XI, 10; *Conf.* X, 6; *Ep. CLXVI*, 4; *De Quant. An.* IV, 6; *De Immort. An.* VII, 13; *De Gen. ad Litt.* VII, XXI, 27; *De Lib. Arb.* II, VIII, 22; *Ep. CXXXVII*, II, 4; *De Vera Rel.* XXX, 55; *Tract. in Ioh.* XCIX, 3; *Liber de Videndo Deo (seu Ep. CXLVII)*, XVIII, 45.

19 Cf. *Tract. in Ioh.* XCIX, 3: 'ulla mole quae in alia parte maior, in alia minor.'

20 *Contra Ep. Man.* XVIII, 20.

21 *De Trin.* VI, VI, 8; cf. *De Immort. An.* VII, 12.

22 *De Trin.* VI, VIII, 9: 'Corpora quippe adiunctione sua crescunt.' Cf. *De Trin.* VII, VI, 11.

23 *De Immort. An.* VII, 12: 'Nam quoniam quodlibet corpus pars est mundi sensibilis, et ideo quanto maius est locique plus occupat, tanto magis propinquat universo: quantoque id magis facit, tanto magis est. Magis enim est totum quam pars. Quare etiam minus sit, cum minuitur, necesse est. Defectum ergo patitur cum minuitur. Porro autem minuitur, cum ex eo aliquid praecisione detrahitur. Ex quo conficitur ut tali detractione tendat ad nihilum. At nulla praecisio perducit ad nihilum. Omnis enim pars quae remanet, corpus est, et quidquid hoc est, quantolibet spatio locum occupat. Neque id posset, nisi haberet partes in quas identidem caederetur. Potest igitur infinite caedendo, infinite minui, et ideo defectum pati atque ad nihilum tendere, quamvis pervenire nunquam queat. Quod item de ipso spatio et quolibet intervallo dici atque intelligi potest. Nam et de his etiam

terminatis, dimidiam, verbi gratia, partem detrahendo, et ex eo quod restat, semper dimidiam, minuitur intervallum, atque ad finem progreditur, ad quem tamen nullo pervenitur modo.' On this whole problem see also Plotinus, *Enn.* IV, 7, 1–3.

24 *De Trin.* X, VII, 10.

25 See the references given in note 18.

26 *Contra Ep. Man.* XVI, 20: 'Neque ullo modo possit (corpus) in loco huius partis simul habere aliam partem.'

27 *De Immort. An.* XVI, 25. See also *De Vera Rel.* XXXII, 60.

28 *Contra Ep. Man.* XVI, 20. Cf. *Tract. in Ioh.* CXI, 3, where Augustine states this law the other way around: locus est cuique rei ubi est (place is where a body is).

   The objection could be raised that there are cases where more than one body occupies the same place, as for instance water in a sponge. However, even in these cases the general law seems to hold, if one approaches the level of their smallest (atomic) parts. For each of these parts of the two bodies seems to be located at its own proper place, and not at that of another part.

29 *De Div. Quaest. LXXXIII*, Qu. VIII.

30 *De Ord.* II, 6, 19: 'de loco in locum transire, quod est moveri.'

31 *De Vera Rel.* XXXII, 60.

32 *De Div. Quaest. LXXXIII*, Qu. VIII.

33 *De Gen. ad Litt.* VIII, XX, 39: 'Omne autem quod movetur per locum, non potest nisi et per tempus simul moveri.'

34 *Ep. XVIII*, 2: 'Est natura per locos et tempora mutabilis, ut corpus.'

35 It goes beyond the scope of our work to investigate critically other *philosophical* conceptions of matter, space and time, such as the notion of the 'event-particle' in the 'four-dimensional space-time manifold.' See Alfred North Whitehead, *The Concept of Nature* (Univ. of Michigan Press, 1957), p. 173 and pp. 99–119. In the present context, we can neither address the problem of whether such conceptions contradict, or rather presuppose and elaborate on, Augustine's view expounded in the text, nor analyze whether their underlying method, which admittedly is an 'extension of thought beyond the immediacy of observation' (p. 106), is justified and adequate to the subject matter in question. Cf. notes 50, 56, 64.

36 Clearly, this law applies only to spatially extended corporeal entities, and not, for instance, to the mathematical point. For though the latter is likewise located at a place in space, it is thereby not contained in space. See note 65.

37 *De Div. Quaest. LXXXIII*, Qu. XX.

38   *Ibid.* 'Locus enim in spatio est quod longitudine et latitudine et altitudine corporis occupatur.'

39   *Contra Ep. Man.* XIX, 21.

40   *De Immort. An.* XVI, 25: 'Moles quippe omnis quae occupat locum, non est in singulis suis partibus tota, sed in omnibus. Quare alia pars eius alibi est, et alibi alia.'

41   A good and concise summary of the bodily properties discussed so far is found in *Ep. CXXXVII*, II, 4: 'corpora, quorum nullum potest esse ubique totum, quoniam per innumerabiles partes aliud alibi habeat necesse est et, quantumcumque sit corpus seu quantulumcumque corpusculum, loci occupet spatium eumdemque locum sic impleat, ut in nulla eius parte sit totum. Ac per hoc densari ac rarescere, contrahi et dilatari, in minutias deteri et grandescere in molem non nisi corporum est.'

42   *De Quant. An.* IV, 6.

43   *Fathers of the Church,* Vol. 4, p. 65: 'I mean the dimension which makes it possible for the interior of a body to be an object of thought, or, if the body is transparent as glass, the object of sense perception.'

44   *De Quant. An.* IV, 6.

45   *Ibid.* 'quanquam (sc. altitudinem) si hoc demas corporibus, quantum mea opinio est, neque sentiri possunt, neque omnino corpora esse recte existimari.'

46   Cf. *De Trin.* VIII, VI, 9; XI, II, 3; XII, XII, 17. Note the modification of this statement given in note 48.

47   *De Quant. An.* VI, 10.

48   See again *De Quant. An.* IV, 6. See also *De Quant. An.* XXXII, 68: 'Cum autem locus et tempus sit, quibus omnia quae sentiuntur occupantur, vel potius quae occupant, quod oculis sentimus, per locum; quod auribus, per tempus dividitur.'

Here Augustine states that all that is perceived by the senses is contained in space and time. For what the eyes see can be divided in space, while what the ears hear is divisible in time. This implies that the object of hearing is not necessarily extended in space. The statement, therefore, that only a body is perceived by the senses is to be modified, in that a body *as* body seems to be perceived only by the senses of sight and touch, while the other senses perceive *qualities* that only a body can have, but that themselves are not bodies.

49   *De Quant. An.* IV, 6.

50   We cannot deal here with certain (philosophical) objections raised against the extendedness of matter on the basis of modern physics and quantum-physics. For this see the critical evaluation of such theories in Seifert, *Leib-Seele-Problem,* pp. 30–7.

51 *Contra Ep. Man.* XIX, 21: 'quantaelibet in eo particulae et innumerabilia frusta alia maiora, alia minora pro cogitantis arbitrio metirentur, ut bipedalis in eo verbi gratia pars octo partibus minor esset quam decempedalis.'

52 *De Immort. An.* VII, 12: 'omnis enim pars quae remanet, corpus est, et quidquid hoc est, quantolibet spatio locum occupat.' See notes 63, 64 and 65.

53 *De Trin.* VI, VI, 8.

54 *De Immort. An.* X, 17.

55 *De Trin.* VI, VI, 8. Certainly, in a sense the color of a body depends on its greatness, in that it might no longer be actually perceivable as this color when the body has gotten too small. In this case one could not even speak of a color to be given at all, since color is understood here as an aspect of the body that comes into existence precisely and only by being perceived. However, if 'color' refers to that property of a body that belongs to it even when it is not perceived, but that, at least in principle, remains accessible to perception, Augustine's thesis holds true, namely that color is independent of a body's greatness.

56 Note that these qualities are *in*corporeal properties of a body. Being essentially grounded in bodies, they themselves are not bodies. This shows that there can, and indeed must, be a number of incorporeal 'elements' belonging to bodies, a fact that becomes further manifest in the light of modern investigations of 'energy fields,' 'events,' 'vibratory entities' found in matter.

57 *De Trin.* VI, VI, 8.

58 *De Lib. Arb.* II, VIII, 22: 'Quidquid enim tali sensu attingitur, iam non unum sed multa esse convincitur; corpus est enim et ideo habet innumerabiles partes.'

59 *Ibid.* 'Sed ut minutas quasque minusque articulatas non persequar, quantulumcumque illud corpusculum sit, habet certe aliam partem dexteram aliam sinistram, aliam superiorem aliam inferiorem aut aliam ulteriorem aliam citeriorem aut alias finales aliam mediam. Haec enim necesse est quamlibet exiguo corporis modulo inesse fateamur, et propterea nullum corpus vere pureque unum esse concedimus, in quo tamen non possent tam multa numerari nisi illius unius cognitione discreta. . . . Cuiuslibet enim corpusculi pars dimidia, quamvis duabus totum constat, habet et ipsa dimidiam suam; sic ergo sunt illae duae partes in corpore ut nec ipsae simpliciter duae sint.'

60 *De Lib. Arb.* II, VIII, 23; see *ibid.* II, VIII, 21.

61 *De Lib. Arb.* II, VIII, 22. Surely, with our eyes we see the number one written on a page and, to mention a modern invention, computers also work with numbers somehow 'recognizing' them. Yet, neither do

our eyes understand the *meaning* of what they see on a page, nor are they able to investigate what is 'oneness' as such. (See our discussions of sense-perception and of the cognition of eternal reasons.) Likewise, a computer can mechanically conduct mathematical processes; but it can do so only because it has been programmed by someone understanding the meanings of numbers and of mathematical laws, which the computer knows nothing about. Hence Augustine's contention that the 'certain truth of number' can only be grasped by the mind.

62   Cf. *De Trin*. XI, II, 3.

63   See also *De Gen. ad Litt*. II, IV, 8: 'nullum esse quamlibet exiguum corpusculum, in quo divisio finiatur, sed infinite omnia dividi, quia omnis pars corporis corpus est, et omne corpus habeat necesse est dimidium quantitatis suae.'

64   The existence of such ultimate simple particles is also acknowledged by modern quantum-physics. See Eyind H. Wichmann, *Quantum Physics*, Berkeley Physics Course Vol. 4 (New York/Düsseldorf: McGraw-Hill Book Company, 1971), p. 11: 'We must conclude that when we study electrons, protons, neutrons, etc., we have reached a limit: it does not appear to be sensible and useful to regard these particles as made up of other more elementary particles. Nobody would attempt today to create a comprehensive theory of matter based on the proposition that matter is infinitely divisible: such an undertaking would be futile.' See also note 65.

65   This distinction has been developed by J. Seifert in his discussion of Leibniz's conception of the monads and Kant's second antinomy (*Leib-Seele-Problem*, pp. 30–7), in which he shows that there is a confusion of at least three basically different *kinds* of simplicity underlying their views. In his *Monadology*, Leibniz had shown that there must be simple substances without any parts, since there are composite ones (§2). Through a similar reasoning, Kant (in the thesis of his second antinomy) comes to the same conclusion. But while Kant, as a necessary contradiction of pure reason, juxtaposes to this argument the antithesis that there can *not* be simple substances because space is infinitely divisible so that each substance, that as a composite being must fill out space, must also be infinitely divisible (*Kritik der reinen Vernunft* 463–71), Leibniz infers that these simple substances (monads) do not have extension, figure, or possible divisibility, though they are 'the veritable atoms of nature' (§3), and that they must be spiritual as the soul also is a simple substance (§16).

In response to these views, Seifert distinguishes between (a) the simplicity of the mathematical point that occupies a place in space without being spatially extended, in which sense there are infinitely many parts (points) in a simple substance (Kant's antithesis); (b) the simplicity of ultimate particles in the sense of being actually indivisible into parts (Leibniz, Kant's thesis), though still being extended in space; (c) the simplicity of the soul which includes the second sense, but which is a far different *spiritual* simplicity that implies individuality, self-consciousness, etc. (See our Chapters 3 and 4). It was Leibniz's mistake to have confused the two latter meanings of simplicity, having concluded from the existence of simple elements of matter to their being conscious spiritual substances, as if a composite being could be constituted by simple 'souls.'

66 Augustine comes close to this distinction when he points out in *De Trin.* XI, X, 17, that our reason does not cease going further and dividing even the smallest parts of a body, though we are no longer able to perceive them actually. Cf. also note 23.

67 *De Musica*, VI, VIII, 21: 'Ita ratio invenit tam localia quam temporalia spatia infinitam divisionem recipere.'

68 Besides spatial extension which provides the basis of mathematical as well as of actual divisibility, a certain material extension also is presupposed for the latter. For an ultimate particle can no longer actually be divided, not because it is not extended in space, but because its material mass does not allow any longer for its being cut into pieces without being annihilated. Augustine mentions these two kinds of spatial and material extension, without however drawing these conclusions: 'quidquid loci spatio continetur, vel quantalibet mole diffunditur' (*Tract. in Ioh.* XL, 4).

69 See the very similar characterization of corporeal 'realities' in Seifert, *Leib und Seele*, pp. 3–12.

It may not be objected that this Augustinian (classic) conception of 'body' must be replaced by a more dynamic view of matter in which matter is considered to be equal to energy according to Einstein's famous equation $E = mc^2$. For this law does not state the *identity* of both matter and energy; rather, it formulates the fact and the proportion of their being *transformed* into each other, thereby precisely presupposing their essential distinctness. However to hold the transformability of matter into energy (and vice versa) does not contradict, but complements, Augustine's investigation of body. See note 56. It would be interesting, in addition, to analyze philosophically the essential features of 'energy' and to distinguish its nature from that of the 'soul.' Yet such an endeavour would obviously exceed the boundaries of the body-soul problem, though it would be analogous to our procedure in this work.

70 *De Trin.* VIII, IV, 7: 'Necesse est autem cum aliqua corporalia lecta

vel audita quae non vidimus credimus, fingat sibi animus aliquid in lineamentis formisque corporum sicut occurrerit cogitanti.'

71   *De Trin.* X, VII, 10: 'Sine phantasiis enim corporum quidquid iussi fuerint cogitare nihil omnino esse arbitrantur.'

72   *De Gen. ad Litt.* VII, XXI, 30: 'Si autem corpus esse dicunt alia qualibet notione omne quod est, id est omnem naturam atque substantiam, non quidem admittenda est ista locutio, ne non inveniamus, quomodo loquentes ea, quae corpora non sunt, a corporibus distinguamus; non tamen nimis est de nomine laborandum.'

73   Cf. *Conf.* VII, 1.

74   See Tertullian, *De Carne Christi*, 9 (*PL* II, 774): 'Omne quod est, corpus est sui generis; nihil est incorporale, nisi quod non est.'

75   *De Gen. ad Litt.* X, XXV, 41.

76   *De Quant. An.* III, 4.

77   *De Quant. An.* IV, 5: 'A. Quid ergo? iustitia, quam non nihil esse confessus es, immo quiddam longe divinius hac longeque praestantius, videtur tibi longa esse? E. Nullo modo mihi iustitia aut longa, aut lata, aut tale aliquid cogitanti potest occurrere. A. Si igitur nihil horum est iustitia, et tamen ipsa nihil non est; cur tibi anima nihil videtur, nisi eius aliqua longitudo sit? E. Age; iam non mihi videtur ex eo nihil esse anima, quod nec longa, nec lata, nec robusta sit.' See the same argument with respect to the beauty of wisdom and justice in *Tract. in Ioh.* XL, 4: 'Cogita, si potes, pulcritudinem sapientiae, occurrat tibi pulcritudo iustitiae. Forma est? statura est? color est? Nihil horum est, et tamen est.'

78   *Tract. in Ioh.* XIII, 5: 'Res est corporea quae videtur oculis corporeis.'

79   *De Immort. An.* X, 17. See also *De Div. Quaest. LXXXIII*, Qu. XLVI.

80   See our section on the *cognitio intellectualis*.

81   *De Quant. An.* III, 4.

82   See pp. 207–12.

83   For this argument see Gangauf, pp. 158–9; Grabmann, *Grundgedanken*, pp. 53–6; Heinzelmann, p. 15.

84   *De Nat. et Orig. An.* IV, XV, 22. See note 88.

85   *Liber de Videndo Deo (seu Ep. CXLVII)*, XVII, 43: 'Quanto magis illa, quae nullam gerunt similitudinem corporum, charitas, gaudium, longanimitas, pax, benignitas, bonitas, fides, mansuetudo, continentia, nulla locorum spatia tenent, nulla intercapedine separantur aut aliqua oculi cordis, quo radios suos mittant et ea videant, intervalla conquirunt! Nonne omnia in uno sunt sine angustia et suis terminis nota sunt sine circuitu regionum? Aut dic, in quo loco videas charitatem, quae tamen in tantum tibi cognita est, in quantum eam potes mentis acie contueri, quam non ideo magnam nosti, quia ingentem aliquam

molem conspiciendo lustrasti; nec, cum tibi intus loquitur, ut secundum eam vivas, ullis perstrepit sonis nec, ut eam cernas, corporalium lumen erigis oculorum nec, ut eam fortiter teneas, corporalium vires praeparas lacertorum nec, cum tibi venit in mentem, sentis eius incessum.'

86 *De Quant. An.* XIV, 23. Similarly, in his article 'Could mental states be brain processes?' (in *The Mind-Brain Identity Theory*, ed. C. V. Borst [Bristol: Macmillan, 1970], pp. 113–22), Jerome Shaffer rightly objects to the mind-brain identity theorists that mental states are not located in the body and do not occur in a volume occupied by a brain. His own attempt at safeguarding the theory, however, is equally untenable and even absurd: to adopt a linguistic convention according to which mental states could be meaningfully located in the brain, while future neurophysiological experiments are expected to verify these localizations. For it is not a matter of language, but a matter of *fact*, that mental states *are* not located in the brain, so that they will not even be found there by future research.

87 *De Gen. ad Litt.* VII, XXI, 27.

88 *De Nat. et Orig. An.* IV, XV, 22: 'dic mihi quam figuram, quae membra, quem colorem caritas habeat, quae certe, si ipse inanis non es, inane aliquid tibi videri non potest.' Cf. *De Trin.* V, I, 2: 'et videat utrum ibi (in nostro intellectu) videat ulla lineamenta formarum, nitores colorum, spatiosam granditatem, partium distantiam, molis distentionem, aliquas per locorum intervalla motiones vel quid eius-modi. Nihil certe istorum invenimus in eo.' See the similar argument in Plotinus, *Enn.* IV, 7, 4.

89 See note 85.

90 See also *De Gen. ad Litt.* XII, III, 6.

91 Cf. *De Trin.* IX, III, 3: 'Sed quoquo modo se habeat vis qua per oculos cernimus, ipsam certe vim, sive sint radii sive aliud aliquid, oculis cernere non valemus; sed mente quaerimus, et si fieri potest etiam hoc mente comprehendimus. Mens ergo ipsa sicut corporearum rerum notitias per sensus corporis colligit sic incorporearum per seme-tipsam. Ergo et se ipsam per se ipsam novit quoniam est incorporea.'

92 *Ep. XVIII*, 2: 'Est natura per locos et tempora mutabilis, ut corpus, et est natura per locos nullo modo, sed tantum per tempora etiam ipsa mutabilis, ut anima, et est natura, quae nec per locos nec per tempora mutari potest, hoc Deus est.' See *De Lib. Arb.* II, XVI, 42.

93 *De Gen. ad Litt.* VIII, XX, 39.

94 *De Gen. ad Litt.* VIII, XX, 39: 'Omne autem, quod movetur per locum, non potest nisi et per tempus simul moveri; at non omne, quod movetur per tempus, necesse est etiam per locum moveri.'

95   *Ibid.*; *Ep. XVIII*, 2.
96   *Ep. CXXXVII*, II, 4; *Tract. in Ioh.* XX, 10: 'multum interest inter corpus et animum.'
97   *Contra Ep. Man.* XIX, 21. Clearly, as should be reminded, this argument is not meant to show the spirituality, much less the substantiality, of the soul. Rather, its scope lies in bringing to light, in a first approach, the lack of corporeal properties in the psychic realities of man given in his inner experience. That this lack is not specific to the soul alone can easily be seen from the fact, mentioned above, that there are various non-spiritual 'entities' lacking corporeal features, such as the greatness or shape itself of bodies or the *rationes aeternae*.
98   *De Nat. et Orig. An.* IV, XII, 17. The question of how an animal-body, though also consisting of 'carnal members,' is distinct from the human body, cannot be discussed.
99   Though Augustine has two terms for 'body' at his disposal, *corpus* and *caro*, he does not always employ them in different technical senses. If there is however a distinction between these two terms, this goes more in the direction of body as part of man's nature (*corpus*), and flesh insofar as it means the corrupted and fallen nature of *man* (*caro*). See for instance note 140.
100 *De Trin.* XV, VII, 11.
101 *De Trin.* VI, II, 3; *De Civ. Dei*, V, 11; *De Mor. Eccl.* I, IV, 6; *Tract. in Ioh.* XXVI, 13; *Sermo CLXXIV*, II, 2; *Ep. CXXXVII*, III, 11; *En. in Ps.* CXLV, 5.
102 *De Mor. Eccl.* I, IV, 6.
103 *Ibid.* 'Quanquam enim duo sint, anima et corpus, et neutrum vocaretur homo, si non esset alterum (nam neque corpus homo esset, si anima non esset; nec rursus anima homo, si ea corpus non animaretur).'
104 *De Trin.* XV, VII, 11: 'non est dubium hominem habere animam quae non est corpus, habere corpus quod non est anima.'
105 *Sermo CL*, IV, 5: 'Nihil est in homine, quod ad eius substantiam pertineat atque naturam, praeter corpus et animam.'
106 *De Civ. Dei* X, 29: 'Corpus vero animae cohaerere, ut homo totus et plenus sit, natura ipsa nostra teste cognoscimus.'
107 *De Civ. Dei* XIV, 4: 'Et ab anima namque et a carne, quae sunt partes hominis, potest totum significari quod est homo.' See *Tract. in Ioh.* XLVII, 12: 'Sed ex quo consortium carnis et animae hominis nomen accepit, iam et singulum atque separatum, utrumlibet eorum nomen hominis tenuit.'
108 *Tract. in Ioh.* XXVI, 13.
109 *Sermo CL*, IV, 5: 'Homo ergo constans ex anima et corpore; sed non qualicumque anima, nam et pecus constat ex anima et corpore: homo

ergo constans ex anima rationali et carne mortali, quaerit beatam vitam.'

110 *De Nat. et Orig. An.* IV, II, 3: 'quisquis ergo a natura humana corpus alienare vult, desipit.'

111 *Sermo CLXXIV*, II, 2.

112 *De Trin.* XV, VII, 11.

113 *Tract. in Ioh.* XIX, 15: 'Anima habens corpus, non facit duas personas, sed unum hominem.' See also *Tract in Ioh.* XLVII, 12: 'Anima et corpus duae res sunt, sed unus homo.'

114 *De Lib. Arb.* II, XVI, 41; *De Trin.* IV, I, 3; *Conf.* III, 6.

115 *De Immort. An.* XV, 24.

116 *Tract. in Ioh.* XXVI, 13; Cf. *De Vera Rel.* XII, 25.

117 *Tract. in Ioh.* XXVII, 6: 'Nam spiritus qui est in te, o homo, quo constas ut homo sis, numquid vivificat membrum quod separatum invenerit a carne tua? Spiritum tuum dico animam tuam; anima tua non vivificat nisi membra quae sunt in carne tua; unum si tollas, iam non vivificatur ex anima tua, quia unitati corporis tui non copulatur.'

118 The main thinkers to be mentioned here are M. Scheler, G. Marcel, J.-P. Sartre, M. Merleau-Ponty. See Richard M. Zaner, *The Problem of Embodiment* (The Hague: Martinus Nijhoff, 1971), Hans-Eduard Hengstenberg, *Philosophische Anthropologie* (Stuttgart: Kohlhammer, 1957), pp. 223–317, and Wilhelm Josef Revers, 'Das Leibproblem in der Psychologie,' in *Philosophische Anthropologie heute*, ed. Roman Rocek and Oskar Schatz (München: Beck, 1972), pp. 130–41.

119 *De Gen. ad Litt.* VII, XVI, 22.

120 *De Quant. An.* XXXIII, 70: 'corpus hoc terrenum atque mortale praesentia sua (anima) vivificat; colligit in unum, atque in uno tenet, diffluere atque contabescere non sinit; alimenta per membra aequaliter, suis cuique redditis, distribui facit; congruentiam eius modumque conservat, non tantum in pulchritudine, sed etiam in crescendo atque gignendo.'

121 *De Gen. ad Litt.* VII, XVI, 22.

122 *Ep. CLXVI*, II, 4.

123 The question whether these functions can be attributed to the 'same' soul, or whether there is a distinction between man's life-principle and his soul as the 'ground' of his feeling, and freely moving, his body, would go beyond the scope of our topic. On this, see Seifert, *Leib und Seele*, pp. 328–36.

124 *De Civ. Dei* XIX, 4.

125 *Ep. CCXXXVIII*, II, 12: 'Item cum homo interior et homo exterior non sint unum, – neque enim eiusdem naturae est exterior cuius interior, quia exterior cum nuncupato corpore dicitur homo, interior

autem in sola rationali anima intelligitur –, utrumque tamen simul non homines duo sed unus dicitur. . . ; et unus homo interior et unus homo exterior et non sunt unum, et tamen propter conexionem vinculi naturalis simul utrumque non duo sed unus homo.'

See also *Contra Faustum Man.* XXIV, 2 and *De Trin.* IV, III, 5–6. In *De Civ. Dei* XIII, 24, Augustine relates that these expressions of inward and outward man for the soul and for the body are taken from Scripture (2 Cor. 4, 16). See also *De Nat. et Orig. An.* IV, XIV, 20, where Augustine distinguishes between the outer, the inner, and the most interior man, which are body, soul (*anima*), and spirit (*spiritus*).

126 *De Immort. An.* II, 2: 'Corpus nostrum nonnulla substantia est.' *De Trin.* I, X, 20.

127 *De Mor. Eccl.* I, IV, 6: 'Sive enim utrumque, sive anima sola nomen hominis teneat, non est hominis optimum quod optimum est corporis; sed quod aut corpori simul et animae, aut soli animae optimum est, id est optimum hominis.'

128 *Conf.* X, 7; *Conf.* X, 17: 'hoc animus est, et hoc ego ipse sum.'

129 *Tract. in Ioh.* XXIII, 10: 'non in corpore, sed in ipsa mente factus est homo ad imaginem Dei.' *De Trin.* XV, VII, 11: 'Et imago est Trinitatis in mente.'

130 *De Div. Quaest. LXXXIII*, Qu. LI, 3.

131 See Plotinus, *Enn.* IV, 8,3.

132 *Solil.* I, XIV, 24.

133 *De Civ. Dei* XXII, 11. See also *Tract. in Ioh.* XLIII, 12, where, using the positive image of a dwelling place, Augustine says about the separation of the soul from the body in death: 'Habitatio iacet, habitator abscessit.' Cf. the late *Sermo CCCLXVIII*, I, 1: 'ipsa (anima) est habitatrix, caro habitaculum.'

134 *De Civ. Dei* XIII, 6.

135 *De Gen. ad Litt.* XII, XXXV, 68: 'quia inest ei (i.e. menti hominis) naturalis quidam appetitus corpus administrandi.' See *De Gen. ad Litt.* VII, XXVII, 38 and VII, VIII, 11: 'anima facta est animans carnem.' See Charles Couturier S.J., 'La structure métaphysique de l'homme d'après saint Augustin,' *Augustinus Magister I* (Paris, 1954), p. 549: 'Unlike the Platonists, Augustine sees the natural appetite that links the soul to the body and the tearing apart which is their separation at death.' In the same way, Richard Schwarz judges about Augustine's view of the ordination of the soul to the body: 'Without doubt this is thought and felt in an antiplatonic manner' ('Die leib-seelische Existenz bei Aurelius Augustinus,' *PhJ*, 63 [1955], 339. See also Margaret R. Miles, *Augustine on the Body* (Missoula, Mon.: Scholars Press, 1979), p. 97. I do not see, however, where in *De*

Civitate Dei XV, 7 she found the image of the soul as 'spouse of the body.' For when Augustine says there 'virum ad regendam uxorem animo carnem regenti similem esse oportere (intelligendum est),' he does not use the husband-wife relation as image for the relation between body and soul. Instead, he merely points out that as the soul rules the body, so the husband should govern his wife, which is the context of this passage. Yet, in another late work Augustine does speak of soul and body as being 'quasi-married': 'Est ergo quasi quoddam coniugium spiritus et carnis' (*De Util. Ieiunii* IV, 5).

136 See *Ep. CXXXVII*, II, 5; *De Vera Rel.* XV, 29; *Conf.* X, 30–4.

137 For Augustine, however, it is not only the body in which vices and other (negative) emotions of the soul originate; they could as well be agitated by the soul itself: 'non ex carne tantum afficitur anima, ut cupiat, metuat, laetetur, aegrescat, verum etiam ex se ipsa his potest motibus agitari' (*De Civ. Dei* XIV, 5).

138 *De Div. Quaest. LXXXIII*, Qu. X. See also Augustine's defense of the goodness of the body against Manichean and Platonic views in *De Civ. Dei* XIV, 5. Cf. Joseph Mausbach, *Die Ethik des Heiligen Augustinus* Bd. I (Freiburg: Herder, 1909), pp. 159–65.

139 *De Doctr. Christ.* XXIV, 24: 'non enim corpus suum, sed corruptiones eius et pondus oderunt.' Cf. Maxsein, p. 29: 'This means a rejection of any attitude that rejects the body in principle; for the body appears at its own proper place in the image of man, in the unity of the whole man that is meant to be eternal.'

140 *En. in Ps.* CXLI, 18: 'Ergo si caro tibi carcer est, non corpus est carcer tuus, sed corruptio corporis tui. Corpus enim tuum fecit Deus bonum, quia bonus est.' Cf. *De Civ. Dei* XXII, 25, where Augustine talks about the state of the (resurrected) body after death: 'Non erit illic ulla corruptio, quod est corporis malum.'

A question much discussed is Augustine's view of marriage, sexuality and procreation. Often he is interpreted as having rejected any sexual activity as being immoral and sinful, that is, as being a mere stimulus of sin. See for instance Dinkler, p. 112: 'He thought that the sphere of sex was as such a sphere of sin, he identified body and sin. In this he committed a *circulus vitiosus* that made impossible in this sphere any harmless view of natural life, any morally indifferent conception of the emotional life and any affirmation of what belongs to the body.' See also Mausbach, *Ethik*, pp. 318–26 and the literature he gives there in favor of this interpretation. Even if it is true, historically speaking, that Augustine did foster such a body-rejecting (*leibfeindlich*) attitude, his final viewpoint on this subject seems to have been more differentiated. For it is not the sexual act, for the sake of procreation, and marriage *as such* that are seen to be immoral, but the cupidity that, as a consequence of original sin, is implied in them (Cf. *De Pecc. Orig.* XXXIII, 38). Thus Michael Seybold comes to the conclusion that 'Augustine, though at first he had a different opinion, considered the bodily union for the sake of procreation something good. . . . It is not bodily union for the sake of procreation which is evil but rather the cupidity implied in it, which is something that ought not to be and which stems from the sin of Adam' (*Sozialtheologische Aspekte der Sünde bei Augustinus* [Regensburg: Pustet, 1963], pp. 87–8). Also Mausbach strongly defends the same conclusion: 'What Augustine deplores about marital relations is the real power and disorder of sexual pleasure (*concupiscentia carnalis*). . . . Marriage as such, however, and the use and enjoyment of the sexual powers for the sake of marriage are never considered evil or bad by Augustine, but always morally good and under certain conditions obligatory' (*Ethik*, p. 319). Nevertheless, it seems questionable how Augustine can, on the one hand, confess the essential goodness of the marital act performed for the sake of procreation, yet, on the other hand, maintain it to be intrinsically connected with sinful concupiscence. He seems to have never settled this problem satisfactorily.

141 *De Lib. Arb.* II, XVI, 42.

142 *De Div. Quaest. LXXXIII*, Qu. X: 'Omne bonum a Deo: omne speciosum bonum, in quantum speciosum est; et omne quod species continet, speciosum est. Omne autem corpus, ut corpus sit, specie aliqua continetur. Omne igitur corpus a Deo.' See *De Vera Rel.* XX, 40.

143 *De Civ. Dei* XXII, 24: 'Iam vero in ipso corpore, quamvis nobis sit cum beluis mortalitate commune multisque earum reperiatur infirmius, quanta Dei bonitas, quanta providentia tanti Creatoris apparet! Nonne ita sunt in eo loca sensuum et cetera membra disposita speciesque ipsa ac figura et statura totius corporis ita modificata, ut ad ministerium animae rationalis se indicet factum? Non enim ut animalia rationis expertia prona esse videmus in terram, ita creatus est homo; sed erecta in caelum corporis forma admonet eum quae sursum sunt sapere. Porro mira mobilitas, quae linguae ac manibus adtributa est, ad loquendum et scribendum apta atque conveniens et ad opera artium plurimarum officiorumque complenda, nonne satis ostendit, quali animae ut serviret tale sit corpus adiunctum? Quamquam et detractis necessitatibus operandi ita omnium partium congruentia numerosa sit et pulchra sibi parilitate respondeat, ut nescias utrum in eo condendo maior sit utilitatis habita ratio quam decoris. Certe enim nihil videmus creatum in corpore utilitatis causa,

quod non habeat etiam decoris locum. Plus autem nobis id appareret, si numeros mensurarum, quibus inter se cuncta conexa sunt et coaptata, nossemus; quos forsitan data opera in his, quae foris eminent, humana posset vestigare sollertia; quae vero tecta sunt atque a nostris remota conspectibus, sicuti est tanta perplexitas venarum atque nervorum et viscerum, secreta vitalium, invenire nullus potest. . . . Qui (numeri) si noti esse potuissent, in interioribus quoque visceribus, quae nullum ostentant decus, ita delectaret pulchritudo rationis, ut omni formae apparenti, quae oculis placet, ipsius mentis, quae oculis utitur, praeferretur arbitrio. Sunt vero quaedam ita posita in corpore, ut tantummodo decorem habeant, non et usum; sicut habet pectus virile mamillas, sicut facies barbam, quam non esse munimento, sed virili ornamento indicant purae facies feminarum, quas utique infirmiores muniri tutius conveniret. Si ergo nullum membrum, in his quidem conspicuis (unde ambigit nemo), quod ita sit alicui operi accommodatum, ut non etiam sit decorum; sunt autem nonnulla, quorum solum decus et nullus est usus: puto facile intellegi in conditione corporis dignitatem necessitati fuisse praelatam. Transitura est quippe necessitas tempusque venturum, quando sola invicem pulchritudine sine ulla libidine perfruamur.' See *De Civ. Dei* V, 11.

144 In his article 'Augustins Interesse für das körperliche Schöne,' *Aug(L)*, 14 (1964), pp. 72–104, Josef Tscholl observes that Augustine often speaks of the beauty of women, and occasionally, of that of children (p. 75).

145 See in Ernst Frankenberger, *Gottbekenntnisse großer Naturforscher* (Leutesdorf: Johannes, 1975) the statements of the German biologists Karl Ernst von Baer (p. 11–12) and Hermann Staudinger (p. 24–5).

146 Similarly, Augustine points out that almost nothing is taken from the body when one eyebrow is shaved off, but how much from its beauty! (*De Civ. Dei* XI, 22.)

147 See Hans Eibl, *Augustin und die Patristik* (München: Reinhardt, 1923), p. 308, where he explains with reference to Augustine's descriptions of the body: 'One could place Augustine's song of praise of the human body among the anatomical drawings and studies in proportion of Leonardo da Vinci. It is the most beautiful thing that a writer of his period has written about the body.' In the light of such accounts, it is surprising how Dinkler can miss the impact that the beauty of the human body left on Augustine when he writes: 'Though the classical idea of the beauty of a body as harmonious once in a while still comes to the fore in him, this occurs very rarely' (*Anthropologie*, p. 109).

148 *De Gen. ad Litt.* VII, XVIII, 24. The very term organ as referring to

a part of the body has its etymological root in the Latin term *organum* (stemming from the Greek term ὄργανον) which originally means instrument, tool.

149 *Tract. in Ioh.* XXVII, 5: 'Unde enim ad nos sonus verbi, nisi per vocem carnis? unde stilus, unde conscriptio? Ista omnia opera carnis sunt, sed agitante spiritu tamquam organum suum.'

150 *De Civ. Dei* I, 13: 'Nec ideo tamen contemnenda et abicienda sunt corpora defunctorum maximeque iustorum atque fidelium, quibus tamquam organis et vasis ad omnia bona opera sancte usus est Spiritus. Si enim paterna vestis et anulus, ac si quid huius modi, tanto carius est posteris, quanto erga parentes maior adfectus: nullo modo ipsa spernenda sunt corpora, quae utique multo familiarius atque coniunctius quam quaelibet indumenta gestamus. Haec enim non ad ornamentum vel adiutorium, quod adhibetur extrinsecus, sed ad ipsam naturam hominis pertinent.' Though Augustine here speaks of the indwelling Holy Spirit, this passage can equally be applied to the human spirit which is the natural condition of the former.

151 *Tract. in Ioh.* XXXII, 3: 'Animus facit decus in corpore ... Decus ergo corporis, animus.'

152 See again note 105.

153 *De Civ. Dei* XXII, 24. See note 143.

154 *De Gen. ad Litt.* VI, XII, 22: 'Congruit ergo et corpus eius animae rationali non secundum liniamenta figurasque membrorum, sed potius secundum id, quod in caelum erectum est ad intuenda, quae in corpore ipsius mundi superna sunt; sicut anima rationalis in ea debet erigi, quae in spiritualibus natura maxime excellunt.' *De Trin.* XII, I, 1; *De Div. Quaest. LXXXIII*, Qu. LI, 3.

155 *De Civ. Dei* XXII, 24. See again note 143.

156 I would agree with Margaret Miles's conclusion that 'despite his own unconscious resistance and that of his culture to the revaluing of the body, Augustine has done a herculean task of integrating the "stone which the builders rejected" ' (p. 131). Cf. also Eugène Portalié, *A Guide to the Thought of St Augustine*, trans. Ralph J. Bastian (Chicago: Henry Regnery Company, 1960), p. 147: 'Thus the body is no longer a stranger to man; it is the man himself. And that is not all. Augustine goes further to restore its good standing by vindicating the worth of the body against the Manichean madness and the exaggerated contempt of the Neoplatonists. He holds that the body is good in itself and he takes pleasure in describing its beauty.'

157 *Ep. CXXXVII*, II, 4. See also the corresponding treatment and further references in our text on pp. 15 ff.

158 See *Conf.* V, 10, where Augustine states his own view of the soul before his conversion.

159 For this argument see Ferraz, pp. 49–50; Gangauf, pp. 162–3; Goldbrunner, pp. 30–1; Heinzelmann, p. 18; O'Connor, pp. 49–51.

160 *Contra Ep. Man.* XVI, 20.

161 *Ep. CLXVI*, II, 4: 'Porro si corpus non est, nisi quod per loci spatium aliqua longitudine, latitudine, altitudine ita sistitur vel movetur, ut maiore sui parte maiorem locum occupet, et breviore breviorem, minusque sit in parte quam in toto, non est corpus anima. Per totum quippe corpus, quod animat, non locali diffusione, sed quadam vitali intentione porrigitur; nam per omnes eius particulas tota simul adest nec minor in minoribus et in maioribus maior, sed alicubi intentius alicubi remissius et in omnibus tota et in singulis tota est. Neque enim aliter quod in corpore etiam non toto sentit, tamen tota sentit; nam cum exiguo puncto in carne viva aliquid tangitur, quamvis locus ille non solum totius corporis non sit, sed vix in corpore videatur, animam tamen totam non latet, neque id, quod sentitur, per corporis cuncta discurrit, sed ibi tantum sentitur, ubi fit. Unde ergo ad totam mox pervenit, quod non in toto fit, nisi quia et ibi tota est, ubi fit, nec ut tota ibi sit, cetera deserit? Vivunt enim et illa ea praesente, ubi nihil tale factum est. Quod si fieret et utrumque simul fieret, simul utrumque totam pariter non lateret. Proinde et in omnibus simul et in singulis particulis corporis sui tota simul esse non posset, si per illas ita diffunderetur, ut videmus corpora diffusa per spatia locorum minoribus suis partibus minora occupare et amplioribus ampliora. Quapropter si anima corpus esse dicenda est, non est certe corpus, quale terrenum est nec quale humidum aut aerium aut aetherium. Omnia quippe talia maiora sunt in maioribus locis et minora in minoribus et nihil eorum in aliqua sui parte totum adest, sed, ut sunt partes locorum, ita occupantur partibus corporum. Unde intelligitur, anima sive corpus sive incorporea dicenda sit, propriam quandam habere naturam omnibus his mundanae molis elementis excellentiore substantia creatam, quae veraciter non possit in aliqua phantasia corporalium imaginum, quas per carnis sensus percipimus, cogitari, sed mente intelligi vitaque sentiri.'

162 *Contra Ep. Man.* XVI, 20: 'ubique tanta est, quia ubique tota est.' This statement must however be modified insofar as the soul is present in *all* parts of the body only *as* animating principle; but it is not able to *feel* each member of the body from within. For there are many organs and bones that we cannot experience from within, though they are 'alive.' Nevertheless, this modification does not touch the validity of the argument under discussion since a variety of bodily

parts *can* be felt interiorly at the same time. The related question of whether Augustine is right in seemingly identifying, or at least not clearly distinguishing between, the animating function of the soul and its power of *sentire in corpore*, cannot be discussed in this context. Cf. Seifert, *Leib und Seele*, pp. 328–36.

163 *Ep. CLXVI*, II, 4. See note 161.

164 *Ibid.* See *De Immort. An.* XVI, 25: 'Ibi tantum sentit ubi fit.'

165 *Ep. CLXVI*, II, 4. See *De Trin.* VI, VI, 8: '(anima) in unoquoque corpore, et in toto tota est et in qualibet parte eius tota est.'

166 *Contra Ep. Man.* XVI, 20: 'Sed cum tota (anima) sentit in digito manus, si alius locus tangatur in pede, nec ibi desinit tota sentire. Atque ita in singulis distantibus locis tota simul adest, non unum deserens, ut in altero tota sit, neque ita utrumque tenens, ut aliam partem hic habeat et alibi aliam, sed sufficiens exhibere se singulis locis simul totam, quoniam tota sentit in singulis satis ostendit se locorum spatiis non teneri.'

167 *De Immort. An.* XVI, 25: 'Cum enim quod dolet in pede, advertit oculus, loquitur lingua, admovetur manus. Quod non fieret, nisi id quod animae in eis partibus est, et in pede sentiret.'

168 See note 166. It may be noted that the argument does not necessarily presuppose the actual feeling of *real* members of the body. It could even be based on the peculiar experience of phantom-limbs. For its decisive premise is that the soul *feels* parts of the body as being locally distinct, independent of whether they are real or not.

169 *De Immort. An.* XVI, 25: 'Anima vero non modo universae moli corporis sui, sed etiam unicuique particulae illius tota simul adest. Partis enim corporis passionem tota sentit, nec in toto tamen corpore ... Nec tamen hoc modo adest tota, ut candor vel alia huiusmodi qualitas in unaquaque parte corporis tota est. Nam quod in alia parte corpus patitur candoris immutatione, potest ad candorem qui est in alia parte non pertinere. Quapropter secundum partes molis a se distantes, et ipse a se distare convincitur. Non autem ita esse in anima per sensum de quo dictum est, probatur.'

170 'Whole body' certainly means here all those parts of the body that *are* accessible to interior sensation (see note 162). Cf. Thomas Aquinas, *Summa Theologiae* I, Q. 76, a. 8 c: 'Sed quia anima unitur corpori ut forma, necesse est quod sit in toto, et in qualibet parte corporis.'

171 Though this term is used in *De Trin.* XI, II, 2 with respect to the soul's faculty of fixing a bodily sense on the (outside) thing that is perceived (*animi intentio quae in ea re quam videmus sensum tenet*) (see our discussion of this faculty in the section on sense-perception), it

may as well be applied to the special inner attention that the soul is able to pay to particular parts of its body.

172 *Ep. CLXVI*, II, 4. See note 161.

173 *Ibid.*

174 *De Gen. ad Litt.* VIII, XXI, 42. The misleading term *commixta* is not meant to suggest a fusion of soul and body, as is clear from the context. In Chapter 5, we will come back to the question of how the union of body and soul is to be conceived.

175 See our section on the individual oneness of the soul. There the sense in which the soul is a (simple, individual, one) whole will further be elaborated on.

176 *De Trin.* VI, VI, 8: 'Nam ideo simplicior est corpore (natura spiritualis) quia non mole diffunditur per spatium loci sed in unoquoque corpore, et in toto tota est et in qualibet parte eius tota est; et ideo cum fit aliquid in quamvis exigua particula corporis quod sentiat anima, quamvis non fiat in toto corpore, illa tamen tota sentit quia totam non latet.'

177 *Ep. CLXVI*, II, 4. See note 161. Cf. Plotinus, *Enn.* IV, 7, 5 and 2, 1, where he uses basically the same argument for the indivisible wholeness of the soul that is present in the many parts of the body.

178 *De Quant. An.* XXII, 40.

179 See Thimme, pp. 39–43.

180 This distinction has been explicated by Seifert, *Leib-Seele-Problem*, p. 47.

181 *Tract. in Ioh.* XXXI, 9: 'Homo enim secundum corpus in loco est.' Plotinus makes a similar distinction when he speaks of the soul as being both indivisible and divisible: indivisible in opposition to bodies that have parts, divisible insofar as it as one whole is present in the divisible body (*Enn.* IV, 2, 1). Cf. Morgan, p. 127: 'The soul, nonspatial in character, is brought, as the result of its connection with the body, into intimate connection with something spatial; the bond of union, however, is non-spatial.'

182 See Chapter 5 where the mysterious union of body and soul that man is will be discussed in more detail.

CHAPTER 2   *The 'rational' incorporeality of the human soul shown by basic faculties*

1 For such a discussion see Anton Maxsein's book *Philosophia Cordis*.

2 The question of whether and in which sense also animals have similar faculties will not be discussed at any greater length. (See the *Introduction*.) The argument is exclusively centered on man's faculties and

what it means for them to have 'rational' features, whereby the term 'rational' is not to be understood, as we will see, in a purely intellectual sense, but is also to include, for instance, man's freedom. In this sense, being 'rational,' together with being 'conscious' to be discussed in Chapter 3, are the two (interrelated) dimensions that constitute the *spirituality of man.*

3   I will not quote the whole chapter which still mentions peculiar acts of dreaming, of phantasizing in delirium or in painful physical states, of visions engendered by outside spirits, and of mystical visionary experiences. Though these acts would as well fall under the broader notion of imagination, they seem too far removed from common experience to be discussed properly.

4   *De Gen. ad Litt.* XII, XXIII, 49: 'Quod autem nunc insinuare satis arbitror, certum est esse spiritalem quandam naturam in nobis, ubi corporalium rerum formantur similitudines, sive cum aliquod corpus sensu corporis tangimus, et continuo formatur eius similitudo in spiritu memoriaque reconditur; sive cum absentia corpora iam nota cogitamus, ut ex eis formetur quidam spiritalis aspectus, quae iam erant in spiritu et antequam ea cogitaremus; sive cum eorum corporum, quae non novimus, sed tamen esse non dubitamus, similitudines non ita ut sunt illa, sed ut occurrit, intuemur; sive cum alia, quae vel non sunt vel esse nesciuntur, pro arbitrio vel opinatione cogitamus; sive unde unde neque id agentibus neque volentibus nobis variae formae corporalium similitudinum versantur in animo; sive cum aliquid corporaliter acturi ea ipsa disponimus, quae in illa actione futura sunt, et omnia cogitatione antecedimus; sive iam in ipso actu, vel cum loquimur vel cum facimus, omnes corporales motus, ut exeri possint, praeveniuntur similitudinibus suis intus in spiritu: neque enim ulla vel brevissima syllaba in ordine suo nisi prospecta sonuisset; sive cum a dormientibus somnia videntur vel nihil vel aliquid significantia.'

5   See also *Tract. in Ioh.* XXXVII, 8 where Augustine talks about the pre-conception of buildings in their artistic idea (*in arte*).

6   *De Trin.* VIII, IV, 7: 'Quis enim legentium vel audientium quae scripsit apostolus Paulus vel quae de illo scripta sunt non fingat animo et ipsius apostoli faciem et omnium quorum ibi nomina commemorantur? Et cum in tanta hominum multitudine quibus illae litterae notae sunt alius aliter lineamenta figuramque illorum corporum cogitet, quis propinquius et similius cogitet utique incertum est.'

7   *De Trin.* XI, X, 17: 'Nec autem quadrupedem memini quia non vidi, sed phantasiam talem facillime intueor.'

8   *De Trin.* XV, XI, 20: 'Omnium namque sonantium verba linguarum etiam in silentio cogitantur, et carmina percurruntur animo tacente

ore corporis, nec solum numeri syllabarum verum etiam modi canti-
lenarum cum sint corporales et ad eum qui vocatur auditus sensum
corporis pertinentes per incorporeas quasdam imagines suas praesto
sunt cogitantibus et tacite cuncta ista voluentibus.' See *Tract. in Ioh.*
XIV, 7.

9   See the section on the *distentio animi* where this anticipating faculty
is more properly treated with corresponding (phenomenological)
literature.

10 *De Nat. et Orig. An.* IV, XXI, 34: 'In somnis enim tibi velut corporeus
apparebis; neque id corpus tuum, sed anima tua, nec verum corpus
sed similitudo corporis erit.'

11 In *Ep. VII*, Augustine talks about the whole forest of images (*tota
imaginum silva*) that we find in us (II, 5). In this context, he gives a
threefold classification of images: those that are taken from sense-
impressions; those that are of things supposed, as when we ask
someone for the sake of an argument to suppose this or that situation;
and those that are of mathematical figures and numbers being thought
(II, 4).

In recent times, much phenomenological analysis has been devoted
to the study of the various acts and kinds of imagination. See especially
Edmund Husserl, *Logische Untersuchungen*, 3rd ed. (Halle: Niemeyer,
1922), II, pp. 499–508, and Adolf Reinach, 'A Contribution Toward
the Theory of the Negative Judgment,' trans. Don Ferrari, *Aletheia*,
2 (1981), 21–27. Husserl mentions 13 distinct meanings of the term
imagination (*Vorstellung*) many of which, however, go in a quite
different direction than what is presented in our text.

12 *Contra Ep. Man.* XVII, 20: 'non sinu aliquo, sed vi potentiaque ineffa-
bili, qua licet eis et addere quodlibet et detrahere et in angustum eas
contrahere et per inmensa expandere et ordinare, ut velit, et
perturbare et multiplicare et ad paucitatem singularitatemve redigere.'
De Vera Rel. XX, 40: 'Nihil enim est corporis, quod non vel unum
visum possit innumerabiliter cogitari, vel in parvo spatio visum possit
eadem imaginandi facultate per infinita diffundi.'

13 *De Vera Rel.* XXXIV, 64.

14 One may interpret Augustine's statement also in the sense that images
are false insofar as they usually do not correspond exactly to the
reality of which they are, being rather distorted at times – a fact made
possible by the 'freedom' mentioned in the text.

15 *De Gen. ad Litt.* XII, XII, 26: 'sicut etiam vigilantes et sani et nulla
alienatione moti multorum corporum, quae non adsunt sensibus corporis, cogitatione imagines versant. Verum hoc interest, quod eas a
praesentibus verisque corporibus constanti adfectione discernunt.'

16   For this argument in Augustine see Gangauf, pp. 160–1; Grabmann, pp. 58–60; Heinzelmann, pp. 18–20; O'Connor, pp. 51–3; Thimme, pp. 36–7.

17   Concerning the problem of animal-souls see notes 2 and 28.

18   *De Nat. et Orig. An.* IV, XVII, 25: 'De his quippe visorum imaginibus maxime anima probatur non esse corporea, nisi velis et illa corpora dicere, quae praeter nos ipsos tam multa videmus in somnis: caelum, terram, mare, solem, lunam, stellas, fluvios, montes, arbores, animalia. Haec qui corpora esse credit, incredibiliter desipit; sunt tamen corporibus omnino simillima. . . . Tam multas igitur et tam magnas corporum imagines, si anima corpus esset, capere cogitando vel memoria continendo non posset, secundum tuam quippe definitionem, "corporea substantia sua corpus hoc exterius non excedit". Qua igitur magnitudine, quae nulla illi est, imagines tam magnorum corporum et spatiorum atque regionum capit?' See *Contra Ep. Man.* XVII, 20.

19   In this context, reference may be made to the problem of the so-called image theory of knowledge according to which we do not transcend in knowledge to the real object, but solely to an image of it in the mind, and to the related question of whether the Scholastic notion of *phantasma* might not have been conceived too corporeally. For this see Husserl, *Logische Untersuchungen*, pp. 421–5, and Josef Seifert, *Erkenntnis objektiver Wahrheit* (Salzburg: Pustet, 1976), pp. 69–72.

20   *De Gen. ad Litt.* XII, VII, 16.

21   *De Gen. ad Litt.* X, XXV, 42: 'sed imago corporis incorporea, . . . quae miro modo sicut in cogitatione formatur.'

22   See also Roman Ingarden's analysis of the 'purely intentional object' in *Der Streit um die Existenz der Welt* (Tübingen: Niemeyer, 1965), II/1, pp. 174–210.

23   *Contra Ep. Man.* XVIII, 20: 'Quid est ergo haec potentia, quae ista (i.e. phantasmata) discernit? Profecto quantacumque sit, et his omnibus maior est et sine ulla tali rerum imaginatione cogitatur. Huic inveni spatia, si potes, hanc diffunde per locos, hanc infinitae molis tumore distende. Profecto si bene cogitas, non potes. Quicquid enim tale tibi occurrerit, iudicas ipsa cogitatione secari posse per partes facisque ibi aliam partem minorem, aliam maiorem, quantum placet; illud autem ipsum, quo ista iudicas, cernis esse supra ista, non loci altitudine, sed potentiae dignitate.'

24   *De Civ. Dei* VIII, 5: 'Hi (i.e. philosophi, qui corporalia naturae principia corpori deditis mentibus opinati sunt) et ceteri similes eorum id solum cogitare potuerunt, quod cum eis corda eorum obstricta carnis

sensibus fabulata sunt. In se quippe habebant quod non videbant, et apud se imaginabantur quod foris viderant, etiam quando non videbant, sed tantummodo cogitabant. Hoc autem in conspectu talis cogitationis iam non est corpus, sed similitudo corporis; illud autem, unde videtur in animo haec similitudo corporis, nec corpus est nec similitudo corporis; et unde videtur atque utrum pulchra an deformis sit iudicatur, profecto est melius quam ipsa quae iudicatur. Haec mens hominis et rationalis animae natura est, quae utique corpus non est, si iam illa corporis similitudo, cum in animo cogitantis aspicitur atque iudicatur, nec ipsa corpus est.'

25 See the very similar argument in Leibniz's *Monadology*, §17: 'Suppose that there be a machine, the structure of which produces thinking, feeling, and perceiving; imagine this machine enlarged but preserving the same proportions, so that you could enter it as if it were a mill. This being supposed, you might visit its inside; but what would you observe there? Nothing but parts which push and move each other, and never anything that could explain perception. This explanation must therefore be sought in the simple substance, not in the composite, that is, in the machine.' (The translation is taken from Gottfried Wilhelm von Leibniz, *Monadology and Other Philosophical Essays*, trans. Paul Schrecker and Anne Martin Schrecker (Indianapolis: The Library of Liberal Arts, 1965), p. 150).

26 *De Gen. ad Litt.* XII, XXIII, 49.

27 *De Gen. ad Litt.* XII, XX, 42. See note 12.

28 *Ibid.* Augustine uses the term *spirituale* or *spiritus* in the twelfth book of *De Genesi ad Litteram* as synonymous with 'incorporeal,' that is, with something that is not a body, but that still *is*: 'quidquid enim corpus non est et tamen aliquid est, iam recte spiritus dicitur' (XII, VII, 16). In this sense, an animal-soul also would be 'spiritual,' since it is incorporeal. However, it would go beyond the scope and the intention of the present study to ask in which sense animals have an imagination, and whether there are not forms of imagination that can only be given in man, as they may imply or ground specifically human acts. As was outlined in the beginning of this section, the starting point of the present arguments is exclusively man's imagination, as it is given in inner experience, which alone is to be shown to presuppose an incorporeal subject.

29 *De Gen. ad Litt.* XII, VII, 16: 'Et utique non est corpus, quamvis corpori similis sit, imago absentis corporis, nec ille obtutus quo cernitur.'

30 *De Gen. ad Litt.* XII, XVI, 33: 'Tamen eandem eius imaginem non

corpus in spiritu, sed ipse spiritus in se ipso facit celeritate mirabili, quae ineffabiliter longe est a corporis tarditate.'

31   *Tract. in Ioh.* XX, 12: 'Primo celeritatem animi ipsius vide. Vide si non vehementior scintilla est animi cogitantis, quam splendor solis lucentis. Solem orientem tu vides animo; motus ipsius quam tardus est ad animum tuum. Cito tu potuisti cogitare quod facturus est sol. Ab oriente ad occidentem venturus est, iam ex alia parte cras oritur. Ubi hoc fecit cogitatio tua, adhuc ille tardus est, et tu omnia peragrasti. Magna ergo res est animus.'

32   *Tract. in Ioh.* XX, 12.

33   *Conf.* X, 8. See Romano Guardini, *Die Bekehrung des heiligen Aurelius Augustinus* (Leipzig: Hegner, 1935), p. 108: 'Great is for him the power of the mind. The treatise on memory in the tenth book with its magnificent beginning in chapter eight is a genuine hymn to it.' Cf. the whole chapter on Augustine's amazement, pp. 108–40.

34   See Guardini, p. 29.

35   See for instance *De Quant. An.* V, 8–9, *De Nat. et Orig. An.* IV, XVII, 25, *Contra Ep. Man.* XVII, 20. The main thrust of these arguments consists in showing that it is impossible for a body to 'contain' in itself as many and as great objects as can be recollected or imagined. See our discussion of the validity of this proof on pp. 51 ff.

36   Augustine himself uses the term *memoria* not only in the context of discussing the act of recollection, as we will see in our sections on the *distentio animi* and on the *memoria sui*. Besides, there is the 'motoric memory' of our body, which Henri Bergson in particular has analyzed and described as 'the memory of the body which is constituted by the whole of sensori-motor systems that habit has organized' (*Matière et Mémoire* [Paris: Alcan, 1903 p. 165]). Again, Roman Ingarden paid special attention to what he called the 'active memory' which is implied in the reading of literary works of art (*Vom Erkennen des literarischen Kunstwerks* [Darmstadt: Wissenschaftliche Buchgesellschaft, 1968], §16. All these and other forms of memory must be excluded from our present discussion which is centered exclusively on recollection proper.

37   *Conf.* X, 8.

38   *Conf.* X, 9.

39   *Conf.* X, 9.

40   *Conf.* X, 8. See Pierre Blanchard, 'L'espace intérieur chez Saint Augustin d'après le Livre X des "Confessions," ' *Augustinus Magister*, I, pp. 535–42.

41   Brigitte Schmitt, *Der Geist als Grund der Zeit (Die Zeitauslegung des Aurelius Augustinus*), (Freiburg, 1967), p. 83: 'Augustine tries to grasp

a thing in images or metaphors, but he has the thing so to speak appear through the image or metaphor.'

42 See also *Tract. in Ioh.* XXIII, 11.

43 *Liber de Videndo Deo (seu Ep. CXLVII)*, XVI, 38: 'Quae autem per corpus videntur, nisi mens adsit, quae talia nuntiata suscipiat, nulla possunt scientia contineri. Et quod nuntiata quasi suscipere perhibetur, foris ea relinquit; sed eorum imagines, id est, incorporeas similitudines corporum incorporaliter commendat memoriae, unde, cum voluerit et potuerit, velut de custodia productas atque in conspectum cogitationis exhibitas iudicet.'

44 *Conf.* X, 8: 'Nec ipsa tamen intrant, sed rerum sensarum imagines illic praesto sunt cogitationi reminiscentis eas. Quae quomodo fabricatae sunt quis dicit, cum appareat, quibus sensibus raptae sint interiusque reconditae?' See also *De Trin.* XI, IX, 16, where Augustine distinguishes four different species involved in remembering. There is first the species of the thing perceived; this species, secondly, produces a species in the sense of the percipient; the latter gives rise to a third species in memory, which, fourthly, brings forth the species that is given in the gaze of thinking (that is, in recollection).

45 Cf. Bernhard Kälin, *Die Erkenntnislehre des hl. Augustinus* (Sarnen: Ehrli, 1920), pp. 23–31.

46 *De Mag.* XII, 39; see note 65.

47 Gareth B. Matthews, 'Augustine on Speaking from Memory,' in *Augustine: A Collection of Critical Essays*, ed. Robert A. Markus (New York: Doubleday, 1972), p. 173. Though Matthews sees the 'paradox' implied in Augustine's account of answering questions about sensible things from memory, his own solution of the problem likewise remains unsatisfactory. He thinks that 'an answer considered confirmable by the evidence of other people's memory reports (*inter alia*)' (p. 174) gives knowledge of the past objects themselves, rather than of the memory image present in someone's mind. The difficulty with this 'solution' is basically the same as with that of Augustine's: it does not explain whether and how the person remembering really perceives the past reality so that he can answer questions about it. The fact that many people give the same account of a past object is as such no greater proof for really perceiving from memory this object itself, and not its image, than a single person's account of it; for each of the many persons, too, has to go into his own memory. Of course, a general consensus, based upon personal memory, about a real historical fact is a strong indication that we do recollect this past fact itself. Yet, such a consensus does not solve the problem implied in

Augustine's account, that is, whether and how we are in touch with a past reality itself in memory, if all we see is an image of this reality.

48   Don Ferrari, 'Retention-Memory. Perception and the Cognition of Enduring Objects,' *Aletheia* 2 (1981), p. 59.

49   Ferrari, pp. 60–1.

50   *De Quant. An.* V, 8.

51   *Conf.* X, 8.

52   *Liber de Videndo Deo (seu Ep. CXLVII)*, XVII, 43: 'Neque enim est, ut opinor, quisquam etiam talibus imaginationibus ita deditus, ut credat sic esse in memoria sua vel in ipso conspectu cogitationis suae solem, lunam, stellas, amnes, maria, montes, colles, urbes, parietes denique domus suae vel etiam cubiculi sui, et quicquid per oculos corporis tale cognovit et tenet, ut locorum spatiis atque intervallis sive stent sive moveantur.' Cf. *Conf.* X, 8.

53   Cf. Gottlieb Söhngen, 'Der Aufbau der augustinischen Gedächtnislehre,' in *Aurelius Augustinus*, pp. 384–91. Though Hermann-Josef Kaiser (*Augustinus. Zeit und 'Memoria'* [Bonn: Bouvier, 1969], pp. 38–9) distinguishes eight different contents of memory according to Augustine, they would basically fit into our more general scheme.

54   Cf. also Wendelin Schmidt-Dengler, 'Die "aula memoriae" in den Konfessionen des heiligen Augustin,' *REAug* 14 (1968), 69–89, on how Augustine stylistically develops the comparison between memory as man's interior and a house.

55   There are passages in Augustine that sound as if he subscribed to Plato's doctrine of reminiscence (developed in the *Meno* 80d–86c). One of these passages is a text in the *Confessiones* (X, 10) in which Augustine holds that we know these ideal reasons because they are in us before we learn them. Other passages are found in *Soliloquia* II, XX, 35 and in *De Quantitate Animae* XX, 34 where he says that learning is nothing but remembering. However, both in *De Trinitate* XII, XV, 24 and later in the *Retractationes* I, IV, 4 and I, VII, 2 Augustine explicitly rejects this doctrine which would imply a pre-existence of the soul. Instead, he corrects himself, saying that the reason why we seem to remember this knowledge lies in the fact that these unchangeable truths are constantly present to us in the light of the eternal reason (*Retract.* I, IV, 4). We can think of them at any time, as we can recall something from memory at any time. Cf. Portalié, p. 104: 'He did have recourse to memory for an explanation of the origin of ideas and he subsequently rejected that error.' See also Kälin, pp. 50–3.

56   *Conf.* X, 9: 'Sed non ea sola gestat immensa ista capacitas memoriae meae. Hic sunt et illa omnia, quae de doctrinis liberalibus percepta

nondum exciderunt, quasi remota interiore loco, non loco; nec eorum imagines, sed res ipsas gero. Nam quid sit litteratura, quid peritia disputandi, quot genera quaestionum, quidquid horum scio, sic est in memoria mea, ut non retenta imagine rem foris relinquerim, aut sonuerit aut praeterierit, sicut vox inpressa per aures vestigio, quo recoleretur, quasi sonaret, cum iam non sonaret.' Cf. *Conf.* X, 10 and X, 15.

57 *Ibid.*

58 It might seem that the distinction between these two classes of objects of recollection is tantamount to Augustine's distinction, previously discussed, between what is contained in memory in the form of an image and what is present as a thing itself. For if a recollected object implies a reference to the past, it appears to be given as an image of something experienced in the past; similarly, if I recall the knowledge of a word of another language (which is not linked to the past act of learning this word), it seems that the word itself is present in memory and not an image of it.

Yet, according to Augustine's own description, these two distinctions are not identical, which can at best be seen in the case of past acts of mine. According to Augustine, these past acts are *self-presently* given in memory, but they are also given *as past* acts. It is easy to see why Augustine thinks so: a past act of learning, for instance, was a *real* part of my consciousness, so that it was stored in memory *as this past real act itself*, and not as an image of itself. If, however, this past act was a perception of an outside thing (which is the primary example of Augustine's image-theory), this thing, remaining *really* outside, enters into memory in the form of its image, according to Augustine. Thus, a recollection implying a reference to the past itself need not necessarily be of images alone, but can also be of objects that are themselves in memory, in Augustine's terminology.

59 *De Trin.* XI, VIII, 13: 'quia meminisse non possumus corporum species nisi tot quot sensimus et quantas sensimus et sicut sensimus ex corporis enim sensu eas in memoria combibit animus.'

60 *De Trin.* XI, VIII, 13: 'Et (solem) tantum memini quantum vidi; si enim maiorem vel minorem memini quam vidi, iam non memini quod vidi et ideo nec memini. Quia vero memini, tantum memini quantum vidi.'

61 *Conf.* X, 8: 'Ibi (i.e. in aula ingenti memoriae meae) sunt omnia, quae sive experta a me sive credita memini. Ex eadem copia etiam similitudines rerum vel expertarum vel ex eis, quas expertus sum, creditarum alias atque alias et ipse contexo praeteritis atque ex his

etiam futuras actiones et eventa et spes, et haec omnia rursus quasi praesentia meditor.' See *De Trin.* XI, VIII, 13.

62 *De Trin.* XI, VIII, 13.

63 See pp. 50 ff.

64 *De Gen. ad Litt.* XII, VI, 15: 'ubi nihil videntes oculis corporis, animo tamen corporales imagines intuemur, seu veras, sicut ipsa corpora videmus et memoria retinemus, seu fictas, sicut cogitatio formare potuerit. Aliter enim cogitamus Carthaginem, quam novimus, aliter Alexandriam, quam non novimus.'

65 *De Mag.* XII, 39: 'Cum vero non de iis quae coram sentimus, sed de his quae aliquando sensimus quaeritur; non iam res ipsas, sed imagines ab iis impressas memoriaeque mandatas loquimur: quae omnino quomodo vera dicamus, cum falsa intuamur, ignoro; nisi quia non nos ea videre ac sentire, sed vidisse ac sensisse narramus. Ita illas imagines in memoriae penetralibus rerum ante sensarum quaedam documenta gestamus, quae animo contemplantes bona conscientia non mentimur cum loquimur: sed nobis sunt ista documenta.'

66 *Conf.* X, 19: 'Tamquam si homo notus sive conspiciatur oculis sive cogitetur et nomen eius obliti requiramus, quidquid aliud occurrerit non conectitur, quia non cum illo cogitari consuevit ideoque respuitur, donec illud adsit, ubi simul adsuefacta notitia non inaequaliter adquiescat. Et unde adest nisi ex ipsa memoria? Nam et cum ab alio conmoniti recognoscimus, inde adest. Non enim quasi novum credimus, sed recordantes adprobamus hoc esse, quod dictum est.'

67 Cf. Ferrari, pp. 62 f.

68 Edmund Husserl, *Zur Phänomenologie des inneren Zeitbewußtseins*, ed. Rudolf Boehm (Haag: Martinus Nijhoff, 1966), pp. 58–9. See also Ferrari, p. 75: 'We grasp the object again by reliving our original experience of grasping it, and the object stands before us in our "past self," not in our "present self," if we may put it that way.'

69 *Conf.* X, 8: 'Ibi (i.e. in aula ingenti memoriae meae) mihi et ipse occurro, meque recolo, quid, quando et ubi egerim quoque modo, cum agerem, affectus fuerim.'

70 *Conf.* X, 14: 'Affectiones quoque animi mei eadem memoria continet non eo modo, quo eas habet ipse animus, cum patitur eas, sed alio multum diverso, sicut sese habet vis memoriae. Nam et laetatum me fuisse reminiscor non laetus et tristitiam meam praeteritam recordor non tristis et me aliquando timuisse recolo sine timore et pristinae cupiditatis sine cupiditate sum memor. Aliquando et e contrario tristitiam meam transactam laetus reminiscor et tristis laetitiam.'

71 Ferrari, p. 79.

72 *Conf.* X, 8: 'Ibi quando sum, posco, ut proferatur quidquid volo, et

quaedam statim prodeunt, quaedam requiruntur diutius et tamquam de abstrusioribus quibusdam receptaculis eruuntur, quaedam catervatim se proruunt et, dum aliud petitur et quaeritur, prosiliunt in medium quasi dicentia: "ne forte nos sumus"? et abigo ea manu cordis a facie recordationis meae, donec enubiletur quod volo atque in conspectum prodeat ex abditis.'

73 Cf. Husserl, p. 48: 'On the other hand, the act of rendering present is something free: it is a free *Durchlaufen*; we can perform the rendering present "faster" or "more slowly," more clearly and explicitly or more confusedly, very fast in one stroke or in articulated steps etc.'

74 *De Trin.* XI, VII, 12. See *Tract. in Ioh.* XXIII, 11: 'Cum vero reflexa est cogitatio tua ad id quod erat in memoria, inde formata est, et visio quaedam animi facta est.'

75 Ferrari, p. 81.

76 Cf. Morgan, p. 77: 'This treatise [i.e. on Memory in the tenth book of the *Confessions*] is most useful because he bases an argument for the spirituality of the soul on the power of Memory.' Unfortunately, Morgan does not develop this argument to any extent.

77 *De Quant. An.* V, 8: 'A. Dic mihi, quaero te, utrum ea quae appelatur memoria, non tibi nomen inane videatur. E. Cui hoc videri potest? A. Animae hanc esse arbitraris, an corporis? E. Et hinc dubitare ridiculum est. Quid enim? exanime corpus meminisse aliquid credi, aut intelligi potest?'

78 Such reasoning underlies the cybernetical thesis that human thinking can ultimately be explained by the operations of electronic machines and computers, which would render superfluous the idea of soul. See Max Horkheimer, 'Zur Idee der Seele,' in *Was weiß man von der Seele?*, ed. Hans Jürgen Schultz (Gütersloh: Mohn, 1972), p. 16: 'The construction of machines whose capacities not only substitute for certain processes of thinking but surpass them in speed and exactness, i.e. automation, is a further guarantee for the scientific penetration and explanation of animal-human actions without having to have recourse to a substantial, not to say immortal, soul.' In the following, our discussion is also directed implicitly against this and similar conceptions. See note 81a.

79 See note 56 and the corresponding elaboration in the text.

80 See note 72.

81 Besides the arguments just developed, it is in particular these imperfections implied in human remembering which show the falsity of Horkheimer's argument cited in note 78. For precisely the fact that machines do operate faster and more exactly than man is able to

think, proves that they *cannot* explain, nor be identified with, the soul as subject of his thinking.

82   Cf. note 23 and the corresponding text, where we presented an argument of Augustine's for the incorporeality of the power of imagination, which could *mutatis mutandis* be applied to memory as well.

The fact that memory is not located in the body is also confirmed by clinical research. See Florian Laubenthal. *Hirn und Seele. Ärztliches zum Leib-Seele-Problem* (Salzburg: Müller, 1953), p. 205: 'Thus, the result of clinical observation is that memory cannot be considered something narrowly localisable.'

83   *Conf.* X, 9.

84   The non-identity of memory and brain is also empirically shown by the fact that, as Laubenthal points out (pp. 202–7), the various parts of the brain assume different 'functions' in each man at different times. For this would be impossible if each part were identical with a specific mental activity, such as remembering, reasoning, hearing, etc.

85   See our discussion in Chapter 5.

86   For this, see Seifert, *Leib und Seele*, pp. 256–66, and the literature given there.

87   *Conf.* X, 14: 'Hic vero cum animus sit etiam ipsa memoria – nam et cum mandamus aliquid, ut memoriter habeatur, dicimus: "vide, ut illud in animo habeas", et cum obliviscimur, dicimus; "non fuit in animo" et "elapsum est animo", ipsam memoriam vocantes animum –.'

88   *Conf.* X, 25.

89   See pp. 199 ff.

90   *Conf.* X, 8: 'Magna ista vis est memoriae, magna nimis, deus, penetrale amplum et infinitum. Quis ad fundum eius pervenit? Et vis est haec animi mei atque ad meam naturam pertinet, nec ego ipse capio totum, quod sum. Ergo animus ad habendum se ipsum angustus est, ut ubi sit quod sui non capit. Numquid extra ipsum ac non in ipso? Quomodo ergo non capit? Multa mihi super hoc oboritur admiratio, stupor adprehendit me. Et eunt homines mirari alta montium et ingentes fluctus maris et latissimos lapsus fluminum et Oceani ambitum et gyros siderum et relinquunt se ipsos nec mirantur, quod haec omnia cum dicerem, non ea videbam oculis, nec tamen dicerem, nisi montes et fluctus et flumina et sidera, quae vidi, et Oceanum, quem credidi, intus in memoria mea viderem spatiis tam ingentibus, quasi foris viderem.'

91   According to our general procedure, the question of whether animals have a memory had to be left undiscussed. It might however be

mentioned that Augustine also attributes memory to the irrational soul, that is, to animals (*De Civ. Dei* V, 11), yet to a limited extent. For at another place he says that certain operations related to memory are not common to man and animals, such as acts of deliberately committing something to memory or of fixing it more firmly in memory by constant recollection (*De Trin.* XII, II, 2). One could list many more features that show the 'rationality' of human memory, as we tried to do in the text. Thus, our present argument, based on man's inner experience, is not to be taken as proving an animal-soul.

92 Cf. *De Musica* VI, *De Gen. ad Litt.* VII.

93 From the very outset it should be noted that time is understood by Augustine as transcendent to and independent of consciousness (contrary to Kant's idealistic conception). That this realistic concept of time underlies modern physics also has been shown by Anton Neuhäusler, 'Augustinus und die Zeitauffassung der heutigen Physik,' *Hochl.* 43 (1950/51), p. 478: 'Therefore it is not Kant's but Augustine's notion of time that is "modern." '

94 Cf. Husserl, *Zeitbewußtsein*, p. 3: 'Even today anyone who wants to deal with the problem of time must study thoroughly chapters 14–25 of book XI of the *Confessiones*. For the modern age, so proud of its knowledge, has not made any very great progress beyond this great thinker, who grappled so seriously with the problem. We can still say with Augustine: si nemo a me quaerat scio; si quaerenti explicare velim, nescio' (*Conf.* XI, 14).

See also Odilo Lechner, *Idee und Zeit in der Metaphysik Augustins* (München: Pustet, 1964), pp. 127–43. Wittmann, *Ascensus*, pp. 200–25 (an excellent analysis of time, measuring of time, and the 'extension' of the mind).

95 *Conf.* XI, 22.

96 *Conf.* XI, 14.

97 *Conf.* XI, 14.

98 *Conf.* XI, 15; *En. in Ps.* LXXVI, 8.

99 *Conf.* XI, 15.

100 *Conf.* XI, 15: 'Nam si extenditur, dividitur in praeteritum et futurum.'

101 *Conf.* XI, 15; XI, 21; XI, 27; XI, 28.

102 *Conf.* XI, 15: 'Quod tamen ita raptim a futuro in praeteritum transvolat, ut nulla morula extendatur.'

103 *Conf.* XI, 14: 'Si ergo praesens, ut tempus sit, ideo fit, quia in praeteritum transit, quomodo et hoc esse dicimus, cui causa, ut sit, illa est, quia non erit.'

104 *Conf.* XI, 14: 'Praesens autem si semper esset praesens nec in praeteritum transiret, non iam esset tempus, sed aeternitas.'

105 For a more comprehensive discussion of this paradox of the existence of the present 'now' see the articles by Walter von Del-Negro, 'Diskussionsbemerkungen zum aristotelisch-augustinischen Zeitparadoxon,' *ZPhF*, 20 (1966), 309–12, and by C. W. K. Mundle, 'Augustine's Persuasive Error Concerning Time,' *Phil*, 41 (1966), 165–8. What follows in our text can partly be seen as a reply to the problems brought up in these articles.

106 *Conf.* XI, 14: 'ut scilicet non vere dicamus tempus esse, nisi quia tendit non esse.' Cf. Erich Lampey, *Das Zeitproblem nach den Bekenntnissen Augustins* (Regensburg: Habbel, 1960), p. 33: 'The only present moment that is has merely a *quasi*-being, insofar as this "being" precisely "consists" in not being.' This passage should be read in context.

107 Ronald Suter, 'Augustine on Time with Some Criticisms from Wittgenstein,' *RIPh*, 61/62 (1962), may have a valid criticism against Augustine in objecting that he did not acknowledge an existence of the past and the future (pp. 388–9). It seems to the author that Augustine emphasized the real actuality of the present so strongly that he neglected the peculiar kind of existence proper both to the past and to the future; but to hold this is not contrary to his view, as we tried to show in the text. The other criticisms Suter raises seem less justified and to rely greatly on equivocations and misinterpretations, which cannot be further discussed here.

108 *Conf.* XI, 21: 'Ex illo ergo, quod nondum est, per illud, quod spatio caret in illud, quod iam non est.'

109 *Conf.* XI, 15: 'Ubi est ergo tempus, quod longum dicamus?'

110 *Conf.* XI, 21. 'Measuring of time' here means for Augustine not the exact scientific determination that a particular stretch of time has a duration of a specific number of time-units (hours, minutes, seconds, etc.), in which sense both the past and the future could be measured; rather, Augustine here refers to the lived experience of shorter and longer periods of time, as will become clear from what follows in the text.

111 *Conf.* XI, 27.

112 *Conf.* XI. 27.

113 *Conf.* XI, 21: 'nec metiri quae non sunt possumus.'

114 *Conf.* XI, 27: 'Non ergo ipsas, quae iam non sunt, sed aliquid in memoria mea metior, quod infixum manet.'

115 *Conf.* XI, 27. In his article 'Time and Contingency in St Augustine,' *RMet*, 8 (1955), Robert Jordan judges about Augustine's approach to the measuring of time: 'His analysis turns up a paradox, the resolution

of which is said to constitute Augustine's contribution to the nature of time.'

116 *Conf.* XI, 26.

117 See also *De Gen. ad Litt.* I, IX, 16.

118 The same can be said from experiencing the beauty of a melody, in which case the melody as this *whole* sequence of tones functions as its 'bearer.' Cf. *De Vera Rel.* XXII, 42.

119 *De Musica* VI, VIII, 21: 'Quamlibet enim brevis syllaba, cum et incipiat, et desinat, alio tempore initium eius, et alio finis sonat. Tenditur ergo et ipsa quantulocumque temporis intervallo, et ab initio suo per medium suum tendit ad finem. Ita ratio invenit tam localia quam temporalia spatia infinitam divisionem recipere; et idcirco nullius syllabae cum initio finis auditur. In audienda itaque vel brevissima syllaba, nisi memoria nos adiuvet, ut, eo momento temporis, quo iam non initium, sed finis syllabae sonat, maneat ille motus in animo, qui factus est cum initium ipsum sonuit, nihil nos audisse possumus dicere.'

120 *De Musica* VI, VIII, 21: 'Non enim sonat secunda, nisi prima destiterit: quod autem simul sonare non potest, simul audiri qui potest?'

121 *Sermo LII*, VII, 19: 'Duas istas syllabas non teneres, nisi per memoriam. Unde enim scires duas esse, si sonante secunda oblitus esses primam?' Cf. *De Gen. ad Litt.* XII, XVI, 33.

122 In his *Zeitbewußtsein.*

123 In the article referred to in note 48. There one can also find further bibliographical references on this topic.

124 Husserl, p. 38. Ferrari, p. 96.

125 Ferrari, p. 95; cf. Husserl, p. 29.

126 Ferrari, p. 94: 'In retention, however, the memorial material is not retrieved, but *retained*.'

Certainly, this structural difference between retention and recollection does not exclude any interaction of the two. For, as Husserl points out (pp. 35–7), there are also retentions in recollection, and this, as it seems, in two ways. First, in presently performing an act of recollection, or of 're-living,' a past act, this past act itself, as we tried to show in the preceding section, stands before our present perceptual gaze as an object enduring in time (since it was performed in time); consequently, its being presently perceived, implied in recollection, has to include retentions, without which any experience of a temporally extended object would be impossible. Secondly, all those retentions that form part of the original past experience have to be re-performed in the present 're-living' of this experience; those temporally enduring objects, therefore, that were experienced in the past are re-experienced in recollection through this very same past experience, which implies also the re-experiencing of the original retentions.

127 Husserl, p. 99.

128 Ferrari, p. 116.

129 For a better understanding of this conscious performing of our acts the reader must be referred to our discussion of the Augustinian *se nosse* in Chapter 3.

130 Ferrari, pp. 116–17. To lack this consciously lived actualization is no contradiction to our argument to be made at the end of the present section, viz. that retention is a *conscious* phenomenon. For as the comparison to memory-contents shows, there are many different states and modes of consciousness. We will come back to these questions in Chapter 3.

131 *De Gen. ad Litt.* XII, XVI, 33: 'Ac sic omnis locutionis usus, omnis cantandi suavitas, omnis postremo in actibus nostris corporalis motus dilapsus occideret neque ullum progressum nancisceretur, si trans-actos corporis motus memoriter spiritus non teneret, quibus conse-quentes in agendo connecteret.'

132 *Conf.* XI, 18.

133 *Conf.* XI, 17.

134 The whole problem that arises here of how it is possible to have some pre-awareness of a thing which does not even exist yet, of how this anticipation of the immediate future is distinct from the foresight of the more distant future with respect to both its direct object and its certainty, of the kind of being, viz. real or imaginary being, possessed by those things which God foreknows in knowing what, from man's point of view, lies in the future – all these questions cannot be investigated in the present context. Therefore, the doubts expressed in the text about the soundness of Augustine's opinion on this matter are meant to be tentative.

135 *De Trin.* XV, VII, 13.

136 *Conf.* XI, 28.

137 See note 4 and our discussion of this passage. Cf. also *De Gen. ad Litt.* XII, XVI, 33.

138 Cf. note 134.

139 *Conf.* XI, 26.

140 Cf. Kaiser, p. 17 note 24: 'To consider this "*distentio animi*" only an image, as Gilson tries to do, seems to us to miss the essence of the *distentio*. More than once Augustine tries to make it clear that the soul extends itself – and this in a very real sense – in order to be able to grasp temporal things.'

141 *Conf.* XI, 28.

142 *Conf.* XI, 28: 'praesens tamen adest attentio mea, per quam traicitur quod erat futurum, ut fiat praeteritum.'

143 Cf. Wittmann, p. 209: 'Without a *distentio animi* a united event could never be kept as a unity, but only as atomically divided.'

144 *Conf.* XI, 20: 'praesens de praeteritis memoria, praesens de praesentibus contuitus, praesens de futuris exspectatio.'

145 Cf. Schmitt, p. 58: 'If presence is understood as extension of the mind, as time-space, it is quite possible that the future is represented in it as "presence of something future" and the past as "presence of something past." ' See also Kaiser, pp. 13–35 on the experience of time and on the *memoria* as securing the experiential continuity of our past, present, and future acts.

146 Augustine does not explicitly develop arguments from these faculties for the incorporeality of the soul. However, they seem virtually contained in his analyses.

147 *Conf.* XI, 20: 'Sunt enim haec in anima tria quaedam (i.e. praesens de praeteritis, praesens de praesentibus, praesens de futuris) et alibi ea non video.' Cf. *De Musica* VI, VII, 19: 'quia unicuique animanti in genere proprio, proportione universitatis, sensus locorum temporumque tributus est.'

148 In this sense, Marilyn E. Ravicz, 'St Augustine: Time and Eternity,' *Thom.* 22 (1959), can rightly say: 'It is in the present-now *distentio* that the soul can be said to be somehow beyond time' (p. 547).

149 Wittmann brings out this point very clearly: 'Through this capability of representing in *memoria*, *attentio* and *exspectatio* the past, present and future at the same time in consciousness, man goes beyond time in a certain sense. For a corporeal being of external reality possesses its existence only in temporal succession. It stands in the present moment between the not yet of its future and the no longer of its past. It is unable to embrace its existence in a *simul*; instead, it constantly changes its future being in the actual moment of the present only to hand it over to the past again' (p. 215).

150 *De Vera Rel.* X, 18: 'Mutari autem animam posse non quidem localiter, tamen temporaliter.'

151 Cf. *Sermo CCXLVII*, 2; *De Gen. ad Litt.* VI, XVI, 27.

152 Cf. Geyser, pp. 63–7 and Joachim Ritter, *Mundus intelligibilis* (Frankfurt: Klostermann, 1937), pp. 67–85 on Augustine's argument against different forms of scepticism.

153 For this see, for instance, Charles Boyer S.J., *L'idée de vérité dans la philosophie de Saint Augustin* (Paris: Beauchesne, 1939), Johannes Hessen, *Augustins Metaphysik der Erkenntnis* (Berlin: Dümmlers,

1931), Ronald H. Nash, *The Light of the Mind. St Augustine's Theory of Knowledge* (Lexington Univ. Press, 1969), and Kälin, and Schöpf, *Wahrheit und Wissen.*

154 *De Gen. ad Litt.* XII, XI, 22. See the whole of book XI, especially chapters 6, 7, 11, 24.

155 *De Gen. ad Litt.* XII, XI, 22: 'Quanquam itaque in eadem anima fiant visiones.'

156 As our main concern is to show the incorporeality of man's soul, the problem of animal-perception will, apart from certain side-remarks, basically be skipped.

157 This approach counteracts de Vries's misgivings that sense-perception, because of its 'determination' and dependence on material processes, would not reveal the 'specific immateriality' proper to spiritual knowledge (pp. 109–28, esp. p. 120). For it shall be shown that in spite of its bodily 'side' sense-perception requires a subject that is just as incorporeal as is the subject of purely intellectual cognition, which will be discussed in the subsequent section.

158 *Ep. CXXXVII*, II, 5; *De Gen. ad Litt.* XII, XVI, 32.

159 *De Trin.* XI, II, 3: 'Gignitur ergo ex re visibili visio, sed non ex sola nisi adsit et videns. Quocirca ex visibili et vidente gignitur visio ita sane ut ex vidente sit sensus oculorum et aspicientis atque intuentis intentio; illa tamen informatio sensus quae visio dicitur a solo imprimatur corpore quod videtur, id est a re aliqua visibili.'

160 *Ibid.*

161 See Winfried Holzapfel, *Mundus Sensibilis* (Freiburg: Oberkirch, 1968), pp. 17–22. W. Ott, 'Des hl. Augustinus Lehre über die Sinneserkenntnis,' *PhJ*, 13 (1900), pp. 45–59 and 138–48.

162 *De Quant. An.* XXIV, 45.

163 See p. 17.

164 *De Quant. An.* XXXII, 68.

165 *De Trin.* XI, I, 1.

166 *De Lib. Arb.* II, III, 8; cf. *Sermo XLIII*, II, 3.

167 *De Lib. Arb.* II, III, 8; *Conf.* VII, 17. On the similarity of Augustine's notion of 'inner sense' to that of Cicero and Aristotle, see Rudolf Schneider, *Seele und Sein. Ontologie bei Augustin und Aristoteles* (Stuttgart: Kohlhammer, 1957), pp. 160–84, and Morgan, p. 184: 'This "interior sensus" ... must be regarded as equivalent to the Aristotelian "commonsense." '

168 *De Lib. Arb.* II, III, 8. See Holzapfel, pp. 49–55.

169 *Ibid.* Cf. *Conf.* I, 20: 'custodiebam interiore sensu integritatem sensuum meorum.'

170 *De Lib. Arb.* II, IV, 10: 'Arbitror etiam illud esse manifestum, sensum

illum interiorem non ea tantum sentire quae accepit a quinque sensibus corporis, sed etiam ipsos ab eo sentiri. . . . Quod si adhuc obscurum est, elucescet, si animadvertas quod exempli gratia sat est in uno aliquo sensu, velut in visu. Namque aperire oculum et movere aspiciendo ad id quod videre adpetit nullo modo posset, nisi oculo clauso vel non ita moto se id non videre sentiret. Si autem sentit se non videre dum non videt, necesse est etiam sentiat se videre dum videt, quia, cum eo adpetitu non movet oculum videns, quo movet non videns, et indicat se utrumque sentire.'

171 *Ibid.*

172 *De Lib. Arb.* II, IV, 10: 'Eundem autem sensum hoc eodem sensu non posse sentiri.'

173 *De Lib. Arb.* II, III, 8. Even though this passage is put in the mouth of Evodius, it is clear from Augustine's response that he agrees with it.

174 *Tract. in Ioh.* XCIX, 3: 'in carne mortali quorumque animalium alibi est visus, alibi auditus, alibi gustus, alibi olfactus, per totum autem tactus.'

175 *Tract. in Ioh.* XIV, 10: 'anima tamen una est quae agit omnia, . . . in aure ut audiat, in oculo ut videat.' See *De Trin.* XV, X, 18: 'Sicut auditio et visio duo quaedam sunt inter se distantia in sensibus corporis, in animo autem non est aliud atque aliud videre et audire.'

176 *Tract. in Ioh.* XVIII, 10: 'In carne tua alibi audis, alibi vides; in corde tuo ibi audis, ubi vides.'

177 Cf. Plotinus, *Enn.* IV, 7,6.

178 See pp. 193 ff.

179 That our nervous system, like the bodily senses, has an indispensable 'mediating function' in the whole act of sense-perception has been shown by Seifert, *Leib und Seele*, pp. 233–43.

180 *De Trin.* XV, VIII, 15.

181 *De Trin.* XI, II, 2. At other places in *De Trinitate*, Augustine refers to the same faculty by the term *voluntas animi* (XI, II, 5), *voluntas animae* (XI, V, 9), and *intentio voluntatis* (X, VIII, 11; XV, III, 5).

182 *De Trin.* XI, II, 2.

183 *De Trin.* X, VII, 10: 'Ea quae oculis aut ullo alio corporis sensu requiruntur ipsa mens quaerit (ipsa enim etiam sensum carnis intendit, tunc autem invenit cum in ea quae requiruntur idem sensus venit).'

184 *De Trin.* XI, II, 2.

185 See Sr Mary Ann Ida Gannon, 'The Active Theory of Sensation in St Augustine,' *NSchol*, 30 (1956), 154–80; Nash, pp. 39–59; Vernon J. Bourke, ed., *The Essential Augustine* (Indianapolis: Huckett

Publishing Company, 1974), p. 68. In brief, this theory attributed to Augustine states that sense-perception is exclusively an act of the soul, without any effect of the body on the soul. Bourke calls the theory a 'one-way interactionism' (p. 68). See notes 187 and 188.

186 *De Musica* VI, V, 9.

187 In this sense, I would reject Bourke's statement that 'this active theory of sensation is one of the weakest elements in the philosophy of St Augustine' (Vernon J. Bourke, *Augustine's Quest of Wisdom* (Milwaukee: The Bruce Publishing Company, 1945), p. 237). Against such an exclusively one-sided interpretation of Augustine's view of the general relation between body and soul see also Robert E. Buckemeyer, 'Augustine and the Life of Man's Body in the Early Dialogues,' *AugSt*, 2 (1971), 197–211. Also Joseph P. Christopher, in his commentary on Augustine's *De Catechizandis Rudibus* (Washington, D.C.: The Cath. Univ. of America, Patristic Studies Vol. III, 1926), states that 'Augustine believed firmly in the reciprocal influence of mind and body' (p. 136). In *De Musica* VI, IV, 7, Augustine himself expresses his amazement at the fact that the body does have an effect on the soul: 'mirare potius quod facere aliquid in anima corpus potest.'

188 It would seem that most of our sense-perceptions are not preceded by a special intention to perceive a thing, but rather that the thing impresses itself on us without us necessarily wanting to perceive it. Indeed, it appears that in sense-perception we are more passively being hit by the impressions from the outside, than actively involved in it, as opposed to Augustine's emphasis. However, one may not overlook, first of all, that there are many degrees of intending to perceive something (a natural scientist has a greater intention to perceive the object of his inquiry than a daydreamer to perceive the world around him); and secondly, that the state of being awake, as opposed to a state of sleeping or of unconsciousness, is as such already an active intention or readiness to perceive on the part of the subject, preceding any actual sense-perception. Without being awake, we could not receive any impressions through the senses from the outside. Thus, it seems that Augustine is right in stressing an active involvement of the soul in sense-perception in the form of this inner intention of perceiving that in some manner must always precede an actual perception.

189 *De Trin.* XI, II, 5.

190 *De Trin.* XI, VIII, 15.

191 *De Gen. ad Litt.* VII, XX, 26.

192 *Sermo CXXVI*, II, 3. It is interesting to observe that such an absent-

mindedness is often expressed in the eyes. When talking to someone I often 'perceive' in his eyes whether he just looks at me, or whether he also pays attention to what I am telling him. The eyes are particularly apt bodily media expressing mental states. See note 216.

193 Even though those objects that are perceived merely 'half-intentionally' are not in the focal point of our attention, they could still 'enter into' our mind. For we often become aware of such a 'background-reality' *after* our act of perceiving it in this peculiar half-intentional manner. We then realize that we perceived something without paying full attention to it, which we can make up for afterwards by re-living the act in recollection.

194 *Ep. CXXXVII*, II, 6.

195 Ep. *CXXXVII*, II, 5: 'Ipsos ergo corporis sensus aliquanto insuetius et vigilantius perscrutetur. Sunt certe quinquepartiti corporis sensus, qui nec sine corpore nec sine anima esse possunt, quia neque sentire est nisi viventis, quod ab anima est corpori. . . . Certe sentire homo non potest, nisi vivat; vivit autem in carne, antequam morte utrumque dirimatur. Quo modo igitur anima, quae sunt extra carnem suam, sentit, quae non nisi in carne sua vivit? An non ab eius carne longissime absunt sidera in caelo? An in caelo non videt solem? An sentire non est videre, cum sit in quinque sensibus excellentior caeteris visus? An et in caelo vivit, quia et in caelo sentit et sensus esse non potest, ubi vita non est? An sentit, et ubi non vivit, quia, cum in sua tantum carne vivat, sentit etiam in his locis, quae praeter eius carnem continent ea, quae tangit aspectu? Videsne, quam sit hoc latebrosum in sensu tam conspicuo, qui visus dicitur?'

196 *De Quant. An.* XXIII, 44: 'Cum autem (oculi) se non vident, non modo cogimur consentire, posse illos videre, ubi non sunt; sed etiam omnino non posse, nisi ubi non sunt.' Cf. the whole context.

197 Cf. *De Trin.* X, III, 5 and XIV, VI, 8.

198 Nash sees in these reasonings 'a hint that Augustine considered the view of a world soul as a possible solution to the problem of sight at a distance' (p. 50). He refers to *De Ord.* II, XI, 30 and *De Immort. An.* XV, 24, where Augustine seems to speak of a Plotinian world soul: 'Per animam ergo corpus subsistet, et eo ipso est quo animatur, sive universaliter, ut mundus; sive particulariter, ut unumquodque animal intra mundum.' I do not see, however, why this statement should necessarily refer to a world-immanent soul ($\psi\upsilon\chi\dot{\eta}$), that is, to the universal soul of all physical reality in Plotinus' system. Augustine could simply have meant here the fact that the world seems in a sense to be alive considering its change in seasons, in growth and decay, in death and birth, which is an animation by the highest uncreated life.

Also, his startling way of discussing the phenomenon of sense-perception does not as such suggest a world-soul, but it is meant to make us realize and be amazed at the mysteriousness implied in an act that is so ordinary and familiar to us.

The question of whether or not Augustine did believe in some kind of world soul remains still open, as Vernon J. Bourke, after having surveyed the relevant texts on the topic, comes to the conclusion 'that he consistently refused either to affirm or to deny its (i.e. the cosmic soul's) existence. All that we can say is that St Augustine was definitely opposed to any divinization of the world soul, if there is such a soul' ('St Augustine and the Cosmic Soul,' *GM*, 9 [1954], 440).

199 *De Quan. An.* XXX, 61.
200 See Heinzelmann, p. 18.
201 I would disagree with Gannon's conclusion that Augustine's 'theory (of sensation) seems effectively to cut off the soul from the object itself' (p. 168).
202 *De Quant. An.* XXX, 60: 'Illud autem quod pati non potest oculus, nisi adsit anima, id est quod videndo patitur, hoc solum ibi patitur, ubi non est? Ex quo cui non videatur, nullo loco animam contineri? Siquidem oculus, quod est corpus, id tantum non loco suo patitur, quod nunquam sine anima pateretur.'
203 *De Trin.* XI, V, 9: 'Sensus enim animantis et voluntas animae est non lapidis aut alicuius corporis quod videtur.'
204 *De Trin.* XI, II, 2.
205 *Conf.* VII, 17: 'ratiocinantem potentiam, ad quam refertur iudicandum, quod sumitur a sensibus corporis.'
206 *De Vera Rel.* XXIX, 53: 'Non solum autem rationalis vita de sensibilibus, sed de ipsis quoque sensibus iudicat: cur in aqua remum infractum oporteat apparere, cum rectus sit, et cur ita per oculos sentiri necesse sit. Nam ipse aspectus oculorum renuntiare id potest, iudicare autem nullo modo.'
207 *De Gen. ad Litt.* XII, XXV, 52: 'unde in omnibus corporalibus visis et aliorum sensuum contestatio et maxime ipsius mentis atque rationis adhibetur, ut, quod in hoc rerum genere verum est, inveniatur quantum inveniri potest.'
208 *Ep. CXL*, XXIII, 56.
209 Clearly, this is not to be identified with the 'inner sense' or the '*sensus communis*' discussed earlier. See note 167.
210 *De Civ. Dei* XIX, 18: 'quoniam miserabilius fallitur qui numquam putat eis esse credendum.'
   In one of his early writings (*Solil.* I, III, 8), Augustine rejects all testimony of the senses. However, by the time of writing *De Gen. ad*

Litt. (401–15), *De Civ. Dei* (413–26), and, above all, *De Trin.* (400–16), Augustine had given up this view. In *De Trin.* XV, XII, 21 he says: 'Sed absit a nobis ut ea quae per sensus corporis didicimus vera esse dubitemus.' For through the senses we have learned of the heavens and the earth and of all God has created for us to know. Certainly, this trust in sense-perception is not identical with the most certain evidence of eternal reasons. The former is more a believing (*credit sensibus*), while the latter is an absolutely certain knowledge (*certissima scientia*) (*De Civ. Dei* XIX, 18). Cf. again *De Gen. ad Litt.* XII, XXV, 52 and *De Trin.* XV, XII, 21. See also Kälin, pp. 33–40, and Boyer, *L'idée de vérité*, pp. 23–59.

211 *De Div. Quaest. LXXXIII*, Qu. IX: 'Non est iudicium veritatis constitutum in sensibus.'

212 *Contra Acad.* III, XI, 26: 'ergone verum est quod de remo in aqua vident? Prorsus verum. Nam causa accedente, quare ita videretur, si demersus unda remus rectus appareret, magis oculos meos falsae renuntiationis arguerem. Non enim viderent, quod talibus existentibus causis videndum fuit.' See also *De Trin.* XV, XXVII, 49.

213 *Liber de Videndo Deo (seu Ep. CXLVII)*, IX, 21. It seems that Augustine has in mind here the same distinction which Reinach, going back to Husserl, makes between intuition (*Anschauung*) and presentation (*Vorstellung*): 'A book is lying in front of me. The entire book is presented (*vor-stellig*) to me, and yet only parts of it are represented intuitively. The back of the book, for example, is not at all intuitively given' ('Negative Judgement,' p. 25).

214 *Tract. in Ioh.* XL, 5: 'duae res ibi factae sunt, discernite illas, auditus et intellectus.'

215 *Ibid.* Cf. *De Musica* VI, IV, 5.

216 *Tract. in Ioh.* XXIII, 9: 'Unde facis nutum? De corpore, scilicet, labiis, vultu, superciliis, oculis, manibus. Haec omnia non sunt quod animus tuus; etiam ista media sunt; intellectum est aliquid per haec signa.' Cf. *De Div. Quaest.* LXXXIII, Qu. 47; *De Catech. Rud.* II, 3; *Conf.* VIII, 12.

217 It might be mentioned that it is the involvement of the rational soul (*mens*) that for Augustine distinguishes human from animal senseperception: 'mens quippe sine oculis carnis humana est; oculi autem carnis sine mente bellvini sunt' (*De Trin.* XIV, XIV, 19).

218 *Conf.* X, 7: 'Est alia vis, non solum qua vivifico sed etiam qua sensifico carnem meam, quam mihi fabricavit dominus, iubens oculo, ut non audiat, et auri, ut non videat, sed illi, per quem videam, huic, per quam audiam, et propria singillatim ceteris sensibus sedibus et officiis suis: quae diversa per eos ago unus ego animus.' See Franz Körner,

'Deus in homine videt. Das Subjekt des menschlichen Erkennens nach der Lehre Augustins,' *PhJ*, 64 (1956), 169–77, particularly p. 175: 'The subject of sense-knowledge is the "inner I" of the self-conscious spiritual soul, which makes use of the senses of the body for this knowledge.'

219 *Sermo CCLXVII*, IV, 4. Cf. *Tract. in Ioh.* XIX, 10: '(anima) est in corpore, praestat illi vigorem, decorem, mobilitatem, officia membrorum.'

220 *Sermo CXXVI*, II, 3.

221 *Tract. in Ioh.* CXIX, 4. Cf. *Sermo LII*, VII, 18; see also *Tract. in Ioh.* XVIII, 10, where Augustine speaks of the one interior emperor who has many ministers: 'vide quam multos ministros habeat unus interior imperator.'

222 Cf. also Blaise Pascal, *Pensées*, in *Oeuvres complètes*, ed. Jacques Chevalier (Bruges: Gallimard, 1954), 355 [C. 37]: 'Qu'est-ce qui sent du plaisir en nous? est-ce la main? est-ce le bras? est-ce la chair? est-ce le sang? On verra qu'il faut que ce soit quelque chose d'immatériel.' ('What is it that feels pleasure in us? Is it the hand, is it the arm, is it the flesh, is it the blood? One will see that this must be something immaterial.')

223 Gilson, p. 65: 'His analysis of sense knowledge makes Manichean sensualism provide a refutation of materialism.'

224 *De Trin.* XI, V, 9. *Retract.* I, I, 4: 'est enim sensus et mentis.'

225 *De Immort. An.* VI, 10. See *De Mag.* XII, 39 and *De Trin.* XV, XII, 21.

226 Kälin, p. 42: 'according to Augustine's teaching man possesses certain knowledge completely independent from sense-perception.'

227 *De Trin.* XII, XV, 25. See also *De Gen. ad Litt.* XII, VII, 16 where the third kind of vision is called the *intellectuale genus visionis*.

228 *De Trin.* XII, XIV, 22. See *De Trin.* XIV, I, 2–3, where Augustine repeats Plato in stating that the philosophers are the lovers of wisdom (*amatores sapientiae*), which is the science of divine things (*divinarum scientia sapientia*). See also Wolfgang Stein, *Sapientia bei Augustinus* (Witterschlick: Schwarzbold, 1973), pp. 107–10.

229 *De Lib. Arb.* II, VIII, 23.

230 *De Lib. Arb.* II, XI, 30 f.; *De Trin.* XV, XII, 21; *De Civ. Dei* XII, 18; *De Musica* I, XI, 18.

231 *De Lib. Arb.* II, X, 28. Cf. *En. in Ps. LVII*, 1.

232 *De Lib. Arb.* II, XVI, 41 f.

233 *Contra Acad.* XIII, 29. See Theodor G. Bucher, 'Zur formalen Logik bei Augustinus,' *FZPhTh*, 29 (1982), 3–45, especially p. 37, note 46.

234 See Geyser, pp. 70–9.

235 For the influence of this treatise see Martin Grabmann, 'Des heiligen Augustinus Quaestio de ideis (De diversis quaestionibus LXXXIII, qu. 46) in ihrer inhaltlichen Bedeutung und mittelalterlichen Weiterentwicklung,' in *Mittelalterliches Geistesleben* Bd. II (München: Hueber, 1936), pp. 25–34. For Augustine's sources see Aimé Solignac, 'Analyse et sources de la Question "De Ideis," ' *Augustinus Magister I*, 307–15.

236 *De Div. Quaest. LXXXIII*, Qu. XLVI De Ideis, 2: 'Sunt namque ideae principales quaedam formae vel rationes rerum stabiles atque incommutabiles, quae ipsae formatae non sunt ac per hoc aeternae ac semper eodem modo sese habentes, quae divina intellegentia continentur. Et cum ipsae neque oriantur neque intereant, secundum eas tamen formari dicitur omne quod oriri et interire potest et omne quod oritur et interit. Anima vero negatur eas intueri posse nisi rationalis, ea sui parte qua excellit, id est ipsa mente atque ratione, quasi quadam facie vel oculo suo interiore atque intellegibili. . . . Quod si hae rerum omnium creandarum rationes divina mente continentur, neque in divina mente quidquam nisi aeternum atque incommutabile potest esse, atque has rationes rerum principales appellat ideas Plato, non solum sunt ideae, sed ipsae verae sunt, quia aeternae sunt et eiusdem modi atque incommutabiles manent. Quarum participatione fit ut sit quidquid est, quoquo modo est. Sed anima rationalis inter eas res, quae sunt a deo conditae, omnia superat et deo proxima est, quando pura est; eique in quantum caritate cohaeserit, in tantum ab eo lumine illo intellegibili perfusa quodammodo et inlustrata cernit non per corporeos oculos, sed per ipsius sui principale quo excellit, id est per intellegentiam suam, istas rationes, quarum visione fit beatissima.' See Lechner, pp. 43–68.

237 *De Ord.* II, XIX, 50.

238 See note 236.

239 *De Trin.* XII, XIV, 23. See also *De Immort. An.* X, 17.

240 See note 236.

241 See note 236. This is one crucial point in which Augustine departed from Plato for whom the ideas are separated from the Demiurge (the shaper of the world) who rather looks up to them. See *Qu. XLVI De Ideis*: 'Has autem rationes ubi esse arbitrandum est nisi in ipsa mente creatoris? Non enim extra se quidquam positum intuebatur, ut secundum id constitueret quod constituebat; nam hoc opinari sacrilegum est.' See Ritter, pp. 33–9, and Hessen, pp. 27–49.

242 See also *De Civ. Dei* XI, 10: 'una sapientia est, in qua sunt infiniti quidam eique finiti thensauri rerum intellegibilium, in quibus sunt omnes invisibiles atque incommutabiles rationes rerum etiam visibi-

lium et mutabilium, quae per ipsam factae sunt.' *Conf.* X, 24: 'Ubi enim inveni veritatem, ibi inveni Deum meum ipsam veritatem.'

In this context, we cannot enter into the disputed question of whether the world can *philosophically* be known to have had a temporal beginning, or to be eternal. Such a discussion would however be presupposed for holding the ideas as being grounded in God; for this view follows from the fact that the world is not eternal but contingent. See Copleston, Vol. II, 1, pp. 292–5, on the controversy between Bonaventure and Thomas on this issue. See also Wittmann, pp. 51–9.

243 *Ep. II*, 1: 'omnia quae corporeus sensus attingit, ne puncto quidem temporis eodem modo manere posse, sed labi, effluere et praesens nihil obtinere, id est, ut latine loquar, non esse.' This non-being (*non esse*) should not be misunderstood to mean that the sensible things we see are in fact not really existing. Rather, this term expresses the essential changeability of these things in that they are never the same at each moment in time. Thus, non-being here means the opposite of that kind of being that the ideas have, that are 'ea quae semper eiusdem modi sunt' (*ibid.*).

244 *De Lib. Arb.* II, XVI, 44 f. Cf. Coelestin Zimara, 'Das Ineinanderspiel von Gottes Vorwissen und Wollen nach Augustinus,' *FZPhTh*, 6 (1959), p. 277: 'It is on the basis of and for the sake of *really existing* creatures that the train of thought postulates divine *"rationes."* '

245 See note 236.

246 *De Div. Quaest. LXXXIII*, Qu. XXIII. See Berlinger, pp. 89–96.

247 Solignac, p. 309: 'Therefore the idea is the *exemplar*, the paradigm, according to which the beings that come into being or pass away are formed, whether possible or real.'

248 *Conf.* I, 6: 'apud te rerum instabilium stant causae et rerum omnium mutabilium inmutabiles manent origines et omnium inrationalium et temporalium sempiternae vivunt rationes.' See *De Lib. Arb.* II, XVII, 45.

In modern philosophy, this 'theory of ideas' has been greatly developed by 'realist phenomenology.' See, above all, Josef Seifert, 'Essence and Existence. A New Foundation of Classical Metaphysics on the Basis of "Phenomenological Realism," And a Critical Investigation of "Existentialist Thomism," ' *Aletheia*, I, 1 (1977), 17–159 and I, 2 (1977), 371–459, where building on traditional and recent investigations he tries to develop a much more differentiated and comprehensive 'theory of ideas' in the context of establishing a 'new foundation of classical metaphysics.'

249 See note 236. See also *Contra Acad.* XIII, 29.

250 *De Vera Rel.* XXX, 56: 'apparet supra mentem nostram esse legem, quae veritas dicitur.'

251 *Solil.* II, II, 2: 'R. Quid illud? Videturne tibi verum aliquid esse posse, ut veritas non sit? A. Nullo modo. R. Erit igitur veritas, etiamsi mundus intereat. A. Negare non possum. R. Quid, si ipsa veritas occidat? nonne verum erit veritatem occidisse? A. Et istud quis negat? R. Verum autem non potest, si veritas non sit. A. Iam hoc paulo ante concessi. R. Nullo modo igitur occidet veritas.'

252 *Solil.* I, XV, 28: 'Nonne tibi videtur intereuntibus rebus veris veritatem non interire, ut non mori casto mortuo castitatem.'

253 For a more systematic treatment of why and how these ideas can also be called truths according to Augustine and Bonaventure see Josef Seifert, 'Bonaventuras Interpretation der augustinischen These vom notwendigen Sein der Wahrheit,' *FS*, 59 (1977), 49–52.

254 See the similar discussion of the eternal ideas in Bonaventure's *Itiner-arium Mentis in Deum*, II, 9.

255 *De Trin.* XII, XV, 24.

256 *Ibid.*

257 *De Immort. An.* X, 17.

258 *De Mag.* XII, 40. See the whole context.

259 *Retract.* I, IV, 4. Cf. *De Trin.* XIV, XV, 21: 'Ubi ergo (regulae immuta-biles) scriptae sunt, nisi in libro lucis illius quae veritas dicitur?'

260 See *De Mag.* XI, 28 f. *Conf.* XI, 3.

261 A good survey of the various interpretations, with corresponding literature, is given by Caroline E. Schützinger, *The German Contro-versy on Saint Augustine's Illumination Theory* (New York: Pageant Press, 1960), and by the same author 'Die augustinische Erkenntnis-lehre im Lichte neuerer Forschung,' *RechAug*, 2 (1962), 177–203. In these studies, she distinguishes four interpretations of Augustine's illumination theory: (a) the *ontologistic* interpretation according to which God acts as the means through which the human reason understands; (b) the *concordant* interpretations that try to reconcile Augustine's view with other theories of knowledge, above all, with that of St Thomas; (c) the *historical* interpretations which are rather the methods of interpreting Augustine on the basis of his texts alone; (d) the *existential* interpretation that using the historical method studies Augustine's teaching in the light of his life and that conceives of the theory of illumination as an explanation of the *interior* God-soul relation.

In our context, a critical discussion of these divisions and of each of these interpretations cannot be offered. For further literature on this much discussed topic may I refer to the following works: Boyer,

L'idée de vérité, pp. 179–249, Cayré, pp. 209–43, Willy Falkenhahn, *Augustins Illuminationstheorie im Lichte jüngster Forschungen* (Köln, 1948), Jakob Fellermeier, 'Die Illuminationstheorie bei Augustinus und Bonaventura und die aprioristische Begründung der Erkenntnis durch Kant,' *PhJ*, 60 (1950), 296–305, Gilson, pp. 77–96, Hessen, pp. 70–113, Bernhard Jansen, 'Zur Lehre des heiligen Augustinus von dem Erkennen der rationes aeternae,' *Aurelius Augustinus*, 120–36, Kälin, pp. 53–66, Franz Körner, 'Abstraktion oder Illumination? Das ontologische Problem der augustinischen Sinneserkenntnis,' *RechAug*, 2 (1962), 81–109, Portalié, pp. 109–14, Ismael Quiles, 'Para una interpretación integral de la "iluminación agustiniana," ' *Augustinus*, 3 (1958), 255–68, Wittmann, pp. 85–115.

On the theme of 'light' in general see Clemens Bäumker, *Witelo. Ein Philosoph und Naturforscher des XIII. Jahrhunderts* (Münster, 1908), pp. 672–73 of the *Sachregister*, where he gives references to this theme in a number of thinkers. See also note 267.

262 *Tract. in Ioh.* XL, 5: 'tamen nescio quid incorporaliter et spiritualiter facit in nobis Deus . . . aliquid est quod sentire facile est, explicare impossibile est.' Cf. also Kälin, p. 60: 'Augustine himself never succeeded in working out to his satisfaction an understanding of how intelligent knowledge through divine illumination occurs.'

263 Jaspers, p. 339: 'It is a fundamental experience in our thinking that a light dawns on us in which whatever is timeless is understood as universally valid and necessary.'

264 *Conf.* IV, 15. See again note 236.

265 *De Lib. Arb.* III, I, 1.

266 *Contra Acad.* III, XI, 25.

267 See note 236. It may be illuminating to outline briefly Bonaventure's interpretation of Augustine and his conception of the divine light. In his *Quaestiones Disputatae de Scientia Christi, Quaestio IV, conclusio*, he gives three interpretations of the statement 'omne, quod cognoscitur certitudinaliter, cognoscitur in luce aeternarum rationum': (1) This statement means that only eternal reasons (and ultimately God) are known with certainty. However, Bonaventure argues, this would allow for no knowledge except in God, which is untenable, since human reason does know earthly things in themselves. (2) It means that only the influences (*influentia*) of the eternal reasons, the created truths, can be known. But to hold that the eternal reasons cannot themselves be known were to contradict Augustine, Bonaventure states, and therefore false. (3) It means a medium between these two positions, namely that for knowledge with certainty an eternal reason is required as *regulans et ratio motiva*, though not as the *only ratio* (as in the first

interpretation), which is 'contuited' (*contuita*) with the created reason not in its complete clarity but 'in part' (*ex parte*) according to our *status viae*. It is this interpretation that Bonaventure adopts since it accounts for both a knowledge of earthly things by human reason as such and for a perception of the eternal reasons themselves: they are not directly 'intuited' but 'contuited' (i.e. seen together) with the created truths (things) formed according to them, whereby it is their immutability that accounts for the certainty of this knowledge. Thus, by 'contuiting' eternal reasons together with the corresponding created things, that is, by perceiving the latter in the *light* of the former, certain knowledge is gained, according to Bonaventure. See also Ignatius Brady, 'St Bonaventure's Doctrine of Illumination: Reactions Medieval and Modern,' *SWJPh*, 5, 2 (1974), 27–37.

268 *De Civ. Dei* XIX, 18.

269 *De Gen. ad Litt.* XII, XXV, 52. Cf. *Enchiridion* XVII. See also Maria Simon, *Gewißheit und Wahrheit bei Augustinus* (Emsdetten, 1938), pp. 19–27.

270 *De Gen. ad Litt.* XII, XXV, 52.

271 Cf. *De Div. Quaest. LXXXIII*, Qu. XXXII: 'Quisquis ullam rem aliter quam ea res est intelligit, fallitur: et omnis qui fallitur, id in quo fallitur non intelligit. Quisquis igitur ullam rem aliter quam est intelligit, non eam intelligit.'

272 See Augustine's very interesting distinctions between different kinds of deceiving and lying in *Enchiridion* XVIII f.

273 *De Vera Rel.* XXXIX, 73: 'Ubi videntur haec, ibi est lumen sine spatio locorum et temporum et sine ullo spatiorum talium phantasmate.' See also note 262.

274 *De Lib. Arb.* II, XII, 34.

275 *De Vera Rel.* XXXI, 57 and 58.

276 *De Beata Vita* IV, 34: 'Veritas autem ut sit, fit per aliquem summum modum, a quo procedit et in quem se perfecta convertit. Ipsi autem summo modo nullus alius modus imponitur; si enim summus modus per summum modum modus est, per seipsum modus est. Sed etiam summus modus necesse est, ut verus modus sit.'

277 *De Lib. Arb.* II, XII, 34.

278 *Conf.* VII, 17. Cf. *De Civ. Dei* VIII, 6; *De Trin.* IX, VI, 10–11.

279 *De Vera Rel.* XXXI, 58.

280 *De Vera Rel.* XXXI, 57: 'Quapropter tanto meliora esse iudico, quae oculis cerno, quanto pro sua natura viciniora sunt his, quae animo intellego.'

281 *De Lib. Arb.* II, XIV, 38.

282 *De Vera Rel.* XXXI, 58.

283 *De Vera Rel.* XXXIX, 72–3: 'Noli foras ire, in te ipsum redi. In interiore homine habitat veritas. Et si tuam naturam mutabilem inveneris, transcende et te ipsum. Sed memento, cum te transcendis, ratiocinantem animam te transcendere. Illuc ergo tende, unde ipsum lumen rationis accenditur. Quo enim pervenit omnis bonus ratiocinator nisi ad veritatem? Cum ad se ipsa veritas non utique ratiocinando perveniat, sed quod ratiocinantes appetunt ipsa sit, vide ibi convenientiam, qua superior esse non possit, et ipse conveni cum ea. Confitere te non esse, quod ipsa est – si quidem se ipsa non quaerit. Tu autem ad eam quaerendo venisti non locorum spatio, sed mentis affectu, ut ipse interior homo cum suo inhabitatore non infima et carnali, sed summa et spirituali voluptate conveniat. . . . Non enim ratiocinatio talia facit, sed invenit. Ergo antequam inveniantur, in se manent, et cum inveniuntur, nos innovant.'

284 Cf. *De Civ. Dei* XIII, 24. That Husserl, when quoting the beginning of this passage from *De Vera Religione* in support of his solipsistic conception of the transcendental Ego (*Cartesianische Meditationen und Pariser Vorträge* [Haag: Martinus Nijhoff, 1963], p. 183) completely misunderstood what Augustine meant by the dwelling of truth in the inner man, has been shown by Seifert, *Erkenntnis*, pp. 256 f.

285 Cf. *Conf.* IV, 15: 'Qualis in me tunc erat nesciente alio lumine illam inlustrandam esse, ut sit particeps veritatis, quia non est ipsa natura veritatis.'

286 *De Lib. Arb.* II, XII, 33: 'Quapropter nullo modo negaveris esse incommutabilem veritatem, haec omnia quae incommutabiliter vera sunt continentem, quam non possis dicere tuam vel meam vel cuiusdam hominis, sed omnibus incommutabilia vera cernentibus tamquam miris modis secretum et publicum lumen praesto esse ac se praebere communiter.'

287 *De Lib. Arb.* II, X, 28. See the whole context.

288 In his extensive presentation of Augustine's theory of ideas, Wittmann interprets Augustine as holding, on the one hand, the receptive transcendence implied in the knowledge of the ideas (against any idealistic conception) (*Ascensus*, pp. 38–44), and, on the other hand, an original self-presence of the ideas in a 'transcendental consciousness' ('All ideas . . . are originally present in the transcendental consciousness of the mind' p. 63). He thinks that there is no contradiction between these two positions: 'The original immanence of the ideas in the mind and their transcendent nature are in no way opposed to each other; for what is transcendent can only be known in its transcendence if it is at the same time somehow present to the mind, i.e. if it is immanent to it' (p. 35). If by 'immanence' Wittmann means the fact that the

ideas are always *interiorly* present *to* the mind without being 'received' through the exterior senses, I would agree with him. However, if he interprets Augustine as holding the ideas to be immanently present *in* the mind, ontologically speaking, as some of his later statements seem to suggest (e.g. on pp. 104 and 127), he is basically wrong, as becomes manifest from our discussion in the text. Unfortunately, he does not explicitly distinguish these two meanings of 'immanence,' for which reason his very profound study suffers from a decisive ambiguity and deficiency on this point.

Cf. also Bonaventure, *Itinerarium Mentis in Deum*, II, 9: 'leges illae . . . sint indelebiles a memoria recolentis tanquam semper praesentes.' See Chapter 2 note 55 on Augustine's view of Plato's theory of reminiscence.

289 For these arguments see Grabmann, *Grundgedanken*, pp. 57–8; Hein-zelmann, pp. 20–1, Körner, *Deus in homine videt*, pp. 178–90.

290 *Tract. in Ioh.* XXXV, 4: 'Intellegit quis in oriente iustitiam; intellegit alius in occidente iustitiam; numquid alia est iustitia quam illa intellegit, alia quam iste? Separati sunt corpore, et in uno habent acies mentium suarum.'

291 *Liber de Videndo Deo (seu Ep. CXLVII)*, XIX, 56: 'Viderunt melius videri mente quam corpore et ea videri mente, quae non continerentur locis nec inter se locorum intervallis separarentur nec minora essent in parte quam in toto.'

292 *De Trin.* XII, XIV, 23. See Nourrisson, p. 175: 'The rational soul is incorporeal; for neither the faculty that judges, nor the wisdom or the truth that the wise contemplates, reveal any corporeal lineaments.'

293 *De Quant. An.* XIII, 22: 'Unquamne igitur oculis istis corporeis, vel tale punctum, vel talem lineam, vel talem latitudinem vidisti? E. Omnino numquam. Non enim sunt ista corporea. A. Atqui si corporea corporeis oculis mira quadam rerum cognatione cernuntur; oportet animum quo videmus illa incorporalia, corporeum corpusve non esse.'

294 *De Div. Quaest. LXXXIII*, Qu. XLVI, 2: '. . . cernit non per corporeos oculos, sed . . . per intellegentiam suam istas rationes.' Cf. Plotinus, *Enn.* IV, 7, 8.

To hold intellectual cognition not to be mediated through the senses is, however, not to exclude the possibility of its being based on sense-perceptions. In fact, most of our insights into immutable ideas are preceded by the (sense-)perception of the corresponding data in the *contingent* world that are shaped according to them. See notes 267 and 280. For this complex relation between the understanding of an idea and the knowledge of what participates in it see Seifert, *Essence and Existence*, pp. 90–4.

295 *Tract. in Ioh.* XXXVIII, 10: 'in veritate quae manet, praeteritum et futurum non invenio, sed solum praesens.'

296 *Conf.* IX, 10.

297 *De Gen. ad Litt.* I, IX, 17: 'temporaliter audiente creatura, quae contemplatione veritatis omnia tempora excedit.'

298 Schmitt, p. 93: 'This moment must be seen as a going beyond time, as a "touching of eternity." ' Cf. Lampey, p. 57, Berlinger, pp. 50–4.

299 See our discussion of the *distentio animi* (pp. 78 f. and 86 f.) in which we tried to distinguish this ontological dimension of really being in time from the peculiar 'extending' of the mind beyond the present moment into the immediate future and past. Though both the *distentio animi* as well as the reaching into the realm of eternity are forms of transcending the underlying ontological relation to time, in a manner being impossible for a body, they are certainly quite distinct from each other; for while the latter precisely means a transcending of *time*, the former essentially presupposes the temporal changes.

300 Such an argument is made by Emerich Coreth, *Was ist der Mensch?* (Innsbruck: Tyrolia, 1973), pp. 92–3, by de Vries, pp. 120–1, and, more elaborately, by Seifert, *Leib und Seele*, pp. 116–22.

301 See note 236.

302 *Tract. in Ioh.* XIX, 14: 'Non enim vitam illam sapientiae sentit corpus, sed mens rationalis. Nam nec omnis anima potest sentire sapientiam. Habet enim et pecus animam; sed pecoris anima non potest sentire sapientiam.' See *De Div. Quaest. LXXXIII*, Qu. V; *De Civ. Dei* V, 11.

303 *De Quant. An.* XXXIII, 75: 'Sed haec actio, id est, appetitio intelligendi ea quae vere summeque sunt, summus aspectus est animae, quo perfectiorem, meliorem rectioremque non habet.'

304 Mary T. Clark, *Augustine, Philosopher of Freedom* (New York: Desclée, 1958), p. 4: 'Augustine's teaching on freedom is both of historical interest and of present-day value.'

305 For a discussion of Augustine's relation to Plotinus on this topic see Clark, pp. 132–56. For the influence of Marius Victorinus on the historical development of the notion of free will in general, including Augustine, see Ernst Benz, *Marius Victorinus und die Entwicklung der abendländischen Willensmetaphysik* (Stuttgart: Kohlhammer, 1932).

306 See Karl Kolb, *Menschliche Freiheit und göttliches Vorherwissen nach Augustin* (Freiburg: Herder, 1908).

307 *De Civ. Dei* V, 9: 'Quod si ita, nihil est in nostra potestate nullumque est arbitrium voluntatis; quod si concedimus, inquit, omnis humana vita subvertitur, frustra leges dantur, frustra obiurgationes, laudes,

vituperationes exhortationes adhibentur, neque ulla iustitia bonis praemia et malis supplicia constituta sunt. Haec ergo ne consequantur indigna et absurda et perniciosa rebus humanis, non vult esse praescientiam futurorum.'

308 *Conf.* VII, 3: '... sciebam me habere voluntatem quam me vivere.'

309 *De Quant. An.* XXXVI, 80: 'Datum est enim animae liberum arbitrium, quod qui nugatoriis ratiocinationibus labefactare conantur, usque adeo caeci sunt, ut ne ista ipsa quidem vana atque sacrilega propria voluntate se dicere intelligant.'

310 See Heinrich Barth, *Die Freiheit der Entscheidung im Denken Augustins* (Basel: Helbing & Lichtenhahn, 1935), pp. 74–111.

311 *Conf.* VII, 3. Cf. *De Duabus An.* X, 14: 'Nobis autem voluntas nostra notissima est: neque enim scirem me velle, si quid voluntas ipsa nescirem.'

312 *De Lib. Arb.* III, I, 3.

313 *De Div. Quaest. LXXXIII*, Qu. VIII: 'Nam si volumus, non alius de nobis vult.'

314 *De Civ. Dei* V, 9: '(dicimus) et voluntate nos facere, quidquid a nobis non nisi volentibus fieri sentimus et novimus.'

315 *De Lib. Arb.* III, I, 3.

316 *De Lib. Arb.* III, III, 7: 'Non enim posses aliud sentire esse in potestate nostra, nisi quod cum volumus facimus. Quapropter nihil tam in nostra potestate quam ipsa voluntas est. Ea enim prorsus nullo intervallo mox ut volumus praesto est.'

317 See Maxsein, p. 134: 'that also man himself in the core of his person, in the center of his nature, is willed by this will, so that there comes about in him that peculiar dynamism by which he possesses something that springs forth from the core of his person as from a fountain and then turns back to this fountain enriching and shaping it.'

318 This aspect of 'self-relatedness' of our willing has recently been studied quite originally by Karol Wojtyla in his *The Acting Person*, trans. Andrzej Potocki (Dordrecht: Reidel Publishing Company, 1979), pp. 105–48. See especially pp. 105–8, where he refers to three ways in which we are related to ourselves in willing: in 'self-possession,' which conditions our 'self-governance,' both of which being the ground of the possibility of our 'self-determination.'

319 See Mancini, p. 265: 'The will determines and effects its own movement, that is it, itself is the cause of its movement and of its activity.'

320 *De Civ. Dei* V, 9: 'humanae voluntates humanorum operum causae sunt.' In the context of this passage, Augustine presents his argument why the fact of man's free will as efficient cause of his actions does not disprove God's foreknowledge of them. For since God knows the

causes of all things, He also knows our wills and actions even 'before' they are performed.

321 *De Civ. Dei* V, 10: 'Multa enim facimus, quae si nollemus,non utique faceremus. Quo primitus pertinet ipsum velle; nam si volumus, est, si nolumus, non est; non enim vellemus, si nollemus.'

322 *De Lib. Arb.* III, XVII, 49: 'sed quae tandem esse poterit ante voluntatem causa voluntatis?' This complete self-determination independent of any exterior cause does not contradict the fact that the will is created by God; instead, it presupposes the latter. For without such 'creational cause' the will would not *be* at all, and it would not *be* as a will that is capable of independent self-determination, since *God* has given to the soul the power of spontaneous movement: 'iste motus animae spontaneus est; hoc enim ei tributum est a Deo' (*De Div. Quaest. LXXXIII*, Qu. VIII). See also *De Spir. et Litt.* XXXIV, 60: 'etiam voluntas . . . dono dei tribuitur, quia de libero existit arbitrio, quod cum crearemur accepimus.'

Discussion of the relation between will and grace, as a very special kind of 'exterior cause,' would go beyond the scope of our philosophical framework.

323 *De Lib. Arb.* III, III, 8: 'Quod si fieri non potest ut dum volumus non velimus, adest utique voluntas volentibus nec aliud quicquam est in potestate nisi quod volentibus adest. Voluntas igitur nostra nec voluntas esset nisi esset in nostra potestate. Porro, quia est in potestate, libera est nobis. Non enim est nobis liberum quod in potestate non habemus, aut potest non esse quod habemus.'

324 *De Duabus An.* XII, 15: 'Si liberum non sit, non est voluntas.'

325 *De Civ. Dei* V, 10: 'Sic etiam cum dicimus necesse esse, ut, cum volumus, libero velimus arbitrio: et verum procul dubio dicimus, et non ideo ipsum liberum arbitrium necessitati subicimus, quae adimit libertatem. Sunt igitur nostrae voluntates et ipsae faciunt, quidquid volendo facimus, quod non fieret, si nollemus.' Cf. the similar thought in Plotinus, *Enn.* III, 1, 8–9.

326 The freedom from being determined exteriorly is an essential feature of man's will not to be identified with what Augustine means by *libertas*, which is the state of 'the true freedom of those blessed ones that adhere to the eternal law' (*De Lib. Arb.* I, XV, 32). See also the long discussion of various stages of *libertas* in *Tract. in Ioh.* XLI, 9–13.

327 *De Lib. Arb.* III, I, 2.

328 *Conf.* VII, 3. Cf. *De Civ. Dei* XII, 7–8.

329 *De Grat. et Lib. Arb.* XV, 31: 'Semper est autem in nobis voluntas libera, sed non semper est bona.'

330 See Augustine's account of the theft of the pears in his early youth

which, as he confesses later, he did solely for the sake of sinning and enjoying sin: 'nec ea re volebam frui, quam furto appetebam, sed ipso furto et peccato' (*Conf.* II, 4).

331 Wittmann, pp. 281–5, points out basically the same three features of the will in Augustine's description: (a) that it is only *my*, *one* soul that is the subject of my will; (b) that the will is caused by itself (*Selbstursächlichkeit*); (c) that it has freedom of choice.

332 See note 321.

333 *Conf.* VIII, 9: 'Imperat animus corpori, et paretur statim: imperat animus sibi, et resistitur. Imperat animus, ut moveatur manus, et tanta est facilitas, ut vix a servitio discernatur imperium: et animus animus est, manus autem corpus est. Imperat animus, ut velit animus, nec alter est nec facit tamen. Unde hoc monstrum? Et quare istuc? Imperat, inquam, ut velit, qui non imperaret, nisi vellet, et non facit quod imperat. Sed non ex toto vult: non ergo ex toto imperat. Nam in tantum imperat, in quantum vult, et in tantum non fit quod imperat, in quantum non vult, quoniam voluntas imperat, ut sit voluntas, nec alia, sed ipsa. Non itaque plena imperat; ideo non est quod imperat. Nam si plena esset, nec imperaret ut esset, quia iam esset.'

334 See also *De Civ. Dei* XIV, 23: 'ipse animus imperat corpori facilius quam sibi.'

335 *Conf.* VIII, 10: 'Iam ergo non dicant, cum duas voluntates in homine uno adversari sibi sentiunt, duas contrarias mentes de duabus contrariis substantiis et de duobus contrariis principiis contendere.'

336 *Conf.* VIII, 10: 'Ego eram, qui volebam, ego, qui nolebam; ego eram.' Wittmann, p. 282: 'It is one single soul, one single I, that wills both things at the same time and is thus torn apart by these two opposing wills and cannot turn with its whole concentration to one end.'

337 See Dietrich von Hildebrand, *Christian Ethics* (New York: David McKay Comp., 1952), Chapters 21, 23, 25 and 26, where these two 'functions,' or, in his terminology, 'perfections,' of the will are much more elaborately discussed and unfolded, particularly with respect to the extent of freedom implied in each.

338 See note 321.

339 As pointed out in note 322, we cannot enter into the question of the relation between grace and free will, which would have to be discussed if the phenomenon of conversion or other existential decisions is to be accounted for more adequately; for in this case, the actual willing itself to perform the act of conversion may be experienced as a gift and not as freely be brought about. However, to show why grace does not exclude freedom would go much beyond our topic.

340 *De Spir. et Litt.* XXXIV, 60. Cf. *Conf.* VIII, 5: 'ego quidem in utroque,

sed magis ego in eo, quod in me approbabam quam in eo, quod in me improbabam.'

341 *De Duabus An.* X, 12. The central passage reads: 'Quibus concessis colligerem nusquam scilicet nisi in voluntate esse peccatum, cum mihi auxiliaretur etiam illud, quod iustitia peccantes tenet sola mala voluntate, quamvis quod voluerint inplere nequiverint.'

342 The following arguments are not explicitly developed by Augustine but clearly implied in what he is pointing out.

343 *De Lib. Arb.* III, I, 2: 'verum tamen in eo dissimilis, quod in potestate non habet lapis cohibere motum quo fertur inferius, animus vero dum non vult non ita movetur ut superioribus desertis inferiora diligat. Et ideo lapidi naturalis est ille motus, animo vero iste voluntarius.'

344 Certainly, this is in no way to exclude that man, besides his free self-determination, is also subject to exterior forces and necessities: he *must* eat, sleep, exercise or finally die.

345 *De Lib. Arb.* III, I, 2: 'Hinc est quod lapidem si quis dicat peccare quod pondere suo tendit in infima, non dicam ipso lapide stolidior sed profecto demens iudicatur; animum vero peccati arguimus cum eum convincimus superioribus desertis ad fruendum inferiora praeponere.'

346 *Tract. in Ioh.* XXXII, 2.

347 *De Civ. Dei* V, 9: 'Corporales autem causae, quae magis fiunt quam faciunt, non sunt inter causas efficientes adnumerandae, quoniam hoc possunt, quod ex ipsis faciunt spirituum voluntates.' See also Augustine's discussions of the *ordo causarum* in the context of this passage, in *De Trin.* III, IV, 9 and in *De Gen. ad Litt.* VIII, XXIII, 44, and see note 322 on the problem of the relation between divine and human causality.

348 *De Trin.* X, VII, 9: 'Et quia sibi bene conscia est principatus sui quo corpus regit, hinc factum est ut quidam quaererent quid corporis amplius valet in corpore, et hoc esse mentem vel omnino totam animam existimarent.'

349 Plato, *Phaedo* 94b–95a.

350 To distinguish various forms of body movements becomes particularly pressing in the light of neurophysiological attempts at 'activating the will electrically' by means of 'stimoceivers' implanted in the brain. See Delgado, pp. 86 ff. and pp. 184–9, where he tries to show how electrical stimuli can cause emotions, sensations and feelings in the person, concluding that all human behaviour could eventually be determined by stimulations of the brain. It would go too far for us to show in detail how Delgado superficially misinterprets causally affected movements of the body as deliberate and *free* motions of the

will, substituting the one for the other, and how in a very undifferentiated manner he identifies moods and feelings caused by bodily processes with intentional experiences which, in order to *be* at all, presuppose a *rational* relation to an object. See the detailed 'philosophical interpretation' of Delgado's experiments in Seifert, *Leib und Seele*, pp. 276–88.

351 *De Spir. et Litt.* XXXI, 53: 'cum enim duo quaedam sint velle et posse – unde nec qui vult continuo potest nec qui potest continuo vult, quia sicut volumus aliquando quod non possumus, sic etiam possumus aliquando quod nolumus –.'

352 *Conf.* VIII, 8: 'quae aliquando volunt homines et non valent, si aut ipsa membra non habeant aut ea vel conligata vinculis vel resoluta languore vel quoquo modo impedita sint.'

353 *De Nat. et Orig. An.* IV, V, 6. A different, yet similar, case is given in bodily movements performed in unconscious states, such as in sleep-walking. For since in such movements one is not fully aware of oneself as cause of the walking, this cannot be a fully volitional act. It must be determined, at least co-determined, by forces or reflexes exterior to one's own free self-determination.

354 *De Civ. Dei* XIV, 24. Augustine gives a number of remarkable examples: some men can move their ears; others can bring up a variety of things they have swallowed by pressing their stomach; some can mimic the voices of birds, beasts and other men; some even seem to sing when freely producing sounds from their bowels.

355 The reason for this lack of complete control of our body Augustine sees in the fall of the first man: 'Sic ergo et ipse homo potuit oboedientiam etiam inferiorem habere membrorum, quam sua inoboedientia perdidit' (*De Civ. Dei* XIV, 24).

356 See *Tract. in Ioh.* XVIII, 8.

357 *De Trin.* IX, VII, 12.

358 *De Div. Quaest. LXXXIII*, Qu. VIII.

359 One may not object that this 'movement' of the will might be accounted for by an incorporeal magnetic force of a body; for not only does such a force affect only specific metals, but evidently, it is also incapable of acting on our body freely and deliberately.

360 *De Gen. ad Litt.* VIII, XXI, 42: 'sed miris modis ipso incorporeo nutu (anima) commixta sit vivificando corpori, quo et imperat corpori quadam intentione, non mole: quanto magis, inquam, nutus ipse voluntatis eius non per locum movetur, ut corpus per locum moveat, quando totum per partes movet nec aliquas loco movet nisi per illas, quas loco non movet.'

361 Cf. *De Quant. An.* XIV, 23.

362 *De Trin.* III, III, 8: 'superiorem causam quae ab anima proficisceretur ad afficiendum corpus quod regit.' *Tract. in Ioh.* XX, 10: 'Imperat tamen animus corpori suo.'

363 *De Trin.* III, II, 8: 'Hoc corpus inspirata anima regit eademque rationalis.' Later in our critique of epiphenomenalism (pp. 210 ff.), we will come back to this argument.

364 *De Civ. Dei* V, 9: '. . . , si tamen voluntates appellandae sunt animarum rationis expertium motus illi, quibus aliqua faciunt secundum naturam suam, cum quid vel adpetunt vel evitant.' See von Hildebrand, *Christian Ethics*, Ch. 22.

365 *De Gen. ad Litt.* VIII, XXIII, 44: 'omne corpus et omnis anima irrationalis non habeat voluntatis arbitrium.'

366 *De Duabus An.* X, 14.

367 In the light of the investigations conducted in this chapter, we feel moved to remark that it seems to be precisely a lack of genuine analyses of mental *facts* which leads to the theory of the identity of mind and brain (see Chapter 1 note 14). For without going into any detailed critique, it appears that identity theorists, such as Feigl, Armstrong, Smart, are more concerned with the language and logic of their arguments, than with an investigation of the *data* in question, which are the acts of thinking, knowing, perceiving, remembering, willing, etc., and their performing subject. If these data would truly be rendered an object of philosophical inquiry, as should of course be done by any theory designed to explain them and as we tried to do following Augustine, their non-identity with bodily organs (the brain) would ever more evidently come to the fore. It seems that such investigations are avoided by the identity theorists precisely for this reason. In fact, they seem to employ almost exclusively an 'extrinsic' manner of arguing, that is, explaining the data in question not by an analysis of themselves, but by reference to alleged analogies in the material world or by anticipation of discoveries that neurophysiology is expected to make in the future. Thus, for instance, the factual identity, yet logical non-identity, of Morning Star and Evening Star, or of light and electrical discharge, are constantly recurring examples meant to explain the factual, and non-logical, identity of mind and brain; and the present scientific impossibility of locating in the brain the inner experiences of mental states is not seen as refuting the theory but as being achievable by future research (cf. Chapter 3 note 163). Apart from its questionable 'success,' it is this 'methodological extrinsicism' which seems to the present author to account for the fundamental falsity of the mind-brain identity theory. See also Seifert,

Leib-Seele-Problem, pp. 58–64, and Eric P. Polten, *Critique of the Psycho-Physical Identity Theory* (The Hague: Mouton, 1973).

368 *En. in Ps.* CXLV, 4: 'Natura animae praestantior est quam natura corporis, excellit multum; res spiritalis est, res incorporea est, vicina est substantia Dei. Invisibile quidam est, regit corpus, movet membra, dirigit sensus, praeparat cogitationes, exserit actiones, capit rerum infinitarum imagines.'

CHAPTER 3   *Knowledge of the self as showing the 'conscious spirituality' of the soul*

1   *De Trin.* XV, XXVIII, 51. Cf. Michael Schmaus, *Die psychologische Trinitätslehre des heiligen Augustinus* (Münster: Aschendorff, 1967), p. 175: 'Thus the Father of the Church has clearly distinguished between faith and science and has granted to each its proper rights.'

2   Josef Seifert contends that Augustine's *De Trinitate* 'contains the deepest philosophical grasp of the nature of the "mind-soul" of man that we possess in Western metaphysics' (*Leib und Seele*, p. 142).

3   For such a study see, above all, John E. Sullivan, *The Image of God. The Doctrine of St Augustine and Its Influence* (Dubuque, Iowa: The Priory Press, 1963), pp. 84–162, Schmaus, pp. 195–420, and Wittmann, pp. 115–98.

4   See Schmaus, pp. 235–64.

5   As far as I can see, these various lines of reasoning making up Augustine's *cogito*-argument have not been treated separately in Augustinian studies.

6   *De Trin.* X, VIII, 11: 'Ergo se ipsam quemadmodum quaerat et inveniat, mirabilis quaestio est quo tendat ut quaerat aut quo veniat ut inveniat.'

7   *De Trin.* X, VIII, 11; See also *Tract. in Ioh.* XL, 4.

8   *Conf.* X, 8.

9   *De Trin.* X, VIII, 11: 'Quid enim tam in mente quam mens est?'

10 *De Trin.* X, VII, 10: 'Quid enim tam cognitioni adest quam id quod menti adest, aut quid tam menti adest quam ipsa mens?'

11 *De Trin.* X, IX, 12: 'Sed cum dicitur menti: *Cognosce te ipsam*, eo ictu quo intellegit quod dictum est *te ipsam* cognoscit se ipsam, nec ob aliud quam eo quod sibi praesens est.'

12 *De Trin.* X, VIII, 11: 'Interior est enim ipsa non solum quam ista sensibilia quae manifeste foris sunt, sed etiam quam imagines eorum quae in parte quadam sunt animae quam habent et bestiae, quamvis intellegentia careant, quae mentis est propria. Cum ergo sit mens interior, quodam modo exit a semetipsa cum in haec quasi vestigia

multarum intentionum exerit amoris affectum. Quae vestigia tamquam imprimuntur memoriaeque quando haec quae foris sunt corporalia sentiuntur ut etiam cum absunt ista, praesto sint tamen imagines eorum cogitantibus. Cognoscat ergo semetipsam, nec quasi absentem se quaerat, sed intentionem voluntatis qua per alia vagabatur statuat in se ipsa et se cogitet. Ita videbit quod numquam se non amaverit, numquam nescierit.'

13 *Ibid.* In our previous section on recollection we have already critically dealt with Augustine's thesis that in going back into the past we perceive merely the images of the real things seen in the past as they are stored in memory. Even though this view is for various reasons not tenable, the ground of the present argument is thereby not destroyed. For there are still many ways, apart from recollection, in which we form genuine mental images on the basis of the perception of outside reality, such as in imaginations based on recollection, in the artistic creation of fictitious persons modelled after real persons, or in planning something on the basis of another's experiences.

14 See our discussion of imagination, esp. pp. 50 f.

15 *De Trin.* X, X, 16.

16 *De Trin.* IX, V, 8: 'Nam et mens est utique in se ipsa quoniam ad se ipsam mens dicitur.'

17 See note 12.

18 See *De Trin.* XIV, XIV, 19; *De Civ. Dei* V, 11 and XI, 27.

19 See note 12.

20 Cf. *De Trin.* XIV, X, 13. The peculiar nature of this kind of constant self-'knowledge' and the reasons why Augustine holds it to be implied in the mind's self-presence will be discussed more fully later in the section on Augustine's notion of *memoria sui.*

21 See again note 20.

22 See p. 156 and p. 170.

23 *De Trin.* XIV, IV, 7: 'Nihil enim tam novit mens quam id quod sibi praesto est, nec menti magis quidquam praesto est quam ipsa sibi.'

24 *Conf.* IV, 7: 'Quo enim cor meum fugeret a corde meo? Quo a me ipso fugerem?'

25 *De Trin.* X, VIII, 11.

26 *Ibid.*

27 See pp. 98 ff.

28 In a sense, however, the experience of feeling the corporeal reality of my body *'from within'* shares in the same privacy as is implied in self-knowledge, since only I have access to my body in this way. Yet, not only is my body, unlike the mind, accessible *also* 'from without' as is any other body, even consisting of parts that are exclusively given

'from without'; above all, the *kind* of privacy and immediacy in which the mind is present to itself is still different from my inner body-feeling; for, as we will more fully analyze in the section on *se nosse*, in the mind's experience of itself as performing subject of its acts (*se nosse*) it is given to itself in such a uniquely intimate manner that, compared to it, even the body is given as something 'outside.'

29 See also Plotinus' discussion of the self-thinking of the νοῦς (*Enn. V, 3*).

30 *De Trin.* XIV, VI, 8: 'Tanta est tamen cogitationis vis ut nec ipsa mens quodam modo se in conspectu suo ponat nisi quando se cogitat, ac per hoc ita nihil in conspectu mentis est nisi unde cogitatur ut nec ipsa mens qua cogitatur quidquid cogitatur aliter possit esse in conspectu suo nisi se ipsam cogitando. Quomodo autem quando se non cogitat in conspectu suo non sit cum sine se ipsa numquam esse possit quasi aliud sit ipsa, aliud conspectus eius, invenire non possum.'

31 *De Trin.* XIV, VI, 8: 'aliquid ad eius (i.e. mentis) naturam sit conspectus eius.'

32 A possible answer to this problem would go in the direction of distinguishing between the mind's consciousness in its awakened form and various states of un- and sub-consciousness in which *actual* (self-) conscious acts cannot be performed, even though the mind itself, as the 'bearer' of consciousness, would still remain within itself, ontologically speaking. On the level of 'awakened consciousness' one could moreover refer to the psychological *human* limitation that man can in many cases not consciously think of more than one object at the same time; this means that his faculty of thinking (*cogitatio*) can, for instance in a case of deep joy, be so 'exhausted' in this act that it becomes impossible (indeed unnecessary, and even destructive) for him still to place himself in his own sight at the same time. But in this case he is not divorced from his power of self-reflection; it is still present to him, however only in the form of an ability that could, but need not always, be actualized. In the present context, these questions cannot be dealt with to any greater extent.

33 See Johann Mader, *Die logische Struktur des personalen Denkens* (Wien: Herder, 1965), pp. 152–87, and Gérard Verbeke, 'Spiritualité et immortalité de l'âme chez Saint Augustin,' *Augustinus Magister* I, pp. 329–34.

34 *De Trin.* IX, XI, 16.

35 *De Trin.* IX, IV, 4. See also *De Trin.* IX, XI, 16.

36 *De Trin.* IX, V, 8: 'Et notitia quamvis referatur ad mentem cognoscentem vel cognitam, tamen et ad se ipsam nota et noscens dicitur; non enim sibi est incognita notitia qua se mens ipsa cognoscit.'

37   *Ibid.*
38   Franz-Maria Sladeczek S.J., 'Die Selbsterkenntnis als Grundlage der Philosophie nach dem heiligen Augustinus,' *Schol*, 5 (1930), p. 344: 'For it is the mind itself that thinks in the act of knowledge; not the act as such is thinking.'
39   *De Trin.* X, IX, 12.
40   *De Trin.* X, IX, 12.
41   *De Trin.* XV, XII, 21.
42   *De Trin.* XV, XII, 21.
43   *De Trin.* X, IX, 12: 'Neque sicut dicitur: "Cognosce voluntatem illius hominis," quae nobis nec ad sentiendum ullo modo nec ad intellegendum praesto est nisi corporalibus signis editis, et hoc ita ut magis credamus quam intellegamus.'
44   *Liber de Videndo Deo (seu Ep. CXLVII)*, XVI, 38: 'sicut voluntatem tuam, de qua ego tibi credere loquenti possum, eam vero, ut abs te videtur, videre ipse non possum.' Cf. *Tract. in Ioh.* XXXII, 5: 'Non enim novi quid cogitas, aut tu quid cogito: ipsa enim sunt propria nostra, quae interius cogitamus.'
45   *De Div. Quaest. LXXXIII*, Qu. XLVII: 'multi motus animi nostri nunc agnoscuntur in oculis.'
46   *De Catech. Rud.* II, 3: 'at si affectus excandescentis animi exeat in faciem vultumque faciat, omnes sentiunt qui intuentur iratum.' See *Tract. in Ioh.* XXIII, 9.
47   For a more detailed argument against the theory that we perceive other persons through inference by analogy with ourselves, stressing the immediacy of this perception of others *through* their bodily expressions, see Dietrich von Hildebrand, *Ästhetik 1* (Stuttgart: Kohlhammer, 1977), pp. 163–7.
48   *De Trin.* XIII, II, 5: 'alterius (voluntas) autem lateat quamvis idem velit, et si aliquibus signis sese indicet, creditur potius quam videtur. Unusquisque autem sui animi conscius non credit utique hanc esse suam sed plane pervidet voluntatem.' Cf. *De Lib. Arb.* II, X, 28.
49   *De Trin.* X, IX, 12: 'Neque ita ut dicitur homini: "Vide faciem tuam," quod nisi in speculo fieri non potest. Nam et ipsa nostra facies absens ab aspectu nostro est quia non ibi est quo ille dirigi potest.'
50   *De Trin.* XIV, VI, 8: 'Ipse quippe oculus loco suo est fixus in corpore; aspectus autem eius in ea quae extra sunt tenditur et usque in sidera extenditur.'
51   *De Trin.* IX, III, 3: 'Neque enim ut oculus corporis videt alios oculos et se non videt, ita mens novit alias mentes et ignorat semetipsam.' *Tract. in Ioh.* XLVII, 3: 'Oculus carnis alia videt, se non potest; intellectus autem et alia intellegit, et seipsum.'

52 *De Lib. Arb.* II, III, 9.

53 See *De Lib. Arb.* II, IV, 10.

54 *De Trin.* X, III, 5: 'numquam enim se oculi praeter specula videbunt, nec ullo modo putandum est etiam rebus incorporeis contemplandis tale aliquid adhiberi ut mens tamquam in speculo se noverit.'

55 Cf. Wladimir Iljitsch Lenin, 'Materialismus und Empiriokritizismus,' in *Sämtliche Werke*, Vol. XIII (Wien-Berlin: Verlag für Literatur und Politik, 1927), p. 145: 'The acknowledgment of the objective regularity of nature and of the approximately correct mirroring of this regularity in man's head is materialism.' See also Nikolaus Lobkowicz, 'Materialism and Matter in Marxism-Leninism,' in *The Concept of Matter in Modern Philosophy*, ed. Ernan McMullin (Notre Dame, Ind.: Univ. of Notre Dame Press, 1978), pp. 154–88.

56 *Ep. III*, 3: 'in imaginibus videmus, quas specula referunt.'

57 It should be kept in mind that self-reflection (*se cogitare*) refers only to the case where the mind knows *itself*, and not an image of itself, as in self-deceptions. Only when the mind alone is the begetter of its own knowledge of itself (*sola parens est notitiae suae*) being both the object known and the subject knowing (*et cognitum enim et cognitor ipsa est*), can we speak of self-reflection in the proper sense (*De Trin.* IX, IX, 18). See also Sladeczek, pp. 343–4: 'According to Augustine the known "I" (*notitia sui*) is simply identical with and equal to the knowing mind itself. If instead self-knowledge were a mirror image it could not possibly be identical with its reflected object but would necessarily have to be distinct from it.'

58 *De Quant. An.* V, 9. *Ep. III*, 3.

59 These contradictions have been pointed out, among others, by Seifert, *Leib-Seele-Problem*, pp. 86–9.

60 See our discussion of sense-perception.

61 *De Trin.* XIV, VI, 8: 'Nec est oculus in conspectu suo quandoquidem non conspicit se ipsum nisi speculo obiecto unde iam locuti sumus. Quod non fit utique quando se mens in suo conspectu sui cogitatione constituit.'

62 *De Trin.* XIV, VI, 8: 'Numquid ergo alia sua parte aliam suam partem videt cum se conspicit cogitando sicut aliis membris nostris qui sunt oculi alia nostra membra conspicimus quae in nostro possunt esse conspectu? Quid dici absurdius vel sentiri potest? Unde igitur aufertur mens a se ipsa, et ubi ponitur in conspectu suo nisi ante se ipsam? Non ergo ibi erit ubi erat quando in conspectu suo non erat quia hic posita, inde sublata est. Sed si conspicienda migravit, conspectura ubi manebit?'

63 See pp. 101–2.

64 The lack of *spatial* aspects in self-reflection certainly does not exclude the possibility that we may perceive ourselves differently at different stages of life, and that we do not possess a constant all-comprehensive grasp of ourselves, as will be discussed later.

64 *De Trin.* XIV, VI, 8.

65 Sladeczek brings out the same point in somewhat different terminology: 'In the *same* act of knowledge the substantial "I" is both opposed to and identical with itself. This apparent contradiction is solved by the fact that "to be known consciously" and "to be a conscious subject" refer only to relations (*esse ad*) which however do not imply *any* negation in the being itself.'

67 *De Trin.* XIV, VI, 8.

68 Cf. Gilson, p. 43: 'But the similarity of the two doctrines is quite evident even to one who does not compare the texts in detail.' For more detailed studies of the similarities and differences between Descartes and Augustine on the *cogito* see Léon Blanchet, *Les antécédents historiques du 'Je pense, donc je suis'* (Paris: Alcan, 1920); Lope Cilleruelo, 'La "Memoria Sui,"' *GM*, 9 (1954), pp. 478–92; H. Leder, *Untersuchungen über Augustins Erkenntnistheorie in ihren Beziehungen zur antiken Skepsis, zu Plotin und Descartes* (Marburg, 1901); Jakob Obersteiner, 'Der Ausgang vom Selbstbewußtsein bei Augustinus und bei Descartes,' *ThPQ*, 102 (1954), 277–88 (a brief, but valuable comparison of the main texts); William O'Neill, 'Augustine's Influence upon Descartes and the mind/body Problem,' *REAug*, 12 (1966), 255–60.

69 *De Trin.* X, X, 13.

70 See his parable of the Divided Line in the *Republic* VI, 509c–511e.

71 See his discussion of sense-deception in which act we have an *opinion* about how the object really is, though being *certain* of the fact that something truly appears to us (*Contra Acad.* III, XI, 26). There Augustine also implicitly refers back to the same distinction in Plato.

72 *De Trin.* X, X, 13.

73 According to Cicero (*Tusculanarum Disputationum*, 10) it was Aristotle who thought that the soul stems from a fifth body, different from the four elements.

74 *De Trin.* X, X, 14: 'Utrum enim aeris sit vis vivendi, reminiscendi, intellegendi, volendi, cogitandi, sciendi, iudicandi; an ignis, an cerebri, an sanguinis, an atomorum, an praeter usitata quattuor elementa quinti nescio cuius corporis, an ipsius carnis nostrae compago vel temperamentum haec efficere valeat dubitaverunt homines, et alius hoc, alius illud affirmare conatus est.'

75 *De Trin.* X, X, 13.

76   *Ibid.*
77   For the following see Salvino Biolo S.J., *La coscienza nel 'De Trinitate'
     di S. Agostino* (Roma: Typis Pont. Univ. Gregorianae, 1969),
     pp. 7–32, and Blanchet, pp. 27–47.
78   *De Beata Vita* II, 7: 'Scisne, inquam, saltem te vivere? Scio, inquit.
     Scis ergo habere te vitam, si quidem vivere nemo nisi vita potest. Et
     hoc, inquit, scio. Scis etiam corpus te habere? Adsentiebatur. Ergo
     iam scis te constare ex corpore et vita. Scio interim.'
     Augustine's major early work against scepticism *Contra Academicos*
     (386) does not state the *cogito*-argument in any developed form, apart
     from the brief remark that it is absurd to think that the wise man
     does not know why, or how, or whether he is living (III, IX, 19).
79   As far as I can see, this is the only place where Augustine extends
     the certainty the mind has of itself to the knowledge of the body.
     That such a step is, on the same grounds, not justified will be pointed
     out in the following section when the ontological conditions of this
     self-certainty in man's consciousness are analyzed.
80   *Solil.* II, I, 1: 'R. Tu qui vis te nosse, scis esse te? A. Scio. R. Unde
     scis? A. Nescio. R. Simplicem te sentis, anne multiplicem? A. Nescio.
     R. Moveri te scis? A. Nescio. R. Cogitare te scis? A. Scio. R. Ergo
     verum est cogitare te. A. Verum.'
81   *De Lib. Arb.* I, VII, 16. The question of animal-consciousness and of
     their possibility of having self-knowledge goes beyond the scope of
     our discussion.
82   *De Lib. Arb.* II, III, 7: 'A. Quare prius abs to quaero, ut de manifestis-
     simis capiamus exordium, utrum tu ipse sis. An fortasse tu metuis ne
     in hac interrogatione fallaris? Cum utique si non esses falli omnino
     non posses. E. Perge potius ad cetera. A. Ergo quoniam manifestum
     est esse te nec tibi aliter manifestum esset nisi viveres, id quoque
     manifestum est, vivere te. Intellegisne duo ista esse verissima? E.
     Prorsus intellego. A. Ergo etiam hoc tertium manifestum est, hoc est
     intellegere te. E. Manifestum.'
83   *De Civ. Dei* XI, 26: 'Nam et sumus et nos esse novimus et id esse ac
     nosse diligimus. In his autem tribus, quae dixi, nulla nos falsitas veri
     similis turbat. Non enim ea sicut illa, quae foris sunt, ullo sensu
     corporis tangimus, velut colores videndo, sonos audiendo, odores
     olfaciendo, sapores gustando, dura et mollia contrectando sentimus,
     quorum sensibilium etiam imagines eis simillimas nec iam corporeas
     cogitatione versamus, memoria tenemus et per ipsas in istorum desi-
     deria concitamur; sed sine ulla phantasiarum vel phantasmatum
     imaginatione ludificatoria mihi esse me idque nosse et amare certis-
     simum est. Nulla in his veris Academicorum argumenta formido

dicentium: Quid si falleris? Si enim fallor, sum. Nam qui non est, utique nec falli potest; ac per hoc sum, si fallor. Quia ergo sum si fallor, quo modo esse me fallor, quando certum est me esse, si fallor? Quia igitur essem qui fallerer, etiamsi fallerer, procul dubio in eo, quod me novi esse, non fallor. Consequens est autem, ut etiam in eo, quod me novi nosse, non fallar. Sicut enim novi esse me, ita novi etiam hoc ipsum, nosse me.'

84 *De Trin.* XV, XII, 21: 'His ergo exceptis quae a corporis sensibus in animum veniunt, quantum rerum remanet quod ita sciamus sicut nos vivere scimus? In quo prorsus non metuimus ne aliqua verisimilitudine forte fallamur quoniam certum est etiam eum qui fallitur vivere, nec in eis visis habetur hoc quae obiciuntur extrinsecus ut in eo sic fallatur oculus quemadmodum fallitur cum in aqua remus videtur infractus et navigantibus turris moveri et alia sexcenta quae aliter sunt quam videntur, quia nec per oculum carnis hoc cernitur.'

85 See Gareth B. Matthews, 'Si Fallor, Sum,' in *Augustine: A Collection of Critical Essays*, ed. Robert A. Markus (New York: Doubleday, 1972), pp. 151–67.

86 *De Trin.* XV, XII, 21.

87 *De Immort. An.* XIV, 23: 'Corporeos enim sensus (somnus) sopit et claudit quodammodo, ita sane ut tali commutationi corporis cedat anima cum voluptate: quia secundum naturam est talis commutatio quae reficit corpus a laboribus: non tamen haec adimit animo vel sentiendi vim vel intelligendi.' Cf. *De Nat. et Orig. An.* IV, XVIII, 26.

88 *De Trin.* XIV, IV, 6: 'ita quamvis ratio vel intellectus nunc in ea (i.e. anima) sit sopitus, nunc parvus, nunc magnus appareat, numquam nisi rationalis et intellectualis est anima humana.'

89 *De Trin.* XV, XII, 21.

90 *Ibid.*

91 *De Trin.* X, X, 14: 'Vivere se tamen et meminisse et intellegere et velle et cogitare et scire et iudicare quis dubitet? Quandoquidem etiam si dubitat, vivit; si dubitat, unde dubitet meminit; si dubitat, dubitare se intellegit; si dubitat, certus esse vult; si dubitat, cogitat; si dubitat, scit se nescire; si dubitat, iudicat non se temere consentire oportere. Quisquis igitur alicunde dubitat de his omnibus dubitare non debet quae si non essent, de ulla re dubitare non posset.' See Biolo, pp. 53–61.

92 See the highly original discussion of the act of doubting in Seifert, *Erkenntnis*, pp. 151–9.

93 *De Trin.* X, X, 14. Cf. *De Trin.* X, X, 13: '*omnes* tamen se intellegere noverunt et esse et vivere.'

94 See Schöpf, *Wahrheit und Wissen*, pp. 154–60.

95 *De Trin.* VIII, VI, 9.

96 *De Trin.* IX, VI, 9: 'Sed cum se ipsam novit humana mens et amat se ipsam, non aliquid incommutabile novit et amat. Aliterque unusquisque homo loquendo enuntiat mentem suam quid in se ipso agatur attendens; aliter autem humanam mentem speciali aut generali cognitione definit. Itaque cum mihi de sua propria loquitur, utrum intellegat hoc aut illud an non intellegat, et utrum velit an nolit hoc aut illud, credo; cum vero de humana specialiter aut generaliter verum dicit, agnosco et approbo.

Unde manifestum est aliud unumquemque videre in se quod sibi alius dicenti credat, non tamen videat; aliud autem in ipsa veritate quod alius quoque possit intueri, quorum alterum mutari per tempora, alterum incommutabili aeternitate consistere. Neque enim oculis corporeis multas mentes videndo per similitudinem colligimus generalem vel specialem mentis humanae notitiam, sed intuemur inviolabilem veritatem ex qua perfecte quantum possumus definiamus non qualis sit uniuscuiusque hominis mens, sed qualis esse sempiternis rationibus debeat.'

97 Cf. Thomas Aquinas, *Quaestiones Disputatae de Veritate*, q. 10, a. 8c, where he discusses the difference between these two forms of knowing the soul.

98 See our section on the cognition of the eternal reasons.

99 *De Trin.* IX, VII, 12.

100 *De Vera Rel.* XXXIX, 73. Cf. *ibid.* XXXVI, 66: 'veritas forma verorum est' and *De Div. Quaest. LXXXIII*, Qu. I: 'Omne verum a veritate verum est.' See also *De Immort. An.* XII, 19, and *Solil.* II, XVII, 3.

101 It has to be left open here what exactly is meant by the term 'truth as such' (*veritas*), and how this relates to the eternal reasons or verities. As Augustine does not explicitly speculate on these problems, and as they are extremely intricate and difficult, they may merely be mentioned here, without any attempt to solve them.

102 *De Trin.* XV, XII, 21.

103 For this argument see Ferraz, pp. 44–9; Gangauf, pp. 169–80; Grabmann, *Grundgedanken*, pp. 51–3; Heinzelmann, pp. 21–3; Herbert Hornstein, 'Immaterialität und Reflexion. Eine Studie zur Geistphilosophie des hl. Augustinus,' in *Erkenntnis und Verantwortung*, ed. Josef Derbolav and Friedhelm Nicolin (Düsseldorf: Schwann, 1960), pp. 285–300; Mancini, pp. 69–74 (with a comparison to Plotinus); Verbeke, *Spiritualité*, p. 330 ff.

104 *De Trin.* X, X, 16: 'Certa est mens autem de se sicut convincunt ea quae supra dicta sunt. Nec omnino certa est utrum aer an ignis sit an aliquid corpus vel aliquid corporis. Non est igitur aliquid eorum. Totumque illud quod se iubetur ut noverit, ad hoc pertinet ut certa

sit non se esse aliquid eorum de quibus incerta est, idque solum esse se certa sit quod solum esse se certa est.

Sic enim cogitat ignem ut aerem et quidquid aliud corporis cogitat, neque ullo modo fieri posset ut ita cogitaret id quod ipsa est quemadmodum cogitat id quod ipsa non est. Per phantasiam quippe imaginariam cogitat haec omnia, sive ignem sive aerem sive illud vel illud corpus partemve ullam seu compaginem temperationemque corporis, nec utique ista omnia sed aliquid horum esse dicitur. Si quid autem horum esset, aliter id quam cetera cogitaret, non scilicet per imaginale figmentum sicut cogitantur absentia quae sensu corporis tacta sunt, sive omnino ipsa sive eiusdem generis aliqua, sed quadam interiore non simulata sed vera praesentia (non enim quidquam illi est se ipsa praesentius), sicut cogitat vivere se et meminisse et intellegere et velle se. Novit enim haec in se, nec imaginatur quasi extra se illa sensu tetigerit sicut corporalia quaeque tanguntur. Ex quorum cogitationibus si nihil sibi affingat ut tale aliquid esse se putet, quidquid ei de se remanet hoc solum ipsa est.'

105 In the present section, the argument focuses exclusively on the incorporeality of the mind, while in the subsequent section basically the same argument is taken up and developed in such a way as to show positively the (conscious) spirituality of the incorporeal mind.

106 See *De Civ. Dei* VIII, 5 and our discussion of this passage on pp. 11 ff.

107 See note 104.

108 *De Trin.* X, X, 14: 'Sed quoniam de natura mentis agitur, removeamus a consideratione nostra omnes notitias quae capiuntur extrinsecus per sensus corporis, et ea quae posuimus omnes mentes de se ipsis nosse certasque esse diligentius attendamus.'

109 *De Nat. et Orig. An.* IV, I–IX.

110 See for instance *De Nat. et Orig. An.* IV, VII, 9.

111 *De Nat. et Orig. An.* IV, VII, 9: 'Ecce modo, modo dum sumus, dum vivimus, dum nos vivere scimus, dum meminisse nos et intellegere et velle certissimi sumus, qui nos naturae nostrae magnos cognitores esse iactamus quid valeat memoria nostra vel intellegentia vel voluntas omnino nescimus.' See *En. in Ps.* LV, 2.

112 *De Nat. et Orig. An.* IV, VI, 8. See *Conf.* X, 16: 'Et ecce memoriae meae vis non conprehenditur a me, cum ipsum me non dicam praeter illam.'

113 Cf. *Conf.* IV, 4 and *Conf.* X, 5: 'confitear ergo quid de me sciam, confitear et quid de me nesciam.'

114 *Conf.* III, 6; *En. in Ps.* LXXIV, 9.

115 On the important topic of self-deceptions see Max Scheler, *Vom Umsturz der Werte* (Bern and München: Francke, 1972), pp. 215–92.

116 Immanuel Kant, *Kritik der reinen Vernunft*, ed. Königlich Preußische Akademie der Wissenschaften, Vol. III (Berlin: Reiner, 1904), A 399–413, and *Prolegomena zu einer jeden künftigen Metaphysik, die als Wissenschaft wird auftreten können*, Vol. IV of the same edition (1903), §46–§49.

117 Edmund Husserl, *Cartesianische Meditationen und Pariser Vorträge* (Haag: Martinus Nijhoff, 1963), §§8–11.

118 Kant, *Prolegomena*, §49.

119 *De Trin.* X, III, 5: 'quod de se fingit hoc amat longe aliud quam ipsa est.'

120 *De Trin.* X, X, 16: 'Certa est (i.e. mens) autem de se sicut convincunt ea quae supra dicta sunt.' Cf. *De Trin.* X, X, 16: 'Qui omnes (who think the mind to be some body or harmony) non advertunt mentem *se nosse* etiam cum quaerit se sicut iam ostendimus.'

121 *De Trin.* X, III, 5: 'Quid ergo amat mens cum ardenter se ipsam quaerit ut noverit dum incognita sibi est?'

122 *De Trin.* X, I, 2: 'quoniam firmissime novimus amari nisi nota non posse.'

123 See Schmaus, pp. 238–9.

124 *De Trin.* X, III, 5.

125 For the present argument it is unessential to pursue the question of what this kind of generic knowledge of the mind really is and in which sense it presupposes an image of other minds. The decisive point is that it is not a knowledge of a concrete self.

126 *De Trin.* X, III, 5: 'Cur ergo cum alias mentes novit se non novit cum se ipsa nihil sibi possit esse praesentius?'

127 *Ibid.*

128 *De Trin.* X, III, 5: 'Et hoc quidem permirabile est nondum se nosse et quam sit pulchrum se nosse iam nosse.'

129 *Ibid.*

130 *Ibid.*

131 *De Trin.* X, III, 5: 'Ubi ergo nosse suum novit si se non novit? Nam novit quod alia noverit, se autem non noverit; hinc enim novit et quid sit nosse. Quo pacto igitur se aliquid scientem scit quae se ipsam nescit? Neque enim alteram mentem scientem scit sed se ipsam. Scit igitur se ipsam. Deinde cum se quaerit ut noverit, quaerentem se iam novit. Iam se ergo novit. Quapropter non potest omnino nescire se quae dum se nescientem scit se utique scit. Si autem se nescientem nesciat, non se quaeret ut sciat. Quapropter eo ipso quo se quaerit magis se sibi notam quam ignotam esse convincitur. Novit enim se quaerentem atequ nescientem dum se quaerit ut noverit.'

132　*De Trin*. X, I, 3: 'Quod nisi haberet cognitum, neque scire se quidquam posset fidenter dicere neque nescire.'

133　See note 131. Cf. the important passage of *De Gen. ad Litt*. VII, XXI, 28: 'cum se nescire non possit, etiam quando, se ut cognoscat, inquirit. Cum enim se quaerit, novit, quod se quaerat; quod nosse non posset, si se non nosset. Neque enim aliunde se quaerit, quam a se ipsa. Cum ergo quaerentem se novit, se utique novit.'

134　*De Trin*. X, V, 7. See *De Trin* XIV, VII, 9. As we will see in the following section, the meaning of Augustine's *se nosse* is not unambiguous, which explains the fact that Augustine shows the difference between *se nosse* and *se cogitare* at the places referred to above by using an example from memory, namely that man still knows (*nosse*) a fact even when he is not presently thinking (*cogitare*) of it.

135　Karol Wojtyla, *The Acting Person*, trans. Andrzej Potocki (Dordrecht: Reidel Publishing Company, 1979), pp. 25–59. For an illuminating presentation and commentary of this work see Josef Seifert, 'Karol Cardinal Wojtyla (Pope John Paul II) as Philosopher and the Cracow/ Lublin School of Philosophy,' *Aletheia*, 2 (1981), 131–81; see also Stephen A. Dinan, 'The Phenomenological Anthropology of Karol Wojtyla,' *NSch*, 55 (1981), 317–30, esp. pp. 319 f.

　　Though the inward unthematic knowing awareness of ourselves as subject of our acts has often been seen and referred to, there does not seem to be a phenomenological analysis of it as careful as that of Wojtyla.

　　It was Husserl who, inspired by Brentano, initiated the discussion of this topic by drawing philosophical attention to and explicating the equivocation of the term *Bewußtseinsinhalt* (content of consciousness). For this term can refer to two completely different data: the *intentional object* of consciousness and the real immanent contents ('parts') of consciousness, for instance, our acts, experiences, feelings, *as* conscious realities. Consequently, 'being conscious' means something quite different in each case, which accounts for the distinctness of conscious intentional relation and inner perception (*Logische Untersuchungen*, Vol. II, 1 pp. 370–5 and pp. 354–6).

　　A further analysis of this inner cognitive awareness was given by Moritz Geiger in his article 'Fragment über den Begriff des Unbewußten und der psychischen Realität,' *JPPF*, 4 (1921), 1–137, where he distinguishes the intentional 'consciousness of' from the inner experiencing of conscious acts: the former is an explicit grasping of something standing over against consciousness, while the latter is an '*Innewerden*' not of an object (*Gegen-stand*), but of an experienced content while it is being experienced (pp. 41–4).

In the same volume of the *Jahrbuch*, Roman Ingarden in his article 'Über die Gefahr einer Petitio Principii in der Erkenntnistheorie' uses the term '*Durchleben*' with reference to the experiencing of conscious acts in opposition to the '*Erlebtwerden*' of the objects of consciousness (pp. 562 and 556 f.).

In his book *Kritik der transzendentalphilosophischen Erkenntnistheorie* (Stuttgart: Kohlhammer, 1969), Walter Hoeres, mentioning the two latter studies, explains his own term '*Daseinsgefühl*,' particularly stressing the fact that the more I consciously perform an act of 'consciousness of,' the less am I conscious of myself as performing this act in the manner of this inward awareness (pp. 36–41).

Dietrich von Hildebrand, especially in his unpublished lectures at the University of Salzburg in 1964 and in his *Ästhetik 1* (pp. 32–4), started to focus more sharply on the difference and the significance of what he called '*frontales Bewußtsein von*' and '*laterales Vollzugsbewußtsein*' of myself and my acts during their performances. His analyses were taken up by Josef Seifert (*Erkenntnis*, pp. 59–67) in his argument that the attempt to identify these two kinds of consciousness and to reduce the one to the other will necessarily lead to intrinsic contradictions and to an infinite regress.

In all these studies, however, an explicit analysis of what this inward self-awareness really is and how it functions is not found to any greater extent. For this reason, Wojtyla's study seems to me to be the most developed in this respect.

136 Augustine talks more extensively about the kind of *se nosse* that we will discuss in the subsequent section under the name of *memoria sui*. See note 134.

137 Wojtyla, p. 28; Cf. Seifert, pp. 146–50.

138 Wojtyla, p. 31.

139 Wojtyla, p. 31.

140 Wojtyla, p. 41.

141 Wojtyla, p. 34.

142 Seifert, p. 148.

143 Wojtyla, p. 42; cf. Seifert, pp. 153–5.

144 Karol K. Wojtyla, 'Person: Subjekt und Gemeinschaft,' in *Der Streit um den Menschen. Personaler Anspruch des Sittlichen*, trans. Jörg Splett (Kevelaer: Butzon & Bercker, 1979), p. 24.

145 Wojtyla, *Acting Person*, p. 36: 'It is to them (i.e. acts of self-knowledge) that every man owes the objectivizing contact with himself and with his actions. Because of self-knowledge consciousness can mirror actions and their relations to the ego. Without it consciousness would be deprived of its immanent meanings so far as man's self is concerned

– when it presents itself as the object – and would then exist as if it were suspended in the void.'

146 Wojtyla, *Acting Person*, p. 37.

147 Cf. Schmaus, p. 243: 'This argument for knowledge of certainty is an original achievement of the great thinker of Hippo for which there was no precedence and which was not understood and developed until long after him.'

148 Cf. *De Vera Rel.* XXXIX, 73: 'Aut si non cernis quae dico, et an vera sint dubitas, cerne saltem, utrum te de his dubitare non dubites, et si certum est te esse dubitantem, quaere, unde sit certum.'

149 See *De Trin.* X, X, 14 and *De Trin.* IX, VI, 9 and our discussion of these passages on pp. 149 f., in which Augustine explains the difference and the relation between the knowledge of my own concrete mind and that of the general nature of the mind as such in doubting.

150 See notes 109–114.

151 See pp. 144 ff.

152 Cf. also *Tract. in Ioh.* XXXII, 5: 'Deus autem scit in nobis et quod ipsi nescimus in nobis.'

153 *De Trin.* XIV, IV, 7: 'Nihil enim tam novit mens quam id quod sibi praesto est, nec menti magis quidquam praesto est quam ipsa sibi.' See our discussion of the immediate self-presence of the mind.

154 Sladeczek, p. 354: 'The mind grasps in its self-knowledge not only the *phenomenon* of its "I," but the *reality* of its conscious (phenomenal) "I" and its act of knowledge itself, and it is conscious of this knowledge. It knows, therefore, an objectively valid truth, that is, the truth that it exists.' See also the extensive discussion of the *cogito* with respect to the transcendental idealism of Kant and the later Husserl in Seifert, *Leib und Seele*, pp. 45–61, and *Erkenntnis*, pp. 203–17 and pp. 233–58, where he distinguishes six very different meanings of the term 'transcendental Ego' which are confused in Husserl.

155 *De Duabus An.* X, 13: 'Liceat mihi me scire vivere, liceat mihi scire me velle vivere: in quae si consentit genus humanum, tam nobis cognita est voluntas nostra quam vita neque cum istam scientiam profitemur, metuendum est, ne nos quisquam falli posse convincat; hoc ipsum enim falli nemo potest, si aut non vivat aut nihil velit.' See *Conf.* XIII, 11: 'Sum enim et scio et volo: sum sciens et volens et scio esse me et velle et volo esse et scire.'

156 See again pp. 152 ff.

157 In the development of this argument of Augustine based on the unique immediate self-awareness of the mind Seifert sees 'one of the greatest epistemological-metaphysical contributions' (*Leib und Seele*, p. 146, note 268).

158 *De Gen. ad Litt.* VII, XXI, 28: 'Quid ergo adhuc se quaerit, si quaerentem se novit? Neque enim si nesciret se, posset quaerentem se scire se; sed hoc in praesenti; quod autem de se quaerit, quid antea fuerit vel quid futura sit quaerit. Desinat ergo nunc interim suspicari se esse corpus, quia, si aliquid tale esset, talem se nosset, quae magis se novit quam caelum et terram, quae per sui corporis oculos novit.'

159 See our discussions on pp. 27 ff. and 35 ff.

160 Peculiarly enough, precisely those organs of our body that, unlike the mind, are not even known from within, but only through exterior research, particularly the millions of brain cells and their interrelations, are widely held to *be* or to 'ground' the mind, as in the mind-brain identity theory and in epiphenomenalism. This again reveals the importance of emphasizing Augustine's point that we ought to distinguish between what I know for sure and what I merely believe. For I am interiorly aware of *myself* with indubitable certainty, as we showed above, but I generally do not even know that I have a brain at all except by relying on the testimonies of scientists whom I *believe* in their empirical judgment that all men have a brain. It seems to be a widespread intellectual tendency tacitly to consider this belief in others (scientists) a more certain form of knowledge than the immediate awareness of oneself. See Chapter 1 note 14.

161 Augustine does not seem to draw out this conclusion explicitly, even though it logically follows from his discussion of the fact that the mind, and only the mind, is most immediately present to itself. In a similar way, Descartes (in the *Sixth Meditation*) arrives at the existence of our body not through the immediate givenness of the *cogito*, but by inference from inner experiences, such as pain, hunger, thirst. See also his 'The Principles of Philosophy,' in *The Philosophical Works of Descartes*, Vol. I, trans. Elizabeth S. Haldane and G. R. T. Ross (Cambridge: University Press, 1978), I, 7, p. 221: 'it is easy to suppose . . . that we possess neither hands, nor feet, nor indeed any body; but we cannot in the same way conceive that we who doubt these things are not; for there is a contradiction in conceiving that what thinks does not at the same time as it thinks, exist.'

162 See p. 49, where we distinguished three different ways of relating to space. The reason why I do not experience myself (the self-conscious subject) as located at a part of my body lies precisely in the facts that 'I' am not extended in space, thus being distinct from, though united to, my body, and that the experience of self-awareness (*se nosse*) is purely of 'myself' excluding any bodily element, unlike for instance the experience of a pain that is felt at a particular part of the body.

163 Cf. *Ep. CXXXVII*, III, 11: 'nam si anima in sua natura non fallatur, incorpoream se esse comprehendit.' This whole argument developed in the text also refutes the claim of Herbert Feigl (in *The 'Mental' and the 'Physical'* [Minneapolis: Univ. of Minneapolis Press, 1967]) that it is 'the scientifically uninformed person' who accepts the idea of mind; for 'when giving phenomenological descriptions (of the awareness of intentionality and of selfhood) [he] does not *know* that he is at the same time describing certain features of his brain processes' (pp. 149–50), even though, as Feigl himself admits, to give 'successor' accounts in physical terms of these awarenesses 'remains to be settled by the future findings of neurophysiology' (p. 150).

In truth, nobody, whether scientifically informed or not, now knows or will know in the future that when speaking about his own awareness of *himself* he is describing his brain, precisely because he is *not* aware of his brain, but of himself. To identify and to substitute the absolutely certain immediate self-awareness of *se nosse* by empirical (future!) knowledge of the brain based on trust in the testimony of scientists (cf. note 160), is the grave philosophical (methodological) fallacy underlying the mind-brain identity theory.

164 *De Trin.* X, X, 16.

165 *De Trin.* XII, I, 1. See *De Trin.* I, I, 1 and II, VIII, 14.

166 Körner, *Deus in homine videt*, p. 188: 'Augustine for the first time has identified this consciousness of the "I" with the consciousness of the substance of the mind-soul: *Ego animus!*'

167 This conclusion obviously does not deny the result gained in the preceding chapter, that the mind is not only incorporeal but possesses rational abilities. On the contrary, both discussions complement each other, positively characterizing the incorporeal mind as a spiritual, that is, self-conscious and rational, being.

168 *De Trin.* X, V, 7: 'Ita cum aliud sit non se nosse, aliud non se cogitare (neque enim multarum doctrinarum peritum ignorare grammaticam dicimus cum eam non cogitat quia de medicinae arte tunc cogitat).'

169 *De Trin.* XIV, VII, 9: 'fierique posse ut noverit homo aliquid quod non cogitat quando aliunde, non inde cogitat.'

170 *De Immort. An.* IV, 6.

171 *De Trin.* XV, XXI, 40.

172 *De Trin.* XIV, VI, 9: 'notitia vero cuiusque rei quae inest menti etiam quando non de ipsa cogitatur ad solam dicatur memoriam pertinere.'

173 *De Trin.* XIV, VI, 8.

174 *Ibid.*

175 *De Trin.* XIV, XI, 14.

176 *De Trin.* XIV, X, 13: '. . . numquam sui meminisse, numquam se

intellegere, numquam se amare destiterit.' *De Trin.* X, VIII, 11: 'numquam se non amaverit, numquam nescierit'; *De Trin.* X, XII, 19: 'quoniam semper *se nosse*.'

177 *De Trin.* XIV, XIV, 18 and XV, III, 5.

178 *De Trin.* XIV, VII, 10: 'Nam si nos referamus ad interiorem mentis memoriam qua sui meminit et interiorem intellegentiam qua se intellegit et interiorem voluntatem qua se diligit, ubi haec tria simul sunt et simul semper fuerunt ex quo esse coeperunt sive cogitarentur sive non cogitarentur, videbitur quidem imago illius trinitatis et ad solam memoriam pertinere.'

179 *De Trin.* XV, XV, 25: 'Sempiternum est enim animo vivere, sempiternum est scire quod vivit, nec tamen sempiternum est cogitare vitam suam vel cogitare scientiam vitae suae quoniam cum aliud atque aliud coeperit, hoc desinet cogitare quamvis non desinat scire.'

180 Augustine argues for the immortality of the mind in *De Trin.* XIII, VII–IX.

181 See notes 168 and 169.

182 See Schmaus, p. 326: 'In all spiritual activities the consciousness of I that exists in the *memoria* resounds.'

183 See again note 176.

184 Schmaus, p. 269. See also Berlinger, pp. 178–80, where he interprets Augustine's *memoria sui* as '*Grundgedächtnis*,' which is 'a "secret" ontic knowledge of oneself' (p. 180).

185 Cf. Gilson, p. 299, note 10: 'The only modern psychological terms equivalent to Augustinian *memoria* are "unconscious" or "subconscious." '

186 Grabmann, *Grundgedanken*, p. 25: 'in the teaching on memory as it is presented in *De Trinitate*, memory is considered an unconscious knowledge that is concealed in the mind. In this way the notion of the unconscious is introduced into psychology.' See the similar judgment of Körner, *Deus in homine videt*, pp. 193–6.

In this context, it is impossible to enter into a general discussion of the nature and the various kinds of 'unconscious' and 'subconscious' states of the mind; nor is it possible to deal with the problem of how these states affect and shape actual consciousness. For this reason, the terms 'unconscious' or 'sub-conscious' used in the text are to be understood exclusively in the light of what Augustine points out in this respect, and not in the light of other (Freudian, Jungian, etc.) conceptions.

Again, a critical evaluation of Karl Delahaye's comparison of Augustine's *memoria* to Kant's transcendental apperception, and particularly of the author's interpretation of Kant, would certainly go far beyond the scope of our work. See Karl Delahaye, *Die 'memoria interior' – Lehre des heiligen Augustinus und der Begriff der 'transzendentalen Apperzeption' Kants* (Würzburg: Becker, 1936).

187   *De Trin.* XIV, VII, 9.

CHAPTER 4   *The mind as a spiritual substance*

1   *De Trin.* XII, I, 1. *De Trin.* II, VIII, 14: 'anima quippe cum sit substantia spiritalis.'

2   Cf. *De Trin.* I, I, 1, where Augustine rejects any attempt at transferring the ideas of corporeal things to incorporeal and spiritual things (substances) (*ad res incorporeas et spiritales*).

3   *De Trin.* II, IX, 16: 'animae substantiam invisibilem.' *Tract. in Ioh.* VIII, 2: 'Haec tamen anima, ut dixi, admirabilis naturae atque substantiae, invisibilis res est et intelligibilis.'

4   *De Trin.* IX, XI, 16: 'in substantia vitali sicuti est animus.'

5   *De Trin.* XII, III, 3: 'ex illa rationali nostrae mentis substantia.' *De Trin.* XV, VII, 11: 'Homo est substantia rationalis constans ex anima et corpore.'

   Already in his early work *De Quantitate Animae*, Augustine speaks of the soul as of a certain substance participating in reason adapted to the ruling of the body (substantia quaedam rationis particeps, regendo corpori accommodata) (XIII, 22).

6   See pp. 175 f.

7   *De Trin.* X, X, 15.

8   As far as I can see, there are merely two places where Augustine vaguely refers to our body as to a substance: in *De Immort. An.* II, 2: 'corpus nostrum nonnulla substantia est,' and in *De Trin.* I, X, 20: 'caro animae meae alia substantia est ad animam meam.'

9   See *De Trin.* X, VII, 9 and our discussion on pp. 11 f.

10   *Conf.* IV, 16.

11   See *Conf.* IV, 16 and *De Trin.* V, VII, 8, where the 10 Aristotelian categories are explained. Cf. Aristotle, *Categories* 5–9, and *Metaphysics*, V, 8 and VII, 3. See also Schneider, pp. 26–34 on the similarities of Augustine's and Aristotle's teaching on being and substance.

12   *De Trin.* VII, IV, 7.

13   *De Mor. Eccl. Cath.* II, II, 2: 'ita veteres qui haec nomina non habebant, pro essentia et substantia naturam vocabant.'

14   *De Lib. Arb.* III, XIII, 36: 'naturam voco quae et substantia dici solet.'

15   *De Trin.* VII, VI, 7; VII, VI, 11; V, IX, 10. However, at other places Augustine translates the Greek ὑπόστασις also by the Latin *substantia*, so that the latter can, with reference to God, mean both His one

nature and His three persons. See note 21. The *theological* consequences which have resulted from this ambiguity cannot be shown
here.

16 *De Trin.* V, II, 3. Cf. *De Mor. Eccl. Cath.* II, II, 3, and *De Civ. Dei*
XII, 2.

17 In this sense, *essentia* is equivalent to the Greek οὐσία which to render
it was coined for (*De Civ. Dei* XII, 2). Cf. Vernon J. Bourke, *Augustine's
View of Reality* (Villanova, Pa.: Villanova Press, 1964), p. 15: 'It (i.e.
essentia) seems to mean *to-be-ness*, which we express as being, in
English.'

18 *De Immort. An.* XII, 19: 'Omnis enim essentia non ob aliud essentia
est, nisi quia est.' *De Vera Rel.* XI, 22: 'quoniam summa essentia esse
facit omne quod est, unde et essentia dicitur.'

19 In his book *St Augustine and Being* (The Hague: M. Nijhoff, 1965),
James F. Anderson rightly points out that 'Augustine's "essence"
(*essentia*) has the same source as Aquinas' "being" (*ens*) considered
as subject of the act of existing (*esse*)' (p. 66).

20 *En. in Ps.* LXVIII, 5: 'Nam quod nulla substantia est, nihil omnino
est. Substantia ergo aliquid esse est.' Certainly, *esse* is employed here
in its widest meaning as that which is opposed to nothing. In this
sense, even qualities, relations, forms etc. are substances, since they
have some kind of being (*esse*).

21 See *De Trin.* VII, VI, 11 and VIII *prooem.*, where Augustine treats
substance and person as interchangeable (*substantia sive persona*, or
tres personas vel tres substantias) in discussing the Divine Persons.

22 *De Trin.* XV, VII, 11: 'Et una persona, id est singulus quisque homo.'
Sermo CL, IV, 5: 'substantia ista, res ista, persona ista quae homo
dicitur.'

See also Paul Henry, *Saint Augustine on Personality* (New York: The
Macmillan Company, 1960), p. 1: 'In the history of thought and
civilization, Saint Augustine appears to me to be the first thinker who
brought into prominence and undertook an analysis of the philosophical and psychological concepts of person and personality.'

23 *De Trin.* VI, IX, 10: 'Si enim mentem recte dicimus principale
hominis, id est tamquam caput humanae substantiae, cum ipse homo
cum mente sit homo.' *Tract. in Ioh.* XXVI, VI, 13: 'Spiritum dico
quae anima vocatur, qua constat quod homo est.' The question of
how the substantiality of the mind relates to the substantiality of *man*
who consists of mind *and* body will be treated in Chapter 5.

24 *De Trin.* X, X, 15 and VII, IV, 9: 'Sicut enim ab eo quod est esse
appelatur essentia, ita ab eo quod est subsistere substantiam dicimus.'
That there is a distinction between these two characteristics of

substance, that is, of being really real and of being a subsisting bearer, is pointed out by Augustine with reference to God. For God is improperly (*abusive*) called a substance if this is to mean that He is the subsisting bearer of His own goodness and other qualities. But He is properly (*proprie*) called essence, or substance, in the sense of being the most real being (*De Trin.* VII, V, 10 and V, XVI, 17.)

25   *De Trin.* VII, VI, 11: 'substantiae vel personae nomine non speciem significari sed aliquid singulare atque individuum.'

26   See notes 16–22 and note 24. Grabmann points out basically the same three marks of the mind's substantiality according to Augustine (*Grundgedanken*, pp. 36–40): (1) its *reality* (which Grabmann, however, tries to demonstrate in a little developed and not fully convincing manner); (2) the standing in itself and the difference (*Selbständigkeit und Verschiedenheit*) of the I (mind) from its acts that inhere in it as in their substance; (3) the endurance of the one same I throughout the changes of becoming and perishing, which accounts for the personal identity. (We will discuss this last feature as one aspect of the mind's individuality.) See also O'Connor, pp. 40–2.

27   Though Aristotle mentions still further marks of substance, such as being capable of taking on opposites without itself having a contradictory opposite, those pointed out in the text are the most fundamental and classic ones, both in Aristotle's and Augustine's view. See note 11. See also Seifert, *Leib-Seele-Problem*, pp. 72–9, where he outlines the classic notion of substance against the background of a number of grave common misunderstandings.

28   These arguments are not explicitly worked out by Augustine, but virtually contained in him. Especially the arguments for the higher substantiality of the mind over the body, though following from Augustine's premises, are not as such developed by Augustine. It was particularly the merit of J. Seifert to have employed these Aristotelian-Augustinian-Thomistic premises for an argumentation of the spiritual substantiality of the soul that, to his mind, is the most convincing of all arguments (*Leib-Seele-Problem*, pp. 99–110 and *Leib und Seele*, pp. 61–6).

29   *De Trin.* VII, V, 10: 'De his enim rebus recte intellegitur in quibus subiectis sunt ea quae in aliquo subiecto esse dicuntur sicut color aut forma in corpore. Corpus enim subsistit et ideo substantia est.'

30   *De Trin.* VII, V, 10. See *De Trin.* VII, I, 2: 'nec omnino ad se dicitur color sed semper alicuius colorati est.'

31   *De Trin.* VII, V, 10. The fact that a substance is in its being independent of its accidents is certainly not to imply that it exists without any qualitative (accidental) determinations. Augustine's point here is not

to deny that there can be, and are, essential features that must necessarily be grounded in a substance, such as color, form, extension, perceptibility, in the case of corporeal substances (cf. *De Trin.* VI, VI, 8; *De Immort. An.* X, 17). His idea is rather that, unlike these features themselves, the underlying body has a kind of being that stands in itself independent of having this or that specific accident. Thus, substantiality here means the metaphysical status of being subsistent, rather than the complete lack of any accidental qualification.

32 *De Trin.* VII, IV, 9: 'ab eo quod est subsistere substantiam dicimus.' For this reason, a substance cannot itself be grounded in some other substance. Itself standing on its own, it cannot be predicated *of* another being, which is a feature proper to accidents alone.

33 *De Trin.* X, X, 15.

34 See Grabmann, *Grundgedanken*, p. 39: 'The psychic phenomena reveal the characteristic of inherence, that is, they inhere in the "I," which is an independent reality, as accidents in a subject.'

35 *De Trin.* XV, XXII, 42: 'Tria ista, memoria, intellectus et amor mea sunt, non sua; nec sibi sed mihi agunt quod agunt, immo ego per illa. Ego enim memini per memoriam, intellego per intellegentiam, amo per amorem.' See *ibid.*: 'Ego per omnia illa tria memini, ego intellego, ego diligo, qui nec memoria sum nec intellegentia nec dilectio, sed haec habeo.'

36 *De Trin.* XV, XVII, 28: 'sicut in nobis aliud est memoria, aliud intellegentia, aliud dilectio sive caritas.'

37 *De Trin.* XV, VII, 11: 'Sed haec tria (i.e. sapientia et notitia sui et dilectio sui) ita sunt in homine ut non ipsa sint homo. . . . Illa ergo excellunt in homine, non ipsa sunt homo. Et una persona, id est singulus quisque homo, habet illa tria in mente vel mentem.'

38 *De Trin.* IX, IV, 5: 'Simul etiam admonemur si utcumque videre possumus haec in anima exsistere et tamquam involuta evolui ut sentiantur et dinumerentur substantialiter vel, ut ita dicam, essential- iter, non tamquam [notitia et amor] in subiecto ut color aut figura in corpore aut ulla alia qualitas aut quantitas. Quidquid enim tale est non excedit subiectum in quo est. Non enim color iste aut figura huius corporis potest esse et alterius corporis. Mens autem amore quo se amat potest amare et aliud praeter se. Item non se solam cognoscit mens sed et alia multa.'

39 *Ibid.* The term *exsistere* may also be used here by Augustine in the sense of coming to the fore, of emerging from something. This meaning, applied to acts of the soul, would add to the mere fact of their existing in the soul the aspect of 'coming out' of the soul, of being able to get into real relation also with outside reality.

40 This unity of the mind with its acts can, however, be realized in various degrees of awareness and intensity. An act of freely making an important decision, for instance, is a much greater manifestation of the performing subject than an act performed merely by habit. See note 46. Nevertheless, the mind-act relation is *as such* structurally different from a body's relation to its accidents, in that only the former is a *conscious actualization* of the subject *in* its acts (to various degrees of perfection), as we will see shortly.

41 *De Trin.* IX, IV, 5: 'Quamobrem non amor et cognitio tamquam in subiecto insunt menti, sed substantialiter etiam ista sunt sicut ipsa mens.' See *ibid.*: 'substantia sit scientia, substantia sit amor.'

42 See Schmaus, pp. 255-6: 'The three members of the trinity (i.e. *mens, notitia, amor*) are not accidents. Rather they participate in the substantial or so to speak essential character of the mind. They do not inhere in a subject as do accidents, such as color or shape, or other accidents of quality or quantity. . . , but exist substantially as the mind itself.'

At this point, a difficulty in interpreting Augustine arises. For, on the one hand, he speaks of knowledge and love as, like accidents, grounded in the mind as in their substance (see notes 35 and 37); but on the other hand, he refers to these acts themselves as substances (see note 41). How are these two statements to be reconciled?

In his interpretation of the latter statement, Schmaus mentions the same difficulty. For him it is both a terminological problem resulting from Augustine's failure clearly to define the term 'substance' (p. 256), and a consequence of his attempt to find trinities in man analogous to the Divine Trinity: *mens, notitia, amor*, being united in the one mind, are thought to correspond to the three Divine Persons (substances) being one Godhead (pp. 263-4).

In a similar way, Kaiser argues that the term *mens* in Augustine carries two meanings: (1) referring to the human person (self, I) as subsisting bearer of its faculties; (2) referring to a member of the trinity *mens-notitia-amor* which in three essences or substances is in the one person (pp. 79-80). One may consider *mens* in this second sense perhaps the person's spirituality, being, analogous to the Father, the origin of its faculties. However, as meaning a substance this sense of the term *mens*, which does seem present in Augustine, appears strongly to be introduced for the sake of establishing an analogy in man most fitting to the Trinity.

Goldbrunner's explanation that the *mens* is not the soul, but that the soul thinks through it as through a part of itself (p. 16), raises many questions that cannot be dealt with here, such as whether it is the soul or the mind which is the *one* self of man, how they are distinct from and related to each other, how those texts can be accounted for in which Augustine speaks of the *mens* as the subject of spiritual acts.

Without attempting to solve this difficulty, one could say, as pointed out in the text, that the acts of the mind (i.e. of the *mens* in the sense of the person, the I) are its 'accidents' in that they essentially presuppose the mind to be their really real subsisting subject. This seems to be also Thomas Aquinas' interpretation of the passage of *De Trin.* IX, IV, 5, when he says that the acts of self-knowledge and self-love 'substantialiter vel essentialiter sunt in anima, quia ipsa substantia vel essentia animae cognoscitur et amatur' (*Summa Theologiae*, Q. 77, A. 1 ad 1). However, insofar as the mind lives and acts through them, they share in its substantiality; they become the 'actualization' of the subsisting mind. In this sense, one could refer to them as substances, or more precisely, as 'substances by participation.'

43 This certainly does not imply the denial of elements of gift or 'grace' received 'from the outside' in acts of love and knowledge. On the contrary, the reception of such gifts precisely proves the point to be made. For obviously, to receive something in love cannot be seen as an accidental attachment to 'myself,' just as a body receives another color; rather, it is of a completely different, conscious and personal, nature, due to the fact that I live and actualize myself in this act.

44 Cf. Wojtyla, *Acting Person*, p. 46: 'This being, which in its ontic structure is basically a real individual object, would never without consciousness constitute itself as the ego. . . . Consciousness in intimate union with the ontologically founded being and acting of the concrete man-person does not absorb in itself or overshadow this being, its dynamic reality, but, on the contrary, discloses it "inwardly" and thereby reveals it in its specific distinctness and unique concreteness.'

See also Seifert's explanation of Wojtyla's notion of constitution in his article mentioned above, pp. 155–7.

45 This is brought out by Seifert in his *Leib-Seele-Problem*. After having pointed out that consciousness is more separable from the person than, for instance, extension from a corporeal entity, he refers to the deep ordination of the person to his actually conscious state of being: 'Rather, psychic being is metaphysically so deeply ordained to consciousness that to separate it absolutely and eternally from consciousness would take from it a feature that is more deeply essential to (though less separable from) it than extension to matter. Only in consciousness does the personal psyche reach its full actuality. The

state of a person who, though objectively existing (like a table), is without consciousness or the possibility of ever becoming conscious again, would be almost tantamount to the annihilation of this person. An eternal sleep of death would not be different in any decisive sense from the destruction of a person. Thus, it is in consciousness that there is the most proper life, the deepest meaning, the fullest being and the destination of the person' (pp. 50–1).

46 See also Ingarden, *Gefahr*, p. 561: 'Experience allows for various degrees of consciousness. These proceed from an experience that is almost "unconscious," that is dark and confused, to kinds of experience that are ever more "conscious," ever brighter and clearer, culminating in an experience that reveals the highest degree of consciousness.'

47 *Conf.* X, 30: 'numquid tunc ego non sum, domine deus meus? Et tamen tantum interest inter me ipsum et me ipsum intra momentum, quo hinc ad soporem transeo vel huc inde transeo.'

48 There are, however, kinds of corporeal 'accidents,' such as a body's 'extensivity' and 'corporeality' themselves, that seem to inhere in their subsisting bearer to a similar degree of unity as acts inhere in the mind. And yet, even though it would go too far in this context to enter into the difficult metaphysical question of how such accidents are distinct, for instance, from color or form regarding the manner of relating to their subsisting body, it appears manifest that even this relation of inherence cannot be compared to the mind-act relation. For the mind *consciously actualizes itself in* its acts in a manner compared to which a body 'expresses' itself, or an aspect of it, much more 'passively' in these accidents. In a similar way, the mind's relation to its acts is also different from its relation to properties such as its 'incorporeality' and 'spirituality' themselves. The peculiar relation of both identity and distinctness which, as we discussed, obtains between the mind and its conscious state of being, and the various forms of 'switching' from sleep to awakeness, are not found in its relation to such 'accidental' determinations of its nature. Thus, without going into further detail, it seems obvious that the *kind* of unity that the mind realizes with and in its acts is completely different from any substance-accident relation occuring in the realm of bodies, and even in the realm of certain dimensions of the mind.

49 The problem of changing states of consciousness is quite different from the question of whether a body can ascend to consciousness, as is maintained by certain theories of evolution. For while the former presupposes the ontological givenness of the 'attribute' of consciousness, since unawakened states also are states of *consciousness*, the latter

concerns the more fundamental problem of whether a body can receive this 'attribute' at all. To enter into such a discussion certainly lies beyond the scope of our work.

50 *Sermo CCXLVII*, 2; *Ep. CXXXVII*, 10; *Tract. in Ioh.* VIII, 1.

51 *De Gen. ad Litt.* VI, XVI, 27: 'et utique ratio est senectutis in corpore iuvenali vel iuventutis in corpore puerili.' *De Civ. Dei* XXII, 24: 'illam vim mirabilem seminum, immo etiam mirabiliorem qua efficiuntur et semina, inditam corporibus humanis.'

52 *De Trin.* XIV, IV, 6: 'ita quamvis ratio vel intellectus nunc in ea sit sopitus, nunc parvus, nunc magnus appareat, numquam nisi rationalis et intellectualis est anima humana.'

53 *De Lib. Arb.* XXII, XXIV, 3: 'Ipse itaque animae humanae mentem dedit, ubi ratio et intelligentia in infante sopita est quodammodo, quasi nulla sit, excitanda scilicet atque exserenda aetatis accessu, qua sit scientiae capax atque doctrinae, et habilis perceptioni veritatis et amoris boni.'

54 This does not exclude a man's being suddenly stripped of his reason or of some particular rational power due to a destruction of specific nerves or organs that serve as its bodily condition, such as parts of the brain.

55 One could still mention a third form of mental awakening that presupposes the two more central ones referred to in the text. For the awakening to actual consciousness can also imply a becoming aware of what is sub- or unconsciously present in the person. While the former is a more 'formal' actualization, the bringing to light of forgotten, repressed, and other unconscious attitudes or feelings is an act of a more 'material' awakening. The person becomes consciously aware of a specific content that was formerly hidden from him. It is, therefore, not merely a (formal) conscious awakening, but to a certain extent it also presupposes a rational awakening, as it is a genuine act of knowledge, more precisely, of self-knowledge.

56 Cf. note 40.

57 *De Trin.* XII, IV, 4: 'Cum igitur disserimus de natura mentis humanae, de una quadam re disserimus.'

58 *De Trin.* VII, VI, 11. See Benz, p. 383: 'The noun "persona", says Augustine, does not refer to the species, but to the "*singulare*" and to the "individuum"; one does not say person as one says "man." '

59 The following various senses of 'individual oneness,' and, above all, the arguments for the higher individuality, and thus substantiality, of the mind over the body, are not explicitly elaborated by Augustine, though they can clearly be gathered and unfolded from many of his observations. Such arguments have been developed by Seifert (*Leib*

und Seele, pp. 62–3, and *Leib-Seele-Problem*, pp. 105–7) in the light of what he calls the three 'directions' of individuality as a mark of substantiality, that is, a substance's being uniquely identical and irreplaceable, its being demarcated from other beings, and its being one and simple (*Leib-Seele-Problem*, pp. 78–9).

60   *De Trin*. X, III, 6.

61   *De Trin*. X, III, 6: 'Quid ergo dicemus? An quod (mens) *ex parte* se novit, *ex parte* non novit? Sed absurdum est dicere non eam totam scire quod scit. Non dico: "Totum scit," sed: "Quod scit tota scit." Cum itaque aliquid de se scit quod nisi tota non potest, totam se scit. Scit autem se aliquid scientem, nec potest quidquam scire nisi tota. Scit se igitur totam.'

62   See notes 69–77.

63   The oneness of the 'I' is not jeopardized, but even confirmed, by cases of schizophrenic personalities. For precisely the fact that such a person experiences *himself* as having a double personality shows that it must be one and the same subject underlying his schizophrenic self-awareness. See Karl Jaspers, *Allgemeine Psychopathologie* (Berlin-Heidelberg-New York: Springer, 1973), p. 105: 'The *one I* experiences itself as *doubled* and is nevertheless *one*; it lives in both emotional states that remain separated from each other, and yet it knows *of both*.' See also the dissertation of Tony Eggel, *Traumleben und Schizophrenie* (Zürich, 1976), pp. 25 f.

64   See pp. 35 ff.

65   For a short summary of the argument see *De Gen. ad Litt*. VII, XXI, 28: 'omne quod novit tota novit: cum itaque se quaerentem novit, tota se novit, ergo et totam se novit: neque enim aliquid aliud, sed seipsam tota novit.'

66   The possible objection that there are many aspects of myself that I do not know while others are known to me, can be answered by referring to our previous discussion of the difference between explicit self-knowledge (*se cogitare*) characterized by cognitive incompleteness, and *se nosse* as the accompanying awareness of myself as subject of my acts during their performance, which alone lies at the basis of the present argument. For through the experience of *se nosse* I am aware of myself *as* being *one* (whole) subject of my acts (*tota*), independent of whether or not I grasp myself in self-knowledge. Cf. pp. 169 f.

67   *De Trin*. X, IV, 6.

68   *De Trin*. IX, IV, 7: 'Fortassis ergo mens totum est et eius quasi partes amor quo se amat et scientia qua se novit, quibus duabus partibus illud totum constat? An tres sunt aequales partes quibus totum unum completur?'

69   *De Trin*. IX, XXII, 42.

70 *Ibid.*
71 See *De Trin.* XV, XXII, 42.
72 *De Trin.* IX, IV, 7.
73 *De Trin.* IX, IV, 7: 'Sed non unius substantiae sunt aqua, vinum, et mel, quamvis ex eorum commixtione fiat una substantia potionis.'
74 *De Trin.* IX, IV, 7: '*Unius* ergo *eiusdem*que *essentiae* necesse est haec tria sint.' (sic!)
75 Cf. Wittmann, p. 171: 'In spite of the triplicity of the spiritual faculties of *memoria, intelligentia* and *dilectio*, there exists in the human mind only one single self-efficacious principle, the personal I, that acts by means of these three faculties. For this reason, one speaks of man as one single person.'
76 See *De Trin.* IX, V, 8.
77 *Liber de Videndo Deo (seu Ep. CXLVII)*, XVIII, 45.
78 *De Trin.* XII, IV, 4. See Schmaus, pp. 246–8.
79 This result is empirically supported by the brain research of the neurophysiologist Sir John C. Eccles who comes to the conclusion that 'the unity of conscious experience is provided by the self-conscious mind and not by the neural machinery of the liaison areas of the cerebral hemisphere' (*The Self and its Brain*, co-author Karl R. Popper [Springer International, 1977], p. 362). See also de Vries, pp. 86–94.
80 It might seem that the ultimate particles of matter are as perfect substances as is the mind, since they too can no longer be divided. However, as we tried to show in Chapter 1, these particles, unlike the mind, are still mathematically or potentially divisible, and they completely lack those kinds of positive simplicity that are found exclusively in the mind and that together account for the latter's superior substantiality, as we will see shortly.
81 For instance, in the *Phaedo* (79a–b) Plato comes close to ascribing immutability to the soul; or in the *Phaedrus* (245c f.) in his argument for the immortality of the soul, he speaks of the soul as of an uncreated, eternal, absolute being.
82 *Tract. in Ioh.* XCIX, 4.
83 *De Trin.* VI, VI, 8.
84 *Ibid.*
85 *De Trin.* XV, VII, 11.
86 Due to Augustine's lack of a specific technical terminology, the terms 'person,' 'individual,' 'man,' 'mind,' 'soul,' are, despite their differences, used in the following as basically interchangeable, referring to the same reality 'in' man. For, as Augustine puts it, as Abraham, Isaac, and Jacob are called three individuals (*individua*), so they are

also called three men (*homines*) and three souls (*animae*) (*De Trin.* VII, VI, 11). Cf. *Conf.* XIII, 11: 'et una vita et una mens et una essentia.'

87   Concerning the question of whether Augustine held a dualistic or a trialistic conception of man, see Chapter 5 note 7. There we point out that, if there is a difference between soul and mind (spirit) in man according to Augustine, this is not a substantial one. He clearly acknowledged the numerical oneness of the self ('I').

Again, this kind of oneness is not jeopardized, even if Seifert is right in his argument (against Thomas Aquinas) that man's biological 'life-principle' is not strictly identical with, though it is deeply 'united' to, his conscious, rational soul (*Leib und Seele*, pp. 328–36). On the problem of multiple personalities see note 63.

88   *De Vera Rel.* XXXIV, 64.

89   *De Trin.* XV, XXII, 42: 'Ista ergo dici possunt ab una persona quae habet tria, non ipsa est haec tria.'

90   *De Lib. Arb.* II, IX, 27: 'tot sunt mentes hominum quot homines sunt.'

91   See p. 20.

92   As we tried to show in our section on recollection, this act of going back into our past can only be an act of the incorporeal mind entering into *its* past. Though the body, particularly the brain, is an indispensable bodily *condition* for the possibility of memory, it itself is not the subject whose acts are re-experienced in recollection. Therefore, it must be the mind, and not the brain, that is the 'locus' of man's temporal endurance as given through recollection.

93   See our discussion on p. 179.

94   *De Trin.* XIV, X, 13: 'Cognitione vero facta cum ea quae cognovimus posita in memoria recordatione revisuntur, quis non videat priorem esse tempore in memoria retentionem quam in recordatione visionem et huius utriusque tertia voluntate iunctionem? Porro autem in mente non sic est; neque enim adventicia sibi ipsa est quasi ad se ipsam quae iam erat venerit aliunde eadem ipsa quae non erat, aut non aliunde venerit sed in se ipsa quae iam erat nata sit ea ipsa quae non erat sicut in mente quae iam erat oritur fides quae non erat, aut post cognitionem sui recordando se ipsam velut in memoria sua constitutam videt quasi non ibi fuerit antequam se ipsam cognosceret, cum profecto ex quo esse coepit, numquam sui meminisse, numquam se intellegere, numquam se amare destiterit sicut iam ostendimus.'

95   In a sense, however, the ultimate particles of matter share in this 'enduring oneness,' since as actually indivisible entities they also remain the same throughout time, being unable to exchange constitutive elements. Yet, even compared to them the mind's 'temporal oneness' can be shown to be more perfect, however only on the basis

of convincing arguments for its immortality. For if the mind can be shown to be immortal, it will endure as this same subject 'eternally,' while an essentially contingent material particle will once have to be annihilated completely.

96 *De Trin.* VII, VI, 11.

97 See also the inspiring *Sermon VI* 'The Individuality of the Soul' by John Henry Newman (in *Parochial and Plain Sermons*, Vol. IV [Westminster, Md.: Christian Classics Inc., 1967] pp. 80–93).

98 The uniqueness of the body as *Leib* becomes especially manifest in spousal love. See, for instance, Dietrich von Hildebrand, *Man and Woman* (Chicago, Ill.: Franciscan Herald Press, 1966), p. 18: 'In spousal love, the body of the beloved assumes a unique charm as the vessel of this person's soul.'

99 In *De Civ. Dei* XXI, 8, Augustine makes a very interesting observation with respect to the unique individuality of each man in relation to the general similarity of all men. On the one hand, he points out, all men are like one another; otherwise, they could not be distinguished from other living beings. On the other hand, they are unlike each other, since each man, as an individual, can be distinguished from another man. Men are thus both alike and unlike each other. Of these features, Augustine continues, the unlikeness is more marvellous, since the common nature of being human seems rather to require similarity. And yet, we are more amazed when we see two men so alike that we can hardly distinguish between them, a fact which Augustine attributes to man's greater amazement at what is rare and uncommon than at what is as such mysterious and wonderful. See also Chapter 5 note 25.

100 *De Lib. Arb.* II, X, 28. See the whole context in which Augustine discusses the peculiar fact that, though everyone has his own intellect and soul through which he understands wisdom, this wisdom itself is one and the same common to all.

101 Cf. *Tract. in Ioh.* XXXII, 5: 'Nam unusquisque homo habet in se proprium spiritum.'

102 Aristotle, *De Anima*, trans. J. A. Smith, in *The Basic Works of Aristotle*, ed. Richard McKeon (New York: Random House, 1941), I, 408 b.

103 See Copleston, *A History of Philosophy*, Vol. II, 1, p. 223.

104 Augustine did, however, know of the similar view of Varro that God is the soul of the world which in its parts has many souls whose nature is divine; cf. *De Civ. Dei* VII, 6. And he was probably aware of Plotinus' theory of the one common soul from which all individual souls stem (*Enn.* IV, 9).

105 *De Trin.* XII, III, 3: 'intellectum nostrum et actionem, vel consilium

et exsecutionem, vel rationem et appetitum rationalem, vel si quo alio modo significatius dici possunt, una mentis natura complectitur.'

106 The problem of how man can see and judge things in the light of and 'with the eyes' of God, the *divine* spirit (cf. *Conf.* XIII, 31), is a completely different one and forms part of the general problem of the relation between nature and grace, into which we can obviously not enter here. Concerning the question of a world-soul in Augustine see Chapter 2 note 198.

107 *De Gen. ad Litt.* X, IV, 7.

108 *De Trin.* I–VII.

109 See the very rich and illuminating study of the nature and the various kinds of community in Dietrich von Hildebrand, *Metaphysik der Gemeinschaft* (Regensburg: Habbel, 1975).

110 Cf. von Hildebrand, pp. 17–105, where he shows that relations of love and communities essentially pre-suppose the individual substantiality of each member: 'In the gazing at each other in love (*Ineinanderblick der Liebe*) both persons remain individual substances in the fullest sense. . . ; and yet, in this gazing at each other . . . there occurs a participation in the other being that is incomparably deeper than anything possible in the material world' (p. 39).

111 See Chapter 5 notes 1–3.

112 See notes 57, 58 and 85.

113 *De Civ. Dei* XII, 2: 'et aliis (Deus) dedit esse amplius, aliis minus; atque ita naturas essentiarum gradibus ordinavit.' *De Lib. Arb.* III, V, 16: 'Omnia enim in ordine suo creata sunt.'

114 See Chapter 1 note 5.

115 *Conf.* III, 6.

116 *Conf.* III, 6. To render the term *certus* by the English term 'real' is, it seems to me, not against Augustine's intended meaning. Also W. Thimme translates it by the equivalent German '*wirklich*' (see *Bekenntnisse* [Stuttgart: Reclam, 1967] pp. 78–9). For, as the context shows, Augustine uses this term with reference to the fact that a being is more certainly, more definitely, grounded in reality.

117 See Joseph Mausbach, 'Wesen und Stufung des Lebens nach dem heiligen Augustinus,' in *Aurelius Augustinus*, pp. 170–80.

118 *De Civ. Dei* XI, 16. To the last point see also *De Vera Rel.* XI, 22: 'sed tantum moriuntur, quantum minus essentiae participant.' Without going into any detail, it is clear that the mortality of *man*, consisting of body and soul, is not opposed to the conviction of the immortality of his soul, as we quoted Augustine's view in note 180 of Chapter 3.

119 *De Civ. Dei* XI, 16. Cf. Karla Mertens, *Das Verhältnis des Schönen*

zum Guten in den Augustinischen Frühschriften (Speyer: Pilger, 1940), pp. 28–30 on the *ordo* in the creation.

120 *De Civ. Dei* XI, 16.

121 *Ibid*. This distinction between 'intrinsic value' and 'relational value' has been strongly developed and elaborated on in modern value-philosophy. Though Max Scheler can be considered its founder, he does not yet draw a clear line between these two very different kinds of value, speaking rather of 'higher' and 'lower' values that motivate us to various degrees. (See his *Der Formalismus in der Ethik und die materiale Wertethik* [Bern: Francke, 1966], pp. 104–17.) It was Dietrich von Hildebrand who introduced the original distinction between three *kinds* of 'importance,' that is, between what gives a being an axiological dimension: the subjectively dis/satisfying, the objective good/evil for the person both of which are constituted by a relation to something outside of themselves, and the value/disvalue in the strict sense which is the preciousness/ugliness that a being possesses in and of itself. (See his *Christian Ethics*, Chs. 1–3 and 7–8).

Recently, John F. Crosby has developed this line of thought against the background of the Thomistic idea of *bonum*, particularly by elaborating on the notion of importance and by showing how a value is grounded in a concrete being realizing a peculiar kind of unity with it. 'The Idea of Value and the Reform of the Traditional Metaphysics of *Bonum*,' *Aletheia* I, 2 (1977), 231–336.

122 In order to prevent misunderstandings it should be pointed out that reality (*esse*) and value are, as such, two distinct, though closely related, 'dimensions of being.' (See the analysis of Crosby, pp. 296–304, built on a distinction by J. Seifert.) Consequently, there are two 'hierarchies of being' that need not coincide. For instance, a painting may have a higher (esthetic) value than a crocodile, but as a living, sentient being the latter is more *real* a part of the world. These two 'hierarchies' can be further differentiated by distinguishing between 'ontological' and 'qualitative' values (a distinction made and elaborated on by D. von Hildebrand in his *Christian Ethics*, Ch. 10), that is, by distinguishing between the value a being has because of *what* it is (τὶ εἶναι – its nature) and the value it has because of *how* it is (ποιὸν εἶναι). The former remains with a being as long as it is, the latter may constantly alter and may even turn into its opposite (disvalue). Developing this distinction one finds that it is only the hierarchy of 'qualitative' values that is independent of that of reality (*esse*); for the 'ontological' value of a being is determined by the same 'whatness' (nature) of the being on which its degree of reality depends. Because man, for instance, is of this particular nature *qua* man, his rank in the hierarchy of both

'ontological' value and reality coincides. In this respect, one may with Augustine speak of the hierarchical structure of God's creation without explicitly distinguishing between reality and value. However, as a general topic these two 'dimensions of being' need to be analyzed much more in their distinctness, and their interrelation; we could only offer an outline here.

123 *De Civ. Dei* XII, 23: 'Talem quippe illi animam creavit, qua per rationem atque intelligentiam omnibus esset praestantior animalibus terrestribus et natalitibus et volatilibus, quae mentem huiusmodi non haberent.'

124 *De Lib. Arb.* I, VIII, 18.

125 *De Lib. Arb.* I, VII, 16. Cf. *De Div. Quaest. LXXXIII*, Qu. XIII.

126 *De Lib. Arb.* I, VIII, 18.

127 *De Civ. Dei* XIV, 4: 'homo ... quod est animal rationale et ex hoc cunctis terrenis animantibus excellentius atque praestantius.'

128 See again notes 123 and 127.

129 *De Lib. Arb.* I, X, 20: 'Iam corpore omni qualemlibet animum meliorem potentioremque esse.' *De Lib. Arb.* IX, IV, 4: 'plus sit ipsa (mens hominis) quam corpus.'

130 *De Gen. ad Litt.* VII, XIX, 25: 'Sicut enim Deus omnem creaturam, sic anima omnem corpoream creaturam naturae dignitate praecellit.'

131 *De Lib. Arb.* II, XVII, 46: 'Quid enim maius in creaturis quam vita intellegens aut quid minus potest esse quam corpus?'

Certainly, this statement is not to imply a negative, rejecting attitude toward the body, which, as created by God, is essentially good (cf. Chapter 1, note 140); but it simply expresses Augustine's amazement at the mind's rank in the hierarchy of being.

132 *De Lib. Arb.* III, V, 16.

133 *De Lib. Arb.* III, V, 16: 'anima ... ad quantamlibet sui decoris deminutionem defectumque pervenerit, omnium corporum dignitatem sine ulla dubitatione superabit!'

134 *De Quant. An.* XXXIII, 73: 'Hinc enim anima se non solum suo, si quam universi partem agit, sed ipsi etiam universo corpori audet praeponere.'

In *De Vera Rel.* XI, 22, Augustine argues for the 'ontological' superiority of the soul over the body on the basis of its immortality. According to the principle that a being possesses less *essentia* the more it tends toward death (see note 118), Augustine tries to show that man's body, in being subject to death, is in its nature closer to nothingness than his soul (corpus ergo magis subiacet morti, et ideo vicinius est nihilo).

135 *De Civ. Dei* XI, 16: 'hominum ... certe natura tantae est dignitatis.'

Augustine's anthropology is ultimately a metaphysics of the person considered as image of the Divine Trinity. Only against this background can the being and dignity of man, whose mind is an *imago Dei*, be fully and properly understood at all. (*De Trin.* XV, VII, 11: 'Et imago est Trinitatis in mente.') Cf. Kaiser, p. 79: 'Man whose most interior being is constituted by his spirituality, is understood as a person precisely on the basis of this background of spirituality which in itself is an image of the Trinity. To be a person, therefore, can only be understood when man is interpreted as "*imago Dei*" in the "*analogia trinitatis.*" '

136 *De Immort. An.* X, 17; *De Trin.* X, VII, 9; *De Civ. Dei* VIII, 5.

137 As far as I can see, there is merely the discussion of *De Immort. An.* X, 17. Plotinus presents some arguments against this theory of soul as harmony of the body in *Enn.* IV, 7–8[4].

138 See, above all, Seifert, *Leib und Seele*, pp. 31–44, and his *Leib-Seele-Problem*, pp. 64–70 and 80–5.

139 See the much more detailed elaboration of this essential difference in Seifert, *Leib und Seele*, pp. 18–26.

140 Plato, *Phaedo* 94b–95a. Cf. also Aristotle, *De Anima* I, 407b 27–408a 34.

141 *De Immort. An.* X, 17.

142 In his *Leib-Seele-Problem*, Seifert defends this argument against a number of objections, which can however not be reiterated here. (See pp. 80–5.) We may only point out that it is no valid objection to say that, just as beauty as an accident of the body can have a 'higher reality' than its bearer, so the mind having a higher reality than the body could as well inhere in the latter. For the argument is not based on degrees of *value*, in which case accidents can indeed be 'higher' than their bearer, but on degrees of *reality*. (See note 122 where we distinguished these two 'dimensions of being'.) In this latter sense, an accident is always inferior to its bearer. See also Brunner's conception of person as substance, pp. 63–84.

143 Schmaus, p. 244: 'In contrast, Augustine emphasizes those aspects which reveal the substantiality of the soul: the reality of the mind as against its activities, its independence from its psychic events, its endurance as compared to the changeableness of the ongoing psychic life. He, in fact, calls the soul a substance.' See also Grabmann, *Grundgedanken*, p. 40.

CHAPTER 5   *The unity consisting of mind and body*

1   *Tract. in Ioh.* XIX, I, 15: 'Anima habens corpus non facit duas

personas, sed unum hominem.' *Ep. CXXXVII*, III, 11: 'in unitate personae anima unitur corpori, ut homo sit.' *Ep. CCXXXVIII*, II, 12: 'Et cum corpus et anima sit unus homo, quamvis corpus et anima non sint unum.' See the number of references given in Chapter 1 notes 101–117.

In his book '*Ex Platonicorum Persona.*' *Études sur les Lectures Philosophiques de Saint Augustin* (Amsterdam: Hakkert, 1977), Jean Pépin refers to Porphyry as a source of Augustine's theory of the unity of body and soul in man (pp. 213–67). In this context, however, one should also mention Porphyry's teacher Plotinus who, in *Enn*. IV, 3, 19–23, struggles very much with the question of how the soul is 'in' the body.

2   *De Trin*. XV, VII, 11: 'Homo est substantia rationalis constans ex anima et corpore.' *Sermo CL*, IV, 5: 'substantia ista, res ista, persona ista, quae homo dicitur.' *De Trin*. V, VII, 8: 'Velut cum dicimus: 'Homo est,' substantiam dicimus.'

3   *De Civ. Dei* XIV, 4: 'Et ab anima namque et a carne, quae sunt partes hominis, potest totum significari quod est homo.' It should be remembered that the terms 'soul' and 'mind' are used in the following, as throughout the course of this work, in reference to the same reality, namely the substantial subject of man's acts.

4   Thomas Aquinas, *Summa Theologiae* I, Qu. 75, introd.: 'considerandum est de homine, qui ex spirituali et corporali substantia componitur.' See also *ibid*. I, Qu. 50, introd.

5   In modern philosophy and science a strong anti-dualistic tendency seems to be prevailing. In his article 'Leib und Seele – Versuch einer systematischen Vermittlung dualistischer Theorie und menschlicher Lebenspraxis,' *ThPh*, 58 (1983), Gerd Pohlenz rightly observes that this tendency, which he traces back to Nietzsche and Feuerbach, often expresses itself in a rather global, emotional, partly polemical rejection of dualistic conceptions of man as irrational and irreconcilable with empirical science. However, he remarks, this attitude is more a 'transparent pretext' of an embarrasing ignorance regarding the body-soul problem, than a serious philosophical penetration of it (pp. 1–16, esp. 10–11).

6   This approach, having been initiated by Augustine himself through his emphasis, against Plato, on the oneness of man and the relations between body and soul, has more elaborately been developed in modern philosophy by Josef Seifert, who thereby, it seems to the author, made a central contribution to a philosophical anthropology. For with this approach he opened up a way of overcoming the opposition between a dualistic and monistic view of man: 'The deeper and

the more determinately we grasp the real difference between body and soul, the more clearly we see the amazing and marvellous "unity" of the *one man consisting of body and soul*' (emphasis his) (*Leib und Seele*, p. 346). See *ibid.* especially pp. 191–7.

Seifert also furthered a more unbiased discussion of the body-soul problem by his distinction of 8 completely different senses of the term 'dualism,' which we may briefly mention here: (1) the position which holds a vague general distinctness of psychic and corporeal realities, while bracketing the problem of their substantiality; (2) the view that acknowledges body and soul as two distinct substances constituting the one man (his own position); (3) positions, presupposing but not necessarily following from the former, that deny a union of the two substances of body and soul or that propose certain questionable theories of their relation; (4) the assumption that the union of body and soul is categorically excluded; (5) the axiological dualism which sees the body to be intrinsically evil and the soul to be good; (6) a dualism that holds the union of body and soul in their distinctness and acknowledges the *possibility* of their being separated in death; (7) the position that there are only two substances in the world at all; (8) a dualism that, opposed to a trialism, holds only the soul and the body to be the substantial 'parts' of man. (See *Leib-Seele-Problem*, pp. 126–30, and *Leib und Seele*, pp. 170–80.)

7   Among Augustinian scholars it is a disputed question as to whether Augustine held a dualistic or a trialistic conception of man. There are passages in favor of each of both interpretations. For instance, in *De Nat. et Orig. An.* IV, II, 3, Augustine says: 'natura certe tota hominis est spiritus, anima et corpus,' and in *De Civ. Dei* V, 11 he speaks of God 'qui fecit hominem rationale animal ex anima et corpore.' (See also notes 1–3.) However, it seems clear to the author that Augustine does not consider the distinction between spirit (*spiritus*) and soul (*anima*) to be as substantial as that between soul and body. In this (substantial) sense he clearly holds a dualistic view of man, yet acknowledging within the soul various 'levels' of 'spirituality' and 'animality.' In this interpretation the author agrees with Dinkler, pp. 255–66; Kaiser, p. 78, note 104; Storz, pp. 119–29. For another interpretation see Delahaye, pp. 132–5.

8   See Goldbrunner, p. 33: 'The body is what it is only through the soul; it subsists through it. The soul as it were takes up matter, descends upon it and from it creates fashions, forms and shapes the human body.'

9   See also Maxsein, pp. 194–203. The author strongly emphasizes the 'holistic' (*ganzheitlich*) conception of man in Augustine.

10   Cf. Maxsein, pp. 114–17.

11   A very original and elaborate presentation of various kinds of psycho-
     physical relations in man 'running' both from the soul to the body,
     from the body to the soul, and obtaining between the two without
     a specific 'direction,' has been given by Seifert in *Leib und Seele*,
     pp. 199–323.

12   In his article 'Augustine and the Life of Man's Body in the Early
     Dialogues,' quoted above, Buckemeyer, after having cited various texts
     of Augustine's, comes to the conclusion that 'Augustine's definition of
     man as a "composite of soul and body" comes as no surprise' (p. 201).
     And Morgan rightly contends that 'it is this union that distinguishes
     Augustine's doctrine from the exaggerated dualism of Plato' (p. 115).

13   For this reason, the whole man can be signified by each of his
     constitutive parts: 'Et ab anima namque et a carne, quae sunt partes
     hominis, potest totum significari, quod est homo; atque ita non est
     aliud animalis homo, aliud carnalis, sed idem ipsum est utrumque, id
     est secundum hominem vivens homo' (*De Civ. Dei* XIV, 4).

14   *Sermo CL*, IV, 5: 'Nihil est in homine, quod ad eius substantiam
     pertineat atque naturam, praeter corpus et animam.'

15   It would go beyond the intention and scope of the present work to
     show how this ordination obtaining between body and soul was one
     main starting point for Augustine's theory of the spiritual body (*corpus
     spiritale*) with which the soul will be united after death. Since our
     body, he holds, is good in and of itself ('caro . . . in genere atque
     ordine suo bona est' – *De Civ. Dei* XIV, 5), yet since it has been
     corrupted, we do not desire to be deprived of it altogether, but,
     knowing its corruption, to be clothed with it in its incorruptible
     immortality ('et adgravamur ergo corruptibili corpore, et ipsius adgrav-
     ationis causam non naturam substantiamque corporis, sed eius corrup-
     tionem scientes nolumus corpore spoliari, sed eius immortalitate
     vestiri' – *De Civ. Dei* XIV, 3). In this, Augustine explicitly rejects
     Plato who thought that souls must necessarily be dismissed from *any*
     body after death (*De Civ. Dei* XIII, 19 and X, 30). On Augustine's
     theory of the nature of this spiritual body see also *De Civ. Dei* XXII,
     11–21.

16   *De Trin.* VI, IX, 10: 'Si enim mentem recte dicimus principale
     hominis, id est tamquam caput humanae substantiae.'

17   Cf. *Solil.* I, II, 7.

18   See Mader, p. 109: 'The unity of the person "out of" soul and body is
     one that is established in and through the performances of the mind.'

19   K. Flasch describes the same double meaning of 'person' in Augu-
     stine, without, however, explicitly mentioning their difference, when

he says on p. 360: 'Subsequently "person" could be understood as the living-correlative spiritual life which Augustine had analyzed under the name of "mind," ' and when he continues on p. 361: 'The word (i.e. person) was for him tantamount to "human substance." '

20 On Augustine's view of the unity of soul and body see also Dinkler, pp. 63–6; Goldbrunner, pp. 26–45; Portalié, pp. 147–8 (a very good brief presentation of this problem in Augustine); Schwarz, pp. 328 f.

21 The most well-known positions to be mentioned here are (a) the *psycho-physical parallelism*, which holds an exact factual correspondance of psychic and physical events without any interaction (Schelling, Schopenhauer); (b) The similar *occasionalistic* theory (Geulincx, Malebranche) according to which it is God who brings about this correspondence at each particular 'occasion'; (c) Leibniz's theory of the *pre-established harmony* which means that the relation of body and soul in man has been pre-established by God in such a way that, like two clocks, they correspond exactly to each other without interacting; (d) the *psycho-physical interactionism* (e.g. von Hartmann, W. James) that views body and soul as causally affecting each other; (e) Descartes' 'solution' of a certain gland that mediates between body and soul. Insofar as these and other theories try to give an account of the 'how' of the body-soul union, they are clearly distinct from the broader problem of the different natures of body and soul as such which all of them answer in a basically dualistic manner.

22 *De Civ. Dei* XXI, 7: 'modus, quo corporibus adhaerent spiritus et animalia fiunt, omnino mirus est nec conprehendi ab homine potest, et hoc ipse homo est.'

23 *De Quant. An.* XXXI, 64.

24 The idea of conceiving the 'how' of the body-soul union as a 'natural mystery,' originating with Augustine, has been adopted by Pascal in his marvellous *Pensée* 84 [72], and by John Henry Newman in his *Sermon XIX* 'The Mysteriousness of our Present Being' (in *Parochial and Plain Sermons*, Vol. IV, pp. 282 f.). Reading these texts, one is led to realize more fully the intricacy of the problem in question, a problem the solution of which goes beyond man's comprehension – 'la preuve de notre faiblesse' (Pascal, *ibid.*). Inspired by these thinkers, Seifert has established and elaborated on the precise *'philosophical category'* of the apory ('natural mystery'), to be applied to the body-soul union: an apory is given when the relation of two realities, which are known *by reason* (unlike supernatural mysteries), is incomprehensible *to man* (not as such, as to a being of higher intelligence), whereby the fact that there must actually be a relation is clearly understood. The exact 'how' alone is 'mysterious.' With this category Seifert tries

to overcome this kind of 'irrationalism' that underlies many body-soul 'solutions,' investigating what *can* be known and acknowledging his ignorance with respect to what goes beyond human comprehension. (See his *Leib und Seele*, pp. 201–8, esp. p. 207, and *Leib-Seele-Problem*, pp. 118–25).

25 Cf. *De Civ. Dei* XXI, 7: '(Deus) fecit mundum in caelo in terra, in aere in aquis innumerabilibus miraculis plenum, cum sit omnibus quibus plenus est procul dubio maius et excellentius etiam mundus ipse miraculum.' See also *De Civ. Dei* XXI, 4 and XXII, 8 where Augustine does nothing but enumerate natural mysteries and miracles that he had observed or had learned about from others. At another place, he laments that man generally loses his sense of amazement as soon as an event gets too common. Man is struck by the raising of a dead, but not by the creation of a new human being happening every day, which is much more mysterious and miraculous since it means the creation of *new* life and not 'merely' the reviving of him who has already been alive. Or he is astonished at the changing of water into wine without realizing that the same process occurs daily in each vine (*Tract. in Ioh.* IX, 1; see also XXIV, 1–2). What becomes common, though in itself being marvellous, is no longer considered to be amazing: 'Quarum vero rerum ante nostros oculos cotidiana documenta versantur, non genere minus mirabili, sed ipsa assiduitate vilescunt' (*De Civ. Dei* XXI, 4).

26 *De Civ. Dei* XXII, 4: 'Si enim animae tantummodo essemus, id est sine ullo corpore spiritus, et in caelo habitantes terrena animalia nesciremus nobisque futurum esse diceretur, ut terrenis corporibus animandis quodam vinculo mirabili necteremur: nonne multo fortius argumentaremur id credere recusantes et diceremus naturam non pati, ut res incorporea ligamento corporeo vinciretur? Et tamen plena est terra vegetantibus animis haec membra terrena, miro sibi modo conexa et implicita.'

This marvellous union of a corporeal with an incorporeal nature is to be admired not only in man, Augustine admonishes, but also in the smallest insects: 'Ipse (i.e. Deus) incorpoream corporeamque naturam, illam praepositam, istam subiectam, miris modis copulans et conectens animantem facit. Quod opus eius tam magnum et mirabile est, ut non solum in homine, . . . sed in qualibet minutissima muscula bene consideranti stuporem mentis ingerat laudamque pariat Creatoris' (*De Civ. Dei* XIV, 4). See W. Montgomery, 'St Augustine's Attitude to Psychic Phenomena,' *HibJ*, 25 (1926), 92–102.

27 Thomas Aquinas also speaks of the union of body and soul as a 'mirabilis rerum connexio' (*Summa Contra Gentiles*, II, 68, 1453). In

this light, it is surprising how a thinker like Gilson can neglect this 'mysteriousness,' accusing Augustine of acknowledging it. He writes on pp. 47–8: 'To justify Christian intuitions he had at his disposal only a Plotinian technique, and the result was that he bequeathed to the Middle Ages formidable problems for which none but Saint Thomas found the solution. Certainly Augustine himself did not find the solution. He felt from the beginning that the body and soul together make man, but he continued throughout his life to reason as though the soul were one substance which uses that other substance, the body. Involved as he was in such a difficulty, it is easy to understand why he found man a strangely mysterious being.' See also note 25 and M. Miles, p. 23, where she expresses her disagreement with Gilson on this point. A critical evaluation of Gilson's statement that none but St Thomas found the solution to this problem would go much beyond the limits of our work. Cf. Bernath, pp. 44–53.

28   *Tract. in Ioh.* XIV, 9: 'Multae animae sunt multorum hominum, et si se diligunt, una anima est.' Cf. *Conf.* IV, 6.

29   *Tract. in Ioh.* XVIII, 4: 'si ergo anima mea et anima tua, cum idem sapimus nosque diligimus, fit anima una, quanto magis Pater Deus et Filius Deus in fonte dilectionis Deus unus est?'

30   *Ep. CXXXVII*, III, 11. Cf. *De Civ. Dei* X, 29.

31   Here it seems to be the case that Augustine is going too far, not only because the unity of Christ is known only through faith in that its very occurrence lies beyond man's reasoning powers, but also because it is not as such evident why a union of two spiritual natures should more readily be possible. However, these speculative questions cannot further be pursued here.

32   Some interpreters of Augustine use this terminology, such as Carlo Boyer, *Sant'Agostino filosofo* (Bologna: Pàtron, 1965), p. 149; Couturier, p. 550; O'Neill, p. 257. Purposely, I avoided speaking in terms of an 'accidental,' 'substantial,' or 'hypostatic' unity of soul and body, since these notions are loaded concepts to employ which would hinder us from grasping the data in question in an original way and not in the light of other theories of man.

33   *De Civ. Dei* X, 12: 'nam et omni miraculo, quod fit per hominem, maius miraculum est homo.'

34   Maxsein, p. 331: 'Personal unity does not mean an obscuring of its substantial constitutive elements, body and soul; rather, in their difference, they constitute the substantial unity of the person in a mysterious manner.'

Bibliography

1 PRIMARY SOURCES

(The choice of the editions of Augustine's work has basically been made according to Eligius Dekkers, *Clavis Patrum Latinorum* [C. Beyaert, Brugis – M. Nijhoff, Hagae Comitis, 1961], in the following manner):
Confessiones (*Conf.*) – *CSEL* XXXIII
Contra Academicos (*Contra Acad.*) – *CSEL* LXIII
Contra Epistolam Manichaei Quam Vocant Fundamenti (*Contra Ep. Man.*) – *CSEL* XXV
Contra Faustum Manichaeum (*Contra Faustum Man.*) – *CSEL* XXV
Contra Fortunatum Manichaeum (*Contra Fort.*) – *CSEL* XXV
De Beata Vita – *CSEL* LXIII
De Catechizandis Rudibus (*De Catech. Rud.*) – *PL* XL
De Civitate Dei (*De Civ. Dei*) – *CC* XLVII–XLVIII
De Cura pro Mortuis Gerenda – *CSEL* XLI
De Diversis Quaestionibus Octoginta Tribus (*De Div. Quaest.* LXXXIII) – *PL* XL
De Doctrina Christiana (*De Doct. Christ.*) – *CC* XXXI
De Duabus Animabus (*De Duabus. An.*) – *CSEL* XXV
De Genesi ad Litteram (*De Gen. ad Litt.*) – *CSEL* XXVIII
De Gratia et Libero Arbitrio – *PL* XLIV
De Immortalitate Animae (*De Immort. An.*) – *PL* XXXII
De Libero Arbitrio (*De Lib. Arb.*) – *CC* XXIX
De Magistro (*De Mag.*) – *PL* XXXII
De Moribus Ecclesiae Catholicae et de Moribus Manichaeorum (*De Mor. Eccl.*) – *PL* XXXII
De Musica – *PL* XXXII
De Natura et Origine Animae (*De Nat. et Orig. An.*) – *CSEL* LX
De Ordine (*De Ord.*) – *CSEL* LXIII

De Quantitate Animae (*De Quant. An.*) – *PL* XXXII
De Spiritu et Littera (*De Spir. et Litt.*) – *CSEL* LX
De Trinitate (*De Trin.*) – *CC* L – L$_a$
De Utilitate Credendi (*De Util. Cred.*) – *CSEL* XXV
De Utilitate Ieiunii (*De Util. Ieiu.*) *PL* XL
De Vera Religione (*De Vera Rel.*) – *CC* XXXII
Enarrationes in Psalmos (*En. in Ps.*) – *CC* XXXVIII – XL
Enchiridion ad Laurentium (*Enchir.*) – *PL* XL
Epistolae (*Ep.*) – *CSEL* XXXIV, XLIV, LVII, LVIII
Retractationes (*Retract.*) – *CSEL* XXXVI
Sermones – *PL* XXXVIII – XXXIX
Soliloquia (*Solil.*) – *PL* XXXII
Tractatus in Evangelium Ioannis (*Tract. in Ioh.*) – *CC* XXXVI
(In our citations, each 'j' of an original source is rendered by 'i,' and each
'u' employed in the sense of 'v' is rendered thus, in order to achieve a
greater uniformity.)

2 TRANSLATIONS

(The English citations of Augustine's are taken, with occasional changes
of mine, from the following available translations):
The City of God. Trans. MARCUS DODS. New York: Random House, 1950.
Confessions. Trans. ALBERT C. OUTLER. In *The Library of Christian Classics*.
Vol. VII. Philadelphia: The Westminster Press.
Contra Epistolam Manichaei Quam Vocant Fundamenti. Trans. R. STOTHERT.
In *The Nicene and Post-Nicene Fathers* (=*NPNF*). Vol. IV. Michigan:
Eerdmans Publishing Company.
Letters of St Augustine. Trans. J. G. CUNNINGHAM. In *NPNF*. Vol. I.
The Soul and Its Origin. Trans. PETER HOLMES and ROBERT E. WALLIS.
In *NPNF*. Vol. V.
The Trinity. Trans. STEPHEN MCKENNA. In *Fathers of the Church*. Vol. 45.
Washington D.C.: The Cath. Univ. of America Press, 1963.
Of True Religion. Trans. J. H. S. BURLEIGH. South Bend: Gateway Editions,
1953.
(Any other quote from Augustine is a free translation of mine.)

3 SELECTED SECONDARY WORKS ON THE TOPICS IN AUGUSTINE

ANDERSON, JAMES F. *St Augustine and Being: A Metaphysical Essay*. The
Hague: M. Nijhoff, 1965.
ANDRESEN, CARL, ed. *Bibliographia Augustiniana*. Darmstadt: Wissensch-
aftl. Buchgesellschaft, 1962.

Augustinus Magister. Congrès International Augustinien. Paris, 1954.

Aurelius Augustinus. Festschrift der Görresgesellschaft zum 1500. Todestage des Hl. Augustinus. Ed. Martin Grabmann und Joseph Mausbach, Köln: Bachem, 1930.

BARION, JAKOB. *Plotin und Augustinus: Untersuchungen zum Gottesproblem*. Berlin: Junker & Dünnhaupt, 1935.

BARTH, HEINRICH. *Die Freiheit der Entscheidung im Denken Augustins*. Basel: Helbing & Lichtenhahn, 1935.

BATTENHOUSE, ROY, ed. *A Companion to the Study of St Augustine*. New York: Oxford Univ. Press, 1955.

BAÜMKER, CLEMENS. *Witelo: Ein Philosoph und Naturforscher des XIII. Jahrhunderts*. Münster, 1908.

BENZ, ERNST. *Marius Victorinus und die Entwicklung der abendländischen Willensmetaphysik*. Stuttgart: Kohlhammer, 1932.

BERLINGER, RUDOLPH. *Augustins dialogische Metaphysik*. Frankfurt: Klostermann, 1962.

BIOLO, SALVINO S.J. *La coscienza nel 'De Trinitate' di S. Agostino*. Roma: Typis Pontif. Univ. Gregorianae, 1969.

BLANCHARD, PIERRE. 'L'espace intérieur chez Saint Augustin d'après le Livre X des "Confessiones." ' *Augustinus Magister*, pp. 535–42.

BLANCHET, LÉON. *Les antécédents historiques du 'Je pense, donc je suis.'* Paris: Alcan, 1920.

BOURKE, VERNON J. *Augustine's Quest of Wisdom: Life and Philosophy of the Bishop of Hippo*. Milwaukee, Misc.: The Bruce Publishing Company, 1945.

BOURKE, VERNON J. 'St Augustine and the Cosmic Soul.' *Giornale di Metafisica*, 9 (1954), 431–40.

BOURKE, VERNON J. *Augustine's View of Reality: The Saint Augustine Lecture 1963*. Villanova, Pa.: Villanova Press, 1964.

BOURKE, VERNON J., ed. *The Essential Augustine*. Indianapolis: Hackett Publishing Company, 1974.

BOYER, CHARLES S. J. *Christianisme et néo-platonisme dans la formation de Saint Augustin*. Paris: Beauchesne, 1920.

BOYER, CHARLES S. J. *L'idée de vérité dans la philosophie de Saint Augustin*. Paris: Beauchesne, 1939.

BOYER, CHARLES S. J. *Sant'Agostino filosofo*. Bologna: Pàtron, 1965.

BROWN, PETER. *Augustine of Hippo*. Berkeley and Los Angeles: Univ. of Calif. Press. 1967.

BUCHER, THEODOR G. 'Zur formalen Logik bei Augustinus.' *Freiburger Zeitschrift für Philosophie und Theologie*, 29 (1982), 3–45.

BUCKEMEYER, ROBERT E. 'Augustine and the Life of Man's Body in the Early Dialogues.' *Augustinian Studies*, 2 (1971), 197–211.

CAYRÉ, FULBERT. *Initiation à la philosophie de Saint Augustin.* Paris: Desclée de Brouwer, 1947.

CHRISTOPHER, JOSEPH, trans. with an Introduction and Commentary. *De Catechizandis Rudibus.* By S. Aureli Augustini. Washington D.C.: The Cath. Univ. of America, Patristic Studies Vol. VIII, 1926.

CILLERUELO, LOPE. 'La "Memoria Sui." ' *Giornale di Metafisica* 9 (1954), 478–92.

CLARK, MARY T. *Augustine, Philosopher of Freedom: A Study in Comparative Philosophy.* New York: Desclée Co., 1958.

COUTURIER, CHARLES S.J. 'La structure métaphysique de l'homme d'après saint Augustin.' *Augustinus Magister,* pp. 543–50.

D'ARCY, M. C., ed. *A Monument to Saint Augustine.* New York, 1930 and 1945; rpt *Saint Augustine: Essays on His Age, Life and Thought.* Cleveland and New York: Meridian Books, 1957.

DELAHAYE, KARL. *Die 'memoria interior' – Lehre des heiligen Augustinus und der Begriff der 'transzendentalen Apperzeption' Kants.* Würzburg: Becker, 1936.

DEL-NEGRO, WALTER von. 'Diskussionsbemerkung zum aristotelisch-augustinischen Zeitparadoxon.' *Zeitschrift für philosophische Forschung,* 20 (1966), 309–12.

DEMPF, ALOIS. 'Die Menschenlehre Augustins.' *Münchener theologische Zeitschrift,* 6 (1955), 21–31.

DINKLER, ERICH. *Die Anthropologie Augustins.* Stuttgart: Kohlhammer, 1934.

DUCHROW, ULRICH. 'Der sogenannte psychologische Zeitbegriff Augustins im Verhältnis zur physikalischen und geschichtlichen Zeit.' *Zeitschrift für Theologie und Kirche,* 63 (1966), 267–88.

EIBL, HANS. *Augustin und die Patristik.* München: Reinhardt, 1923.

ESCHER DI STEFANO, ANNA. *Il Manicheismo in S. Agostino.* Padova: CEDAM, 1960.

FALKENHAHN, WILLY. *Augustins Illuminationstheorie im Lichte der jüngsten Forschungen.* Köln, 1948.

FELLERMEIER, JAKOB. 'Die Illuminationstheorie bei Augustinus und Bonaventura und die aprioristische Begründung der Erkenntnis durch Kant.' *Philosophisches Jahrbuch,* 60 (1950), 296–305.

FERRAZ, MARTIN, *De la psychologie de saint Augustin.* Paris: Durand, 1862.

FLASCH, KURT. *Augustin: Einführung in sein Denken.* Stuttgart: Reclam, 1980.

GANGAUF, THEODOR. *Metaphysische Psychologie des Hl. Augustinus.* Augsburg, 1852.

GANNON, SR MARY ANN IDA. 'The Active Theory of Sensation in St Augustine.' *The New Scholasticism,* 30 (1956), 154–80.

GEYSER, JOSEPH. 'Die erkenntnistheoretischen Anschauungen Augustins zu Beginn seiner schriftstellerischen Tätigkeit.' *Aurelius Augustinus*, pp. 63–86.

GILSON, ETIENNE. *The Christian Philosophy of St Augustine*. Trans. L. E. M. Lynch. New York: Random House, 1960.

GOLDBRUNNER, JOSEF. *Das Leib-Seele-Problem bei Augustinus*. Kahlmünz: Laßleben, 1934.

GRABMANN, MARTIN. *Die Grundgedanken des Hl. Augustinus über Seele und Gott: In ihrer Gegenwartsbedeutung dargestellt*. Köln: Bachem, 1916.

GRABMANN, MARTIN. 'Des heiligen Augustinus Quaestio de ideis (De diversis quaestionibus LXXXIII, qu. 46) in ihrer inhaltlichen Bedeutung und mittelalterlichen Weiterentwicklung.' *Mittelalterliches Geistesleben*, Vol. II, München: Hueber, 1936, pp. 25–34.

GUARDINI, ROMANO. *Die Bekehrung des heiligen Aurelius Augustinus: Der innere Vorgang in seinen Bekenntnissen*. Leipzig: Hegner, 1935.

HEINZELMANN, WILHELM. *Über Augustins Lehre vom Wesen und Ursprung der menschlichen Seele*. Halberstadt, 1868.

HENDRIKX, EPHRAEM. 'Platonisches und biblisches Denken bei Augustinus.' *Augustinus Magister*, pp. 285–92.

HENRY, PAUL. *Saint Augustine on Personality: The Saint Augustine Lecture 1959*. New York: The Macmillan Company, 1960.

HERTLING, GEORG FREIHERR VON. *Augustin*. Mainz: Kirchheim, 1902.

HESSEN, JOHANNES. *Augustins Metaphysik der Erkenntnis*. Berlin: Dümmlers, 1931.

HOFFMANN, WILHELM. *Augustinus: Das Problem seiner Daseinsauslegung*. Münster: Aschendorff, 1963.

HOLMAN, MARY J. *Nature-Imagery in the Works of St Augustine*. Washington, D.C.: Cath. Univ. of America, 1931.

HOLZAPFEL, WINFRIED. *Mundus Sensibilis: Die Analyse der menschlichen Sensualität nach dem heiligen Augustinus*. Freiburg: Oberkirch, 1968.

HORNSTEIN, HERBERT. 'Immaterialität und Reflexion: Eine Studie zur Geistphilosophie des hl. Augustinus.' In *Erkenntnis und Verantwortung*. Ed. Josef Derbolav und Friedhelm Nicolin. Düsseldorf: Schwann, 1960.

JANSEN, BERNHARD. 'Zur Lehre des heiligen Augustinus von dem Erkennen der rationes aeternae.' *Aurelius Augustinus*, pp. 111–36.

JASPERS, KARL. *Die großen Philosophen*. Vol. I. München: Piper, 1957.

JORDAN, ROBERT. 'Time and Contingency in St Augustine.' *Review of Metaphysics*, 8 (1955), 394–417.

KAISER, HERMANN-JOSEF. *Augustinus: Zeit und 'Memoira.'* Bonn: Bouvier, 1969.

KÄLIN, BERNARD. *Die Erkenntnislehre des hl. Augustinus*. Sarnen: Ehrli, 1920.

KOLB, KARL. *Menschliche Freiheit und göttliches Vorherwissen nach Augustin.* Freiburg: Herder, 1908.

KÖRNER, FRANZ. 'Deus in homine videt: Das Subjekt des menschlichen Erkennens nach der Lehre Augustins.' *Philosophisches Jahrbuch,* 64 (1956), 166–217.

KÖRNER, FRANZ. *Das Sein und der Mensch: Die existenzielle Seinsentdeckung des jungen Augustins: Grundlagen zur Erhellung seiner Ontologie.* Freiburg/ München: Alber, 1959.

KÖRNER, FRANZ. 'Abstraktion oder Illumination? Das ontologische Problem der augustinischen Sinneserkenntnis.' *Recherches Augustiniennes,* 2 (1962), 81–109.

LAMPEY, ERICH. *Das Zeitproblem nach den Bekenntnissen Augustins.* Regensburg: Habbel, 1960.

LECHNER, ODILO. *Idee und Zeit in der Metaphysik Augustins.* München: Pustet, 1964.

LEDER, H. *Untersuchungen über Augustins Erkenntnistheorie in ihren Beziehungen zur antiken Skepsis, zu Plotin und Descartes.* Marburg, 1901.

MADER, JOHANN. *Die logische Struktur des personalen Denkens: Aus der Methode der Gotteserkenntnis bei Aurelius Augustinus.* Wien: Herder, 1965.

MANCINI, GUIDO. *La Psicologia di S. Agostino e i suoi elementi neoplatonici.* Napoli: Ricciardi, 1919.

MARKUS, ROBERT A., ed. *Augustine: A Collection of Critical Essays.* New York: Doubleday, 1972.

MATTHEWS, GARETH B. 'Augustine on Speaking from Memory.' In *Augustine: A Collection of Critical Essays.*

MATTHEWS, GARETH B. 'Si Fallor, Sum.' in *Augustine: A Collection of Critical Essays,* pp. 151–67.

MAUSBACH, JOSEPH. *Die Ethik des Heiligen Augustinus.* Freiburg: Herder, 1909.

MAUSBACH, JOSEPH. 'Wesen und Stufung des Lebens nach dem hl. Augustinus.' In *Aurelius Augustinus,* pp. 169–96.

MAXSEIN, ANTON. *Philosophia Cordis: Das Wesen der Personalität bei Augustinus.* Salzburg: Müller, 1966.

MERTENS, KARLA. *Das Verhältnis des Schönen zum Guten in den Augustinischen Frühschriften.* Speyer: Pilger, 1940.

MILES, MARGARET R. *Augustine on the Body.* Missoula, Mon.: Scholars Press, 1979.

MONTGOMERY, W. 'St Augustine's Attitude to Psychic Phenomena.' *Hibbert Journal,* 25 (1926), 92–102.

MORGAN, JAMES. *The Psychological Teaching of St Augustine.* London: Elliot Stock, 1932.

MOURANT, JOHN. 'St Augustine's Quest for Truth.' *The New Scholasticism*, 5 (1931), 206–18.

MUNDLE, C. W. K. 'Augustine's Persuasive Error concerning Time.' *Philosophy*, 41 (1966), 165–8.

NASH, RONALD H. *The Light of the Mind: St Augustine's Theory of Knowledge*. Lexington: Univ. Press, 1969.

NEUHÄUSLER, ANTON. 'Augustinus und die Zeitauffassung der heutigen Physik.' *Hochland*, 43 (1950/51), 472–82.

NOURRISSON, JEAN-FÉLIX. *La philosophie de Saint Augustin*. Paris: Didier, 1866.

OBERSTEINER, JAKOB. 'Der Ausgang vom Selbstbewußtsein bei Augustinus und bei Descartes.' *Theologisch-Praktische Quartalschrift*, 102 (1954), 277–88.

O'CONNELL, ROBERT J. 'The Plotinian Fall of the Soul in St Augustine.' *Traditio*, 19 (1963), 1–35.

O'CONNELL, ROBERT J. *St Augustine's Early Theory of Man*. Cambridge, Mass.: The Belknap Press of Harvard Univ. Press, 1968.

O'CONNOR, W. *The Concept of the Soul According to St Augustine*. Washington D.C., 1921.

O'NEILL, WILLIAM. 'Augustine's Influence upon Descartes and the mind/body Problem.' *Revue des Études Augustiniennes*, 12 (1966), 255–60.

OTT, W. 'Des hl. Augustinus Lehre über die Sinneserkenntnis.' *Philosophisches Jahrbuch*, 13 (1900), 45–59 and 138–48.

PALMERI. PASQUALE. 'La persona umana nel pensiero di Sant' Agostino.' *Studia Patavia*, 1 (1954), 370–99.

PÉPIN, JEAN. *'Ex Platonicorum Persona.' Études sur les Lectures Philosophiques de Saint Augustin*. Amsterdam: Hakkert, 1977.

PORTALIÉ, EUGÈNE. *A Guide to the Thought of St Augustine*. Trans. Ralph J. Bastian. Chicago: Library of Living Catholic Thought, Henry Regnery Company, 1960.

PRZYWARA, ERICH. *Augustinus: Die Gestalt als Gefüge*. Leipzig: Hegner, 1934.

PRZYWARA, ERICH. *An Augustine Synthesis*. New York: Sheed & Ward, 1936.

QUADRI, GOFFREDO. *Il pensiero filosofico di S. Agostino, con particolare riguardo al problema dell'errore*. Firenze: La Nuova Italia, 1934.

QUILES, ISMAEL. 'Para una interpretación integral de la "iluminación agustiniana." ' *Augustinus*, 3 (1958), 255–68.

RANLEY, ERNEST W. 'St Augustine's Theory of Matter.' *Modern Schoolman*, 42 (1964/65), 287–303.

RAVICZ, MARILYN E. 'St Augustine: Time and Eternity.' *Thomist*, 22 (1959), 542–54.

RIEF, JOSEF. 'Liebe zur Wahrheit. Untersuchungen zur Ethik des jungen Augustinus.' *Theologische Quartalschrift*, 141 (1961), 281–318.

RITTER, JOACHIM. *Mundus intelligibilis: Eine Untersuchung zur Aufnahme und Umwandlung der neuplatonischen Ontologie bei Augustinus.* Frankfurt: Klostermann, 1937.

SCHMAUS, MICHAEL. *Die psychologische Trinitätslehre des heiligen Augustinus.* Münster: Aschendorff, 1967.

SCHMIDT-DENGLER, WENDELIN. 'Die "aula memoriae" in den Konfessionen des heiligen Augustin.' *Revue des Études Augustiniennes*, 14 (1968), 69–89.

SCHMITT, BRIGITTE. *Der Geist als Grund der Zeit: Die Zeitauslegung des Aurelius Augustinus.* Freiburg, 1967.

SCHNEIDER, RUDOLF. *Seele und Sein: Ontologie bei Augustin und Aristoteles.* Stuttgart: Kohlhammer, 1957.

SCHÖPF, ALFRED. *Wahrheit und Wissen: Die Begründung der Erkenntnis bei Augustin.* München: Pustet, 1965.

SCHÖPF, ALFRED. *Augustinus: Einführung in sein Philosophieren.* Freiburg/München: Alber, 1970.

SCHÜTZINGER, CAROLINE E. *The German Controversy on Saint Augustine's Illumination Theory.* New York: Pageant Press, 1960.

SCHÜTZINGER, CAROLINE E. 'Die augustinische Erkenntnislehre im Lichte neuerer Forschung.' *Recherches augustiniennes*, 2 (1962), 177–203.

SCHWARZ, RICHARD. 'Die leib-seelische Existenz bei Aurelius Augustinus.' *Philosophisches Jahrbuch*, 63 (1955), 223–360.

SEIFERT, FRIEDRICH. *Seele und Bewußtsein.* München/Basel: Reinhardt, 1962.

SEIFERT, JOSEF. 'Bonaventuras Interpretation der augustinischen These vom notwendigen Sein der Wahrheit.' *Franziskanische Studien*, 59 (1977), 38–52.

SEYBOLD, MICHAEL. *Sozialtheologische Aspekte der Sünde bei Augustinus.* Regensburg: Pustet, 1963.

SIMON, MARIA. *Gewißheit und Wahrheit bei Augustinus.* Emsdetten, 1938.

SLADECZEK, FRANZ-MARIA. 'Die Selbsterkenntnis als Grundlage der Philosophie nach dem hl. Augustinus.' *Scholastik*, 5 (1930), 329–56.

SÖHNGEN, GOTTLIEB. 'Der Aufbau der augustinischen Gedächtnislehre.' In *Aurelius Augustinus*, pp. 367–94.

SOLIGNAC, AIMÉ. 'Analyse et sources de la Question "De Ideis."' In *Augustinus Magister*, Vol. I, pp. 307–15.

STEIN, WOLFGANG. *Sapientia bei Augustinus.* Witterschlick: Schwarzbold, 1973.

STORZ, JOSEPH. *Die Philosophie des Hl. Augustinus.* Freiburg: Herder, 1882.

SULLIVAN, JOHN E. *The Image of God: The Doctrine of St Augustine and its Influence.* Dubuque, Iowa: The Priory Press, 1963.

SUTER, RONALD. 'Augustine on Time with Some Criticisms from Wittgenstein.' *Revue internationale de Philosophie,* 61/62 (1962), 378–94.

THEILER, WILLY. *Porphyrios und Augustin.* Halle: Niemeyer, 1933.

THIMME, WILHELM. *Augustins erster Entwurf einer metaphysischen Willenslehre.* Berlin: Trowitzsch, 1908.

TOWNLEY, FRED LORD. *The Unity of Body and Soul: The Value of the Body in Christian Teaching and Modern Thought.* London: Unwin Brothers Limited, 1929.

TSCHOLL, JOSEF. 'Augustins Interesse für das körperliche Schöne.' *Augustiniana,* 14 (1964), 72–104.

VERBEKE, GÉRARD. 'Pensée et discernement chez saint Augustin: Quelques réflexions sur le sens du terme "cogitare." ' *Recherches Augustiniennes,* 2 (1962), 59–80.

VERBEKE, GÉRARD. 'Spiritualité et immortalité de l'âme chez Saint Augustin.' In *Augustinus Magister,* Vol. I, pp. 329–34.

WITTMANN, LEOPOLD. *Ascensus: Der Aufstieg zur Transzendenz in der Metaphysik Augustins.* München: Berchmans, 1980.

WÖRTER, FRIEDRICH. *Die Geistesentwicklung des Hl. Aurelius Augustinus bis zu seiner Taufe.* Paderborn, 1892.

ZIMARA, COELESTIN. 'Das Ineinanderspiel von Gottes Vorwissen und Wollen nach Augustinus.' *Freiburger Zeitschrift für Philosophie und Theologie,* 6 (1959), 271–99 und 361–94.

4   OTHER WORKS CONSULTED

AQUINAS, THOMAS. *Quaestiones Disputatae de Veritate.* Ed. Raymundi Spiazzi. Taurini/Romae: Marietti, 1949.

AQUINAS, THOMAS. *Summa Theologiae.* Madrid: Biblioteca de Autores Cristianos, 1951.

AQUINAS, THOMAS. *Summa Contra Gentiles.* Taurini/Romae: Marietti, 1961.

ARISTOTLE. *Basic Works.* Ed. Richard McKeon. New York: Random House, 1941.

BERGSON, HENRI. *Matière et Mémoire.* Paris: Alcan, 1903.

BERNATH, KLAUS. *Anima Forma Corporis: Eine Untersuchung über die ontologischen Grundlagen der Anthropologie des Thomas von Aquin.* Bonn: Bouvier, 1969.

BONAVENTURA. *Opera Omnia.* Ad Claras Aquas (Quaracchi) prope Florentiam ex Typographia Collegii S. Bonaventurae, 1891.

BORST, C. V.Ed. *The Mind-Brain Identity Theory.* Bristol: Macmillan, 1970.

BRADY, IGNATIUS. 'St Bonaventure's Doctrine of Illumination: Reactions Medieval and Modern.' *Southwestern Journal of Philosophy*, 5, 2 (1974), 27–37.

BRUNNER, AUGUST. *Der Stufenbau der Welt: Ontologische Untersuchungen über Person, Leben, Stoff.* München: Kösel, 1950.

BUYTENDIJK, FREDERIK J. J. *Prolegomena einer anthropologischen Physiologie.* Salzburg: Müller, 1967.

CICERO. *Tusculanarum Disputationum.* Bologna: Zanichelli, 1935.

CONRAD-MARTIUS, HEDWIG. *Die Geistseele des Menschen.* München: Kösel, 1960.

CONRAD-MARTIUS, HEDWIG. 'Die "Seele" der Pflanze.' in *Schriften zur Philosophie*, Vol. I. Ed. Eberhard Avé-Lallement. München: Kösel, 1963, pp. 276–362.

COPLESTON, FREDERICK. *A History of Philosophy.* Garden City: Image Books, 1962– .

CORETH, EMERICH. *Was ist der Mensch?* Innsbruck: Tyrolia, 1973.

CROSBY, JOHN F. 'The Idea of Value and the Reform of the Traditional Metaphysics of *Bonum.*' *Aletheia*, 1, 2 (1977), 231–336.

DELGADO, JOSÉ M. R. *Physical Control of the Mind: Toward a Psycho-civilized Society.* New York: Evanston, London: Harper & Row, 1969.

DESCARTES, RENÉ. *Philosophical Works.* Trans. Elizabeth S. Haldane and G. R. T. Ross. Cambridge: Univ. Press, 1978.

DINAN, STEPHEN A. 'The Phenomenological Anthropology of Karol Wojtyla.' *New Scholasticism*, 55 (1981), 317–30.

ECCLES, JOHN C. See Popper, Karl R.

EGGEL, TONY. *Traumleben und Schizophrenie.* Zürich, 1976.

FEIGL, HERBERT. *The 'Mental' and the 'Physical'.* Minneapolis: Univ: of Minnesota Press, 1967.

FERRARI, DON. 'Retention-Memory: Perception and the Cognition of Enduring Objects.' *Aletheia*, 2 (1981), 65–123.

FLEW, ANTONY, Ed. *Body, Mind, and Death.* New York: Macmillan Publishing Co., 1964.

FRANKENBERGER, ERNST, Ed. *Gottbekenntnisse großer Naturforscher.* Leutesdorf: Johannes, 1975.

GEIGER, MORITZ. 'Fragment über den Begriff des Unbewußten und der psychischen Realität.' *Jahrbuch für Philosophie und phänomenologische Forschung*, 4 (1921), 1–137.

HENGSTENBERG, HANS-EDUARD. *Philosophische Anthropologie.* Stuttgart: Kohlhammer, 1957.

HILDEBRAND, DIETRICH VON. *Christian Ethics.* New York: McKay Comp., 1952.

HILDEBRAND, DIETRICH VON. *Man and Woman*. Chicago, Ill.: Franciscan Herald Press, 1966.

HILDEBRAND, DIETRICH VON. *Metaphysik der Gemeinschaft*. Regensburg: Habbel, 1975.

HILDEBRAND, DIETRICH VON. *Ästhetik 1*. Stuttgart: Kohlhammer, 1977.

HOERES, WALTER. *Kritik der transzendentalphilosophischen Erkenntnistheorie*. Stuttgart: Kohlhammer, 1969.

HORKHEIMER, MAX. 'Zur Idee der Seele.' In *Was weiß man von der Seele?* Ed. Hans-Jürgen Schultz. Gütersloh: Mohn, 1972, pp. 11–19.

HUONDER, QUIRIN. *Gott und Seele im Lichte der griechischen Philosophie*. München: Hueber, 1954.

HUSSERL, EDMUND. *Logische Untersuchungen*. 3. ed. Halle: Niemeyer, 1922.

HUSSERL, EDMUND. *Cartesianische Meditationen und Pariser Vorträge*. Haag: Martinus Nijhoff, 1963.

HUSSERL, EDMUND. *Zur Phänomenologie des inneren Zeitbewußtseins*. Haag: Martinus Nijhoff, 1966.

INGARDEN, ROMAN. 'Über die Gefahr einer Petitio Principii in der Erkenntnistheorie.' *Jahrbuch für Philosophie und phänomenologische Forschung*, 4 (1921), 545–68.

INGARDEN, ROMAN. *Der Streit um die Existenz der Welt*. Tübingen: Niemeyer, 1965.

INGARDEN, ROMAN. *Vom Erkennen des literarischen Kunstwerks*. Darmstadt: Wissenschaftliche Buchgesellschaft, 1968.

JASPERS, KARL. *Allgemeine Psychopathologie*. Berlin-Heidelberg-New York: Springer, 1973.

KANT, IMMANUEL. *Prolegomena zu einer jeden künftigen Metaphysik, die als Wissenschaft wird auftreten können*. Ed. Königlich Preußische Akademie der Wissenschaften, Vol. IV. Berlin: Reimer, 1903.

KANT, IMMANUEL. *Kritik der reinen Vernunft*. Ed. Königlich Preußische Akademie der Wissenschaften, Vol. III, Berlin: Reimer, 1904.

LAUBENTHAL, FLORIN. *Hirn und Seele: Ärztliches zum Leib-Seele-Problem*. Salzburg: Müller, 1953.

LEIBNIZ, GOTTFRIED WILHELM VON. *Monadology and Other Philosophical Essays*. Trans. Paul Schrecker and Anne Martin Schrecker. Indianapolis: The Library of Liberal Arts; Bobbs-Merrill Educational Publishing, 1965.

LENIN, WLADIMIR ILJITSCH. 'Materialismus und Empiriokritizismus.' In *Sämtliche Werke*, Vol. XIII. Wien-Berlin: Verlag für Literatur und Politik, 1927.

LOBKOWICS, NIKOLAUS. 'Materialism and Matter in Marxism-Leninism.' In *The Concept of Matter in Modern Philosophy*. Ed. Ernan McMullin. Notre Dame, Ind.: Univ. of Notre Dame Press, 1978, pp. 154–88.

NEWMAN, JOHN HENRY. *Parochial and Plain Sermons*. Westminster, Md.: Christian Classics, 1967.

PASCAL, BLAISE. *Oeuvres complètes*. Ed. Jacques Chevalier. Bruges: Gallimard, 1954.

PEGIS, ANTON C. *At the Origins of the Thomistic Notion of Man*. New York: Macmillan Co., 1963.

PIEPER, JOSEF. *Tod und Unsterblichkeit*. München: Kösel, 1968.

PLATON. *Sämtliche Werkse*. Ed. Ernesto Grassi und Walter Hess. Hamburg: Rowohlt, 1957–59.

PLESSNER, HELMUTH. *Die Stufen des Organischen und der Mensch*. Berlin-New York: de Gruyter, 1975.

PLOTIN. *Schriften*. Trans. Richard Harder. Hamburg: Meiner, 1956–1967.

POHLENZ, GERD. 'Leib und Seele – Versuch einer systematischen Vermittlung dualistischer Theorie und menschlicher Lebenspraxis.' *Theologie und Philosophie*, 58 (1983), 1–33.

POLTEN, ERIC P. *Critique of the Psycho-Physical Identity Theory*. The Hague: Mouton, 1973.

POPPER, KARL R. and ECCLES, JOHN C. *The Self and its Brain*. Springer International, 1977.

REINACH, ADOLF. 'A Contribution Toward the Theory of the Negative Judgment.' Trans. Don Ferrari. *Aletheia*, 2 (1981), 9–64.

REVERS, WILHELM JOSEF. 'Das Leibproblem in der Psychologie.' In *Philosophische Anthropologie heute*. Ed. Roman Rocek und Oskar Schatz. München: Beck, 1972, pp. 130–41.

RYLE, GILBERT. *The Concept of Mind*. London: Hutchinson, 1949.

SCHELER, MAX. *Der Formalismus in der Ethik und die materiale Wertethik*. Bern: Francke, 1966.

SCHELER, MAX. *Vom Umsturz der Werte*. Bern und München: Francke, 1972.

SCHULER, BERTRAM. *Pflanze-Tier-Mensch: Wesensart und Wesensunterschiede*. München/Paderborn/Wien: Schöningh, 1969.

SEIFERT, JOSEF. *Lieb und Seele*. Salzburg: Pustet, 1973.

SEIFERT, JOSEF. *Erkenntnis objektiver Wahrheit*. Salzburg: Pustet, 1976.

SEIFERT, JOSEF. 'Essence and Existence: A New Foundation of Classical Metaphysics on the Basis of "Phenomenological Realism," And a Critical Investigation of "Existentialist Thomism."' *Aletheia*, 1, 1 (1977), 17–159, and 1, 2 (1977), 371–459.

SEIFERT, JOSEF. *Das Leib-Seele-Problem in der gegenwärtigen philosophischen Diskussion*. Darmstadt: Wissenschaftliche Buchgesellschaft, 1979.

SEIFERT, JOSEF. 'Karol Cardinal Wojtyla (Pope John Paul II) as Philosopher and the Cracow/Lublin School of Philosophy.' *Aletheia*, 2 (1981), 130–99.

THUM, BEDA. 'Theorien des Bewußtseins.' In *Geist und Leib in der menschlichen Existenz*. Ed. Görres-Gesellschaft. Freiburg/München: Alber, 1961, pp. 60–75.

VRIES, JOSEF DE. *Materie und Geist*. München: Pustet, 1970.

WHITEHEAD, ALFRED NORTH. *The Concept of Nature*. Univ. of Michigan Press, 1957.

WICHMANN, EYIND H. *Quantum Physics: Berkeley Physics Course Vol. 4*. New York/Düsseldorf: McGraw-Hill Book Company, 1971.

WOJTYLA, KAROL. *The Acting Person*. Trans. Andrzej Potocki. Dordrecht: Reidel, 1979.

WOJTYLA, KAROL. 'Person: Subjekt und Gemeinschaft.' In *Der Streit um den Menschen: Personaler Anspruch des Sittlichen*. Trans. Jörg Splett. Kevelaer: Butzon & Bercker, 1979.

ZANER, RICHARD M. *The Problem of Embodiment*. The Hague: Martinus Nijhoff, 1971.

Name index

Ambrose, 3, 80
Anaximenes, 11, 230
Andersen, J. T., 305
Andresen, C., 223
Aquinas, Thomas (Thomistic), 7, 183, 213, 248, 274–5, 295, 306, 309, 314, 320, 324–5
Aristotle (Aristotelian), 183, 203, 213, 230, 266, 292, 304, 306, 315, 319
Armstrong, D. M., 231, 286
Avé-Lallement, E., 228
Averroes, 203

Baer, K. E. von, 245
Barion, J., 225
Barth, H., 281
Bastian, R. J., 246
Bäumker, C., 276
Benz, E., 280, 311
Bergson, H., 254
Berlinger, R., 226, 274, 280, 303
Bernath, K., 227, 325
Biolo, S., 293–4
Blanchard, P., 254
Blanchet, L., 292–3
Boehm, R., 258
Bonaventure, 6, 274–7, 279
Borst, C. V., 231, 239
Bourke, V. J., 268, 270, 305
Boyer, Ch., 225, 265, 271, 275, 325
Brady, I., 277
Brentano, F., 298
Brown, P., 225–6
Brunner, A., 228, 319
Bucher, Th., 272
Buckemeyer, R. E., 268, 322

Cayré, F., 225, 276
Chevalier, J., 272
Christopher, J. P., 268
Cicero, 3, 115–16, 266, 292
Cilleruelo, L., 292
Clark, M. T., 280
Conrad-Martius, H., 228
Copleston, F., 230, 274, 315
Coreth, E., 280
Couturier, Ch., 242, 325
Crosby, J. F., 317

Delahaye, K., 303–4, 321
Delgado, J., 231, 284–5
Del-Negro, W. von, 262
Dempf, A., 225
Derbolav, J., 295
Descartes R. (Cartesian), 6, 26, 142–3, 189, 292, 301, 323
Dinan, St, 298
Dinkler, E., 225, 243, 245, 321, 323

Eccles, J., 231, 313
Eggel, T., 312
Eibl, H., 245
Einstein, A., 237
Epicurus, 11
Escher di Stefano, A., 224
Euclid, 7
Evodius, 16–17, 22, 40–1, 61, 72, 145, 267

Falkenhahn, W., 276
Feigl, H., 231, 286, 302
Fellermeier, J., 276

Subject index